Defining Moments

Defining Moments

AN AUTOBIOGRAPHY

MARIUS BARNARD

WITH SIMON NORVAL

Published by Zebra Press
an imprint of Random House Struik (Pty) Ltd
Reg. No. 1966/003153/07
80 McKenzie Street, Cape Town, 8001
PO Box 1144, Cape Town, 8000 South Africa

www.zebrapress.co.za

First published 2011

1 3 5 7 9 10 8 6 4 2

PUBLISHER: Marlene Fryer
MANAGING EDITOR: Robert Plummer
EDITOR: Beth Housdon
PROOFREADER: Lisa Compton
COVER DESIGNER: Michiel Botha
TEXT DESIGNER: Monique Oberholzer
TYPESETTER: Monique van den Berg
INDEXER: Sanet le Roux
PRODUCTION MANAGER: Valerie Kömmer

Set in 10.5 pt on 14 pt Minion

Printed and bound by Paarl Media, Jan van Riebeeck Drive, Paarl, South Africa

ISBN 978 1 77022 154 3 (print)
ISBN 978 1 77022 201 4 (ePub)
ISBN 978 1 77022 202 1 (PDF)

Over 50 000 unique African images available to purchase
from our image bank at www.imagesofafrica.co.za

To my beloved parents for the enormous sacrifices they made for me,
and for their unwavering love and devotion;
to my beloved wife, Inez, who, with her guidance and loyal support,
has endured me through thick and thin for sixty years;
and to my brother Chris, without whom this book
would not have been written

Contents

Foreword

'SCALPEL!'

This single command sets the tone for the life story of my father, Dr Marius Stephanus Barnard.

Born to missionary parents of modest means in the desolate Karoo town of Beaufort West, he dreamt of seeing the wonders of the world and achieving great things, and these he certainly did.

Defining Moments follows his extraordinary life, beginning with his early days in racially divided Beaufort West and his medical studies in Cape Town and following him to Southern Rhodesia, where he practised as a general practitioner and started a family. It documents his surgical research at Cape Town's Groote Schuur Hospital and in Houston, and tracks his return to South Africa, where he was an integral member of the surgical team, led by his brother Chris, that performed the world's first human-to-human heart transplant. With candour and humility he describes the preparation, execution and aftermath of this historic operation – and those that followed – and reveals the full impact on his life and his family's of being thrust suddenly onto the world stage.

As he recounts his triumphs and defeats, opinions and personal anecdotes, he highlights the defining moments of his life from three perspectives: medicine, politics and medical insurance. He tells of the experiences, frustrations and achievements of his life as a cardiac surgeon in communist Romania and Poland, a member of parliament in Cape Town and a critical illness insurance pioneer all over the world, commenting on his increasingly difficult and ultimately untenable relationships with hostile Nationalist Party government officials, hospital authorities and his brother Chris, with whom he had a complex and at times acrimonious relationship.

As the book reveals, he has also played the role of part-time writer, speech giver and raconteur, has been involved in the work of a number of organisations and has established or officiated over several worthy funds.

My father writes with searing honesty and his accounts, peppered with his typical sense of humour, are always underpinned by an unwavering religious faith. The book portrays a man with boundless compassion, relentless energy and dry wit, someone who has long courted controversy and shunned the trappings of fame to fulfil his father's wish to treat his fellow man with respect, dignity and God-given love.

Today, Dr Marius Barnard, my father, is eighty-three years old. His extraordinary life journey, with all its twists and turns, has been undertaken with determination, dignity and grace.

This is the personal account of a man who is finally at peace with himself and the world, and one that reflects the rich and rewarding legacy of his life's defining moments.

ADAM HENDRIK BARNARD
CAPE TOWN
JANUARY 2011

Preface

'You only live once – but if you do it right, once is enough.'
— JOE E. LEWIS

I HAVE BEEN MEANING TO WRITE A BOOK FOR MANY YEARS NOW. AT last, it has become a reality and, as I look back, I really have to say, 'Boy, what a life it has been!'

I grew up surrounded by the beauty and wonder of the extraordinary Karoo and, paradoxically, endured intolerance and hardships during my youth in the small Karoo town of Beaufort West.

My years of medical training started at the University of Cape Town's medical school, after which I engaged in medical research and practice in the United Kingdom, Southern Rhodesia, Cape Town and Houston before returning to Cape Town and later Johannesburg.

My active participation in the historic first human heart transplantation at Groote Schuur Hospital was an extraordinary moment in my life and gave rise to a number of unique opportunities. It paved the way for me to be able to improve cardiac surgery techniques, methods and standards in our country and in other parts of the world. I led highly competent teams of South African medical colleagues to Romania and Poland to pass on the knowledge and experience we had gained, at a time when it was considered politically unthinkable for a South African to enter and operate from behind the Iron Curtain.

My involvement in South African politics was largely circumstantial, but the injustices and pure wickedness of apartheid motivated my service as a member of parliament during one of the country's bleakest periods.

What grew out of experiences with patients worldwide – and particularly during my time in private practice – was the realisation that a new protection insurance policy was required to provide financial security for patients diagnosed with life-threatening diseases. Eventually the concept of critical illness insurance became a reality, both in South Africa and abroad, and it remains a thriving policy today.

All of these experiences have been professionally and personally challenging, enriching and rewarding. I would like to think that I have been driven by a singular sense of purpose – to better the lives of people and to advance medical knowledge where I was able to do so.

But my greatest gift is to have received great love and direction from my missionary parents. My father set a wonderful example for me and his simple yet powerful statement, 'God is love', is an enduring truth that has been a guiding influence throughout my life.

So, too, have I been blessed with a lifelong marriage to my beloved wife, Inez. She has been the perfect partner, companion and mother to our three children, and has always supported me, through thick and thin.

For all these experiences – my defining moments – I give thanks to the Almighty God, who gave me life and made all things possible.

MARIUS BARNARD
'BERG 'N SEE', HERMANUS
JANUARY 2011

Acknowledgements

I WISH TO ACKNOWLEDGE THOSE PEOPLE WHO HAVE PROVIDED both material and moral support in the compilation of this book, as well as the sources of information used.

My sincere appreciation is extended to my son, Adam Hendrik, for writing the foreword and for assisting significantly by digging out tracts of information which may otherwise have been forgotten, and which subsequently proved to be of such importance to this book.

I also wish to thank my editor, Simon Norval, for his able support and persistence during this busy process.

I would like to extend my grateful thanks to Reverend Dr James Gray, for writing the introduction to Part I of this book; to Petre Ghidu, a previous patient of mine from Romania, whose letter to me provides an introduction to Part II; to my friend and former colleague Ray Swart, for the introduction to Part III; and to our great friend and critical illness insurance stalwart Marcia Johnson, for the introduction to Part IV.

I would not have been able to write this autobiography without the able and willing assistance of my wife, Inez.

I also wish to thank Zebra Press of Random House Struik, not only for publishing this book but for making all efforts to expedite its release. Similarly, I would like to thank Zebra Press's editorial staff, in particular Beth Housdon, their editor, for her excellent efforts.

I wish to thank Dr Joe de Nobrega, a former medical colleague of mine at Groote Schuur Hospital, for his supporting information on Robert Sobukwe.

My special thanks go to Paul Thesen, one of Groote Schuur Hospital's heart transplantees, who kindly provided details of his operations, and to local television broadcaster e.tv, which interviewed Paul Thesen and myself at the Heart of Cape Town Museum, Groote Schuur Hospital, recently.

I wish to thank Hennie Joubert, curator of the Heart of Cape Town Museum, for providing invaluable information on the history of the heart transplants performed at Groote Schuur Hospital, as well as on Hamilton Naki. In a similar vein, I would like to thank Natasha Bolognesi, a researcher at the Heart of Cape Town Museum, for her permission to include her research material on the first heart–lung machine and immunosuppression drug development and applications.

I would like to thank Lieutenant Colonel Malcolm Fraser for providing me with a copy of *The War Cry*, official organ of the Salvation Army in South Africa, in which the article 'The Barnard Story' appeared on 10 February 1968. This material went a long way in confirming my father's activities while he served in the Salvation Army.

My appreciation is extended to Caroline Bedeker of the Beaufort West Museum for providing recent historical information on my father's church and its parsonage.

In researching the life of Louw Geldenhuys, *Die Afrikaner Familie-naamboek* (1954) and the *Standard Encyclopaedia of Southern Africa* (1972) were consulted, and in the description of my grandfather's background, a reference has been made to the titles of two books written by Dalene Matthee, namely *Circles in a Forest* and *Fiela's Child*. The book *The Heart of My Child* by Cecilia Anghelescu-Sămărghitan is also referred to by name only, and Peter Hawthorne's *The Transplanted Heart* is referenced.

I have quoted from the book *Every Second Counts* by Don McRae. I have also referred to two books written by my late brother, Chris: *One Life* and *The Second Life*. For this, I thank him in absentia.

Two articles of mine, 'A Piece of Bread' and 'Soul of His Feet', which appeared in the *Reader's Digest* in February 1975 and December 1976 respectively, have been published in this book verbatim.

I have cited *Karoo*, a book I published with Anthony Johnson, who has kindly granted permission to reproduce some of his photographs in this book. Selected photographs have been reproduced with the kind permission of Don McKenzie, including the image on the front cover.

A selected stanza from the poem 'The Blind Boy' by Colley Cibber has also been included.

I have taken the liberty of including a recent email sent to me by one of my previous patients at the Red Cross Children's Hospital, Cindy le Roux, who coincidentally re-established contact with me during the process of writing this book. I have also incorporated two letters sent to me by a former Romanian medical colleague and long-time friend, Dr Daniel Constantinescu, as they add value and substance to the accounts of my time spent in Romania. Similarly, I have incorporated several excerpts from a manuscript written by a former Romanian medical colleague and friend, Dr Theadora

('Dora') Petrila, which provide considerable insight into the socio-political situation that prevailed in Romania during my visits.

Supporting information relating to critical illness insurance has been very kindly provided by the wonderful insurance friends I made during my roadshows: Alphonso Franco from Canada; Marcia Johnson from the United States of America; Peter Dodd from the United Kingdom; Johnny Timpson and Jane Flett from Scotland; and Howard Davy from Australia.

I would like to thank our special friend, Tessa Marks, for reviewing and providing critique on sections of the manuscript.

In verifying certain medical facts, concepts and terminology, the following websites were consulted, for which we make formal acknowledgement: the American Heart Association, Medline Plus, a service of the United States National Library of Medicine Science and the National Institutes of Health; New York State Department of Health; MedicineNet.com; and bestdoctors.com.

In confirming key historical facts regarding South African history, www.sahistory.org.za and www.southafrica.co.za were consulted. When researching historical information concerning the admission of black medical students to the University of Cape Town and the University of the Witwatersrand, I have quoted from the medical faculty board minutes of 12 May 1927, discussed in 'Truth and Reconciliation: A Process of Transformation at the UCT Health Sciences Faculty', published by the Faculty of Health Sciences, University of Cape Town.

Selected headlines and article excerpts have been quoted from the following local and overseas newspapers and referenced where appropriate: the *Cape Times*, the *Cape Argus*, the *Sunday Times*, the *Sunday Tribune*, the *Star*, the *Zoo Lake Advertiser*, the *Hillbrow News*, the *New York Times*, *Het Vaderland*, the *Guardian*, *The Economist*, the *Chicago News* and the Scottish *Herald*. The newspapers *Die Burger*, the *Citizen*, the *Daily Dispatch*, the *Rand Daily Mail* and *Rapport* are mentioned by title only, and single headlines and article extracts have been quoted from the following international magazines: *Life* magazine and *Money Marketing*. They have been referenced accordingly.

Die Burger and *Rapport* have generously granted permission for the reproduction of cartoons.

To the best of my knowledge, this book is an accurate representation of my life and all the events that have taken place in it.

Editor's Note

WHEN I WAS FIRST APPROACHED BY MY FRIEND AND FORMER schoolmate Adam Barnard to assist with the compilation of his father's autobiography, I was astonished that it had not already been published.

Initially I was daunted by the prospect, but I was driven by an overwhelming sense of urgency to ensure that the extraordinary life of one of South Africa's great sons was brought into the public domain, both locally and internationally.

Throughout my twelve years at school with Adam, which commenced in 1965, I was aware of his father's activities and achievements. During Adam's sporting events, at which Marius was always an avid supporter, I would observe this larger-than-life figure from afar with great admiration. Adam's classroom orals and playground conversations invariably touched on his father's exploits, travels and triumphs.

Even as an adolescent I was aware of the immensely supportive role played by Adam's mother, Inez. Her devotion as both wife and mother was obvious to me and to anyone else who visited the Barnards' home in Newlands during this period.

In parallel with the above, I was able to monitor Marius's professional achievements closely via the local press. My late father, Ronald, held various editorial positions on the Cape Town daily newspaper, the *Cape Times*. Through the flow of his pen and those of others, the roles of Dr Marius Barnard both as pioneering cardiac surgeon and as anti-apartheid politician were revealed. My awareness of his activities, which are forever etched in my childhood memories, was an integral part of my upbringing.

Marius's invention of critical illness insurance has filled a niche in the worldwide protection insurance industry. Stemming from his acute awareness of and concern for his patients, the development of this essential and successful policy has justifiably bestowed on him international recognition and gratitude.

In addition, he has made significant contributions to medical science and has to his name an array of awards and honours and lists of humanitarian initiatives – too many to cover in one book.

This account chronicles the traits, opinions, beliefs and inherent nature of Marius Barnard, the man. His writings reveal a life of professional dedication and excellence as well as a fearless championing of the oppressed, an unflinching commitment to healing and supporting the sick, and ceaseless dedication to justice and fair play.

Equally evident are his fond memories of his beloved parents; his enduring love for his wife, Inez, his family and his fellow man; and, ultimately, his recognition of and love for his Creator.

SIMON NORVAL
CAPE TOWN
JANUARY 2011

'Do all the good you can,
By all the means you can,
In all the ways you can,
In all the places you can,
At all the times you can,
To all the people you can,
As long as ever you can.'

— JOHN WESLEY, CHURCH OF ENGLAND
CLERIC AND FOUNDER OF THE
METHODIST CHURCH

PART I

Heritage

Many South Africans associate Beaufort West with coffee and petrol. En route to the great cities they stop, fill their tanks, grab a cup of coffee and move on. To some, the Karoo town reminds them of the question once contemptuously asked of Jesus Christ and his home village: 'Can anything good come out of Nazareth?'

Marius Barnard's fascinating book answers that sneering question. Beaufort West may not be the destination of choice for restless youth, but like so many dusty villages and *dorpe* of the South African *platteland*, it has produced countless people who have made significant contributions to the life of the nation.

Growing up in a conservative Karoo town was never going to be an easy experience for the bright young Marius, who bristled against much of what he witnessed. Much to the chagrin of the status quo, the Barnard family did not conform to the expectations of a culturally narrow and politically exclusive community. Marius's father, Adam, was a fighter who could no more turn a blind eye to injustice than he could deny his God. He loved the coloured people among whom he worked and stood up to those who looked down their noses at them. He was a true shepherd of his despised flock.

In a town like Beaufort West, such stands on behalf of the voiceless had profound consequences, not least for the children of such a fearless man of God. Two things often strike me about Marius: he remains in awe of his beloved father, and he has never quite worked through the sadness he feels for what the Afrikaans establishment of Beaufort West did to his Afrikaner dad.

The Karoo is a unique place. It is a place you have to 'feel'. It is a vast and empty landscape, but it is filled with presence. It is a silent place, but those with ears to hear may yet discern the 'still small voice'. Nightly, the Karoo sky stretches both the eye and the imagination to unrealised worlds of endless possibilities.

That is the beauty of the Karoo: it instils a sense of 'otherness' in her children. It allows them to dream dreams. The Karoo is a deep and formative place. In the socio-political and ecclesiastical cross-currents of life in Beaufort West, so acutely felt in the Barnard home, a young life was being shaped; a dream was being imparted. In that godly home in the Karoo was born a hunger to see right prevail.

That hunger has remained with Marius throughout his life and, although life has presented him with challenges, what he learnt from his father in that hardy Karoo landscape will anchor his soul for the days of uncertainty that may lie ahead: 'act justly, love mercy and walk humbly with your God' (Micah 6:8).

REVEREND JAMES GRAY
UNITED CHURCH, HERMANUS
JANUARY 2011

Humble Roots

THERE IS A PART OF OUR COUNTRY THAT I FIND MORE BEAUTIFUL than any other in South Africa, if not in the whole world. Having visited many places during the course of my life, I have to say that not one of them surpasses its exquisite beauty. I am, of course, referring to our famous Garden Route. I do not, with certainty, know where its exact geographical boundaries lie, but if one drives from Cape Town, it starts at George and ends at the Storms River Mouth.

It is not possible to describe here all the towns, villages and hidden seaside resorts within this area, but Victoria Bay, the Wilderness, Brenton-on-Sea, Knysna, Knoetzie, Plettenberg Bay and Nature's Valley are a few. Add to this the spectacular coastline along the Garden Route as well as the majestic inland mountains and forests, and one has scenic wonder and perfection on earth.

This stretch is blessed by God to be the only area in South Africa with both winter and summer rainfall, which has resulted in the vast indigenous forests known as the *Tsitsikamma*, a Khoi word meaning 'place of much water'. The tall, ancient trees of these sprawling forests form an immense canopy of branches, which prevents the sun from shining through and conceals within its dark shadows the diverse habitat below. Many of these trees were living organisms when Christ walked the earth, the most famous of which are the stinkwood, yellowwood and ironwood. I owe a lot to the trees of these forests: with their solid trunks and entwined branches, they were crucial to my forefathers' existence, providing them with shelter and work. It was among the trees of the nearby Knysna forest that my grandparents lived and raised their eight children, the youngest of whom was my father, Adam Hendrikus Barnard.

During my father's youth, small deer such as duikers and tawny bushbuck lived in the forests, as well as wild pigs aplenty, which often destroyed the vegetable gardens. My father, whom I affectionately referred to as my *Deddie*, related to me how the mighty African elephant roamed in abundance then. He told me many a story of his narrow escapes, including how he was stormed by angry cows protecting their young.

Tragically, owing to man's greed, these giants were destroyed, shot for their ivory and the damage they wrought on properties. Some people claim that there are three or four elephants still roaming this forest, but the most reliable evidence suggests that there is only one ancient cow remaining. So much for civilisation.

The trees did not fare better: they were indiscriminately logged to supply wood to shore up the roofs of mines, to provide telephone poles and sleepers for railway lines, and for crafting into elegant furniture. Sculpted from these ancient trees and treated with oils and varnish, such furniture remains in great demand today and is, in many instances, priceless. In large areas where there was forest, there now exist vast plantations of pine and bluegum trees, sourced from as far afield as Australia.

In my father's time, the dense, lush foliage and high branches provided the haunt and breeding grounds of a variety of birdlife, including the famed Knysna loerie, a large, beautiful green bird with a short bill and brilliant red wings. This bird, as well as the emerald cuckoo, the narina trogon, the Knysna and olive woodpecker, the chorister robin and many other feathered species, still inhabits the forest today.

I never knew my paternal grandparents, Johannes Wilhelm and Anna Dorothea Elizabeth Marthina Barnard, both of whom were born in 1836. I do, however, know that my grandmother's maiden name was also Barnard. She and my grandfather must have been related in some way; possibly they were cousins. It was joked in those days that if you walked down a street in Knysna during this period and you knocked into a pole or a tree, you had to say, 'Sorry, Mr Barnard!' The woodcutters of Knysna formed a small community and intermarriage was common practice.

My father described to me his family's daily struggle to eke out an existence. My grandfather and his kin were part of a group of people who were uneducated but hard-working and God-fearing. They were known as *poor whites*. Incidentally, we never spoke about *poor blacks*, as it was accepted that the vast majority of black people were poor. As a youngster, I never let on that I had originated from such stock when people referred to 'poor whites' in derogatory terms. In those days I was ashamed of my forefathers; today I am extremely proud when I hear talk about 'poor whites'. I never hesitate to tell anyone who wants to hear that my grandfather and his family were classified as such.

Although I was told little about my grandfather, I was at least informed that he was powerfully built, as one could expect from a man who swung an axe for most of his life. Felling the trees and then working with the wood was labour intensive, requiring great precision. It has been said that the craftsmanship of these men surpassed anything produced by machine. My grandfather had very little education and could barely read, but he and my grandmother lived by the Bible and, when he was discovered dead outside his humble dwelling early one morning, the Holy Scriptures were lying open next to him.

I recently discovered from the South African Department of Agriculture, Forestry and Fisheries that a permit had to be obtained during those times to cut down stinkwood and yellowwood trees. The permit cost £4 and, in addition, a span of oxen was required to remove the logs from the dense forest. There were, of course, no roads leading in and out of the forest in those days. It is amazing that so many people who signed those contracts were Barnards. Although I have examined a list of permit holders dating back to 1899, I have not been able to recognise or identify the names of relatives or my grandfather. I am certain that they were among those permit holders, however.

One of South Africa's best-known authors, Dalene Matthee, wrote several books, including *Circles in a Forest* and *Fiela's Child*, about the lives and daily struggles of the woodcutters and craftsmen who existed in this forest. It is perhaps appropriate that the main characters in *Circles in a Forest* were also Barnards. In fact, if I had the ability, I could have written those stories myself, because the characters and places were just as my father described them to me.

The inhabitants of the forest had little chance of a better future. The agents who bought the wood that they logged were far better educated and exploited them unmercifully. Owing to the dishonest system used by the buyers, my grandfather's people were always in debt and had to sell timber at any price to buy provisions and other necessities.

Adam Hendrikus, my father, first saw the light of day on 20 March 1875. At the time of his birth, his parents were already approaching forty. They died around the early 1900s, never having left their forest dwelling. Of the rest of his family I have little knowledge, although I am aware that four of my father's cousins died while fighting in the First World War, at Flanders and Delville Wood. I do recall meeting an uncle of mine, Oom Koos, who worked at some time or another as a 'tug pilot' in the Knysna harbour. He wasn't a tug pilot in the conventional sense of the term: his particular brand of vessel was a rowing boat. He would leave the harbour, row out to sea and guide the steamships over the shallow sandbars, through the narrow, dangerous channel between the famous Knysna Heads and into the safety of the placid lagoon.

Being a difficult port to enter, a harbour pilot was employed in those days to assist large vessels. The best-known harbour pilot during this period was, of course, John Benn, a shipwright from Mossel Bay who came to Knysna in 1868 to direct the salvage of the *Musquash*, which had been wrecked in the Heads. Although the ship broke up before he could rescue her, Benn decided to stay in Knysna when he was offered a commission to build a new ship, the *Rover*, for a local merchant.[1]

I have never established whether Oom Koos and John Benn worked together. I doubt this was the case as Benn would have been considerably older than my uncle, whose services were possibly motivated by Benn's retirement or death.

In describing his birthplace, my father always spoke of an area just north of Knysna called *Ou Plaas*. If one passes the turn-off to the Heads today, one ascends a small incline on the N2, which passes through Knysna, and this particular area is situated on the immediate left-hand side of the road. My father must have spent most, if not all, of his youth there.

While my parents were still alive, we visited my father's relatives in the small shacks that my grandparents and their fellow forest dwellers had previously occupied. The small, two-roomed, corrugated-iron dwellings would have offered little comfort. With ten or more people crowded into such confined spaces, the rigours of living on top of one another and the lack of privacy must have been barely tolerable. The dwellings were, therefore, home for only a few reasons: they provided shelter against the elements and protection against hostile intruders and wild animals. There was, of course, no running water or electricity, and my memories of such visits are limited to the cramped, harsh conditions and dense smoke.

But living in that area could not have been without some fun. My father told me how he frequently sighted ghosts while walking back to Ou Plaas after a night on the town, and of how he ran away when he saw these apparitions. As a boy, I would dream about these ghoulish figures throughout the night; I could not believe that my father – a man of God – would ever lie to me. Now, of course, I know it was simply his way of amusing us. Whether he actually ever saw them, I will never know.

I never really knew the reason for our visits, but I have an idea. When my father heard *boeremusiek*, he would start dancing and, much to my mother's disgust, demonstrate how one danced the *sitee*, the *vastrap* and the *Hotnot's riel*.[2] It was below my mother's dignity ever to join him. My deduction from my father's antics was that the old man had been a bit of a 'lad about town' in his youth.

I remember well how my father pointed out to me the factories in which he had worked while growing up. Thesen's wood factory was located on the island bearing the same name along the Knysna lagoon, while another factory, Parkes, was situated near to the town's main street. I will always remember the special, unique smell of the wood and the noise made by the machines while cutting and shaping spade and pick handles. The crafting and smoothing of the wood was a sight that amazed me, and my Deddie would show me where he had stood and what he had made, telling me of the long hours that he had spent on his feet.

At home, my father was an expert when wood had to be chopped for the hungry Esse stove. I loved watching him, but he always admonished me by saying that it was better to watch a dog urinating against the trunk of a tree than a man chopping wood with an axe. I didn't see the connection then, nor do I see it now, but it was his way of warning me of the danger of flying woodchips and protecting me from losing an eye.

My father told me many stories about the ships that entered the harbour to deliver all kinds of provisions and then, loaded with all the precious wood, sailed to far-off, unknown destinations. He met many interesting people during these years in Knysna, and it is no wonder that all three of my aunts were married to seamen. The men must have found either their beauty, or the beauty of Knysna itself, too much to resist, and jumped ship. I can still remember their surnames: Stopforth, from Scotland; Iverson, from Norway; and Thomas, from Wales. We actually stayed with all of them for short periods of time on different occasions. Thomas in particular was notorious in my family for living up to the reputation of a sailor: he was often inebriated and apparently could tell wild and woolly stories about his life on the high seas and the experiences he had gained all over the world.

When staying in Knysna we never failed to visit the picturesque Heads. Perched on the rocks, my father would explain the difficulty that boats experienced when entering the lagoon through the dangerous channel, describing Oom Koos and his rowing boat and the shipwrecks that litter the treacherous coastline.

But my father's greatest joy was when he and I fished from the wharf on Thesen Island or at the Heads. Even then, fish were scarce – or possibly we were just poor fishermen – as I cannot remember catching a thing. We had better luck when we went onto the lagoon by boat at night. Under a full moon, with the tranquil waters lapping at the sides of the small vessel, we would cast our nets into the clear night air and pull in a fish or two.

My father's other great love was the forest and he could identify all the trees and vegetation. Between Knysna and Plettenberg Bay was a small area through which one could walk in the dense, indigenous Outeniqua Forest. Today, its name is still the *Garden of Eden*. As a child raised on readings from the Bible, I could imagine the biblical Adam walking there and hiding from God in the many concealed places. Today, this area and its surroundings represents to me a small piece of heaven on earth.

In December 1957, I visited my father and mother while they were living in Knysna. On the day prior to our departure, I took my parents, my wife, Inez, and our two daughters to the Keurbooms River, near to Nature's Valley. We had a picnic in the Garden of Eden and stopped at the Heads for a short while. My father's cancerous body could hardly manage the walk up the tricky steps, but he remained steadfast and so brave, beaming with pleasure at his beloved surroundings and at being able to enjoy one last opportunity with his family.

That was the last time I saw my Deddie. He died the following year, on 18 July 1958, aged eighty-two, four days after his grandson – who carries his grandfather's name, Adam Hendrik – was born. I think the knowledge that his name would live on through my son is the last thing he experienced on earth.

* * *

From an early age my father had aspirations of bettering himself and seeing the outside world. I believe it was then that he felt the need to serve his God. So he turned his back on his youthful woodcutter existence to seek God's teachings. The image of my father walking out of the Knysna forest, and the profound significance of that decision in his life, remains one of my own defining moments.

On 10 January 1899, my father entered the Salvation Army ranks in the small Karoo town of Oudtshoorn as Cadet Adam Hendrikus Barnard. Six months later, on 15 June 1899, he was promoted to the rank of Probationary Lieutenant.

It is fascinating, but not surprising, that my father joined the Salvation Army, a Christian organisation founded by one-time Methodist minister

William Booth and his wife, Catherine. This decision of my father's was to have the greatest influence on his spiritual life, and it is fitting that during the final months of my mother's life she was lovingly nursed in the William Booth Memorial Hospital in the suburb of Gardens, in Cape Town, where she subsequently died.

But my father wasn't to stay in Oudtshoorn long: with his promotion came a posting to the Claremont Corps in Cape Town. Around this time, British and Imperial troops were already massing in Cape Town in anticipation of the outbreak of the Anglo-Boer War, which finally began on 11 October 1899. It was a bloody war that raged for nearly three years, and one that left emotional scars and enduring antagonism between the Afrikaner and the colonial British.

Despite such upheavals, my father's career continued to develop. More appointments followed, both from within the Corps and socially. After lying extremely ill with typhoid fever in East London for two months, he recovered in time to serve at the Kimberley Soldiers' Home while guns were still booming between Kimberley and Mafeking.[3]

On 5 July 1900, my father was promoted to the fully commissioned field rank of Lieutenant. Before her departure to the relieved town of Mafeking, one of his female fellow officers was quoted as saying that my father 'was a real friend of the children', as he was enthusiastic about anything concerning children's work. His devotion to his four sons would later be proof of this.

My father's first appearance 'in print' was, perhaps, the *War Cry* issue of 25 August 1900, in which he provided an obituary notice for a soldier of Kimberley. '[T]he death angel,' he wrote, 'has taken from us our dear comrade ...' And in Kimberley he is recorded as having testified that he was 'saved at an early age, and that grace had kept him'. I forever thank God that this was indeed the case.

In 1902, my father was promoted to the rank of Captain and put in charge of the Kenilworth Corps in Cape Town. During this turbulent period he would regularly visit Bulawayo in what was then Southern Rhodesia, travelling through British lines to reach the town, which was several hundred miles away. With martial law still in force, travelling was restricted. However, he found himself in possession of a military rail permit that allowed him a certain degree of freedom of movement. I can remember my father showing me the 'passes' that the British army issued to him allowing his transit through the border posts. On completion of such visits, he would return to Cape Town, passing through Mafeking and Kimberley. My father loved telling me about his experiences of working in Bulawayo. When he visited us while I was practising as a general practitioner (GP) in what was then Salisbury, he would recall his memories and express how he loved that particular part of the world.

From the time of his taking charge at the Kenilworth Corps, enthusiastic reports of his activities were heard and, during November of the same year, he was leading Salvation Army open-air meetings in the suburb of Mowbray. In this very area, on a Sunday morning sixty-five years later, his two doctor sons would make medical history.

A month later, in December, ill health saw him boarded and he was compelled to take leave of the Salvation Army. This may well have been due to the after-effects of his previously contracted typhoid fever. In any event, my father was never able to resume the extremely exacting and exhausting life of a Salvation Army officer.

A valedictory speech from the Kenilworth Corps speaks of the high esteem in which my father was held:

> … we are sorry to say that it was the farewell of Captain Barnard who is leaving on furlough[4] through his health failing him. The farewell meeting was a very touching one as the comrades, one and all, testified to the fact of how God has made him a means of blessing to many a soul, and while we will miss the Captain very much, the prayers of all the comrades and of many Christian friends in Kenilworth follow him and, one and all, pray that God may spare him and use him to the salvation of many a precious soul.[5]

This He did, as the following chapters testify.

2

My Father, the Missionary

IN 1903, AFTER FIVE YEARS WITH THE SALVATION ARMY, MY twenty-seven-year-old father set out to resume his formal education at the Missionary Institute in the Western Cape town of Wellington.

He travelled via Knysna to Cape Town by tramp steamer. Departing in very rough seas, the ship navigated with great caution through the treacherous Heads. It waited patiently between the large swells, keeping well clear of the countercurrents that threatened to drag the ship and its passengers onto the jagged rocks. Then, at just the right moment, it headed at best speed over the bar and out into the open ocean. Once well clear of land, it headed west. But the mighty Cape rollers buffeted the small vessel mercilessly and my father was horribly seasick all the way to his destination.

I never established how my father's studies were funded, but I suspect it was by a certain Dominee Louw from the Little Karoo town of Robertson, a man who apparently played a significant role in the formative years of his life. Many of the early pupils of the Missionary Institute had received no formal education; they were admitted simply because they exhibited a need to serve God. This need, recognised by those in charge, ensured that no applicant was ever turned away.

Those who were still in the throes of boyhood were sent to the public school to further their education. Some, however, were already grown men and it was deemed unfair to expect them to sit and learn among young boys. The education of the older men was, therefore, undertaken by the Institute.

My father realised that his education was limited, but he would take no credit even for the little he'd already received. Years later he related to me how, on his arrival, they had asked him where he would like to start. He simply stated: 'From the beginning.' It seems that he took just one year to complete his schooling to the required level. To embark on his tertiary education at the Institute he was then required to take a year out to prepare for an admission exam. His subjects included Dutch, English, Greek, general history, the history of theology and school administration. Although he struggled with Greek, he persisted with it. He duly wrote the exam the following year and gained entrance to the Missionary Institute.

The next four years were spent focusing on theological studies, on completion of which the graduates had a choice: they could become either teachers or missionaries.

While at the Institute, my father had been required to undertake short periods of community service during the holiday breaks. The intention of this was that the pupils of the Institute would apply practically the theory they had learnt in their classrooms, so they were sent to various outlying stations of the church.

During a practical session that took place in the small town of Joubertina in the Eastern Cape, my father met a young woman named Maria Elizabeth de Swardt. She was a teacher in the town as well as the organist of the church in which he'd been sent to work. Elizabeth was ten years younger than he was, a tall, good-looking woman with brown eyes and striking features. Her parents were well-to-do farmers from the Blanco area near George, a town not very far from Knysna. A courtship in the manner typical of the time soon followed: circumspect, restrained and discreet.

My father's spirits must have soared as the pair became better acquainted. Aside from their disparate upbringings, they had much in common. Maria too had trained in Wellington, at the sister school of the Missionary Institute – the Huguenot Seminary for Women – and, like my father, she was deeply religious. A well-educated woman, she was also well versed in the skills required of the wife of a future missionary. As tends to happen, they fell in love.

But prejudice knows no bounds. For my parents, it was a union literally made in heaven, but, for Maria de Swardt's family, their future son-in-law was not quite what they had in mind. For a start, my father's background was frowned upon. Their daughter was, after all, from far superior stock than that of Adam Hendrikus Barnard. How, they wondered, could a man of such humble credentials provide the kind of future they desired for their daughter? One can only imagine the murmurs of concern and the chatter of prejudiced minds. But my father was not one to give up when he had set his mind on something, nor was his sweetheart easily dissuaded. In 1908, after a short courtship, they became husband and wife.

My parents' marriage took place at the Dutch Reformed Church in Robertson. The reason they chose this town in which to get married remains something of a mystery to me. The *dominee* who married them, Dominee

Louw, is also an elusive figure in my inherited memory of events. I know he was important to my father, who saw him as a surrogate parent, I think. My mother's parents and family felt that *sy het benede haarself getrou* – she married beneath her station in life. Coincidentally, years later I gained the impression that my wife's parents felt the same way about me.

Two years later, my father graduated from the Missionary Institute at the relatively advanced age of thirty-two and decided to become a missionary. My parents moved to the Eastern Cape town of Graaff-Reinet, where my father served as an assistant missionary in the Dutch Reformed Mission Church.[1] He started on a stipend of £4 a month – a pittance, even in those days. The life of a missionary, though spiritually rewarding, would never see him earn the kind of money that would make him financially comfortable. Although my father would certainly find himself earning more than his own father had, our family always struggled to make ends meet. On his meagre monthly income, he had to support a wife and, some months later, a son – my eldest brother Johannes.

The birth of Johannes brought with it an unfortunate casualty: Johannes's twin, a girl, was stillborn. The death of an infant in our family was to be followed by another – my brother Abraham. Throughout their lives, the deaths of these two children remained a source of enduring sorrow for my parents.

3

Beaufort West

I N 1911, MY FATHER WAS CALLED TO MINISTER TO THE COLOURED community of the town of Beaufort West in the Dutch Reformed Mission Church. He was now a fully fledged missionary with his own congregation. Although it didn't occur to me during my youth, I realise now that by the time my father arrived in Beaufort West it was a town already divided.

The last few decades have seen numerous divided cities and countries: Berlin, until recently, was separated into East and West by the Iron Curtain; North and South Korea remain divided by ideological hatred; and the sabre-rattling by communist China towards Taiwan is ongoing. But Beaufort West, in the heart of the Karoo, was already divided when the people of Berlin were loyally standing together, their right arms diagonally raised with flattened hands. Beaufort West was split long before the people of Korea experienced the wrath of communism.

The town of my childhood was carved in two not only by the Gamka River, but also along racial lines. From the time my father entered its precincts, he took a stand against everything he perceived to be an injustice suffered by those in his own congregation and others. Poor was poor, regardless of skin colour. To my father, these were the people who required the most help: they needed comfort and they needed ministry, and he believed it was an essential part of his calling to provide such services. The objective of the Salvation Army was to minister without discrimination, and this principle was forever his guide. My father's uncompromising stand against racial prejudice meant, however, that he soon found himself subjected to much hostility and tireless attempts from certain sectors of the community to have him banished from his church.

* * *

The Gamka River is like the Karoo itself: dry and dusty, with minimal vegetation along its banks. If good rains fall in the catchment area, the river – for a day or two – becomes an angry torrent of brown and muddy water rushing headlong towards the sea many miles away.

On one occasion during my childhood, after a cloudburst in the mountains, the river, no longer able to contain its gushing flood, burst its banks and came pouring through the town. Strangely, no rain had fallen in Beaufort West itself. I remember the incident well because it happened on a Sunday morning. Whereas motor cars a few hours earlier had raised clouds of dust behind them, Donkin Street – the main street of the town – soon became a fast-flowing river. Petrol drums, outside lavatory buckets and all other forms of flotsam and jetsam were swept down the streets in the flood. With most of my father's congregation unable to get to church, he had a rare morning off.

But aside from this occasion and other isolated incidents like it, the Gamka was dry and of little practical use, except to serve as a haven for the town's wine and brandy drinkers. They would buy their bottles of courage from a hotel situated on the river's edge and then hide from a disapproving society – as well as an alert police force – under the few trees and bushes that grew along the banks of the river.

The geographical divide created by the river was mirrored in the town's racial divisions. To the east of the Gamka was an area occupied by the privileged white society. It boasted the main business centre, the magistrates' court and the post office. To the north, east and south of this important hub stretched Beaufort West suburbia, consisting predominantly of large houses with spacious grounds.

The west, by contrast, was occupied by the poorer, less privileged coloured people, living in their uniformly distributed flat-roofed square houses set on bare, postage-stamp-sized plots. The location was a bleak place with no electricity. The streets were uneven, potholed and without pavements, and no trees adorned their edges.

But on both sides of the Gamka River there were pockets of land occupied by members of the other group. A large section of the western side's northern territory was taken over by the South African Railways. The railway station was situated just west of the Gamka, and further to the west were the houses built by the Railways for its white workers. Uninteresting dwellings on small plots, the exteriors of these houses were all coated black with soot from the passing coal-burning locomotives.

In the *Bo-Dorp* – the 'Upper Town' – of the eastern zone, and spread along the banks of the outflow of the dam, the better-educated coloureds clung desperately to small areas, where they lived in better homes and under better conditions than those in the location. These people – the Wepenaars, the Standers, the Morkels and the Van der Rosses, among others – were well respected by the whites. This was perhaps due to the fact that they could often claim more 'white blood' in their veins than some of those living in the 'pure-white' areas. This is not an insignificant truth: the degree of 'whiteness' or 'blackness' in one's blood has always been a factor in South Africa, and it was no less so in Beaufort West in those days. An interesting facet of our history is that some of these coloured people succeeded in having themselves reclassified as whites in later years, during the apartheid era.

I remember my father telling me of one such instance during a holiday spent in Cape Town after I had completed Standard 6 (today's Grade 8). One Sunday morning, my father returned from church smiling to himself. I asked him what had happened, and he told me that he had gone to the *Groote Kerk* (also called the *Mother Church* of the Dutch Reformed Church in South Africa) in Cape Town's Adderley Street.[1] To his surprise, he observed that the man who had been his head deacon at the coloured mission church in Beaufort West was now the head *ouderling* – the head elder, a necessarily 'white' position – of this exclusively white church!

But the houses of the better-off coloured people in Beaufort West were not the only 'intrusions' into the white area. Situated in the best part of the town were two other isolated 'invasions'. The first was the coloured primary school in Bird Street, opposite the back of the Dutch Reformed Church. The second was the Dutch Reformed Mission Church and its parsonage. They were situated in the middle of Donkin Street, sandwiched between the town hall and Beaufort West's largest shop, Mortimer and Hill (later to become the Merino Co-Op), and opposite the magistrates' court and post office.

Although the Dutch Reformed Mission Church and its parsonage occupied a central position in the town, they could not compare in size or magnificence to the Dutch Reformed Church and *its* parsonage. Situated a block further north, this white church was on the same side of Donkin Street as the coloured church. But here the similarity ended.

The Mother Church was built in the shape of the holy cross. It seated at least a hundred more people than the narrow, rectangular coloured church and it possessed a magnificent steeple that rose high above the town. The steeple is an important landmark of many small towns in South Africa: it can be seen from great distances and, for travellers, it is a recognisable indicator that they are soon to come upon some form of civilisation. In our town, the steeple served other functions. To the citizens, it was a constant reminder that they should remain wise to the laws of their God. It was also the place that housed the only functioning public clock in the town. Dutifully, the clock struck the quarter-hour, the half-hour and the hour, day and night, summer, autumn, winter and spring. If the clock ran slow, all of Beaufort West proceeded at a pedestrian pace; if it ran fast, the town distinctively speeded up its life and activities.

On Sundays, the bells of the Dutch Reformed Church pealed for so long and so loudly that they drowned out those of its competitors, the Anglican and Catholic churches. The Mother Church's offices were separated from the church itself and a large hall was used for social gatherings, bazaars, concerts and, on occasion, political events. These buildings were all sur-rounded by spacious grounds that contained one or two monuments in memory of past well-respected and loved *dominees*.

Compared to its white counterpart, the mission church was an also-ran. It was significantly smaller and had no steeple, no clock or bells, and no church hall. Not even its organ, which my mother played every Sunday, was able to rise to the same volume as that of the Mother Church's organ during the singing of psalms and hymns to the glory of God.

In the same grounds as my father's church, connected to the vestry as if by an umbilical cord, was the parsonage. Number 77 Donkin Street was a roomy house with large bedrooms and living rooms, set in a sizeable garden that stretched from Donkin Street to Bird Street at the back. Our family lived here rent-free, and it was the house in which I, as well as two of my brothers, was born.

With the house came a car: a black Model T Ford. As a teenager in the 1940s I was ashamed to be seen in it because by then it was already of vintage classification. It was also the car in which I later learnt to drive. There were no automatic gears to glide smoothly into place; instead, foot pedals had to be manoeuvred to change gears. A lever on the side of the steering wheel provided for the accelerator and, on the other side, there was one for the choke.

Starting this car was quite an experience. One first had to advance the choke and then, with the car in neutral, run to its front to turn the crank handle as fast as one could. Once combustion was achieved, the engine would splutter to life and one had to then rush back and jump into the car to advance the accelerator and retard the choke. The crank handle was, unfortunately, very unforgiving. If the engine didn't start while one was building up compression, its handle would swing back rapidly and forcefully. If a hand or arm was in the way, a fracture or severe bruising could very easily result.

I wonder how many people today can, like me, claim that not only did my early driving experiences take place in a Model T Ford, but I actually obtained my driver's licence in it. My driving test was supervised by the local hairdresser, who didn't have his own car nor could he drive. The test took the form of his telling me that I had been spotted driving the car around the town. When I admitted to this, he gave me the licence. It remains valid today – nearly seventy years later.

Although my father possessed a licence, he didn't drive the Model T. He said that he never felt confident behind the wheel, which was hardly surprising, since he'd had several hair-raising experiences. In the last of his near-accidents, he turned off Donkin Street to enter the garage of the parsonage. Something went drastically wrong, however, and he found himself steering the car up the steps and through the front doors of the church. This was the first and only time that he entered his church by car.

After that experience, my father never again touched the steering wheel of a car. The Model T was placed in the hands of a driver, Jan ver Hoog. My father's assistant and sometime friend Oom Fred Bastiaanse, however, made the most use of the vehicle, as it was his duty to transport my father to outlying farms when he conducted his services there.

* * *

My father was referred to as *meneer* by the members of his church and as *eerwaarde* by those whites who respected him. But he was also known as *die Hotnot predikant* – 'the Hotnot minister' – by those whites who disapproved of him. The term *Hotnot* was, and indeed remains, a derogatory term used by some whites when speaking of a member of the coloured population.

The *eerwaarde* thus ministered to the coloured community and the *dominee* ministered to the white, largely Afrikaans, community. Whereas the position of *eerwaarde* was considered inferior to that of the *dominee* of the Dutch Reformed Church, they were both called *reverend*, neutralising the apparent disparity in status.

When I was a child, my father's stipend was raised from £4 to £20 per month. As part of his duties, he would visit the local jail on a weekly basis to spread the Word. For this, he was paid an extra £1 a month. He performed this function not only because he considered it an adjunct to his calling, but because the extra amount he was paid was an added incentive. When my father told people about prison visits, he jokingly said that he was the only man of God who had to go to jail once a week.

Every Sunday morning, convicts of all races would be told of God's love and caring, even for them, and how they might be saved or provided for. Often, when the prisoners were released and found the outside world harsh and hostile, with no one to take care of them, they would remember my father and his message of faith and the love of God and arrive at the parsonage for counselling and reassurance.

It was customary at the time that the whites knocked on the front door while the non-whites came to the back door. Requests were many: a place to sleep, clothing for children, and food or medicine for sick fathers and mothers. Where he could, my father would help, but the pleas were, for the most part, for cash. My father was experienced enough to recognise those in true need; those that weren't in desperate need were summarily sent away, but not before a short, sharp sermon that was usually based on the evils of alcohol.

I remember such an occasion one New Year's Eve, when one of his parishioners, by that point well inebriated, approached our back door to ask for a *dop*. I was always amazed that this man chose my father as a possible benefactor for his desperate thirst. After incurring the full wrath of my father and a couple of strong words, the man departed with the following New Year's good wishes: '*Ek hoop die Here sal meneer spaar solank as wat u lewe*' – 'I hope God will spare you for as long as you live.' My father often related this incident, a favourite of his, afterwards.

Although he was to live and minister in Beaufort West for many years, my father's stipend never exceeded £20. The earnings of the white *dominee*, by contrast, were much higher, and he enjoyed other privileges not afforded to my father, including a better house and car. His education was also of a much higher standard – no Missionary Institute for him. The *dominee* was required to spend seven years at a university to complete his studies and entered his calling with a degree behind his name. This should come as no surprise because bringing Christ to the coloured community was considered to require a lower level of education than that necessary for the whites – yet another example of the absurd racial discrimination that prevailed at the time.

Despite the inequalities, my father diligently tended to the spiritual well-being of the members of the Dutch Reformed Mission Church for thirty-seven years. He loved his calling as he loved his flock, and I don't think he would have changed such circumstances for anything in the world.

* * *

In those of us who have been blessed to have lived in the Karoo there exists a deep passion for this beautiful corner of God's creation. For others – and there are many – it is ugly, barren and undesirable. Often I have heard friends describe, when travelling by road from Cape Town to the north, their frustration that for many hours and miles they had to drive through this sweltering, arid landscape. What they do not understand is that the beauty and splendour of the Karoo is not what one sees, but what one *fails* to see.

My seventeen years of living and experiencing the Karoo – walking in the veld, observing the drought-resistant succulents surviving in dry, rocky ground – opened my eyes, ears and nostrils to the daily wonders of the soil on which I was born, bred and educated. The story that follows conveys my sentiments about the bewitching magic of the Karoo and some of its inhabitants:

It is a dry, windy dusk in one of the most isolated and drought-stricken parts of the Karoo. The freezing mid-winter south wind is chilling the poor shepherd so that his teeth are chattering. His clothes are soiled and torn, and insufficient to keep him warm and protected from the long, frosty night that lies ahead. While guarding his small herd of merino sheep, especially the lambs, against jackals, caracals and other hungry predators, he needs food and warmth.

Regular, severe drought across the Karoo has resulted in a largess of cinder-dry dead bush and trees. It will take only a few minutes for the shepherd to collect enough firewood and dry *bossies* to start a fire, which will provide heat for cooking his evening meal and warmth during the night. Soon his small black kettle is boiling and he brews himself a cup of *rooibos* tea. The liquid – piping hot and without sugar or milk – gives him immediate relief from the cold as he cooks his dinner.

Sitting on a comfortable rock, which he chooses from the hundreds scattered on the parched ground around him, he hears a distant whistle and, with it, the gradually increasing thundering of an approaching steam engine. The sound of the wind whistling through the sparse Karoo trees and bush is suddenly eclipsed by the hiss and clatter of a black monster. As it roars towards and past him, its foul-smelling black smoke replaces the clean air of his beloved Karoo.

It is dinner time in the Blue Train and, as it flashes past the shepherd, a Johannesburg chief executive has just finished his first course of poached salmon and is waiting for the main meal of roast beef, potatoes and seasonal vegetables. He sips chilled French champagne as he reclines in the comfortable leather-covered seat of the five-star hotel on wheels.

Dispassionately, he looks through the window and cannot believe that anybody could live surrounded by this desolation of rocks, ankle-high bushes, dotted Karoo *doringbome*, dry rivers and occasional lonely farmhouse with hardly a green patch around it. It is nothing compared to Illovo.

In his mind, he sees his large double-storey house on its two-acre property, with a swimming pool and tennis court where friends and business acquaintances are entertained. The garden has rolling green lawns, beds of colourful flowers and tall, leafy trees. His wife is a society beauty and over the holidays he relaxes by the sea with his family. 'How lucky I am to be able to live such a life of luxury,' he thinks to himself. 'I could never live in this barren desert.'

As the noisy iron train clatters west towards Cape Town, the Karoo shepherd enjoys steaming-hot spoonfuls of *mieliepap* and looks with distaste and a certain amount of fear at the passing train. What he sees is so unlike his surroundings that he cannot believe, or understand, how people can travel in its confined space, the continuous clanking filling the air.

In the Karoo stretch distant horizons and at night the moon and the millions of stars in the sky are clear and bright, in a stillness he can almost touch. Surrounding him are yellow-flowered *gannabos* and Karoo thorn bush, with its yellow miniature powder-puffs in flower at the base of long, white thorns.

'Those people in the train cannot hear the *kelkie-wyn … kelkie-wyn* call of the flock of sand grouse flying overhead from the waterhole,' he thinks. 'They cannot experience the smells, sounds and all the wondrous beauty around me.'

Finishing his meal and wrapping himself in his blanket next to the glowing embers, he cannot but think of the unfortunate passengers in the rumbling train. He knows that, unlike them, he will wake up tomorrow morning in the same place. And, after counting his sheep, he will spend this day and many more in this rich, arid land.

My Youth

I T WAS MY PARENTS' BELIEF THAT, APART FROM THEIR BASIC parental responsibilities, there were two prerequisites to raising children: they should know the Lord their God in all His many facets and they should receive the best possible education.

Unlike my paternal grandfather, they believed learning to be essential to success, whatever that success might eventually be. This particular conviction must have had my grandfather turning in his grave. Had he been alive, I imagine he would have thought that my father and his daughter-in-law had taken leave of their senses.

My grandfather on my mother's side, Abraham Jacobus de Swardt, was born in 1861. My grandmother, born in 1866, was named Magdalena Sophia de Swardt (née Lamprecht). The Lamprechts were a prominent family from George, a town some twelve miles from my grandfather's farm near Blanco. My mother had three brothers and three sisters. One of her sisters, Lenie, was married to a farmer with the surname Botha, and they farmed in the Cango Valley on the southern end of the Swartberg Pass, near Oudtshoorn. We would stay over with Auntie Lenie and her family on our way from Beaufort West to the Wilderness on holiday, as it was a convenient stopover point and made for pleasant family reunions.

Lenie and her husband had a daughter, Naomi, who was my age. I was very fond of Naomi and we would play together next to the river furrows and lush grass, which was completely different from the arid Beaufort West veld with which I was familiar. In 1935, I remember my parents receiving a telegram informing us that Naomi had died of diphtheria at the tender age of six years. Her death upset me terribly, and I still think of her often. Here I am, at the advanced age of eighty-three, having led a rich, full life, and it forever saddens me that she was never given the opportunities of life that I have had.

I was fortunate to meet both my maternal grandmother and great-grandmother when I was a boy, although I never met my grandfather, who had died several years previously. We didn't visit them often because the drive from Beaufort West to George was arduous. The journey along the dusty gravel road between Beaufort West and George took about twelve hours, as many stops had to be made along the way. These were generally as a result of some or other problem with our car, most frequently punctures.

My great-grandmother was the oldest woman I had ever seen. It was customary upon arrival at the farm to greet my grandmother and great-grandmother with a kiss. For me, this was a nightmare. My grandmother had a moustache and my great-grandmother a rodent ulcer on her forehead, which seemed to be eating her head away. At that age, my compassion had not yet found its potential, but I'd conform to the ritual because the reward for my counterfeit affection was a glass of cold buttermilk and a slice or two of homemade brown bread, spread thickly with homemade butter – elixir to a tired and dusty boy.

To this day, buttermilk is one of my favourite drinks, much to the disgust of my children and grandchildren. But then, they don't make buttermilk like they used to – and that's the difference.

* * *

My parents' marriage produced five sons: Johannes, Abraham, Dodsley, Christiaan and me. I was born on 3 November 1927, the youngest son of missionary parents. I don't know the time of my birth offhand, but since it was summer I know it must have been hot, dusty and dry. Our house would have smelt of – and been covered in – coal dust, because the prevailing west wind would have been blowing the smoke and dust in our direction from the railway station with its steam trains, shunting yards and work shed.

Beaufort West owed its existence to that station, and to the large sheep-farming community that it served. When there was sufficient rain, it was a flourishing community, but when there was drought – which was most of the time – the townsfolk were miserable. Topics of conversation in those periods were limited to the lack of rain, sheep deaths and poverty.

I remember very little about the first few years of my life. Perhaps this is because I don't want to remember. One thing I do recall as an infant is pushing the hand of my mother or father away when they tried to force egg into my mouth. Although I must have been very young at the time, I vividly remember a spoon of foul-smelling, nauseating yellow glue being pushed through my lips. I gagged, spat and fought to stop this. This total aversion remains with me today. I have never eaten the yolk of an egg on its own and cannot bear to watch people eating it. Call it an allergy, a psychological phenomenon or plain stupidity, but for me it is impossible even to attempt it. Should I ever suffer a heart attack, no one will be able to place the blame on eggs.

I can remember my early birthdays, in particular one where I stood at the gate of our front garden waiting for Miss Mary Dodsley Flamstead. A dear friend and confidante of my parents, she is the reason for my third-eldest brother's acquisition of such a fancy English name – Dodsley. I awaited her arrival with great eagerness because she gave me the most wonderful books as presents. One in particular I will never forget: *Wonders of the World*. As a young boy in the featureless Karoo, I was introduced to the most amazing places on earth. I gaped at the pyramids, feasted my eyes on the Victoria and Niagara Falls, walked the streets of London and New York, and much, much more.

At the time, Beaufort West had few, if any, cultural heroes. Mary was an influential force in my life as she was the only person in the town who showed an interest in broadening my horizons. As a teacher, she possibly found that Beaufort West did not provide her with many opportunities to feed a hunger for knowledge. By some fluke, I was fertile soil for her 'intellectual gardening'. Do not ask me why. Perhaps at that early stage of my education I was already throttled by the intellectual poverty of the society in which I grew up and she recognised this. I still find Mary's influence a miracle and impossible to explain.

The library was virtually next door to us and, thanks to Mary introducing me to the joys of reading, I became an avid reader of cowboy books, travel books, biographies and books on many other topics. I learnt about famous people, great wars and wonderful countries, and, later, I indulged in a few love stories. With these revelations came a fierce determination to escape Beaufort West and live these dreams. Many of them later came true. I have been lucky enough in my life to have visited some of the places that I read and dreamt about in my youth. I have since lost that amazing book, but it remains with me in my fondest memories. I often page through it mentally and think back to its significance and the profound influence that Mary Dodsley Flamstead had on my life.

When I was born, my eldest brother, Johannes, was seventeen years old and had already left home. He was studying at the University of Cape Town (UCT), where he was completing a degree in mechanical engineering. In those days, this was considered to be an exceptional qualification and achievement. After university, Johannes joined a company in Johannesburg that reprocessed spent fuels. During his time with them, he slipped in hot oil and burnt his legs severely. Once he had recovered, he returned to Cape Town and joined the South African Railways as a mechanical engineer, eventually becoming Chief District Engineer for the Western Cape. His area extended from Cape Town in the south to Upington in the north, including Beaufort West and the Eastern Cape coast to George. Within his field, Johannes was an extremely creative individual. He invented a funnel that prevented sparks from being thrown from coal-burning locomotives. This had been a great problem, as the glowing cinders had all too often caused large veld fires that burnt acres of grazing land in rural areas.

One of Johannes's duties was to establish boreholes and pumps for the supply of water to the hungry tanks of steam locomotives. Another important role of his was to investigate train accidents. On such occasions, his coach, which served as his living quarters, was coupled to the caboose – the last coach on the train – and unhooked at a siding or station until the investigation was complete. This suited him well, as he didn't have a happy marriage. Just as a sailor has a girl at every port, I suspect that Johannes – who had an eye for the ladies – had a woman at every station.

My second-eldest brother, Abraham, was born four years after my parents arrived in Beaufort West. He was a 'blue baby'. My father told me that he constantly struggled for breath, that his complexion was blue and that he was a sickly infant. We knew that his condition was in some way heart-related. From what I know today, it was more than likely what is termed a *tetralogy of Fallot*.[1] Ironically, in later life I would repair this heart lesion many times in infants. I often wonder whether Abraham's condition led both Chris and me – perhaps subconsciously – to our professions as heart surgeons.

When Abraham arrived in this world, not much could be done for him. My parents did everything they possibly could to save his life and travelled many miles to Cape Town with him to consult specialist doctors. In a desperate but futile attempt to improve his health, my father took him to Muizenberg, a southern coastal suburb between Cape Town and Cape Point, where he hoped the fresh sea air could improve his little son's condition. Their search for a cure, or even some kind of relief for Abraham, was unfortunately in vain. He died there at the age of two years.

My father told me that Abraham's last words before he died were *ta-ta*, accompanied by a tiny wave of the hand. He was buried in a cemetery in the Cape Town suburb of Plumstead. My mother subsequently requested that, when she died, she too be buried there. This wish was granted many years later.

Abraham's death deeply affected my parents. All his life, my father kept a pair of Abraham's shoes and a small piece of icing sugar that still bore his tiny teeth marks. He was always a presence in their lives and my father spoke of him often.

Then my parents' 'problem child' arrived. Dodsley was born in 1917 and, unlike the rest of us, he struggled at school. At the end of Standard 8, he performed so badly that my parents sent him to Outeniqua High School in George as a boarder. It was a very good school with an excellent track record. The principal at the time had a reputation for *dondering* his students to get them to pass their subjects. My parents hoped that this move would set Dodsley on the right path. How they managed to send him there financially, I do not know, but it paid off because Dodsley eventually passed matric.

Johannes was able to arrange employment for Dodsley at his company in Johannesburg during his first year after school. He couldn't have liked it very much, because the following year Dodsley returned to enrol at the University of Cape Town to study mechanical engineering. But, being Dodsley, he failed every subject and dropped out. He now had to find employment, and an opportunity arose in the Eastern Cape coastal city of Port Elizabeth. Dodsley took up the post and started work at General Motors but, soon afterwards, at the outbreak of the Second World War, he joined the Kaffrarian Rifles in East London. There he met a young woman, Marge, married her, and within days had to leave with a South African army unit for East Africa to take part in the Abyssinian Campaign.

After the Italians were soundly thrashed in both Abyssinia and Eritrea, Dodsley went on to North Africa with the Allied forces to join the fight against General Erwin Rommel's 'Desert Rats'. Shortly afterwards, he was captured by the Germans in Tobruk. Dodsley spent four years behind barbed wire in several concentration camps, firstly in Tobruk itself and then in Italy. When the Italians capitulated, he was taken to Poland to see out the last stages of the war, and, as the Allies marched in at the cessation of hostilities, his captors fled and Dodsley simply walked through the open gates to freedom.

Shortly after his departure from East to North Africa, however, my parents had been informed, by the feared telegram arriving at the front door, that Dodsley had been reported missing and was believed to be a prisoner of war. For more than a year, we heard no further news of him.

During this time my parents, like so many others, worried constantly about their son's well-being. There was no radio and no telephone in the house: we were virtually cut off from the world.

The most reliable source of information at my parents' disposal was the *Cape Argus*, a newspaper that arrived daily after a long train journey from Cape Town. My father would read it hungrily, willing the Allies to victory and desperately hoping that that would win freedom and a safe homecoming for his son. When major battles were being fought, Sunday church services were often cut short so that my father could get to his newspaper. Fortunately for his congregation, it seldom arrived before the service commenced; otherwise he would almost certainly have been late.

During most nights of the war, and especially because Dodsley was a prisoner of war, my father would walk to Mr Rossouw's house in Bird Street about a mile away. The house, named *Petra*, was built on a rock, and it was there that he would listen to the BBC's 6 p.m. news. I remember accompanying him and hearing the strong, beautiful voice of Ken Dimbleby speaking in a strange-sounding English accent. But what was even more impressive on the radio was the time signal, the booming chimes of London's Big Ben, which, on the second, vibrated around the Rossouws' sitting room and through the open window into the hot, dry silence of the Karoo.

Via our radio and newspaper news sources we fought the major battles with the Allies through the deserts of North Africa; we rejoiced when we heard of the great victory at the Battle of El Alamein; we invaded Italy; and we were depressed by the news of Pearl Harbour. And then came the final victorious assault on the beaches of Normandy. The confident, arrogant faces of our town's Nazi sympathisers soon changed to depression, and their claims of victory slowly turned to acceptance of defeat. This gave us great pleasure and, because we were in the minority, it became *our* moment of triumph.

On Dodsley's return to South Africa, Johannes found him employment as a bookkeeper at the South African Railways office in Beaufort West. He and his wife had a child, but the marriage soon ended in divorce. Dodsley then left for greener pastures and qualified in the then Transvaal as a bookkeeper-cum-accountant, a profession he would follow for the rest of his working life.

Dodsley never spoke about his war experiences, the exception being the story of his capture, when his German captor had apparently informed him: 'Sergeant, your war days are over.' He had also become withdrawn and, at dinner times, would simply finish his food and retire to his room without a word being spoken.

Chris was born in 1922 – like me, in the month of November. Chris's life and career, which were interwoven with mine to greater and lesser degrees for the duration of our lives, have been well documented elsewhere and will emerge as this book unfolds.

When I arrived five years later, in 1927, my mother was already aged forty-two and my father was fifty-two. It can be argued that, due to their relatively advanced years, my parents were more like grandparents to me than parents. This, however, made no practical difference to our upbringing: they both loved their sons unreservedly and equally.

Having three brothers with such large age gaps between us meant that we could never be referred to as a 'close' family. Though separated by only five years, Chris and I never got on with one another. We fought incessantly all our lives. As youngsters we used our fists; later words and other means were our weapons of choice.

* * *

After my birth, my mother developed a condition known as *otosclerosis*, an affliction involving the growth of spongy bone in the capsule of the ear's labyrinth, leading to deafness. Eventually, various kinds of hearing trumpets and hearing aids were dotted around the house. My mother fought constantly with these buzzing devices; her preference was to keep them switched off. As a result, she must have become a very good lip-reader.

All their lives, my parents remained wholesome Calvinists, never straying from this path. It was their habit to start their day in prayer. My bedroom wasn't far from theirs and, given my mother's deafness, my father had to speak forcefully. So I was always privy to their conscientious intercessions. They would begin with a reading from the Bible, followed by prayer, mentioning each of us by name. Finally, there would be the singing of a psalm.

When I was asked in later life about the reasons for our success, I would say that it was due to these daily intercessions made by my parents to God for our future well-being and safe-keeping. I'm also convinced that these actions served to instil in me a moral discipline necessary for a world in which I would one day have to make my way.

Religion was in our very marrow. Every day at lunch and dinner with our parents we played an active part in devout meditation. As my parents had done in the morning, we too would participate in reading from the Bible and singing and praying in the afternoon and evening.

When we prayed, we had to kneel. This often gave rise to a prank that we, as young children, enjoyed very much: on occasion, my elder brothers would bring their lady friends to our house and, because they too had to kneel, we never missed the opportunity to slip off one of their shoes and hide it away – resulting, of course, in much confusion and laughter.

In company and among their children, my parents were the picture of a decorous, upstanding couple. Though they were unquestionably devoted to one another, I don't think I ever witnessed a physical display of love pass between them.

When I reflect on my mother, I experience a duality of feelings. She had an immense influence on my life – of that there is no doubt. But there were other peculiarities to her character that were unsettling. She had such a forceful nature that I always felt predisposed to please her, to be the dutiful son. It was indoctrination of a kind that is hard to explain. By the time I became aware of her as a person, she was already post-menopausal – an elderly woman, anxious, deaf and leaning strongly towards hypochondria. This inclination saw my father tending unceasingly to her needs, and there was always a bottle of some or other medicine or tonic displayed around the house. She used to believe that she had some incurable disease, such as cancer, but her concerns were unfounded and she lived to the ripe old age of ninety-four.

She was an exceptionally dutiful wife and mother. She worked all her life, cooking, cleaning and running a large house. Being a mother to four boys could not have been easy. Most white people at the time had servants – children were cared for by a *kindermeid*. But we seldom had a maid in the house; it was a luxury my parents simply could not afford. To keep an eye on me while she was doing her chores, my mother would tie me to the leg of the kitchen table so that I couldn't stray without her becoming aware of it. It didn't worry me in the least; I would happily play there for hours.

With older parents and a mother who was hard of hearing, it may come as no surprise that I only started speaking when I was more than three years old. This so concerned my parents that they took me to the local doctor, as they thought I was deaf and dumb. People who know me today will certainly vouch for the fact that I made up for this misconception in later life.

Mother was not an affectionate person. In fact, my perception of her was that she was quite emotionally cold. I think this lack of warmth was largely due to her own very orthodox upbringing and perhaps because of her lack of hearing, which detached her to a large degree from the outside world.

Although she was a devoted mother, she was driven by a burning ambition for her boys. She was also the family disciplinarian. Once, while in high school, I slipped from the top position in the class. This made her terribly angry – I received a hiding I never forgot. I didn't lapse again. While he shared my mother's ambition for her sons, my father was not prone to corporal punishment; he would shy away from delivering any form of it. Although he never interfered with her particular brand of discipline, he was more inclined to talk through a problem.

Because my mother had been educated to become a teacher, she was indispensable to us when we had problems with schoolwork. Had it not been for her investment in our lives and her aspirations for our future, I doubt I would ever have left Beaufort West.

Money was always scarce. My father's parishioners were not wealthy and most of the money that found itself onto the plate on a Sunday was used not only for my father's stipend but also for the running of the church. In order to increase church funds, a variety of avenues had to be explored. At least once a year there would be a church bazaar, and Mother would set to this task with purposeful enthusiasm, cooking, baking and making preserves. Then there was the annual church concert, for which she would write a play and select congregants to participate. These were, in essence, 'morality plays' with strong social and religious messages. Other congregants would perform song-and-dance routines, but, if the women's dresses were too short or they kicked their legs too high, my father would step in and bring an immediate end to the frivolities. For these duties, as well as her responsibilities as organist, my mother received no compensation, but she performed them with diligence and grace for many years.

* * *

Often I would lie awake at night due to the oppressive summer heat. I was frequently awakened by the buzzing, dive-bomber attacks of bloodthirsty mosquitoes. During these seemingly endless nights, I would marvel at the mechanical clanking of the windmills in the gardens of our neighbourhood.

The windmill is the man-made sunflower of the Karoo. Drought – and more drought – is one of the realities of existence in this region. Grazing lands are destroyed by the lack of water and, with no food available, sheep and other animals perish. Lucerne and other fodder, if obtainable, can stave off large *vrektes*, but drinking water is essential. If unavailable, major disaster looms: riverbeds run dry and dams simply become empty craters of cracked mud.

This is where the windmill makes its great contribution to our arid land. Two things are crucial for its efficiency: large underground reservoirs and the wind. God may have denied the Karoo rain, but He gave it a bountiful supply of artisanal water. Wind is also in abundant supply. After a diviner has established the exact position of the water, a few dry holes are sunk with a bore machine. The first glimpse of water makes the operation worthwhile and brings relief to the anxious farmer. Round cement dams can then be built and filled with clean, but very brackish, water that has been sucked up and deposited in the dams by the dutiful windmill.

We believed that, in order to bring the drought-breaking rain we so desperately needed in summer, a consistent, three-day east wind was necessary. On the afternoon of the third or fourth day, rain would come – or so we prayed. It would be unbearably hot but the east wind would blow and, by midday, clouds would appear over Bulthouers Bank, our highest mountain peak, in the north-west. But, as the clouds thickened, the wind would change direction and the west wind would pick up, strengthening by the minute. Soon the clouds would disperse – and another day of hope would be blown away. This sequence would be repeated day after day.

So the wind was our hope and our despair but, throughout it all, our windmills would use both the good and the bad winds as indicators to our advantage. They turned their faces to the rain-bringing east wind and, when the wind changed, they simply swivelled their faces towards the west wind, picking up speed and continuing their delivery of water from the depths of the earth. The area around our windmill and its cement dam was lush and green, with a garden, fruit trees, vegetables, lucerne and cement troughs filled with water, from which the sheep could drink – an oasis in the parched land.

As a son of the Karoo, what I observed and learnt from the windmill taught me a valuable lesson: whatever the circumstances in my future life, whether good or bad, I would use them to my and my fellow human beings' benefit so that all around me there would be the fertile soil of compassion, love, hope and laughter.

* * *

From a young age, playing games with friends was an important part of my life. My first playmates were mostly black children from my father's congregation. They made very good friends because, since I was white, I was always the leader and always allowed to win. My playmates were simply following the example set by their elders. I loved playing with them, but from my early teens they slowly disappeared and were replaced by white children only. The biscuits and cooldrink they had been given by my mother were no longer worth the sense of inferiority that I had inadvertently conferred upon them.

We had no televisions, CDs, DVDs, iPods or computers, which today seem to dominate my grandchildren's free time. Our entertainment predated the digital era by many decades. Our large garden, with the outhouse and the two paths leading along either side of the house from the front garden to the back, was an ideal spot for playing Hide and Seek. In fact, our house and garden, with so many places to hide, was the Wembley Stadium of Hide and Seek. I loved it.

A water furrow ran from the northern side of the town to the southern end alongside the pavements on either side of Donkin Street, disappearing under the side roads. When irrigation water was supplied from the town's dam, my great friend Ray de Villiers and I would throw sticks or matches into the swirling water and race our floating objects for great distances. When they disappeared underneath the road, we'd wait with great anticipation to see whose would be the first to appear on the other side. Incidentally, my father always used to say that he grew the best *dagga* in town because of these furrows. Some of the families of those awaiting court cases would sit, smoking, on the pavement opposite the magistrates' court, which was right in front of our house. The flow of water in the furrow next to the pavement would be diverted into our garden, carrying with it *dagga* seedlings, which would subsequently germinate into large plants.

Our dam was seldom full and often dry, and was overlooked by a *koppie*. There we spent many happy hours, especially during the school holidays, playing games. The *koppie* was used for an exciting race: we removed used tyres from the backyard of the shop next door and, with great effort, rolled them up to its highest point. We then lined up the tyres and, with a push, watched them roll down the sharp incline as far as they could go. I will never forget how they picked up speed and bounced over rocks and shrubs until they eventually rolled over in great puffs of sand. The boy whose tyre went the furthest was declared the winner. Then we would rush down to gather them, clamber up the *koppie* again and repeat the process until we tired.

One of the earliest games I played was Ring a Ring o' Roses:

> Ring a ring o' roses,
> A pocketful of posies.
> A-tishoo, a-tishoo!
> We all fall down.

Many years later I discovered that this game we so innocently played originated from one of the worst plagues in history, the bubonic plague of London in 1665, which killed approximately a hundred thousand people – 20 per cent of London's population at the time. The lyrics to the nursery rhyme have their origin in a children's ring game and represent the symptoms, 'cures' and stages of the plague. Symptoms included a raised red rash on the skin, as well as violent sneezing and coughing. People carried pouches of sweet-smelling herbs, as it was believed that the disease was transmitted by bad smells. The scourge was halted by the Great Fire of London in 1666, which killed the flea-ridden rats carrying the disease.

As we became older, we ventured further. In summer, swimming in the dam and swimming pool – if there was water – in the sweltering heat of a Karoo summer was a favourite pastime. We became boat builders, using corrugated-tin sheets normally used for roofs to construct these boats. After much beating with a hammer and bending, we would fashion a bottom with enough space in which to sit. The boat ends, however, proved to be the major problem. Approximating the bent sheet into a canoe-like structure meant that the two points where the left and right halves met had to be watertight. With the use of mud, newspapers and hessian sacks, the openings were closed up and we would proudly carry our boat to the dam. When launched, it almost always sank – even before we could climb in!

Nearly every upturned stone in the veld produced a scorpion, giving rise to another childhood game. Each of us would catch a scorpion and place the now very angry creature in a shoebox with the others. With nothing else to fight, they attacked one another, which often resulted in their deaths.

As time passed, my friend Ray taught me how to play chess. Although we played often, I seldom won. Testosterone began to make its presence known, and girls entered my life. But as school became a more serious consideration and I had to study more, my carefree days slowly came to an end.

I believe that my grandchildren, born into the digital era, have missed out a lot on the wonderful games we played. But I'm sure they'll disagree!

* * *

One of the highlights for our dusty little town, which was rarely brought outside entertainment, was the visits of the merry-go-round and circus. We would wake up one morning and, as if by magic, the swings, rides and other attractions would be in place on a piece of common ground that, on the previous night, had been a bare patch of rocky Karoo earth. I have to admit that the merry-go-round didn't hold much attraction for me – it was noisy and, in any event, I couldn't afford to pay for the various swing rides.

But the circus was a different matter altogether. We were visited by two touring circuses, Boswell's and Pagel's. Again, the bare piece of ground with no vegetation, visited only by the odd mangy dog, was transformed overnight by the presence of a large tent and cages with lions and tigers, Shetland and other ponies and, best of all, elephants.

We couldn't wait for the school bell to ring, releasing us from our 'book prison' to rush to the small African jungle that would be part of the town for the next twenty-four hours. We stared, open-mouthed, at the big cats and watched with amazement how the gigantic elephants ate straw by daintily picking up armfuls of it with their trunks and depositing it into their large mouths.

But gaining access to the actual circus performance was a major problem. Since we did not have enough money to buy tickets, we had to find devious ways and means to get inside the big top. We could try to slip in past the ticket attendant when she was distracted by one of us asking her questions, but this seldom succeeded, as the attendants were wise to our sly antics. A better and more successful method was to gain entrance by lifting the side flaps and crawling inside the tent at a spot hidden from the circus staff's view. The most opportune time to attempt this was when the trapeze artists had everybody looking skywards. This method was, unfortunately, less effective when we tried it at some of the performances of Pagel's Circus. Old Mrs Pagel must have been in her eighties, but she ruled the circus with an iron fist. We children feared her, as stories abounded of what she would do to us if we were caught. I certainly did not want to be fed to the lions! When she was on duty – which was all the time – we very seldom managed to gain admission to the circus shows.

But, when we were successful and were safely hidden behind a pole or chair inside the tent, we were in wonderland. I will never forget the trapeze artists flying through the air or the lion tamer alone in the ring with snarling lions that jumped through hoops and rolled on the ground. I could hardly watch when the lion tamer put his head into the mouth of the biggest male. What utter joy for us youngsters starved of entertainment!

The highlight for me, however, was the clowns' act, especially one clown called *Ticky*. When he entered the ring with his face painted white, a large red nose and big ears protruding from under the silly, small hat perched on his head, we would cheer madly. Ticky's baggy trousers were a good few sizes too big for him, and were held up by suspenders. His tricks and antics had us literally rolling in the aisles. The best-loved act was when he ran up the steps to choose an overweight matron, on whose lap he'd sit. As he raced up the steps the people in the matron's immediate vicinity would scatter in all directions to get out of his way, falling over each other in the process.

The next morning, the tent, the animals and Ticky would be gone and the bare, dusty patch was as lonely as before. I wonder what happened to Ticky the clown, and whether he ever knew just how much pleasure he gave me and my young friends.

Beaufort West also received 'culture injections' from touring theatrical companies. The Hanekoms, André Huguenet and Wena Naudé were some of the prominent pioneers of Afrikaans theatre who visited our town at regular intervals. I cannot remember an English group ever coming to Beaufort West to entertain us, but since it was an almost exclusively Afrikaans town that is hardly surprising.

I seldom found the money to buy tickets to the plays, which were performed in the cinema. Most of the plays were about the suffering of the Afrikaners during and after the Anglo-Boer War, the Great Drought and other calamities. I recall attending one such performance, which told of a girl from a poor family who found herself pregnant before marriage, how she was banished in shame and how she struggled in the city before her lover, now a successful farmer, came to take her back into his bosom. We all left the hall sniffing and blowing our noses. These plays, however, did form a part of our education, in that they provided rare glimpses of a world outside Beaufort West.

On one occasion, Beaufort West was abuzz with expectation and excitement. The *ossewa-trek*, commemorating the Great Trek – known to the Afrikaners as *die Groot Trek* – that took place more than a hundred years earlier, was on its way from Cape Town to Pretoria – and it was set to pass through our town.

The Great Trek, which started in 1835, saw more than 10 000 Boers – termed *Voortrekkers* – leave the Cape Colony with their families by ox-wagon to proceed into the northern and north-eastern parts of the British colony and beyond. The mass exodus was caused in part by the Boers' economic problems and the threatening danger of conflict with the Xhosas, who settled on the other side of the Fish River. But they left largely because of their discontent with the English colonial authorities. The Great Trek led to the founding of numerous Boer republics, including the prominent Natalia Republic, the Orange Free State Republic and the Transvaal.

The determination and courage of these pioneers has become one of the most important elements of the folk memory of Afrikaner nationalism. Great entertainment was planned in our town for this celebration, including speeches, *volksspeletjies*, *boeremusiek* and concerts. Ladies were making their own *Voortrekker* dresses and hats, and the flags of the republics were draped all over Donkin Street.

Even more important was the swell of Afrikaner pride and nationalism that this event created. It provided a great opportunity for Afrikanerdom in general, and the National Party in particular, to dredge up the battles of the past – Slagtersnek, Blood River, Majuba and the Anglo-Boer War – and to resuscitate all the bad things and wrongs of the hated *rooinekke* and jingoes – those Afrikaners who took the side of the English.

As always, Beaufort West was divided. The blacks and coloureds were excluded from the celebrations, although they could cook, clean and do the work that was reserved for them. The English were, not surprisingly, also unwelcome, and the jingoes didn't really feel part of the celebrations either. It should, of course, come as no surprise that during these celebrations the Union Jack was banned.

For us youngsters – whether English, Jewish or children of jingoes – this was not a problem; we gladly took part in the celebrations. After all, when last had Beaufort West hosted such festivities? I can still remember the horsemen advancing down Donkin Street on beautiful *ryperde* with the colourful flags of the Transvaal and Orange Free State republics swirling in the hot, dry breeze. The streets were lined with cheering people; inquisitive blacks and coloureds were tolerated. Next marched the bearded *ooms* and the *tannies*, wearing traditional multicoloured jackets, pants and dresses. Then came the span of beautiful red, long-horned *osse* pulling the creaking wagon. Beaufort West had never seen anything like it, and everybody in town watched the procession in awe and amazement. All except one – my father, who had announced that he was staging his own personal boycott. While we stood in the parsonage garden on Donkin Street and watched the ox-wagon pass, my father planted watermelon seeds in the vegetable garden. None of the seeds germinated. His explanation for this was that he could not see why God should bless anything relating to this day.

The 'Trek' stayed over for one night, and the following morning there was an official breakfast. My father was asked to attend and to offer a prayer. He refused, saying that he could not ask God's blessings if the people he represented were excluded from the occasion.

Prophetically, this would be the beginning of bad times for our country. This *ossewa-trek* contributed significantly to an upsurge of nationalism, stunted for a few short years by the Second World War. But it resumed with fervour immediately after the war, resulting in the defeat of Jan Smuts's government three years later and the installation of a party led by D.F. Malan. Over the next few decades, the policy of apartheid caused not only unnecessary suffering with its immoral laws, but an immense division between blacks and whites, which, even today – seventeen years into democracy – is still a major problem and a day-to-day reality that hinders our progress towards full racial reconciliation.

How did my father know that this would come to pass? I believe that, working with black people and witnessing their daily struggles, he must have sensed their determination to rise up against this suppression. I pray that, in heaven, he is aware that his sacrifices were not in vain.

* * *

Growing up in a parsonage as the son of strict Calvinistic parents, most things were considered a sin. Drinking was a sin, smoking was a sin, dancing was evil and any form of sex before marriage was a sin. A girl who fell pregnant before she was married had fallen into sin, and she became subject to the censure of the Dutch Reformed Church – and especially my father. Such girls were forbidden to take Communion and could not be married in the church.

With my parents being so strict and so much older, I grew up without any real knowledge of girls or sex. (I discovered that girls menstruated only when taking biology classes during my first year at university.) In my teenage years, however, as my male hormones kicked in, I became more aware of the female species. At first it was look, then look and kiss, and eventually touch became a new experience, which was very pleasant – but there it ended.

In my matric year, I became 'cased' to a girl named Hettie. 'Cased' was a term used by us to indicate that there existed a special relationship between two youngsters – she was 'your girl'. This was often unspoken and unwritten – an understanding of sorts. Hettie was sweet, with a good figure, large eyes and a permanent smile. She was a year behind me at school and very clever. But there was one serious problem: her father was very strict. She was not allowed to meet or go out with boys. An even bigger problem was that her father was a large man and our police sergeant. He patrolled the streets of our town on a bicycle. So our moments together were few and furtive – I was constantly on the lookout for a police uniform.

But love always finds a way. Hettie's friend's mother went out to play cards on Friday nights, which enabled us to meet at the friend's house. Soon after she left, the lights in the room were switched off and the fun started. Afterwards, I would walk Hettie halfway home, as I was always fearful of encountering her policeman father. Our romance ended when I went to university.

* * *

Holidays for my parents lasted for, at the most, a period of two weeks, and they were always taken annually over the New Year. This was the only time when both of my parents were free of other responsibilities. For my mother, the time must have been a godsend.

My father owned a holiday house at the Wilderness, a tiny coastal town situated between George and Knysna. How my father acquired the place, or where he found the money to do so, I have never established. All I know is that it cost £700. Today, it is a bed and breakfast with a restaurant where our garage used to be. But out front, the Cape mahogany and *melkbos* trees, which my father and I once planted, still stand.

During our youth, the Wilderness consisted of about twenty houses. We went there most years, except during the war, when petrol restrictions were particularly severe. On the last day of the 'old year', the car would be packed. Before we set off, my father had to conduct the New Year's midnight service, so we would sit waiting in the car, our anticipation barely tolerable. At one minute past twelve on the dot, my father would pronounce his final 'Amen' of the year. He would then put a white coat over his vestments and off we'd go.

Between Beaufort West and Meiringspoort the road was badly corrugated, which typically resulted in at least five or six punctures. In certain parts, it was entirely unlevelled and we would find ourselves tilting and pitching around in the car, often with the serious threat of broken bones. Often we'd come to a standstill and the car would need to be cranked back to life, after which, once again, we'd proceed on our bumpy journey.

At about eight o'clock in the morning we would reach Meiringspoort, where we'd stop for breakfast – usually in the form of a *braaivleis* – at the waterfall. Then, after several more hours of driving, we'd stop over at my grandmother's farm. The next day we would arrive at our promised destination. For one last time the old motor car would negotiate the bridge over the Kaaimans River, splutter up a short incline and then, wonder beyond wonders, the sight of the Wilderness would unfold before our eyes. The smell of the sea air and the sight of rolling sand dunes and the waves crashing onto the endless white sandy beaches was the ultimate experience of paradise.

When we opened the house, it would smell damp and musty. The windows would be opaque with the sticky accumulations of sea mists and relentless coastal winds. Soon the unforgettable smell of the ocean would come rolling in, along with the roar of breaking waves. These sensations would be the prelude to days of easy-going happiness.

One of the many wonderful experiences in the Wilderness of my youth was caddying at the local golf course, which we did to make extra pocket money. I would stand outside the hotel waiting for those guests who wanted to play golf. Because I was the youngest, I had to wait till last. But when I eventually got my chance to carry a bag, I was rewarded with a ticky – the equivalent of three pennies, or three pence.

The first five holes of the golf course were situated on the Knysna side of Wilderness and the remaining four were on the George side. But we hardly ever completed the last four holes: the players had to walk through the hotel after the fifth and generally stopped in the bar for drinks, seldom returning to see out the rest of their game.

We often made extra money by selling lost golf balls. As the course was very sandy, we developed a favourite trick for finding players' balls in the rough, which was usually dense bush: we purposely trod them into the sand and then, at the end of the day, retraced our steps, recovered the balls and sold them back to the players.

With a ticky in my pocket after a day of caddying, I'd run to the bottom of the fairway of the first hole, where there was a little shop that sold everything.

I'd buy ju-jubs; liquorice, which we called *donkey drops*; little sweets with love inscriptions on them; and sour sweets called *suurklontjies*. But my favourites were n****r balls. These were totally black on the outside and, as one sucked them, they changed colour: to red, blue, pink and finally white before they melted away completely. Maybe, just maybe, they foretold what was going to happen to South Africa in the then distant future.

Since I was still only a *laaitie* then, I did not play the game of golf myself until many years later. But, I profess that I was a better caddie than I am golfer.

* * *

Despite spending years hewing trees, my father, with his signature moustache, was quite a sickly person. He suffered all his life from pernicious anaemia. Part of his diet was to eat raw liver disguised as watercress sandwiches. Often I would join him in a show of support – it was the only way I could think of helping him through this particular form of gastric torment. Though he was not a pushover – he was considered by many people to be quite prickly, and was always in conflict with the immoral stand taken by certain quarters of the white community – he was an extremely compassionate and generous person. I loved my Deddie without reservation, and was always very close to him.

One memory of him that is particularly dear to me was a habit of his on our birthdays. At lunchtime, he always put a flower at our place at the table. He never forgot. When one of us was ill, it was he who comforted us or looked after our needs, and I believe that it was from his unique approach to life that we learnt what compassion was all about.

My early years coincided with the end of the Great Depression. To make matters worse, the Karoo was hit by *die Groot Droogte* – the Great Drought – which resulted in great hardships for those people of Beaufort West who were dependent on the farming community. Flocks of merino and Persian sheep were decimated and the farmers had to give up their livelihood. This, of course, resulted in many job losses, particularly among farm labourers, many of whom formed part of my father's parish. They could no longer afford their weekly offerings, the fundraising bazaars failed financially and my father's church could no longer pay his stipend.

With no income, my father had to look for some other form of employment. He found it as a temporary minister serving among the white community at a place called Vanwyksvlei, situated very close to Oudtshoorn.

As a result, my mother, Dodsley, Chris and I relocated to the Wilderness during this period to be closer to him. I was too young to attend school at the time, but Dodsley and Chris attended one at nearby Harkerville, a *dorp* situated on a small plateau above the Wilderness. For my brothers, getting there and back required a long walk up and down the hill.

During this period, large areas of this part of South Africa were bought by the Dutch Reformed Church for the purpose of relocating destitute farmers and 'poor whites', who farmed pigs and cows and, for sustenance, planted sweet potatoes and *mielies*. They supplemented their income by rowing onto the nearby lagoons at night to catch fish, especially *harders* and *springers*. Attracted by a strong light, the fish would jump into their boats and later be roasted in a pan, making for delicious eating. They also collected *Hotnotsvye* on the sand dunes, and we would make jam from the pulpy fruit. Even today, I can remember those young, poorly dressed white boys and girls venturing down the hill carrying Oros bottles filled with milk, sweet potatoes, green *mielies* and buckets full of *Hotnotsvye*.

* * *

In 1935, when I was eight years old, my father developed double pneumonia and became desperately ill. Everyone thought he was going to die; in those days, infections of all kinds were commonplace and often fatal. To add to this illness, and as a result of a lack of adequate oral hygiene, he developed an infection in both of his parotid glands.

His face and neck swelled up like a balloon, which threatened to block the air passage from his throat to his lungs. To relieve the pressure and to stop him from suffocating, the doctors had to lance both sides of his face to drain the pus from these glands. It was a drastic medical intervention which, later on, had an interesting and uncommon physical consequence.

During surgery, some nerves were severed. The first type, the parasympathetic nerves, stimulate the salivary glands to keep the mouth moist, while the second kind, the sympathetic nerves, stimulate sweating when one is overexerted or frightened. Unfortunately, after my father's surgery some of the nerves stimulating saliva ended up being connected to those that stimulated perspiration, and vice versa. The regrettable outcome of this was that my poor father would subsequently sweat profusely when eating, while struggling to chew his food as a result of a dry mouth. This condition stayed with him until the day he died.

During his period of recovery from pneumonia, a certain irony raised its head. As was the habit every year on Reformation Sunday, preachers of the Dutch Reformed Church, or any other church that fell under its jurisdiction, were required to deliver sermons on the evils of Catholicism. My father was no exception. But while he lay sick in bed, it was the local Catholic priest and the Jewish rabbi who visited him and comforted him with prayer. Not once during that time did the town's *dominee* darken his door. The *dominee*'s lack of common courtesy – and Christianity, in fact – left an indelible impression on me, and I came to realise the extent to which my father's stance on racial issues had angered this *dominee* and some of the Dutch Reformed Church's conservative white congregation.

It would have been interesting to observe my father's reaction to one of his granddaughters, Marie, who is married to and practises as a devout Catholic. She and her husband, Darryl, have produced three beautiful daughters and one son, all of whom are Catholic. Knowing my father, I think that he would, decades ago, have changed his view and shown his love and devotion to those of this faith.

My father consistently had to stand up to the town's bullies. When Dodsley was fighting in the Second World War, these same people decided to apply the jackboot. He already over sixty years of age; one would have thought that they would have refrained from bullying him. Not them. At the time, South Africa was experiencing a rise in Afrikaner nationalism. In Beaufort West, the *Ossewabrandwag*, an Afrikaner cultural group, had mutated into a paramilitary organisation and members fast aligned themselves with the National Socialist ideals that Adolf Hitler was propagating with fervour.

My father spoke out against their anti-British, pro-Nazi madness and openly supported the Allies in their quest to free the world of Nazism. He also publicly backed the entitlement of independent opinion among all dwellers in Beaufort West. As a consequence, he was continually harassed and intimidated. Even the Dutch Reformed Church's *ringkommissies* actively attempted to have him dismissed from his position.

One day, for a few hours, my father had – apart from us – an unlikely ally in his support for the English cause. He was a pupil at my school, Pieter Maritz, nicknamed *Piet Cock-eye* because he had a permanently crooked neck and could therefore never look directly at you. There had been a heavy battle between the Allies and the Germans in which the latter were trounced. In celebration, Piet arrived in class waving a Union

Jack. His proud affiliation did not last long and he was given a thorough hiding. Despite this, and with tears streaming down his face, he continued to wave the flag defiantly.

When these incidents were taking place, I was already in high school and well on my way to completing my secondary education. Naturally I was conscious of what was occurring politically and of the direct repercussions for our family, for which certain groups of people in our town were responsible. Eventually the opportunity to voice my own displeasure arose. I was sixteen years old, and I was due for confirmation in the Dutch Reformed Church. All candidates, who were required to appear before the *dominee* and other appointed elders of the church, were obliged to answer questions that would determine the candidates' suitability for taking Communion and becoming full members of the church. There was, in particular, one important question that would be asked: 'Can you honestly declare that you are a Christian and that you will follow a Christian way of life?' Usually the answer was 'Yes.' Mine, however, was 'No.'

The church elders were obviously shocked at my response and asked me why I felt this way. I replied that I couldn't believe in a church that treated my father the way theirs did. This, of course, threw the cat among the pigeons, and a lengthy and heated debate followed. Eventually they decided to confirm me because, I was told, I'd at least had the decency to be honest.

On one occasion, my father stood as a candidate in the municipal election but received very few votes. I suppose one could argue it was to his advantage that this happened: he now knew, unambiguously, that he would find few allies among the town's white Afrikaans community. This fact, however, didn't faze him; it merely spurred him on. Where moral principle was concerned, my father never wavered. It remained a constant source of worry to him, however, what his adversaries might try next.

As a result of my father's hard work and insistence that there should be a good school for the non-white children in Beaufort West, a primary school was opened in 1931, in Bird Street. As part of his duties, my father was superintendent of both the coloured primary school and the coloured high school. This meant, among other things, that he played a major role in the appointments of the principals and teachers of both schools. The teachers were all coloured. Although these were mission schools, their principal and vice-principal were better qualified than their counterparts at the white schools. This, no doubt, was yet another thorn in the flesh of the antagonists, who eventually decided that the coloured primary school and the mission church, which occupied prime positions in white Beaufort West, should be moved to the coloured section of town. My father was appalled and took up the cudgel on behalf of his people.

One of the principal agitators of this view was Fred Bastiaanse, my father's assistant. A robust man with a wide girth, Oom Fred had hair that was closely shorn at the sides but stood up like a fright on top. Poor Oom Fred desired only one thing: my father's job. He was not without position or influence among the white community, and the more conservative of them saw him as the perfect replacement for my troublesome father. Should Oom Fred occupy my father's position, they knew they would have no problem relocating my father's school and his church from the middle of the town to the coloured location.

The local authorities tried every mean ploy they could think of to have the church and school moved, but my father resisted with all of his being. They went so far as to have an ordinance passed in the municipality to enforce the removals. When my father heard about this, he sought to stop them in their tracks. He immediately, and at his own expense, took the matter to the High Court in Cape Town.

I was a second-year medical student at the University of Cape Town at the time. Two days prior to the hearing, my father sent me a telegram asking me to meet him at Cape Town Station the following day. I was obviously surprised by his unexpected visit. On his arrival, he explained what had happened and said that he wanted an interdict from the Cape High Court against the ordinance. He succeeded: the court ruled that the school and parsonage were to remain in their current location.

The interdict didn't stop the local authorities, however, who simply bided their time. Although frustrated, they never gave up on pursuing their agenda. When my father eventually retired, they saw that the road was clear and succeeded: in 1953, the primary school was moved to the location and named *Excelsior*. It provided education for the children of the coloured and black communities. In 1962, due to the enforcement of the Group Areas Act, the school was moved to Rustdene, where, today, dedicated teachers of the A.H. Barnard Primêre Skool continue to provide excellent education to the children of the town.

* * *

My father's church was closed as a place of worship in 1964. After an eight-year tussle between Beaufort West's municipality and the Dutch Reformed

Mission Church, the church and its parsonage were sold to the municipality for R40 000.

From 1967 to 1975, the church was used as a sports centre (for badminton and other indoor sports) and the parsonage was apparently occupied as an office. Between 1975 and 1977, artefacts were moved to the mission church, and the church and the parsonage were declared a national monument on 22 February 1980.

Ms Caroline Bedeker of the Beaufort West Museum recently informed me that the upgrading of exhibits in the mission church is still in the planning phase, but that the curators will concentrate on re-establishing the history of this church and its missionaries. To date, the museum has traced the broad history of religious leaders in the town and included other ancient paraphernalia, including old rifles (which, I am pleased to hear, are soon to be removed – what these weapons had to do with the religious history of our town I fail to see).

My father's contribution to the spiritual upliftment of his congregation and the significant role he played as a missionary for thirty-seven years has, however, been reduced to just a few photographs: the dominant exhibits of the Dutch Reformed Church *dominees* of that era eclipse all other exhibits in the mission church.

The parsonage in which I was born is adorned with pictures of my parents, the family, our youth and other family memorabilia from this period. While my parents' bedroom has been correctly featured, little care has been taken over the photographic displays: Johannes is frequently described as 'Marius', for example, and Dodsley is often labelled 'Chris'.

I believe that the mission church ought be dedicated to my father, who served God and its parishioners for a lifetime. My dream is that this church will be reconverted into a place where people of all races and religions can worship together; where its open doors will enable people to come inside at any time to pray and to feel the presence of their God.

To this day, I have never been able to forgive Beaufort West for what some of its locals did to my father and how they desecrated his church. The way in which he spoke out for what he believed was right taught me my own lessons, however, and for that I will always be proud of, and very grateful to, my father.

* * *

45

It is hard to believe that the amenities installed in our houses today are so taken for granted. They are so vastly different from those with which I grew up. When I say *our*, I am unfortunately referring to the privileged minority of South Africa's citizens and not to the vast majority, who still have to endure accommodation far worse than I have ever experienced. I shudder to think how people exist in the tin-and-cardboard houses that they call home. I can see absolutely no future for South Africa until the majority of our people have decent homes, primary education, work, primary health care, potable water and proper sanitation.

But back to our house, where I lived for seventeen years. Instead of an indoor, flushing toilet, we made use of an outhouse with the bucket system. Until I left home, I had never experienced the luxury of a waterborne toilet. The outhouse was situated about fifty yards from the house. As the garden was well treed, a walk in the dark at around midnight to tend to nature was a scary experience.

Twice a week, we were awoken by the sound of the municipal bucket carriers opening the gate, finding their way to the location of the outhouse and replacing the bucket. What a dreadful job. On a few occasions on their way back to the street, they would trip up in the dark and literally leave a bad smell on their way out. When this occurred, it was my duty to clean up. I can still recommend Jeyes Fluid for this unpleasant task. On the positive side, a month or two later a patch of the garden would produce an abundance of vegetables.

Attending to personal hygiene, especially in winter, was most unpleasant and we tried to avoid it at all costs. Since there was no hot-water system in the house, washing one's hands and face during those cold months was an icy experience. In the Karoo, the temperature at night frequently drops to below zero degrees. When this happened, the next morning's ablutions were met with freezing water. Brushing one's teeth was, in itself, a painful undertaking. But bathing was the really tricky problem, especially during winter. With no geyser in the house, bathing was an outdoor ritual that took place on Saturday mornings. A big black pot was filled with water and, once boiling on the Esse stove, it was poured into a large zinc bath. Cold water was then added to achieve the right temperature. *Kaalgat*, with teeth chattering and gooseflesh prickling, we were in and out: quickly we would soak, scrub and rinse before jumping out again to return to the relative warmth of the house. Fortunately this was a weekly torture only.

Saturday was also *maagskoon maak* using a generous dose of liquid from 'the blue bottle' – castor oil. This foul-tasting oily substance was believed to clean one's blood. I still do not completely understand why, but it certainly resulted in a few sprints to the little house in the garden.

During the very hot summers there was no air-conditioner, and during the freezing winters there was only a small wood-burning fireplace that smoked too much, making breathing indoors difficult. My father, who suffered from bad asthma, could not tolerate the smoke-filled house, so the fireplace was never used.

The summer heat was often unbearable. When the municipal swimming pool had water, we could take a dip to cool off, but, since the pool was a good few miles away, when we walked back home we were hotter and sweating more than when we had left. As I have mentioned, it was not only the heat that made sleeping an ordeal in summer but the mosquitoes, which attacked nightly in fearsome swarms. The bites were not the problem but rather the continuous, well-recognised warning that these dive-bombers sounded before their attack. As a repellent, we used a spray called *pumo*, but its odour was obnoxious and very irritating to the nose and throat. The mosquitoes, after a while, loved it and increased their savage nocturnal assaults. When one couldn't take it any longer, the only option was to switch on the light and search for them on the walls and ceiling. A well-aimed, flat-handed smack obliterated the whining insects. If one was unable to reach the ceiling, an accurate throw of a cushion would kill them as they sat there. In the morning, the walls and ceiling looked as if Michelangelo had been painting there all night. Since they were seldom painted, we could observe our nightly victories for months – even years – afterwards.

* * *

Without a telephone or radio, we corresponded via telegram or the postal service and acquired news either by going to those friends who owned a radio or by reading the *Cape Argus*. As an avid reader, I could hardly wait for my father to finish reading about the day's events in the newspaper. As soon as he put it down, I rushed to get it from him and retired with the paper to my bedroom.

As a young, sports-mad Afrikaans boy, it was the back pages that most interested me. At that time there were no scantily clad, bosomy ladies peering from these pages, but rather sports news. I read every single line and had a thick scrapbook into which I pasted photographs of my boyhood sports heroes.

Wrestling was very popular in those days. The muscular Jim Londos and our local favourite, *Die Gemaskerede Wonder* – 'The Masked Marvel' – were greatly admired. The latter's identity was well hidden. He made a promise that only when he was beaten would he reveal his true identity. But he kept on winning, more often than not by way of his famous 'paralysing mule kick'. But all things come to an end, and when he eventually lost and was obliged to remove his mask, he was, much to our pride, found to be one of us – an Afrikaans boy.

In the world of boxing, Joe Louis – the formidable 'Brown Bomber' – Max Baer and Max Schmeling reigned. Schmeling, a German, was Hitler's pride, but he was loathed by us. To everyone's delight, the German boxer was pulverised by Louis in their rematch after a few seconds in the first round of the world heavyweight boxing title – another blow against Nazi Germany and a small victory for those of us supporting the Allies in Beaufort West.

But rugby was, by far, our most popular sport. We knew most of the teams in South Africa, especially those in Cape Town – Gardens, Maitland, Hamiltons, Villagers and Van der Stel, to name a few of the more prominent teams. But the two 'Varsity' teams captured our imagination the most: Stellenbosch University – the 'Maties' – and the University of Cape Town – the 'Ikeys'. Every Monday I would wait eagerly to read the results, and would be terribly unhappy if the Ikeys lost, particularly as I had an older brother studying at UCT at the time. Each and every member of the Springbok rugby team was known to me by name, as were the positions in which they played: Gerry Brand – fullback; Bennie Osler – flyhalf; Boy Louw and his brother Fanie – front-rankers; and several others. These were my heroes, and I can still recall each member of the 1937 series-winning team that defeated the mighty All Blacks in New Zealand.

In those days, soccer among white South Africans was hardly known in the rural areas, so it remains a mystery to me why I, as a young boy, took such an interest in this game, especially those matches played in Cape Town and the United Kingdom. I followed the results and log positions of my favourite teams keenly. In Cape Town, there was Clyde, Liesbeek Park, De Beers (known as the *Dynamiters*, as their players were composed mainly of employees from the De Beers Dynamite Factory in the Strand) and my favourite, Marist FC. Most of the names of my favourite players have, unfortunately, disappeared from my memory. Most amazing for me, however, is the great interest that I developed for English and Scottish football history. I picked Arsenal (the Gunners) and Glasgow Rangers, teams that still receive my loyalty and support. Why I chose them will always be a mystery to me.

* * *

Given the geography of his birthplace, it is not surprising that my father was a great lover of nature. It was his custom to take a daily walk after lunch and longer walks on Sundays. I accompanied him often and he would use these opportunities to teach me about his life philosophy, the Karoo and, above all, his boundless love for his fellow man.

Because Beaufort West was such a small town, it took only a few minutes for us to be out in the open veld, with its *koppies* and scrub-land. My father had an extraordinary knowledge of the flora of the Karoo and he would teach me the names of the plants we came upon. Eventually I found myself caught up in his enthusiasm and I constructed a rockery in our back garden where, with my father's help, I grew and nurtured the plants we had identified.

It goes without saying that my father was a keen gardener. He cultivated a vegetable patch, but his success in this endeavour was dependent on the amount of water in the municipal dam, which provided the town with water. If there was a drought and the dam's water levels were low, vegetables didn't grow. But he also tended our garden's many fruit trees. When in season, walnuts, plums, figs, apricots, almonds and lemons were plentiful.

People talk about the featureless, ugly Karoo, and much of this is true. We who lived there have to concede that we missed green mountains, forests, rivers and rolling fields. But the Karoo has its own beauty, which my father showed me from an early age. As I have mentioned, what the untrained eye sees is perhaps not spectacular, but it is in that which one *doesn't* see that the Karoo's true beauty lies. In the Karoo veld there live scorpions, spiders, beetles, ants, snakes and lizards. The vegetation is sparse. Thorn trees are typical Karoo bushes but, for me, it was the succulents that made those walks with my father all the more worthwhile. Even today I remember some of their Latin names: *Lithops lesliei, Stapelius, Euphorbia* and a few more. These little plants are the real children of the Karoo. They exist because they adapt to the dry conditions by becoming water-storage plants – each leaf or root a reservoir. They are usually small but can take the form of various sizes and shapes and, if one is lucky enough to see their flowers, one will observe that even they adapt to ensure their continued existence. I became an enthusiastic collector of succulents and my rock garden became so admired and well known that we had visitors from all over South Africa as well as from overseas coming to see it. I still miss my succulents garden.

When Chris and I were at school, we were each delegated a tree for which to care. Chris's tree was the apricot, mine the methley plum, a tree that bore an astonishing amount of small, sweet, delicious fruit, which I'd sell for pocket money. It was also the tree to which my mother referred when I returned home from school one afternoon boasting of some or other achievement. She responded by saying, 'Go to the plum tree and take a look. The branches with the most fruit are the ones closest to the ground.' It was a valuable piece of advice: the more one achieves, the humbler one must be. One of the many things my mother instilled in me was the importance of humility, irrespective of one's achievements and accolades. This has been a lasting guide for me.

* * *

There were a few places in the Beaufort West of my growing-up years that were havens to me, one of which was the department store.

Situated on the right-hand side of our house was Mortimer and Hill. The store had three departments: one for women – mainly clothing and perfumes – another for men's clothing and a third for hardware and groceries. It was the men's department that attracted me most, but not because of its clothing. It was the possessor of a small instrument of magic – the gramophone.

We'd go there often to listen to the records being played. The gramophone was advertised with a picture of a squat wooden box with a little dog, Nipper, listening intently to the music from its horn-shaped 'speaker'. The 'His Master's Voice' records and others would magically produce the popular music of Bing Crosby, Al Jolson and other vocal luminaries of the day.

My favourite theme was Hawaiian music. The lilting melodies of 'My Little Grass Shack in Kealakekua, Hawaii', 'Hawaiian Wedding Song' and several others were captivating, and I dreamt of visiting these exotic islands. I had such expectations after these boyhood dreams that years later I would promise Inez that I'd take her there.

The manager of Mortimer and Hill was Mr Rossouw. He had two sons, Laurie and Mitchell. Although Laurie was more Dodsley's contemporary and Mitchell Chris's, I also tagged along. They were our best friends and, to me, Mitchell was something of a hero. There was a fence between our house and the department store, at the back of which were storage places with sufficient parking space for the transport lorries. From here, Mitchell would slip into the shop and help himself to Vienna sausages, tins of bully beef and sardines, condensed milk and bottles of Oros. These foods never entered our house – they were delicacies my parents couldn't afford. We would toss the pilfered goods over the fence and a feast would ensue. To our palates, this was gourmet delight – absolute heaven. Even today I'm extremely partial to such foodstuffs.

5

Schooling Years

I SPENT ALL OF MY SCHOOLING YEARS IN BEAUFORT WEST, STARTING at the preparatory school in 1934. Located near the municipal stores on the eastern edge of the town, this school covered our initial education – Sub A, Sub B and Standard 1 (the equivalent of today's Grades 1 to 3). For reasons unknown to me, I completed the first two grades in only one year. I would like to believe that it was because I was so very clever! From there I graduated to the primary school, where I completed Standards 2 to 6, and then attended the high school from Standard 7 to my final year of school, *matric*, as South Africans tend to call it.

The primary and high schools were situated in the same grounds, close to the railway station. Both were built from local granite rock and, in winter, the classrooms were ice-cold. There were attempts to warm the schools in the cold months by installing fireplaces in the classrooms, but, since they served only to fill the rooms with smoke, this initiative proved to be a failure and was soon abandoned.

One of the more pleasant moments at school occurred during playtime, when the poorer children were given a cup of hot vegetable soup in winter and chunks of cheese in summer. As I was considered to fit into this social category, I could also take part in the bonanza. The cheese, as a rule, was old, mouldy and very sharp. Today, roughly eight decades later, I still ask my wife to buy offcuts of this kind of cheese to match the flavour that I so savoured during those early schooldays.

When the weather allowed, I went to school barefooted – right up to matric – and had to wear old school clothes, darned and patched, as handed down from my older brothers. My first suit I acquired only when I was confirmed in the church at the age of sixteen. It was made by the local tailor, who had no idea how to make it: it fitted me like a rag, resembling a *gooingsak*.

As I was always the youngest in my class, I was very aware of the large age differences among my classmates. In Standard 6, for example, I was twelve years old, whereas two of my classmates were over twenty years of age. Many of these boys grew up on farms far away from town and were brought to school for the first time when they were twelve years old or even older. Then, unlike now, failures were common. In primary school, my results were average, but in high school I progressed rapidly and was placed top of my class for the final two years, matriculating with a first-class pass. At sport, I was an achiever – but then, there was not much competition, given the relatively small number of pupils at the school.

My parents aside, the only other noteworthy academic influence in my life was Mary Dodsley Flamstead, who introduced me to the geographic wonders of the world. A single woman, Mary arrived in Beaufort West in 1910, around the same time as my parents. She suffered from tuberculosis (TB), and the dry, clean Karoo air was considered beneficial for her health. This was actually proved true: she made a remarkable recovery soon after her arrival in the town. Mary became the principal of the girls' high school. She was English, very religious, was perceived to be a little on the 'outside' politically and had a close relationship with my parents.

The notion that the Karoo conditions were beneficial to people suffering from chest conditions such as TB and asthma became so popular that the Nelspoort Sanatorium was built some thirty miles north of Beaufort West and attracted sufferers from all regions for treatment. This, of course, was before modern therapeutic agents capable of destroying the TB germ became available.

My last year at primary school coincided with the first year of the Second World War. As mentioned earlier, the community was deeply divided into the anti-war camp of the National Party and the pro-war camp of General Jan Smuts's United Party. As supporters of the latter, we were a minority in an overwhelmingly pro-Nationalist community. Among the Afrikaans-speaking people, we were an even smaller minority and were extremely disliked as a result. Our local member of parliament was one of the few Nationalist representatives in parliament during the war years. He was an arrogant man who later became foreign minister in the government of Daniel François Malan – an ordained minister and the grand architect of apartheid.

At school, the majority of our teachers were pro-war Nationalists, none more so than the school principal. Whenever he could, he would punish us by keeping us back after school to write out 'lines' and, at any opportunity, he would mete out unfair hidings. We disliked him intensely and, although he was an excellent arithmetic teacher, he showed his true colours towards my father and me in a most stupid way.

After I had completed my Standard 6 exams, my father arranged for us to go on my first ever holiday to Cape Town. We were booked to leave by train the day before the close of the term. He asked the principal's permission, but it was refused. More attempts failed. My father then took the situation into his own hands and we duly left the day before term ended.

On our return, my report was waiting in the post. I had achieved a good pass but had 'failed' because of my absence from school on the last day of term. As a result, I would not be allowed to advance into Standard 7. No amount of pleading would change the principal's mind. Fortunately, the principal of the high school, Tommy Anderson, was pro-war, having fought on the side of the British during the First World War. He told my father to ignore the report and permitted me to continue with my education. So today, with a few medical degrees, government awards and two honorary doctoral awards to my name, I have yet to pass Standard 6!

By the time I commenced high school in Standard 7, I had started coming into my own. My schoolwork improved and, in Standard 8, I was appointed captain of the swimming team. This achievement was something of a damp squib, as it were. Our pool was dependent on its own borehole, and my three years of captaincy were served during a severe drought – so severe that the borehole was constantly dry. Like Gilbert and Sullivan's admiral who never went to sea, this schoolboy captain never once swam during the entire period of his captaincy!

In high school I was a cadet. Mr Anderson never forgot Armistice Day and, to commemorate this day, we cadets marched up Donkin Street to its intersection with Meintjies Street, where there was a war memorial for the sons of our area who had fallen in the 'Great War'. We would be splendidly attired in our uniforms and had to wear puttees, or gaiters, over our socks, which stayed up with great difficulty: often they came loose while we were marching and would eventually give up the battle. After trailing behind on the dusty road for a few yards, they would soon be left behind. In disgrace, we'd continue with one puttee still secured and the other leg covered with a reddish-brown sock. As hard as I tried, I never arrived at the memorial with both of them in place.

In Standards 9 and 10, I began to excel in all areas, becoming the top student in the school, the best athlete, captain of the rugby team and a lieutenant in the cadets. In my final year, I was made head boy of the school. Despite claims to the contrary, I was the only one of my brothers to be placed top of my class academically, and the only one to be voted head boy.

Chris was a promising tennis player and athlete at school but was never made captain of any team.

When I was in matric, my father was sixty-nine years of age and my mother fifty-nine. They never once attended any sport or school meeting in which I was involved. This was not out of disinterest but rather because of the controversial issues that so often surrounded our family. I believe that they probably felt that their presence there would have embarrassed us. More importantly, however, they considered our exam results, not our sporting or social events, to be of most relevance and importance.

All my brothers had already left home during the last four years of my schooling and, because my parents were not great socialisers, I grew up studying with few friends. I was shy and had a definite inferiority complex. I matriculated in 1944.

* * *

I had initially entertained the idea of becoming a marine biologist, as I've always loved the sea. But in my final years at school, and with Chris already in his concluding years of university training to become a doctor, I developed a keen interest in medicine. Whenever possible, especially during holidays, I would accompany our local doctors to farms and railway sidings to treat the sick. I was useful for opening gates when they made forays out to the farms. During my outings with them, I picked up some of their medical talk, of which I could never get enough.

There was the added incentive of comparing their lifestyles with ours. Medicine paid well: doctors had big houses and sleek, modern cars.

6

Pocket Money

E VEN IN BEAUFORT WEST, A YOUNG BOY NEEDED POCKET MONEY – for sweets, chocolates, condensed milk and other delicacies. We also required money for toys, such as yo-yos, Dinky Toys and toy soldiers, which we used to fight the battles of the Boer Wars. Marbles were essential as we spent so much time playing games with them. If one lost, however, one could lose all one's marbles (literally) and would need to buy more.

Money was needed, too, to buy a ticket to attend the Saturday-afternoon matinee at the local Star cinema. Although there were evening shows, our preference was for those screened on Saturday afternoons, at a ticket price of four pennies. In those days, we referred to the cinema as the *bioscope*. This was long, long before television and, as mentioned, we didn't even have a radio while I was living at home. Pocket-money initiatives were essential not only for ensuring our entrance to the bioscope, but because they covered that 'other' part of going to the movies: a little erotic sustenance customary on such outings, in the form of an extra ticket for a partner. When the lights went off, we paired off, each with his own fancy. It was here that I practised 'surface anatomy' for the first time and discovered that girls were indeed very different from boys.

Connected to the bioscope was the Good Hope Café. With leftover pennies, we were able to buy sweets, cold drinks and ice cream there during the interval. Very often, when the owners' backs were turned, we would sneak out without paying.

One Saturday afternoon during the interval, I went to the urinal and had the dreadful experience of witnessing my first dead person. He was lying on the toilet floor, neither moving nor breathing. His body was lifeless and his face blue. I was the first to stumble upon the corpse and will never forget the fright I received. I was so overcome with emotion that I went straight home rather than stay to watch the second part of the movie. Later in life, I would see hundreds of corpses, but I will never forget the nightmares I endured long after this frightening episode.

Our bioscope was, to me, one of the local wonders of the world. Here, my world changed. I was mesmerised by the big-band music of Joe Loss,

Edmundo Ros and Xavier Cugat, as well as the Waldorf Astoria orchestra, the Harry James orchestra and many others. What was especially fascinating to me was when each section – trumpets, saxophones and trombones – stood up and played a specific part of the tune. They then sat down and the rest of the orchestra would take over.

I shot crooks with Roy Rogers and the Lone Ranger; visited Morocco, Hawaii and other countries with Bing Crosby, Bob Hope and Hedy Lamarr with their *On the Road* movies; and loved the hilarious Marx Brothers. We had the usual fractures of arms and legs when attempting to imitate Johnny Weissmuller's Tarzan swinging through the trees on his way to rescuing 'Just Jane', as our trees weren't suitable for such daring escapades.

Where did my money come from? At high school, I had a thriving business. The department store, Mortimer and Hill, bought bones, scrap iron and used bottles. These items could be found all over, in the veld, streets and gardens. I collected as much as I could, sold it all to the store and, when money was very short, I would climb over our boundary fence, repossess these items and then sell my spoils back to them. Not very honest, but very profitable for a boy in his teens.

Another source of income was rats and mice. The Beaufort West municipality had a programme called *Vermin Control* and paid anyone who caught and delivered these rodents to their store. After trapping them, we'd pop them in a bag and off we'd go. The catch would be entered in a book and then dropped into a forty-four-gallon drum brimming with Jeyes Fluid. We'd receive one penny for every mouse caught and nine pennies for every rat.

The girls' school was situated close to our garden, and the results of their domestic science cooking classes attracted these creatures aplenty, providing a dependable source of supply – and income. The period from November to December, however, was when this vermin was most prevalent and was, therefore, my most profitable time of the year. Even today, any mouse or rat that dares to invade our house has a very short life expectancy. But instead of pennies, I have the reward of a shrieking wife when I proudly remove the dead rodent invader.

Another means of obtaining pocket money was by selling fruit. As mentioned, our large garden had a variety of fruit-bearing trees, and my chosen tree was the methley plum. Karoo fruit is the sweetest, most flavourful fruit you could ever wish to taste, and my brothers and I would sell the surplus fruit from our trees. When in season, the branches of my plum tree were so laden that I feared they would break. The harvest was plentiful and the plums juicy and delicious. I sold them for five pence for twenty, and ten pence for fifty, and I made a small fortune, which provided me with sufficient money for the bioscope.

When Giuseppe Tornatore's *Cinema Paradiso* and Federico Fellini's *Armarcord* were screened years later, I observed striking similarities between some of the people depicted in these movies and the inhabitants of Beaufort West.

There was the electrician, Fransie Hattingh, for example. At the time, electricity had just become available to households in Beaufort West, and Fransie installed the connections. It is not surprising, therefore, that he became known as *Fransie Connection*. Unfortunately, Fransie suffered from a major speech impediment: he was a very bad stutterer who 'connected' better with electricity than he did with humans.

Then there was the 'smoothie', who was always combing back his Brylcreemed hair, and the young woman who was known to please in more ways than one. We had a *Boetie Visbek* – literally 'Brother Fishmouth' – whose facial contortions when he spoke closely resembled those of a fish. *Mal Piet* – 'Mad Piet' – was mentally disabled and had delusions of being a magician. When you asked him to perform a trick, he'd oblige by zipping down his fly and showing all and sundry his magical wand.

Oom Jannie Viviers was the local storekeeper on the corner of Donkin Street. We called him *Oom Jannie Blikkanery met die hout poephol*. Unfortunately, there is no conceivable English translation for this, but I will try: 'Uncle Jannie tin canary with a wooden anus'. I still do not know why he was insulted with such a title, but there were, of course, even worse descriptions that I cannot put into print.

We Karoo *japies* were certainly a rough crowd, and youth didn't spare us from rude name-calling and jokes. I remember once repeating to my parents an extremely obscene rhyme that I thought was very funny. They did not laugh; instead, I was rewarded with a good hiding. At the time I didn't understand the reason for my punishment, but later I discovered that I had described the sexual act in a most graphic and offensive manner.

And not even Beaufort West was immune to the odd paedophile lurking in the shadows, from whom our mothers would warn us to keep at a safe distance. Our greatest fear was a pair of brothers who were reputed to be so afflicted. Whenever we saw their car, we ran as fast as our legs could carry us.

A small town with the occasional rumour of husbands visiting others' wives, and vice versa, Beaufort West was also a real 'Peyton Place'. I am fairly sure that nothing has changed.

7

Sunday Services

I WAS TAUGHT BY MY FATHER THAT, ACCORDING TO THE BIBLE, ONE
worked hard for six days and rested on the seventh. In most of the
Christian world, that day is a Sunday. My father's work, however, followed
the opposite of this teaching: for six days, he did very little, leading the
weekly prayer meeting on Wednesday nights, performing the odd weekday
wedding or funeral service, conducting house visits to the sick, old and
needy, and preparing his Sunday sermons.

But Sunday was his day of real toil. It usually started at 7 a.m., when
he went to the jail to conduct the weekly service. On his return, he would
have a quick breakfast and then spend a few minutes in his study, praying
and doing some revision of the morning sermon. His sermons were never
written in full. Instead, he would jot down on a piece of paper three or four
main points relating to the chapter or verse of the Bible from which he was
going to read. They were, otherwise, spontaneous. He would often joke that
many preachers, when starting their sermons and asking God to help them
preach His Word, should rather pray that God prevent them from going
blind during the delivery of the sermon.

At nine o'clock sharp, the bells of the Dutch Reformed Church began
their pealing, announcing that worship would commence in one hour. The
Anglican Church bells in the north and the Catholic Church bells in the
south bravely competed, but could do little to drown out the superior
bells of the Afrikaans Mother Church. Although their collective tolling rang
out the same uniting message to all four corners of the town and beyond,
their calls excluded the small Jewish community, who worshipped on Friday
nights and Saturdays in the synagogue in Union Street.

Inside their houses, people dressed in their Sunday best: the men in their
finest suits, shirts and ties; the women outfitting themselves in special girdles,
bodices, dresses and hats. Showers of perfume and powder and hair cream
were sprayed and dusted and rubbed onto all colours and textures of skin
and hair.

At 9.30 a.m., the bells resumed with greater urgency. All over the town,
people were on the move, a single young man or woman or child here,

whole families there. Colours and creeds mixed freely on their way to their separate churches.

At ten o'clock, the Dutch Reformed Church's verger would muster all his skill to ring out three or four sharp, short peals announcing that Beaufort West was now united before God and worship should commence. The whites would be ensconced in the Dutch Reformed, Anglican, Catholic and Methodist churches, and the non-whites would be gathered in the mission church.

While my father and his church council discussed important matters in the vestry, my mother and I walked from our house to the church building, through the vestry, into the church and straight down the aisle to the front door, almost as though we were leaving. I often wished I could carry on walking out of the church, but we always turned to climb the stairs to the gallery, where the organ was situated.

Because she was very deaf, my mother could hear neither the short ring of the bell that started the service nor my father's announcement of the psalms and hymns to be sung. She couldn't hear the deacon's completion of the collection round either. It was my duty to indicate to her when she was to start or to stop playing, either by nodding my head or by placing a hand on her shoulder.

Her handicap meant that I had to attend church at least twice, sometimes three times, on Sundays and that I had to be present for most weddings and funerals. Unlike today's youth, who are familiar with all the latest pop music, I was brought up on a diet of psalms and hymns. I could whistle the wedding and funeral marches before I was ten years old. At the last knell of the Dutch Reformed Church verger's terse tolls a block away, my mother would respond to my signal by starting to play the opening hymn.

There were often complications with the organ music and the singing of the congregation downstairs parting company. This was due firstly to my mother's deafness and secondly to the congregation's love of lingering on their favourite notes or words. My mother, playing strictly in time, would be unable to hear the consistent lagging of the singers downstairs. Slowly but surely she'd race ahead of the congregation, often finishing while those below still had a verse or two to go. No signal from me could have rectified things.

Depending on his mood, my father would often let matters slide, but sometimes a sharp reprimand would follow the unorthodox singing of the hymn. He would request that the congregation sing the errant verse or

verses again, thereby absolving my mother of any blame. The repeat performance was always much better. Mother would slow down and the
congregation would speed up, my father enthusiastically leading the whole
affair from the height of his pulpit like an orchestral conductor.

There was, however, another interesting facet to the congregation's vocal
renderings. Although they sang as a whole, certain members were apt to
compete with one another. The better known and more melodious the
hymn, the stronger the whole congregation; the lesser known the hymn, the
more prominent the voices of certain individuals. It was routine to stand
when we sang, and I'd be able to peek out from the gallery and observe
most of the singers.

I would see tall Miss Avenant, a teacher at the coloured school who was
in her forties and unmarried, singing a forceful contralto, always ending
later than the rest of the congregation so that her voice alone might be
heard. I'd find myself fantasising that this quirk was her love-call – though
late in life and in church, she still emitted a strong and unambiguous call.

There was Basie Boer, a hefty six-footer who worked for the municipality. Two stretches in jail for being drunk and disorderly had not spoilt his
deep and devout bass voice. Alone, he had the ability to keep the male voices
together, at convenient moments encouraging the tenors to harmonise.

The inevitable showy high soprano was also present: Mrs Witbooi, who
was tone-deaf, weighed nearly 300 pounds, almost obliterating from view
poor Mr Witbooi, who beside her appeared starved and emaciated. Now
and then her false warblings would receive disapproving stares from those
close to her, but there was no doubt that, even if no one else did, she
thoroughly enjoyed her own voice. Oblivious of church, people or tune, she
unashamedly sang along with discordant and piercing utterances.

There were those who could not read but were ashamed to admit it.
With hymn books upside down and open at the wrong page, they would
'sing' lustily. Though their mouths stretched wider than anyone else's, no
sound emanated. Then there were the honest ones, not afraid to admit that
they couldn't read. They held no hymn books. With eyes closed, they'd sway
to the music, carefully listening for familiar words. When these arrived they'd
join in enthusiastically, only to become mute again as the hymn continued.

In spite of these eccentricities, it was well known that the members of
my father's congregation sang much better than their white counterparts
a block away. Often on a Sunday evening when my father had preached
a little longer than usual, the last hymn was still being sung as the white

congregation, heading for their homes, passed our church. They would stop and listen as their weekday servants gave full voice in praise of their Almighty God.

'Rock of Ages', 'Nearer My God to Thee', 'At the Cross', 'Jesus Loves Me' and many other hymns were well loved among my father's congregants, and their words are still fresh in my memory. Separated though they were from their white brothers and sisters, I was sure that as the sound reached Heaven, God judged it to be as pleasing, as worthy and as equal to any other.

* * *

An important event in the church calendar was Temperance Sunday. It occurred in summer, when Beaufort West is uncomfortably hot. I remember one such episode vividly.

The seating arrangements in the church conformed to a hierarchical structure, and this particular Sunday was no different. Although the seating protocol took the form of an unwritten agreement, anybody who unknowingly broke it by, for example, sitting on a bench that had been occupied by a family for twenty years or more, would be unceremoniously removed by the rightful owners when they finally arrived, often with the aid of a threat from a walking stick.

In front, below the pulpit, sat the church council. From my perch above, the elders were on my left, the deacons on my right. Like my father, they were dressed in black suits and white shirts with high, stiff collars. Some of the shirts had been worn for many, many years and were beginning to fray at the collar. Being at a time before the appearance of whitening detergents, shirts were often more brown than white in colour. The black suits, too, revealed various states of fit and wear: some were too big, others too small; some were still black, while others, after twenty or thirty years of use, were more green than black.

At the age of seventy-six, Gert Appolis, who had been a deacon and was at this point an elder, had been a member of the church council for more than fifty years. As the senior member, he sat in the place of honour on the elders' benches – first row, first on the right. His shrivelled faced appeared from his ill-fitting suit like the head of a Karoo tortoise protruding from its shell. Though a poor and infirm old man, he was loved by all. Inside that body, covered by wrinkled brown skin, was a heart of gold. Oom Gert had almost nothing, but, as is traditional in the Karoo, he shared what little he did have with friend and stranger alike.

The two front benches, in their own block and closest to the pulpit on the right, were reserved for the reverend's family or any other white people who might attend a service. If no whites turned up, this piece of territory would remain respectfully unoccupied, even if there were no other seats available.

The rest of the church belonged to the congregation. In the first three or four front benches sat the so-called better-class coloureds. On what basis this social status was accorded was difficult to judge, but it included the degree of whiteness of skin, the neatness of dress, the standard of education and, above all, the occupant's residential address and his proprietorship of an English surname.

Sometimes, a new family would be admitted to the front benches. On this particular Sunday, I witnessed such a move up the social ladder: the Standard family was being honoured for the first time by being allowed to occupy the row third from the front on the left. Mr Standard had recently moved from the coloured location to the Bo-Dorp. The move, incidentally, had also resulted in a change of surname – from Stander to Standard – thereby ensuring he and his family became an instant social success.

Behind the front rows, the disparate social standings of the coloured community were reflected in diminishing order. Right at the back were the people who lived in shanties. They were illiterate and poverty-stricken, and dressed in an assortment of second-hand garments. A few of them had no shoes. These were the people who concerned my father the most. He visited them regularly, trying to ease their lot by giving all the warmth, comfort and food the limited funds of his church could afford. Often on his walks with me, he would voice his worries for these forgotten people: 'How can I go to them and tell them of God's love when they are hungry and cold and sick?' he would ask desperately.

A church, my father taught, was the temple of God. It was, therefore, to be respected: no talking and no laughing. Too much coughing was frowned upon. When one sat, it had to be upright, eyes respectfully drawn to the preacher in the pulpit. When one stood in prayer, the head was to be bowed, eyes closed. Above all, there was to be no fidgeting.

The church doors were always shut at the beginning of the service to keep out inquisitive passers-by. The small windows were situated up high, and could be opened only with ropes on pulleys. At any one time, more than half of them were out of order.

On this particular Temperance Sunday, it was unbearably hot and dry.

The summer sun beating down on the church from above, combined with the body heat of the worshippers inside, saw the poor ventilation of the building unable to cope. As my father read the lesson, the congregation, especially the overdressed, overweight matrons, started to become restless.

The concentration of the boys, who stood with the men when prayer was in session, began to waver. Pennies for the collection became toys. Soon, the sound of coins being tapped on benches resonated around the church. As the noise escalated, some mothers gave their offenders a fierce jerk, pulling them onto the benches. A penny or two flew through the air, clattering to the floor and rolling beneath the benches. There followed much noisy scrambling around as the boys hunted their vanished coins.

Then it was the turn of the infants, the sound of their crying increasing in volume as desperate mothers rocked them forwards and backwards in an attempt to quiet them. Even the grandmothers offered advice in loud voices: '*Gee hom die pram*' – 'Give him the breast.' Dress buttons were hastily unfastened and a full, bare breast popped out. A nipple disappeared into the hungry mouth and the baby was immediately silenced. If these methods proved unsuccessful, the crying baby was passed along the bench to a younger brother or sister. Baby in arms, they'd stumble out of the pew and march down the aisle, the infant's crying receding as it was carried outside into Donkin Street. Soon, a shuttle service developed – babies were removed to be soothed, others returned in folded arms where they'd fallen asleep.

On this special Sunday, the Temperance band provided the music for the collection. Before the service began, the band, dressed in their suits with red sashes draped over their chests, banners aloft, marched from the coloured location up Donkin Street and into the mission church. They took their place in the gallery next to my mother and me.

Their leader, Johannes Brander, played the trumpet, while the other eleven members played an assortment of brass instruments. They gave it all they had. Although the players were not accomplished, what they lacked in ability they made up for in enthusiasm. Because they sat next to me, I received the full blast of the music – at times it seemed like the roof would lift off and the walls would fall down.

While the band was busy blowing away some of the congregation's alcohol blues, the deacons collected the humble offerings. For the most part pennies were given; here and there was a ticky. (It was only on rare occasions that a sixpence, or even a shilling, was donated.) When the collection had been completed, the band bravely ended their rendition, all twelve instruments at full volume. My ears recovered just in time for me to give my mother her cue as the next hymn was announced.

The hymn over, the congregation settled down. My father read the text and began the sermon. I listened attentively as he explained how Joshua, by carefully following God's instructions, organised his people and, with the aid of trumpets, managed to bring down the walls of Jericho. In my imagination, Johannes Brander became Joshua and his Temperance band the Israelites.

The church was becoming hotter and hotter. Beneath me, the congregation was trying to cool itself through all means possible. Bibles, hymn books and other pieces of paper were being used as fans, vigorously waved up and down, from side to side, to cool perspiring faces. Distracted by the restlessness below him, my father slowly began to lose his own concentration. He paused for a few seconds, sternly looking down on his congregation in exasperation. He continued with less confidence than before.

Eventually, no longer able to control himself, he stopped mid-sentence and said: 'I am trying to bring you the Word of God, but I find it very difficult if you all sit there waving your Bibles and hymn books. From here you look like a large flock of birds preparing to fly towards me and attack me.' Lackadaisically, the flock of birds gave up their attempt at flight and settled down. The waving stopped and the sermon continued.

From my eyrie, I was able to observe other happenings below. I was amazed by some of the things people had brought with them to church – clearly a lot of preparation and planning had gone into the morning's attendance. Mr and Mrs Cupido and their ten children took up an entire row about eight pews from the front. They were all clean and neat and well, if not lavishly, dressed. Their ages ranged from newborn to sixteen. During the service, the unfortunate parents had a major task to perform in keeping all of their ten children happy and silent. Two or three handkerchiefs, which were passed up and down the row as required, served the whole family. Just before the collection, five pennies – all the family could afford – were carefully handed out. The parents kept one each, and the other three were distributed in a manner that satisfied all.

For coughs, Vicks drops appeared like magic. For the restless, heart- and diamond-shaped sweets, white and pink in colour with sentimental verses inscribed on them – 'My love is true' and 'Forget me not' – were distributed. These not only kept the older children busy reading, but were also slowly licked away, word for word, until only a sticky wet lump remained. The lump was then passed to a younger brother or sister.

The battle for peace and quiet continued, for the most part successfully. Here and there there'd be a complete breakdown, but a general '*shhhhh*' from all corners of the church succeeded in hushing the perpetrator. Thankfully, the sermon was heading towards its predictable conclusion – how the ungodly would be punished, but those who believed would share in the bounty.

When the service had been in progress for an hour, the odours of the congregation became extremely pronounced. Various face powders and perfumes and soap smells mingled with those from hair plastered down with an assortment of oils and creams – the sharp scents of bay rum and lavender oil mixed freely with the heavy smells of coconut oil and Brylcreem. It was a multiple olfactory experience – but not all of the odours were pleasant: here and there could be detected the sickly reek of the previous night's overindulgence in wine and spirits.

The wave of unrest was rippling through the church again, my father's reprimand forgotten. I think he realised this, for as the clock in the church steeple struck eleven, he ended his sermon with a final 'Amen'. Hurriedly, my mother readied herself for the final hymn.

As the last bars of music faded, my father, with arms outstretched, gave the congregation the final blessing: 'In the name of the Father, the Son and the Holy Spirit, Amen.' This was the signal for the Temperance band to swing into action for the last time, more or less blowing the departing worshippers from the church to the location. My father disappeared from the pulpit and was followed into the vestry by the church council. Finally, with the church empty, my mother and I were left to wend our way back to the parsonage.

PART II

Medicine

Dear Dr Marius Barnard,

First of all, I would like to mention that, by Dr Daniel Constantinescu's kindness, I obtained your address and hope you'll have the time and patience to read these few lines.

From a crucial date for me – June 30, 1975 – I have gathered plenty of thoughts in my mind and heart which, since then, have imprinted on it (the latter) the pattern of your delicate hands, [those] of the person to whom I'm daring to send this timid letter today.

I'm thinking of the delicate hands and compare them to those of the famous Italian instrument makers in the old city of Cremona who created unique violins. In the same way, you approached hundreds of patients and, with the skill of a jeweller, worked on the human mechanism called the heart in order to fix it, to make it function better and to help it resume its normal beating.

I was one of your patients, the Romanian Petre Ghidu, from Marasesti – Vrancea County. God helped me to travel overseas … and reach the shore washed by two oceans, in the city at the end of the world – Cape Town, at the famous Groote Schuur Hospital. That was the place where two brothers, famous surgeons, opened a new era of the surgical interventions, getting their international recognition with the heart transplant.

I went through such a complex surgery and the author of its success was the doctor and human being Marius Barnard, who was and is still for me a second father, better said a second mother, and even more. My mother who gave me birth and life has never literally touched my heart. The only person who really put his hands on my heart was Marius Barnard, the man and doctor who helped me return to my life, which could have brutally ended at the age of forty.

Many words can be written, but I must admit there is no way to express my gratitude that you ... certainly deserve. I have beside me the family: my wife Viorica, my daughter Rodica (BA in foreign languages, working in Bucharest) and my son Victor (future PhD in organic chemistry at Case Western Reserve in Cleveland, Ohio). My 'clan' salutes you and sends the best wishes of health and happiness to you and your family! And especially for Mrs Barnard – as the Romanian habit is, I kiss her hands!

I have met you a couple of times in Bucharest, but unfortunately I've only seen you on TV in autumn 2002. I would like to congratulate you for the prizes and honours you received in recognition of your tremendous results and success. Hopefully maybe next time you are in Romania we'll have the chance to meet, even just to say 'Hello'!

I've just remembered that when I was a young boy I read a novel, *Against the Thunder.* Its action took place over fifty years ago in Cape Town. It was the love story of a young African native for a beautiful blonde girl, but her father was against their affection so he brutally separated them. Associating these ideas with my situation, Doctor Marius Barnard, the man in white, providentially came against the thunder that could strike me.

Finally, I cannot but thank the man and Doctor Marius Barnard!

PETRE GHIDU
FOCSANI, ROMANIA
JUNE 2004

8

Medical School

ONE OF THE DEFINING MOMENTS OF MY LIFE WAS LEAVING
Beaufort West to embark on my medical studies in Cape Town. On
a hot, dry summer afternoon towards the end of February 1945, I stepped
through the front door of the house in which I had been born, walked along
the narrow footpath to the front gate of the parsonage, turned right into
Donkin Street and headed for the train station.

If I never saw this town again, it would be too soon. I was leaving behind
the unpleasant memories of drought, heat and coal ash and heading
towards a new life of advancing my studies in a world far removed from
Beaufort West.

When my eldest brother, Johannes, had matriculated from school several
years earlier, there had been insufficient funds to send him to university, so
he had earned an income driving large trucks carrying forty-four-gallon
petrol drums between Mossel Bay and Beaufort West. This income, supplemented by a study loan from the Helpmekaar,[1] an organisation that had
established a fund for Afrikaans boys who required financial assistance for
academic study, had enabled him to enrol for mechanical engineering at the
University of Cape Town – the same university that my brother Chris and
I later attended. Chris and I were also sponsored by the Helpmekaar, and I
am forever indebted to the organisation for funding my brothers and me.

Being accepted to study medicine at the prestigious UCT was a dream
come true for me. It was an opportunity for freedom, along with boundless
challenges and the potential for exciting opportunities. It had taken hard
work to get there, but the unwavering support and the many sacrifices made
by my parents had made it possible.

When I started at UCT, Chris was already in his fifth year, so my parents
had the added financial burden of having two sons studying at university.
The total annual cost per student in those years was £60. Both Chris and I
had been awarded bursaries of £20 a year each from the Bolus Scholarship
and the same amount from the Helpmekaar. The remaining £20 required for
each of us was provided by my parents. Where they obtained this money
from, other than by way of personal sacrifice, I will never know. But they

firmly believed that God would provide if one believed and asked. And that He certainly did.

When I finally arrived at Cape Town Station, all I had were the clothes on my back and a tog bag – I had two shirts, two pairs of trousers, a few other personal belongings and five shillings' pocket money for the term that lay ahead. I remember taking the bus to the suburb of Observatory and then having to walk up steep Clee Road to the boarding house that would be my home for the next two years. The boarding house was run by a Mrs Mellet, who provided full digs, three meals a day and laundry – all for the princely sum of £8 a month, which was not inexpensive in those days.

The house was situated just below Groote Schuur Hospital,[2] half a mile from the medical school but a lengthy distance from the university, where I attended my first-year lectures. Not having enough money for transport, I had to walk to lectures daily, through fair and foul weather, quite often getting soaking wet through my old, torn raincoat.

Chemistry, biology, physics and botany were my first-year subjects. Lectures were delivered in English and, since I had spoken very little English up till then, I found my first year very difficult. Physics, in particular, was a nightmare, but somehow I managed to pass all my subjects.

During the middle of the year, many former servicemen returning from the war enrolled for medical studies. As a result, my class of 120 swelled to over 200 people and there were several students in my class who were forty years of age and older.

For the first four years that Chris had been studying in Cape Town, I saw him only during certain holidays in Beaufort West, during which time he spoke a lot about medical school. Until I arrived in Cape Town, he stayed with our elder brother, Johannes, in Pinelands – a suburb about three miles away from UCT and one in which I would reside with my family many years later.

Johannes, who was often away from home due to his employment with the South African Railways, had a wife who was difficult, moody and aggressive. She had burning-red hair, was full of freckles and everything she said was repeated at least twice. From our first meeting I developed an intense dislike for her. She was so argumentative that one had to stay away from her if possible. How Chris stayed there for four years is hard to fathom. Johannes, however, helped Chris by providing him with companionship, academic support and free board and lodging.

For the two years spent in Clee Road, I shared a room with Chris – a brother I hardly knew. We had nothing in common and I don't think either of us enjoyed the experience. He met Aletta ('Louwtjie') Louw during my first year at university and his romance with her was very stormy – I witnessed many arguments and tears. During this time, I experienced a patent lack of support and generosity from Chris. Perhaps I wasn't particularly generous towards him either.

Chris was very comfortable with people who supported and praised him; he was equally at ease with people to whom he felt superior. This created problems in our relationship that stemmed back to the sibling rivalry of our youth. Chris and I had often fought like cat and dog in fist-fights when he had returned home during university vacations. He was older and taller, but I was stockier. It's perhaps difficult to believe today, but I was very well built in those days!

I often had the feeling that Chris manipulated things, even my parents – especially my mother. Whenever anything went wrong between us, I received the blame – my mother was extremely partial towards Chris.

From my third year at university, I lived on the corner of Main and Hospital roads. My room was situated on the front veranda of the dwelling and had a zinc roof and walls made of plywood. When it rained, water from the gutter ran straight through my room, which meant that, when I studied, I had to keep my feet in the air so that they didn't get soaked.

The landlady had ducks in her yard, which was adjacent to my bedroom. I experienced foul smells twenty-four hours a day and virtually every meal included a serving of duck. Not surprisingly, I have not been fond of duck as a dish since.

On one occasion, my father visited me and was horrified by the state of my lodgings. He implored me not to stay there a second longer, so I moved to new accommodation near Observatory Station. Even in those days this area was dangerous, particularly so at night. In my fifth year, I moved into the medical residence, which was an unbelievable improvement.

Academically I was always one of the better students, but, to my great disappointment, I was never top of my class. Life as a student wasn't easy and I was constantly afraid of failing. Failure would mean that everything my parents had sacrificed would be lost. I was not going to let this happen.

I had arrived at UCT as a school rugby captain and a well-regarded first-team scrumhalf. I naturally assumed that making the UCT Under-19A side would be a pushover. Great was my disillusionment when I was selected for the B side. I found attending rugby practices very difficult because I had to walk several miles between the practice fields and Clee Road and, after practice, I generally arrived at my digs in the dark. My togs, like all my other clothes, were of inferior quality: my boots had studs with the nails poking through the soles of my feet, and my jerseys were old and tattered.

During my second year I again played rugby for the varsity B team, but had a stroke of luck when the A side's regular scrumhalf was injured and I was drafted into the team for the rest of the season. To crown this, I had the distinction of scoring a try against the Hamilton RFC at Newlands – the hallowed ground of South African rugby – in the left-hand corner next to the railway stand, a feat that I proudly mentioned to anyone who would listen when we lived in the suburb of Newlands years later.

With the significant increase in my study workload in my third year, I gave up playing rugby, a game I love to this day – even more so when the Western Province Stormers or the Springboks win. At one point I tried my hand at baseball, making the second team, but I never had a real feel for the game and soon packed it in.

Prior to entering medical res, I was often hungry and seldom ate wholesome food. It was a struggle merely to keep my clothes clean. Even taking girls out was difficult without money or transport. But I was a good sponger! Even today I don't spend money if I can help it – a fact to which my wife and children can, with great amusement, attest.

* * *

After my first year in Cape Town, I returned to Beaufort West for a long, hot and dry holiday at home. As the holiday drew to a close, I could not wait to start my second year. We would no longer attend classes at the university but continue our studies at the medical school just below Groote Schuur Hospital.

On the medical campus my class finally felt a part of the community of students hoping to become doctors. At last, we were permitted to study the human body. The second-year subjects were anatomy, a one-year course that had to be passed at the end of the year, and physiology, an eighteen-month course running into the middle of our third year.

Although I had already experienced the body of a dead person in the toilet of the Beaufort West bioscope, nothing could have prepared me for the sight that awaited me the first time I walked into the anatomy laboratory. Rows of cadavers preserved in formalin were stretched out on marble-slab tables. There must have been at least thirty cadavers of all sizes, shapes and colours – in death there was no apartheid in the laboratory. Some of the corpses were people who had donated their bodies to research, but the majority were paupers whose bodies had never been claimed by relatives or anyone else. They were now considered to be the 'property of the state' and if they were not used by us they would be buried in a pauper's grave.

Armed with *Gray's Anatomy*, we had to study the human body by dissecting it from skin to bone. Four of us were allocated to a body and, equipped with scalpels, we commenced our studies. We all prayed that our body would be very thin, because fat corpses are considerably more difficult to dissect. Mine was a winner – he had so little fat that he looked as if he had been starved to death.

We studied the nerves, vessels, muscles and bones as well as the organs, learning a completely new vocabulary. A multitude of foreign words such as *platysma*, *cuneiform* and *pituitary* entered my life, and I had to be able to verbally state if a bone was from a male or female and if it was left- or right-sided. We also had to be able to describe in great detail the origins and destinations of nerves and how they find their way from the brain down the body to the tip of the big toe. These were formidable tasks that required many hours of poring over the famous anatomical handbook that we referred to as our *Body Bible*.

We had to understand the complex relationships between nerves, vessels and other structures. This was very difficult to memorise and we used little rhymes or sayings to try to remember them. The lingual nerve presented such a difficult anatomical problem that we remembered its anatomy with the following rhyme: 'The lingual nerve took a swerve around the hypoglossus. "Well, I'll be f****d," said Wharton's duct, "the bugger double-crossed us."' There were several others that were most helpful in this regard but are best not repeated.

So, with our 'Body Bible', dissections and lectures, we learnt the anatomy of God's greatest creation – the human body. And slowly my cadaver disappeared: by the end of the year, he was the proverbial 'skin and bone'. I still wonder who he was and if he was mourned by anyone. But I am grateful to him because he helped me to develop a sound knowledge of anatomy and this, of course, would be of great benefit during my later years as a practising surgeon. Unfortunately, I could never thank him personally.

A highlight for me was the lecture series presented by Matthew ('Maxi') Drennan, a professor of anatomy. With his broad Scottish accent, he made the subject come alive on the large blackboard. When he lectured on any part of the body, he drew – with coloured crayons – exactly how the anatomy appeared when we dissected it out of the cadaver. Amazingly, he could draw with both hands simultaneously, and the diagrams he produced were incredibly accurate, with nerves in yellow, arteries in red, veins in blue, muscles in brown and bones in white. His lectures were a joy, and my only regret is that I never thought of photographing this genius's anatomically perfect blackboard drawings. It will come as no surprise that, having been instructed by such a teacher, I passed anatomy.

Physiology, too, was very interesting and I enjoyed it, but the professor was no Maxi Drennan, and neither were his fellow lecturers. After eighteen months, I once again passed and was well set on the long road to becoming a doctor.

* * *

During our fourth year, pathology was my main concern, and I found it very difficult. There was no patient involvement; it entailed examining specimens of hearts and many other organs in bottles and slides that had to be studied under a microscope. You could say that it was a 'dead' subject.

At the same time, we started our clinical years of surgery, medicine, and gynaecology and obstetrics. It was while studying these subjects that I spent most of my time in hospitals examining patients. It was a major ego-boost when some of the patients called me 'Doctor'.

At the end of the year, we had to write our final pathology exam and, if we failed, we were condemned to repeat the entire year. I had left my swotting a bit late and, just as I had sat down to revise this subject, my name appeared with nineteen others on the noticeboard at the medical school. I had to go to the Peninsula Maternity Home (PMH) to do a month's practical in obstetrics.

This assignment allowed me very little time to study, as the hospital was in District Six and we were obliged to stay there. It had a noisy and dirty residence for students – and the food was atrocious. As a start, we would attend 'confinements', when patients were in their final phase of pregnancy. When we had obtained sufficient experience we'd go out into the surrounding suburbs to do our stint of 'baby catching'. Uncomplicated confinements were not admitted to the hospital, but once a patient went into labour, a midwifery nurse and the student on call were sent out to assist.

The areas allocated for our practical experience consisted of District Six,

Woodstock and Salt River. District Six, which was named the sixth municipal district of Cape Town in 1867, has a tragic history that had not yet fully unfolded when I was placed there as a medical student. Located on the lower slopes of Table Mountain, the area became a melting pot of different cultures, languages, religions and creeds. But by the 1940s, when I was carrying out my practical experience there, these suburbs were downmarket, dirty and crime-ridden. Theft, mugging, murder, poor housing, and alcohol and drug abuse were the social problems of the day. It was not safe to wander around at night, especially if one was white. For medical students, however, the area was considered safe as long as we were accompanied by a nurse in uniform. When walking with her, the greetings would be friendly and she would regularly be greeted with a 'Good evening, Nurse'. At times, we were even promoted to 'Doctor'.

Later, the homes of more than 60 000 people living in District Six would be bulldozed to conform to the apartheid government's 'separate development' plan.[3] In the 1940s, however, it was merely a shabby, dangerous place. Such was the nature of the area in which I had to spend the whole of November 1948.

When a new group of students arrived, there were always problems as none of them, by that stage, was sufficiently qualified to accompany the nurse into District Six to assist with the confinements. We could only be trusted once we had delivered three babies under supervision in the hospital – don't ask me how this magic number was worked out!

We decided to expedite the process by drawing lots. The first name drawn would do three deliveries as soon as possible; the rest would deliver on a rotation basis. My name came up first, and that very day I delivered three infants. Since the rotation process for the rest of the students took a long time, I was out every night doing deliveries for ten days at a stretch.

Entering into the area's hovels was a new experience for me. Most were dirty and overcrowded, and the male partner was either missing or passed out on the floor. One night, I experienced a protracted labour in a particularly unpleasant room in the nearby suburb of Woodstock, just above the railway line. After a few hours, I was so tired that I stretched out at the foot of the bed and shared it with the woman in labour. I have to admit that I fell asleep and woke up only when the sister informed me that the infant's head was crowning and that I had to wash my hands and put on my gown and gloves.

Fortunately, the baby was delivered with ease and we were soon ready to leave. I asked the husband to phone the PMH to call our transport. To my utter amazement, he told me he didn't know how to use the public telephone, which was a short distance away. I went to make the call and, while waiting, I asked him his surname. 'Barnard,' he replied. I must admit that, deterred by the state of his dwelling and his inability to use the telephone, I didn't go on to establish whether we were in any way related.

Once back in my room, I stripped down to have a bath. Suddenly, I was enveloped in a massive cloud of fleas, which had found my blood a welcome change of diet. I was left with red skin on my legs and in the groin region, and I could retaliate only by throwing all my clothes into boiling water and having a steaming-hot bath.

The night I delivered that baby in Woodstock was a special night in my life for another reason: it was 3 November, my twenty-first birthday. I believe I must be the only person in the world to have celebrated this occasion in bed with a strange woman who was in labour, while being sucked dry by fleas. Instead of drinking champagne and looking into the loving eyes of my beautiful girlfriend, the fleas were drinking my blood.

While at PMH, one of the nurses told us of an interesting experience of hers. She had been assisting with a very difficult and protracted delivery of the first baby of an eighteen-year-old mother. The nurse had attended to her when the new mother was returned to the ward. On the second day after the baby was born, a tearful and tired-looking patient had asked the nurse if she could post a letter for her when she next went to town. Being inquisitive, the nurse had opened the letter, as she had seen that it was addressed to a man. It was short and to the point: 'Dear Taliep,' the girl had written. 'If this is what married life is about, the engagement is off.' We never found out what his response was, if any!

Our obstetrics and gynaecology course was made highly memorable by Professor Crichton, a man who was much loved by all of his students. The unforgettable tales about him were often repeated years later by many of us. Whether they are true or not I have never found out, but I still enjoy telling them!

On one occasion, a high-society lady brought her attractive, private-school-educated daughter to see him. The daughter, who was seventeen years old, had missed her periods for the previous three months. After examining her, Prof. Crichton (or *Pappa Crichton*, as we affectionately called him) had to inform the mother that her daughter was pregnant. The mother retorted that this was impossible, but Prof. Crichton had to

© Anthony Johnson

The Karoo, where I was born and grew up, in a common state of drought

© Anthony Johnson

The windmill known as 'the sunflower of the Karoo' awaiting a rare thunderstorm

My parents, Maria Elizabeth Barnard (née De Swart) and Adam Hendrikus Barnard, c. 1910

My father's church and parsonage: 77 Donkin Street, Beaufort West. For thirty-seven years my father tended to the spiritual well-being of the parishioners of the Dutch Reformed Mission Church

On the beach in 1930 at the Wilderness on the Garden Route, where my family holidayed annually. Back row, from left: Mammie, Johannes, my eldest brother, Deddie and a friend. I am standing in the front row (far left) with Chris (second from left) and two others

Collecting succulents in the veld with my father, who opened my eyes to the extraordinary beauty of the Karoo

My father and me with our faithful Model T Ford, the car in which I learnt to drive, *c.* 1944

The Barnard family at the parsonage in Beaufort West, 1946. Clockwise from top left: Dodsley; Dodsley's wife, Marge; Johannes's wife, Joyce; Johannes; me; my father; my mother; and Chris. My mother is holding Shirley, Dodsley and Marge's daughter

Me as a third-year medical student in 1947

My MBChB graduation from the
University of Cape Town, December 1950

© Don McKenzie

Groote Schuur Hospital, Cape Town, where I served as a houseman, medical researcher and, for thirteen years, cardiac surgeon. Groote Schuur is where the world's first human heart transplant was performed in 1967

Inez and me on our wedding day,
1 December 1951. We were married by my
father in Worcester, in the Cape

Inez Barnard (née Naude),
my beautiful bride

Number 10 Dunoon Road, Honour Oak Park, London, our first apartment and
where we started our married life

Three spinsters, the Viviers sisters of Beaufort West, in later years. The sister on the extreme right was my first schoolteacher

My parents in advanced years

My beloved parents at the Heads in Knysna, close to the forest from which my father's family originated, December 1957. This was the last time I saw my father

Fruits of our labour (from left to right): Marie, Naudéne and Adam, 1961, in Salisbury, Southern Rhodesia, where I practised as a general practitioner for almost ten years

Reverend Tom and Doris Sumners, my wonderfully supportive 'adopted' parents while I was training in Houston, Texas, in the 1960s

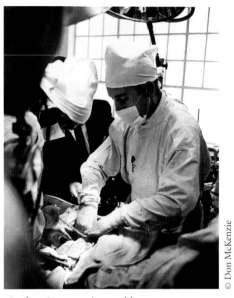

With Chris and my three children, who were supporting me at my Master of Surgery graduation from the University of Cape Town, June 1966

Performing experimental heart surgery on dogs at Groote Schuur Hospital in the mid-1960s

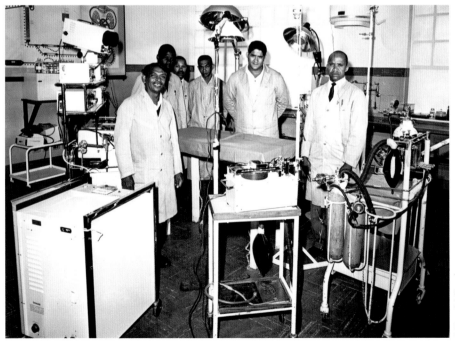

My supporting team in the dog laboratory at Groote Schuur Hospital

insist that the girl was indeed with child. Eventually the mother made her own diagnosis – that what Prof. Crichton had detected was merely water. To this he agreed, but informed her that there was a large trout swimming around in it.

A similar story describes a mother who emphatically denied that it was possible for her daughter to have had sex. Pappa Crichton went to the window, opened it wide and stared intently up to heaven for a few minutes.

'What are you doing?' the indignant mother enquired.

'I am looking for the Star of Bethlehem,' he replied.

Another very funny episode involving the legendary professor relates to a pompous surgeon who tried to assert his superiority by wearing a monocle, which, he must have believed, made him look distinguished. The story goes that he had been invited to a fancy-dress party and had asked Pappa Crichton what he should go as. The response was typical: 'Shove another monocle up your backside and go as a microscope.' Professor Crichton's lectures were always filled with humour, which served to enhance rather than detract from his brilliant teaching.

Despite having spent so much time at PMH, to the detriment of my studies, I somehow managed to pass the end-of-year pathology exams when I returned to medical school at the end of November.

* * *

While I had had brief encounters at university with girls – more particularly nurses – such dalliances were never serious and were very few and far between. For a start, I had no money. I was also quite self-conscious and shy, and I believe I had an inferiority complex. Furthermore, I had no car.

All of this ended during my fifth year, ironically on Friday 13 May 1949, when I met Inez Naude on a blind date. She was studying speech therapy at Mowbray Teachers' College at the time. It was instant electricity and, although she was at first reluctant, I pursued her with such determination that today, more than sixty years on, we are still together. We have been married for fifty-nine of them and have three children, nine grandchildren and four great-grandchildren.

Inez was born on 29 July 1930 on the farm Excelsior in the Over Hex, Worcester, a farming district near Cape Town. She was the youngest of six children, and her father, David, was a wine farmer in the district. After first attending a small farm school near their town, she went on to the Worcester Seminary for Girls as a weekly boarder. On completing school,

Inez enrolled at Mowbray Teachers' College – a convenient fifteen-minute walk from the medical residence in which I was staying.

Inez has her own proud heritage. Her grandmother, Emmarentia, was married to the famous Louw Geldenhuys, a man who left an indelible mark on this country and a significant historical legacy. There are certain parallels in the lives of our families that I find interesting. Given my union with Inez, the genes of the Barnard lineage and those of Louw Geldenhuys form an inherent part of my children's – and their offspring's – make-up.

Louw was a kind and decent man who took pity on the downtrodden, specifically the Boers returning from war. My father, *die Hotnot predikant*, also championed the poor, weak and wretched while nurturing the souls of the Beaufort West coloured community. Louw built schools in Johannes-burg for the underprivileged, while my father was superintendent of his community's coloured schools in Beaufort West.

Both Louw and my father had similar political convictions and were opposed to the rise of racist Afrikaner nationalism and its exclusion of other racial groups. Louw served fourteen years in the South African Party for the constituency Johannesburg North. This party later evolved into the United Party, from which several members, in 1959, broke away to form the Progressive Party. The latter, in turn, became the Progressive Federal Party (PFP), which, years later – and half a century after Louw had left politics – approached me to stand as their candidate for Parktown. I therefore rep-resented some of the same constituency that Louw had served – a strange coincidence. Unfortunately, my tenure in parliament was of a far shorter duration – and rather less significant! We shared the political ideals of opposing a racist government, however, and fought to uphold common decency and values for this country and for all those who live here.

There is also an interesting and somewhat symbolic twist to this parallel. A stream from Melville flows under one of Johannesburg's major highways down to Emmarentia Dam. I find it fitting that the great anti-apartheid cleric, Dr Beyers Naudé,[4] with whom I had one or two happy associations later, is by name linked to the land of Louw Geldenhuys by this highway – Beyers Naudé Drive[5] – and the confluence of Inez's family heritage. Our youngest daughter, Marie Emmarentia, shares her second name with the first name of Louw's beloved wife. Even today, the spirit of his liberal traditions endures with the presence of his great-granddaughter, Anchen Dreyer, in the Democratic Alliance.

* * *

Some people say that Friday the thirteenth is an unlucky date, but my personal experience proves that this is a fallacy. Inez and I met on a blind date and I always jokingly say that I was blind and she was the date. This beautiful, vivacious eighteen-year-old woman certainly blinded me the first time I saw her from across the room.

Our meeting was an accident. As the daughter of a well-to-do wine farmer from the Over Hex, she mixed in a totally different circle of family and friends from mine. I think she, like her three sisters, was raised with the intention that she should marry a wine farmer. Inez not only was physically attractive but also exuded a wonderful personality – certainly a good catch for any young wine farmer. As a fifth-year medical student, my circle of friends consisted of fellow medical students, and my contact with females, as I have mentioned, was limited to nurses. Our chance of meeting was basically zero but, thanks to the game of rugby, such an opportunity arose.

One of my best friends – and I only had a few then – was Lex Krogh. He hailed from Usakos, South West Africa (now Namibia). I knew of Usakos as my brother Chris had worked as a doctor there doing a locum for a month in January 1947. One day, Lex came to me with his arm in plaster of Paris. He'd fractured it in a rugby match the previous Saturday. He had a problem and appealed to me to help him sort it out: he had accepted an invitation to a social evening at Mowbray Teachers' College that Friday night but now couldn't go due to his injury. He had been invited by one of his friends, who had a girlfriend there. Since it was the university holidays, there was a general shortage of men, so Lex's friend, a medical student, had had to recruit a few others for this party. Because our holidays were shorter than those of the other students, we were the only people available.

When I heard it was a 'blind-date' party, I refused immediately. In my experience it was often the less attractive girls who were the blind dates. In spite of Lex's pleading, I steadfastly refused. He was most likely refused by other friends for the same reason, because the next day he was back, pleading with me to go. Against my better judgement, I eventually agreed.

The Friday night arrived and, as I was waiting for a lift at the entrance to the medical residence, one of my friends asked me where I was heading. When I mentioned Mowbray Teachers' College, he said that, should I meet Inez Naude, I was to give her his regards. When I finally arrived, everyone was wearing fancy clothes except for me. I think that most people who saw my old, ill-fitting clothes would have thought I was actually in fancy dress.

And then followed one of the most defining moments of my life. As

I walked into the hall, I saw a young girl standing against the opposite wall. She was of average height with a beautiful figure. Her hair was dark brown and plaited into two thick ponytails. A smiling face and beautiful complexion completed the picture.

From the moment I set eyes on her, I was smitten. I quickly crossed over to her and, after a shy greeting, told her that she would be my partner for the evening. I'm not so sure that her first impression of me was the same as mine, as she responded firmly that this was a blind-date party and there were no partners. There and then, I claimed her for myself, telling her that, although the other girls may not have had partners, she did – me. From that moment, I did everything to 'dominate' her, allowing no other boy to dance with her. I then told her about my friend's request to say hello to Inez Naude from him. She surprised me by saying 'I am Inez.'

She was dressed in red with 'Danger' written on pieces of paper stuck to her dress. I can still remember the first time I took her in my arms: it just felt right. Looking back to this moment, the wonderful strains of 'Some Enchanted Evening' from the musical *South Pacific* come to mind. The song speaks of seeing a stranger across a crowded room and knowing that she is the one you've been looking for, and that you'll never let her go. After sixty-one years, I have certainly never let her go! I had a great evening but gained the distinct impression that Inez would have been happier had I given her the opportunity to mix with others. But I wanted nothing of that.

I had a problem. I definitely wanted to see Inez again – and soon. Less than an hour after meeting her, I tried to arrange a date with her for the following evening. But as hard as I tried, I ran into persistent refusal. She already had a date and would not cancel it. Being the desirable female that she was, one of her boyfriends had bought tickets for them to go to a movie she dearly wanted to see. I discovered then that Inez was a movie addict.

My next ploy was to tell her that I would buy tickets and take her to the movie myself. I can still remember its name – *The Snake Pit*. I could not believe my good fortune when, after much persistence, she agreed to drop her date and go with me instead.

The evening at Mowbray Teachers' College ended all too soon. I walked back to the medical residence and my route took me along Main Road. On turning up towards the medical res, the last 300 yards passed between two graveyards, which were situated on opposite sides of the road. Walking between them was usually terrifying. As I was not exactly the bravest of the brave, I usually sprinted this distance in the middle of the road, hoping that if the ghosts of these two graveyards were to have some serious disagreement, or were attempting to invade each other's homes, the fight would not be in the vicinity of where I was sprinting. But on this night, I had no thoughts of ghosts; I had only Inez on my mind. Since I had no pocket money, I faced a dilemma: how was I was going to afford seats at the cinema?

The next evening I arrived at Inez's residence and rang the doorbell. She was called, and if she had looked beautiful the previous evening, *that* evening she was absolutely stunning. But I had a sad tale to tell. The very popular movie was fully booked; there were no more seats available. Inez was more than disappointed but soon cheered up when I told her we would instead visit my friend Lex Krogh, the very man who had made my meeting with her possible.

What really made her happy was when I told her that he had a great collection of records. When she heard that one of them was *Oklahoma!*, a musical that was a great hit at the time and playing in Cape Town, we made off on foot for his digs in Mostert Street, Observatory, just above the Main Road and almost directly below Groote Schuur Hospital.

When we arrived and Lex opened the door, I said to him that I had come to show him what he had missed out on the previous night. Inez enjoyed the music and I enjoyed being with her. After an hour or so, we walked back to her residence and said goodnight at the same door at which we had met earlier that evening. I risked my first kiss – and she certainly responded! So ended our first evening in each other's company.

It was at least twenty years after we were married that I admitted to Inez I had told her a lie. I had never even tried to get tickets for *The Snake Pit* because I didn't have enough money to buy them. Her wry response was, 'You can never trust a man.'

* * *

Except for meeting and courting Inez, my last two years at medical school were largely uneventful. These were our clinical years and most of our time was spent examining patients who did not take kindly to us and resisted being disturbed. I had great sympathy for them, but this was the only way of obtaining patient experience.

In addition, we had to study what were called 'minor subjects' and pass an exam on each of them. Ear, nose and throat is an example. The lecturer was ancient and boring. He walked into the lecture theatre every Friday at

12 p.m. and, with his head facing the floor, mumbled through the lecture. He forced our attendance by having us sign an attendance register. It was signed as fast as possible and, after we'd filled it in, one after another left. The lecturer never once raised his head, proceeding with his hour-long lecture uninterrupted. When he had finished, the class had, by now, dwindled from a hundred to twenty students. I actually felt sorry for him, so I sat through each ordeal.

Then there was ophthalmology. We were told that if we spelt it correctly we would pass. Other subjects included venereal disease (better known as VD), dermatology, psychiatry – with visits to the nearby Valkenberg Mental Hospital – and public health, where we visited the Cape Town sewerage plant. This utility is still situated on the N2 highway opposite the old electrical power station, and its foul smell persists to this day – especially when the south-easterly wind is blowing. Our visit to a reservoir where the city's water supply was stored remains a blur in my memory, as it was the morning after I had met Inez. Water supply and purification were hardly priorities for me at that point in time.

Strangely, of all these subjects, medical jurisprudence interested me the most. We had to visit the government mortuary, where there was a display of the outcomes of the fatal knife fights from drunken brawls that had taken place the previous night. I was greatly impressed by the skill of the forensic doctors in accurately diagnosing the time of death and determining the poisons in corpses years after they had been buried, and by their identification of other concealed evidence that helped to convict criminals.

We studied several famous cases. The murder trial of Daisy de Melker was particularly interesting. This woman had specialised in poisoning her husbands – and even her own son – for insurance money. Eventually she went too far and the exhumation of the corpses revealed that this frail, middle-aged woman had used arsenic to expedite her claim for a life insurance policy. She was one of the few white South African females who paid for their crimes at the gallows.

My interest in medical jurisprudence persists today. The television programme *Crime Scene Investigation* is one of my favourites – I marvel at how murderers are caught and found guilty years after having committed a crime. But, of course, the development and refinements of fingerprinting, DNA matching and other such methods have made true the saying, 'There is no place to hide.'

* * *

After thirty-seven years of serving his congregation, my father – exhausted and chronically ill – finally retired. He would dearly have loved to retire to Knysna and his beloved forest but, on a princely pension of £12 a month, this was not possible. So he chose a more modest town that was still in the Karoo but nearer to the sea. Seated at the foot of the Swartberg mountains, the town of Prince Albert would, from 1948 to 1953, be my parents' home.

Most of my holidays were spent there during my last years at medical school. In those days, it was a small village that owed its existence to a large farming community. The hamlet didn't boast the trappings of the typical Karoo towns of today – the smart bed and breakfasts, the olive farms, the cheese factories and the posh restaurants serving retirees and wealthy tourists. But, of course, the dominating landmark of the Dutch Reformed Church and its towering steeple *was* there, as was the jail in the main street and a few general stores. It was actually a very boring town in which to spend the long summer holidays.

As was my habit, however, I made friends with the one and only GP in the area and accompanied him on his calls into the district and farms. I soon discovered that he was a rather special character. Well over six feet tall and very thin, he was known by all as *Ou Riem* – hardly surprising, as he had a distinctly leathery appearance.[6]

Prior to 1928, South Africans had to complete their final clinical years in the United Kingdom or Europe to qualify as doctors. But Riem had been in the first group at UCT that had not had to go abroad in order to qualify. As to be expected in this part of the world, he was doctor, dentist and vet, and he was so respected that he was made mayor of the town. (The other two professions we Afrikaners admired and looked up to back then were those of the magistrate and the *dominee*.)

Riem's term of office coincided with the first landing of an aeroplane at Prince Albert. An airstrip was cleared in the veld a few miles out of town and the entire community was eager to witness this historic event. Being the mayor, Riem was, of course, there waiting to give a speech. Soon a tiny dot appeared on the northern horizon and, shortly afterwards, the plane landed in a cloud of dust. The mayoral speech was duly delivered, and Riem was offered a short flip in the aircraft. Not impressed by this kind offer, Riem flatly refused. But after much persuasion, he eventually gave in and accepted the invitation.

As he later recalled, given his height they had had to 'fold' him into the rear cockpit. Strapped in – much to his discomfort – they were soon airborne. The pilot did a few circuits and then came in to land. And then Riem's worst fears came true: on landing, the plane hit the runway, bounced once, bounced twice – and flipped over. With stones and dust flying in all directions, it came to a sudden halt, Riem still strapped into his seat, looking straight up to heaven.

A rescue party arrived not long afterwards and Riem was unstrapped and lifted out. Fortunately he was not badly injured, but he experienced unbearable pains in his back. Helping hands soon had him in a car, which despatched him home, where he was carried inside and lowered onto his bed. He took pills to relieve the pain and had to stay in bed for the next few weeks. But being the only person in the town and district who could treat sick people, aching teeth and animals, poor Riem had to consult on such issues from his bed. A few days after the accident, still convalescing in his four-poster, he literally came back to earth when he had to deal with a most unusual case.

Oom Giel, the owner of one of the best and biggest local farms and a prominent figure in society, came to visit him. He was rumoured to be very wealthy, owning hundreds of sheep and a large flock of ostriches. The reason for the visit was not his wife or his children, but his favourite saddle horse. The stallion had developed a large dental abscess in its right lower jaw and Oom Giel insisted that the offending tooth be extracted.

The doctor-cum-dentist-cum-veterinary-surgeon refused. Due to his sore, stiff back he couldn't leave his bed, nor was he prepared to have the horse enter his bedroom. But as is the way of the inhabitants of the Karoo, a plan was soon devised. It required a compromise for both Riem and the horse: the doctor's bed was moved to the open window and the horse was led into the garden. Its neck and head were then pushed through the window.

With the horse's head and the doctor now in reach of one another, it was easy for Riem to grab the offending tooth with a large pair of dental tongs. The horse, of course, did not take kindly to the sudden excruciating pain in its mouth. Not only did it retract its head, but it pulled back its entire body as well, doing so with such force that the combined pull in opposite directions resulted in the tooth being easily extracted. Of course, Oom Giel was very grateful, but the horse dentist now suffered back pain more severe than ever.

On one of our visits to a neighbouring farm, we had an amusing experience. The patient in question was a baby of a few months – the child of one of the wool shearers. Riem was on to the problem within a few minutes and remarked to me that the patient looked like a 'syphilitic kind', to which the old granny hovering behind us indignantly replied, 'Nee, dokter, sy is eintlik 'n meisiekind' – 'No, doctor, she is actually a female child.' In actual fact, both doctor and granny were correct. Infants with congenital syphilis had diagnostic facial features which Riem had immediately recognised – and it was indeed a little girl.

During one of my holidays we visited a farm some fifty miles away. It was January, when the sweltering heat was around 40 °C. We entered a small, one-roomed shack with brick walls and a roof covered with corrugated-zinc sheets. Other than the door, there existed only one postage-stamp-sized window to ventilate it. The room felt like a furnace – the temperature must have been approaching 50 °C inside.

On a dilapidated single bed lay a young coloured girl, sweating, hyper-ventilating and obviously exhausted and weak. Her history was diagnostic; in other words, one could diagnose her condition from just taking her history. It was her first pregnancy and she had been in labour for more than two days. On examination, it was obvious that, unless she was helped, she would die. She had what is termed an *arm presentation*. Most births are accomplished with the unborn child's head presenting first. Slightly more complicated than that is a breech presentation. The buttocks presentation is a difficult birth, but manageable. An arm presentation, however, if not treated, results in the death of the child and its mother, because it is impossible to pull the child's arm and head in this position through the small pelvic passage.

In the case at hand, the best treatment option would have been to perform a Caesarean section. This, however, was impossible, as we didn't have the necessary equipment and instruments at our disposal, nor did we have expert assistance. The closest hospital was in Oudtshoorn, many miles away.

The only other method available to Riem was to push the arm and shoulder back into the uterus, find the legs and pull them down, thereby achieving a breech delivery. This was not an easy procedure and could only be done under anaesthetic. The baby was already dead, but the mother's life could be spared if we acted quickly.

As I had already completed my fourth year of medicine, which included anaesthetics, I was the only candidate for the job at hand. A face mask and bottles of chloroform and ether appeared like magic from Riem's medical

bag. Anaesthetising a patient with a chloroform induction is very dangerous. If too much is administered, the patient will pass from the first stage of
anaesthesia to the fourth stage – death – within a few minutes.

Having placed the mask over the young woman's face, I slowly dropped
the chloroform onto the mask using a dropper. As I had been taught, I
was counting each drop – one drop, two drops – until the patient was well
anaesthetised, when I would switch to the much safer ether to keep her
under until the procedure was completed.

But nothing happened: the patient was still awake after five minutes.
Riem was now getting impatient and asked me to increase the rate of drops,
which I reluctantly did. But instead of the patient losing consciousness, I
was now beginning to feel very sleepy and weak. Finally, the penny dropped.
Instead of being in an air-conditioned theatre, I was in a little hut with
a tin roof and no ventilation – a veritable hothouse. As I was dropping the
chloroform, it was evaporating so fast that I was inhaling more of it than
the patient was.

Against all my teachings, I poured the chloroform onto the mask in a
constant stream and kept my face far away. This worked, and I soon switched
to ether. A gloved Riem was then able to push the baby's arm and shoulder
back, rotate the baby and deliver it – legs first.

After the anaesthetic was discontinued, the mother woke up and we were
able to leave. The ease and correctness with which Riem performed this
difficult procedure increased my admiration for this experienced doctor
and remarkable man. Such doctors are few and far between today. Medicine
is the poorer for it.

* * *

My sixth and final year ended with examinations on the three major clinical
subjects: medicine, surgery, and gynaecology and obstetrics. The year consisted of lectures, seeing patients and studying pages upon pages of notes
and textbooks – and, importantly, protecting Inez from other men. I was
successful in all of these endeavours and, on my twenty-third birthday,
I completed my final exams. I passed with two seconds and a third, which
in those days was quite good. I finished in the top ten of the class. These
were better results than I had hoped for and, to be honest, deserved.

With Inez at my side, I was awarded my medical degree in UCT's Jameson
Hall in early December 1950. My greatest regret is that neither of my parents

was able to witness the event given their advanced age and failing health. But I am sure that they were with us in spirit on that special day.

After forty years of marriage, they had raised their sons under the most difficult of circumstances and had made great sacrifices in order to send them all to university. Their dream of ensuring that their children would be well educated had finally become a reality. Their eldest son was a mechanical engineer with a BSc degree and their two youngest were both doctors with MBChB degrees.

I hope they realised that all their devotion, prayers and sacrifices were not in vain. All I can say today is, 'Thank you, my dearest Mammie and Deddie. Your mission was accomplished.' I pray that somewhere in heaven they can feel my gratitude and love for them.

Six years after leaving the mission church parsonage in Beaufort West and walking down the pathway into Donkin Street to face a totally new world, I had achieved what I had set out to do: I was now a doctor and had the world at my feet. I also had at my side the woman with whom I wanted to share my life and, together, we would fulfil our dreams. What a defining moment!

9

Houseman

IN EARLY 1951, I WAS FORTUNATE ENOUGH TO BE APPOINTED houseman at Groote Schuur Hospital under Professor J.R. Brock, head of medicine, and Professor J. Erasmus, head of surgery. These appointments were highly sought after because being an intern in these professorial firms had a certain amount of prestige. Unfortunately, I only discovered later that it was actually a mistake to work there because we essentially served the function of clerks.

In retrospect, it would have been far better to have gone to, for example, a mission hospital, where one could have gained practical experience by way of diagnosing and treating patients and performing surgery. Nevertheless, this appointment gave me my first opportunity to engage with and treat patients.

I started my working life as a doctor in whites-only Ward F1 early on a Monday morning. The beds stood in rows against the walls on either side of the ward. If my memory serves me correctly, there were two rows, each consisting of eight beds. In those days, we still had to wear a suit to work. I was given a long-sleeved white coat that reached below my knees to wear, and duly reported to the office of the sister in charge. A staff nurse was on duty and immediately stood up when she saw me, a book containing all the patients' records in her hand. She accompanied me on my first ward round. How different it was from today, when doctors have to conduct the rounds on their own, seldom accompanied or even greeted by the nursing staff.

One of the first initiations in my life as a doctor was to perform an electrocardiograph (ECG). Today, a technician or doctor will do an ECG in a few minutes; it is difficult to believe what a major procedure it was for us sixty years ago. However, with perseverance we succeeded. But our work had only started because, as housemen, we also had to do our patients' blood groupings and blood counts and urine tests ourselves. There were no laboratory assistants available to come and collect the specimens and return the results to us the same, or the next, day.

On some days, we had to admit up to five patients in addition to looking after the other ward patients, and twice a week we were required to attend to the hordes of outpatients seeking treatment of one form or another. I will never forget my first patient, Mrs Moses. She had just been admitted and, when the round was finished, I had to 'clerk' her. This meant that I had to take her history (past and present), examine her from top to bottom and perform certain routine tests and other investigations in preparation for the more formal round that would be done afterwards by the professor.

Mrs Moses was a greying, plump lady about fifty-five years old. Employed by the Cape Town municipality, she was the caretaker of the public toilets on the Grand Parade. This is the same venue where, decades later, thousands of people would gather to listen to Nelson Mandela give his first speech to the nation from the steps of the City Hall after his release from prison.

Mrs Moses displayed the typical symptoms of a heart attack. She had moderate hypertension, was obese and her urine tested positive for sugar. First, I had to take her blood. For this purpose, glass syringes and thick needles were provided. After selecting one of each, I looked for a nice worm-like vein. No such luck: she had a thick, plump forearm and the veins were hiding from me in the fat. All attempts to make them visible failed as the veins continued to play Hide and Seek with me. My only remaining option was to plunge the needle through the skin at the site our anatomy book said they were located. Unfortunately, Mrs Moses's veins had not read that book. After several failed attempts, however, I eventually found a vein, leaving poor Mrs Moses's arm looking like a dartboard – and black and blue!

Having checked Mrs Moses, I proudly presented her to Professor Brock on his ward round later that day. The obvious diagnosis of a moderate heart attack was confirmed, treatment was ordered and she was given instructions that three weeks' bed rest was required. During this period, we became great friends, and she used her time in the hospital to knit me a pair of socks. That they were twice the actual size of my feet I'm sure was unintentional. Bless her heart, I will never forget her.

* * *

As a houseman, I gained my first experience as a doctor treating patients with cardiac valvular diseases. I was one of two housemen serving in Ward A5, which was reserved for black patients. I worked there for only one month, but my lasting impression was of the many coloured patients, especially young females, in total cardiac failure due to rheumatic heart disease that had given rise to incompetent heart valves.

Rheumatic fever was a common disease in those days among people with poor nutrition and living in damp, overcrowded conditions. It would start as a streptococcal sore throat and then, as a result of poor treatment, develop into the most painful arthritis – mainly of the large joints. Patients would scream in pain when you touched their beds. It was easy to understand why so many coloured people developed this disease in the light of the conditions they lived under in District Six and on the Cape Flats at the time. Unfortunately, this disease did not disappear after the acute arthritis settled: we used to say that rheumatic fever 'licked the joints but bit the heart'.

In many cases, the disease damaged the heart valves, most commonly the mitral and aortic valves. Over a period of years, they would leak increasingly or became obstructed, resulting in a heavier workload on the heart. Blood would dam up in the lungs, resulting in congestion and the accumulation of fluid in the lungs – known as *pulmonary oedema*. Patients would also experience an increasing shortness of breath, or *dyspnoea*.

These patients, especially the young girls, had to sit and sleep on three to four cushions, gasping for breath, their livers so enlarged that they filled their abdomens. Their lower legs became so swollen that the skin burst and a bloody, watery fluid oozed out continuously. The only treatment we could offer them then was to administer oxygen and mercury injections in an attempt to remove the excess fluid. We could just as well have given them water: despite our best intentions and medical care, they all died.

I can still see them struggling to breathe, becoming restless, irrational and then comatose, and finally their last few gasps as death came to them, the only effective treatment to remove their symptoms completely. I will always remember my frustration and sadness, and a burning desire to perform some kind of miracle to cure them.

* * *

Inez and I already had plans for our future. During my year as a houseman, Inez was commanded by her mother to spend the year on their farm. The excuse given was that Inez had to learn the duties of a housewife, but I think it was her mother's last attempt to separate her from me and perhaps to get her involved with a young farmer – and marry him.

Fortunately, this never transpired. We were engaged on Inez's twenty-first birthday and married by my father on 1 December 1951 in the Dutch Reformed Church in Worcester – Inez's hometown. Unfortunately, I do not remember the names of the two classmates that acted as my groomsmen.

What I do remember is that the tails I hired fitted very badly: my pants tried to fall down throughout the ceremony. The reception was held on the veranda of Inez's parents' farmhouse in the Over Hex.

Inez and I then departed for the Wilderness Hotel, where we spent our honeymoon. This hotel was very popular as a getaway for young couples. I had such fond memories of the Wilderness, where I had spent much time during my youth, and the area and its surroundings remain for me one of the most beautiful places on earth.

* * *

After completing my year of internship at Groote Schuur Hospital, Inez and I spent the following eighteen months in the United Kingdom. In January 1952, we left Cape Town on a passenger liner, the *Windsor Castle*. In those days, the most popular form of travel between South Africa and the United Kingdom was on the so-called mail ships of the now long-gone Union-Castle Line.

Looking back, I am still amazed at our carefree spirit and obstinacy at the time. We simply left South Africa and headed abroad, not really knowing what we'd be doing or where we would end up. But nothing could suppress my desire to see the world, a yearning instilled in me in my youth in Beaufort West, when I had paged through my treasured book on the world's wonders. For Inez and me, it was, of course, an extended honeymoon, but it was the first time that I had ever travelled by ship, or been at sea for that matter. For the first few days, we had great difficulty keeping our food down, but we soon recovered to enjoy the three meals that were provided on a daily basis as well as to participate in several of the sporting and recreational activities offered on board. We both thoroughly enjoyed the trip.

After eleven days at sea, we arrived in Southampton with very little money. We took the train to Waterloo, where we were met by an old friend of Inez, the son of a neighbouring farmer of her family. He kindly directed us to a private hotel where we would spend our first night on English soil. It was mid-February and, for the first time, I experienced the dark, cloudy and cold weather of England and had to get used to not seeing the sun for days and weeks on end. I could not believe that people could live in such miserable conditions.

Our first challenge was finding accommodation. We soon found a small room with full boarding in one of the cheapest parts of South East London on the old Croydon Road, in Penge. The term 'full boarding' was somewhat of a misnomer, as the food – breakfasts in particular – was abominable. This was probably due to the strict rationing that was still being applied, despite the fact that the war was long over. Breakfast consisted of a slice of nauseating bread fried in fat, fried rotten tomatoes, an apology for an omelette, fat for bacon and tasteless baked beans. In most instances, the food was entirely inedible and, when no one was looking, Inez and I would simply deposit it in a little bag. When we went out into London, we would then discreetly dispose of it in the grounds of an old bombed-out church.

Our room was bitterly cold. There was gas heating, but it was on a meter which we seldom used, so we made good keeping warm under the blankets. Downstairs in the lounge we found the unbelievable novelty of a television set. Although its picture was in black and white, Inez and I found the television fascinating and thoroughly enjoyable to watch.

But the worst part of our living conditions was the fact that our room overlooked a very noisy road. For this reason – and the others – we looked for, and found, better accommodation – a flatlet in Honour Oak Park, just off Forest Hills Station. I can still remember the street address today: Number 10 Dunoon Road.

We were very happy there, and after about eight months I accepted the post of Senior Surgical Houseman at St Martin's Hospital in Bath. My intention had been to specialise afterwards, but it didn't work out that way. I had seen an advertisement for a post in Akron, Ohio, as a trainee pathologist and, on impulse, had applied. I was accepted and even obtained a work permit for the United States. But Inez wanted to go home.

I often wonder how she would have adapted to living in the United States and how my future would have turned out. But before the year was out, we were on our way back to South Africa, this time on another Union-Castle passenger liner, the *Carnarvon Castle*.

On a subsequent trip to Akron years later, I realised that Inez actually did me a great favour: the ice-cold weather would have been unbearable and my recollections are of a dirty little city that was overcrowded and noisy.

10

A GP in Southern Rhodesia

W HEN WE ARRIVED HOME FROM ENGLAND AT THE END OF 1952, Inez and I were penniless. I had to borrow money from my father-in-law to tip the ship's porter, who helped us with our luggage while we were disembarking. Fortunately, we were able to stay on Inez's parents' farm in Worcester. Inez's mother was always more than generous and gave her some money to tide us over. There was obviously a great sense of urgency for me to find employment. I was very eager to obtain a higher degree in surgery, so I went to Cape Town to see Professor Erasmus, for whom I had worked in surgery for six months in 1951, while I'd been a houseman at Groote Schuur Hospital.

He was very sympathetic, but unfortunately there were no vacant positions. He promised me the first vacancy available, however. As an aside, he mentioned that he had recently received a letter from an army colleague who was practising in Salisbury, Rhodesia – now Harare, Zimbabwe – and who was looking for an assistant. Although he was practising as a GP, this doctor was also a Fellow of the Royal College of Surgeons (FRCS) and performed surgery.

This option was very attractive to me. The salary on offer was £120 for the first three months and £150 for the next six. But at that stage I hardly knew where Rhodesia was and had no knowledge of its climate or its people. *Salisbury* was only a name from my school geography book.

I went back to the farm and discussed the situation with Inez. She was entirely supportive, as she has been her whole life, but not particularly enthusiastic, as she had no idea where or to what we were heading. Since Inez was the darling of her family and the youngest daughter, her parents were naturally very upset, as were her three sisters. But I had a positive feeling about this opportunity and, the next day, I contacted Professor Erasmus and accepted the position in Rhodesia for six months. Little did I then realise that we would spend more than nine of the happiest years of our lives in that beautiful, vibrant country. Salisbury, in particular, was booming at the time.

A month later, after two days and nights of travelling and with £500 borrowed from Inez's mother, I was welcomed at Salisbury Station by the doctor whose practice I was to join. Although a GP, he called himself *Mister* because he had an FRCS, a higher surgical degree that allowed one to practise as a specialist.

I stayed with his family for a few nights and then rented a furnished flat in Mabelreign, a suburb about three miles from the city centre. The flat was in one of three separate blocks named after large rivers that flow through the southern part of Rhodesia – the Tokwe, the Lundi and the Sashe. I stayed in the Sashe block.

Because of our financial situation, and to soothe her parents' unhappiness, Inez had stayed on the farm while I went ahead to Salisbury. But another reason for my going alone was that I had to confirm that my occupational prospects were favourable before getting her to join me.

My next step was to purchase a car. I found a brand-new front-wheel-drive Citroën with a novel hand-gear on the dashboard and bought it for £310. Southern Rhodesia had many miles of tar strip roads, which were generally dangerous as they were very narrow. If the car left the road it would veer onto dirt-gravel, and the loss of traction on the tyres could easily result in the car's ploughing into the veld or overturning.

With a flat to live in and a car to drive, I was now ready to start my practice. I was fortunate in that I never had to build one: it was already built and waiting for me. There was a large Afrikaans community in the area that consisted mainly of farmers. Since there was only one other Afrikaans-speaking doctor (who was not well liked), my practice grew rapidly.

Within the first few weeks I was invited to a party where I met many of Salisbury's prominent Afrikaners, including Luther van Zyl, a local Afrikaans-speaking accountant. We immediately struck up a friendship and he became a daily visitor to our house.

Luther handled my tax assessments. He did this without payment until I left Southern Rhodesia. When Luther married his wife, Oni, I proposed their toast. I also delivered their first child and proposed the toast at her wedding. Luther is godfather to my son, Adam, and today, fifty-seven years on, Luther and Oni remain our best friends. After all this time, Luther still looks after my taxes and if they or any of their family members have medical problems, they seek my advice. Luther himself will have no treatment unless I am in agreement.

* * *

Inez arrived in Salisbury in early November 1953, on my twenty-sixth birthday. Ten months later, Naudéne was born, and ten months and three weeks thereafter, Marie arrived. Hormones were rampant in those days and our son, Adam, was born three years later.

My practice did so well that after five months I became a full partner. Soon, a Mercedes Diesel replaced the Citroën and then a Jaguar followed. Almost annually I acquired a new car, as I covered many miles in my practice, and soon Inez could show off her own car. We had many friends and enjoyed a wonderful, full social life. I even became a partner in two farms. I hate to admit it, but both were tobacco farms. My bank balance grew and after four years I bought a five-bedroomed house with three bathrooms, a big living area, a tennis court and a swimming pool in a good neighbourhood opposite the Royal Salisbury Golf Club. Not too bad for a young Afrikaans doctor!

Things were going well – perhaps too well. But I very seldom had a holiday; over the summer holidays Inez and the children would travel by train to visit her parents at their holiday home in Hermanus. For a young GP, I had a sizeable obstetrics practice and, once I took on a patient who was pregnant, I felt duty-bound to attend to her from the earliest stage of her pregnancy until her baby was born.

I enjoyed this part of my practice immensely and considered it an honour that the patient trusted me enough to help her bring this precious little gift into the world. It was, to me, a miracle that from the first examination the slightly enlarged and soft uterus would increase in size as a perfectly formed human being grew and matured and finally escaped from the womb nine months later. The first cry, the first suck, but especially the loving, devoted smile of the mother, who had just undergone a painful labour, was to me a reward that no money could buy. I felt as if I was God's partner in the miracle and gift of life.

These experiences created a great bond between the patient, her family and the doctor. Even today I meet patients and their children – now adults – whom I treated and delivered.

* * *

We arrived in Salisbury during the early days of the Federation of Rhodesia and Nyasaland. The three countries under British rule – Southern Rhodesia, Northern Rhodesia and Nyasaland (soon to become Malawi) – formed a federation with a federal government. Each territory had its own local government.

It was a system imposed upon the black population by Britain and the local whites, and, although blacks were given a role in government, they exercised very little power. I initially had limited knowledge of what was going on, but certain names soon became familiar: Sir Godfrey Huggins, Sir Roy Welensky, Kenneth Kaunda and Hastings Banda were the most prominent.

We were aware of the mounting black 'resistance', particularly those activities led by Banda and Kaunda. As strong black nationalist organisations started to emerge, accompanied by an increasing number of demonstrations and riots, we whites continued with our happy lives, either blissfully unaware of or insensitive to the reality of the political situation and the consequences that would later follow.

We soon had a nanny for the children, a 'cook boy' and a 'garden boy', all of whom had quarters in our backyard. If you think we employed juveniles, you would be wrong: these were the names given to blacks even if they were grey-haired and elderly. We bought them *mielie meal* for their *sadsa* and 'boys' meat', an extremely derogatory description of meat – bones, in fact – that was their ration.

We believed then that they were lucky to have a job and shelter, and they served us with devotion and loyalty. So we could have our social gatherings, play golf and enjoy our sundowners at the Royal Salisbury Golf Club and other prestigious venues. This idealistic British-style colonial system was very pleasant for us. And we thought it would never end.

But the blacks were restless and a small germ of concern and insecurity niggled at the back of my mind: our privileged, selfish, white supremacy was being seriously threatened. I suspected that our future could change dramatically in the near future and become a nightmare. The events taking place in the Belgian Congo to the north certainly suggested the latter.

As the 'wind of change', so aptly described several years later by British Prime Minister Harold Macmillan, was already sweeping through Africa, the Belgians in 1960 decided to give the Belgian Congo its independence. Patrice Lumumba, previously a postal worker, was the popular political leader and became its first president.

The locals of Katanga, with its rich copper fields, were not in favour of this. With the aid of white mercenaries their leader, Moise Tshombe, broke away from the rest of the Congo to declare Katangan independence. This action provoked a civil war, and the whites were seen as the common enemy. Their dreams were not only shattered overnight, but they had to flee at once without any of their possessions, leaving their houses, their farms and even their clothes behind. Some were less lucky and were murdered in the riots that followed the Declaration of Independence and black-majority rule.

The fleeing colonials arrived in Salisbury in great numbers. One couple I remember fled from their wedding reception and arrived with the bride still in her wedding dress. Some we took into our homes; others were accommodated in hangars at the then uncompleted new Salisbury Airport. Here they found safety and shelter and were brought food and clothes. We, as doctors, went to treat them for both medical and psychological conditions. A few stayed in Southern Rhodesia, but the large majority were repatriated home.

Many of us never believed that we would end up in the same situation, but if you listened and looked carefully, it became clear that it was only a matter of time before the pressure of 'black nationalism' would bring about change, either by way of a peaceful settlement or by way of an armed struggle. When Inez asked me if I thought this could happen to us, I would say, 'Yes.' When she wondered how long it would take, I'd reply that it would be within twenty years. And how right I was proved to be.

* * *

Our house was open to patients who, for some or other illness, needed somewhere to wait for their medical management. Some of these were young unmarried girls who either wanted to hide from their families or had no other means at their disposal. One such girl had a major impact on our lives. She was young, blonde and pretty and was a new patient of mine. She was about twenty-two years old and had left England two months earlier to come to work in Africa.

Her farewell from her then boyfriend was a passionate affair and although she arrived safely in Salisbury her period stayed behind in the UK. It was not difficult to establish that she was two months' pregnant. Abortions were illegal and she could not continue working once her pregnancy became conspicuous. She had no relatives or friends in Rhodesia or South Africa, and my heart went out to her. After a phone call to Inez, who agreed without hesitation, we had a solution: when the girl could no longer work, she could come to stay with us. In tears of relief she agreed, and when she was about five months' pregnant she moved in with us. Inez and the children adored her and so did our friends. She was a cheeky young lady and we soon called her Barbara Castle after the outspoken, leftist British politician.

We needed to determine what would happen when her baby was born, however. After explaining the pros and cons of the various options, she decided on adoption. When she went into labour, Inez took her to the Lady Chancellor Maternity Home, where she had an easy, uncomplicated delivery. As the head crowned, we gave her a light anaesthetic so that when the baby was born she would not hear the cry or see the beautiful little girl her amorous farewell night in London had produced. When she woke up, her baby was gone.

On my way home from the hospital, I considered the adoption. I was keen that this little girl should go to the best possible parents, and my thoughts immediately turned to our neighbours, a prominent and respectable couple. The husband was manager of a large South African newspaper company. They were middle-aged with a nine-year-old daughter who was a great playmate of our two daughters. The wife had previously confided in me that she would have dearly loved a sister or brother for her daughter but complications had rendered her sterile. Well, I now had their daughter. Before I went home, I turned into their driveway, which was opposite ours. My knock on the front door brought the lady of the house to the door.

Her husband was playing golf, but I decided to tell her about the baby anyway. She had been aware of the pregnant girl staying with us but had no knowledge of the circumstances. She appeared keen on the idea, but had to discuss it with her husband. An hour later, there was a knock on my door: they wanted to adopt the baby.

Before the adoption could become a reality, we had a few problems to sort out. When I told the young mother the next day that I had found excellent parents for her child, she had second thoughts and became tearful. I left the choice to her and, the next day, after weighing up all the possibilities, she agreed to the adoption.

With her child having been officially adopted and living in the house opposite us, there was no way the girl could come back to us, so Inez's best friend, June Teubes, took her in. After a few weeks she was able to go back to work and a few months later she returned to the UK. The adoptive parents were transferred back to South Africa shortly afterwards, and there I thought the story would end. But fate intervened.

About a year after she had returned to England, I received a letter from her telling me that there was a new man in her life. She wrote that she had been honest with him and had told him about the adoption. I was not surprised that this did not alter his love for her, as she was a special, warm person. A few months later, I received their wedding photograph, which I filed somewhere among my papers.

Many years later, in 1980, we went to live in Johannesburg. My move was in the news, as I was entering parliament. The couple who had adopted the baby contacted me and invited us to dinner. Although their adopted daughter was not there, we heard that she was a much-adored child, had been educated at a private school, excelled at sport and was crazy about nature and wildlife.

A few years later, we were invited to her wedding in the magnificent garden of her parents' home in Illovo, Johannesburg. When the bride came through the door on the arm of her father, it was as if I had been transported back to my rooms in Salisbury many years ago, when her biological mother had first consulted me. She was the spitting image of her natural mother: same face, smile, hair and figure. I relived the loneliness, desperation and uncertainty felt by the mother on the day of her child's birth. Here was her daughter, getting married, surrounded by her family and friends, with a bright future.

Unfortunately the marriage did not work out, and she again disappeared from my life. I had not heard from the biological mother since receiving the wedding photo. I was informed that her biological daughter knew she was an adopted child but had no knowledge of who her real mother was or where she lived, and never showed any interest in finding out. The family never spoke about it.

We made many moves after leaving Salisbury. First we relocated to Cape Town, where we lived in Pinelands, then Rondebosch, then Pinelands again, then Newlands and eventually Clifton. From there, we moved to Milpark in Johannesburg and then Auckland Park before finally moving down to Hermanus, near Cape Town. After our last move, forty years after leaving Salisbury, and having moved house and belongings eight times, I was searching among my files one day for some information when the wedding photograph fell out from between some pages. It brought back so many memories, and I could not help wondering what had happened to mother and daughter over all these years.

A few months later, I received a phone call from a man who introduced himself as the daughter's new husband. Both her adoptive father and mother were now dead. While they were alive, she had never wanted to stir up the past, but she had always wanted to know who her real mother was. She knew that I had something to do with her past and now felt free to try to find out who her biological mother was.

Fortunately, I remembered that the mother, in her last letter to me, wrote that she had told her husband all about her pregnancy and the adoption. Since the daughter and her husband lived in a nearby town, I had no hesitation in asking them to come and see me. Over tea the next day, I told her the whole story and said that she could be her mother's twin so close was the resemblance between them. I made certain that she could handle the possibility of meeting her mother and carefully explained the reasons for her adoption and my choice of her adoptive parents. She, in turn, expressed her gratitude to me for what I had done for her and said that she had had the most wonderful, devoted parents, had wanted for nothing and that she and her adoptive sister had had a most happy childhood. At this stage, all of us – the daughter, her husband, Inez and I – were all in tears. Only then did I bring out the wedding photo. For the first time she could look at her mother and hold her photo in her hands.

The burning issue now was to trace her mother. I knew and remembered the mother's first and maiden names and her approximate age, but the best clue of all was the name and address of the photographer on the back of the wedding photo. The daughter and her husband knew about a tracing agency in London and left with the photograph.

Within a month, the mother had been traced. Later, she told me that when she answered the call and realised that it was an attempt by her long-lost daughter to find her, all she could say was, 'I have been waiting for and expecting this call for so many years.' She was still married to the man in the photo and had two daughters.

Contact was made by telephone and soon mother and daughter met for the first time at Heathrow Airport. A few months later, and after all those years, I met 'Barbara Castle' again – not in a labour ward but in the garden of our house in Hermanus. Of course, she was older, but still the same bubbly personality, talking nineteen to the dozen and smiling her warm, friendly smile. With so much to share from the past, it was as if nothing had happened in between. She and her husband were now comfortably retired, lived near London and travelled all over the world, playing golf at every opportunity. We renewed our friendship and she and my daughter Naudéne, whom she often babysat in Salisbury many years ago, are now great friends who live near each other.

The daughter, who had no children and expressed a firm conviction that she did not want any, was not practising contraception but she was unable to conceive. But then nature intervened: a few months after she was reunited with her mother, she fell pregnant and gave birth to a boy. Proudly, she visited our house to introduce me to the 'young man'. She explained to me that I had always been a presence in her life – not near, but somewhere in the back of her mind – and that she was very grateful to Inez and me.

This gratitude summed up a lot of the work I felt I had accomplished in Southern Rhodesia and reminded me of the lyric from *The Sound of Music* – that, in the process, I must have done something good.

* * *

By 1956 my practice was growing rapidly, not only in numbers, but also in geographical area. I never refused a call, day or night, whatever the distance, sometimes travelling more than a hundred miles away to the farming districts around Salisbury. Whenever I received a long-distance call, I would finish my consultations, return home for a light meal and then set off. Frequently there would be thunderstorms and my passage would be impeded by flooded rivers. The rural roads were rough and dangerous. When the rivers were in flood, the farmer would arrange a car on the opposite bank. Holding my medical bag above my head, I would wade through torrents of water to continue my trip in the vehicle waiting on the other side.

Often my patient would be too sick to stay on the farm and I would have to bring him or her back to Salisbury to be admitted to hospital. Otherwise they would be treated at my house, where Inez would always feed them and make them comfortable. On principle, I never refused a call. Sometimes they would prove to be unnecessary, but my patients obviously didn't have my medical knowledge: to them, their discomfort was very real.

My training in Cape Town and England did not, however, prepare me for some of the diseases I often had to diagnose and treat in Southern Rhodesia: malaria, tick-bite fever and bilharzia. I even had a case of leprosy, and once saw the effects of a non-fatal crocodile attack – the patient had suffered a clean amputation of his left hand and left foot and the resulting infection very nearly killed him.

All consultations were rewarded with the princely sum of twelve shillings and six pence, while for visits I charged fifteen shillings. It was common practice to add two shillings for each mile when travel was more than four miles. A circumcision cost £2 2s, confinements £15 and an appendectomy £12.

I never charged a minister of religion, a doctor or a dentist, or any member of their families.

There were times in my first few years when I was worked off my feet. During a polio epidemic, every mother with a young child showing the slightest signs of not being well – a slight temperature, cough or poor appetite – would call me out. My phone rang night and day and I would have to go out and attend to each of them. Beautiful children, who had been laughing and playing a few days earlier, quickly developed paralysis as a result of the disease, and some even died. We had very little in the way of treatment and those that recovered were often left with paralysed limbs. I remember, immediately after the Salk vaccine had become available, administering 120 polio injections, which included twenty-six house calls – all in one day. Fortunately, the vaccine brought an end to this dreadful disease.

As my practice in Southern Rhodesia grew, it became necessary to employ an additional partner. We found one and started a satellite practice for him in Hatfield. But soon, and I think with good reason, I became resentful because I was seeing twice as many cases as my partners, but receiving the same salary.

One morning, it all came to the boil. I was consulting with a waiting room full of patients when my original partner casually strolled in, an hour late. When I complained, he dismissed my unhappiness with an uncalled-for snide remark. That was it; I had had enough. I went into his office, sat him down and told him that the partnership was over. Either he or I would have to move to new premises. At first he did not take me seriously, but quickly he realised that, as far as I was concerned, the decision was final.

There was, however, another reason that I could no longer continue the partnership with him. Although he was practising predominantly as a GP, he was very keen on surgery because of his membership with the FRCS. I gained the distinct impression that some post-war FRCS degrees, and particularly those awarded to former servicemen, had been easily obtained and, although he might have had this qualification, he could not have had much practical experience. My partner could never tell me where he had gained his clinical experience. No other doctors referred patients to him; he operated on his own patients only. As his partner, I was expected to refer my surgical cases to him.

This was reasonable for minor surgery: appendectomies, tonsillectomies, hernias and varicose veins – although he struggled even with these. But he considered himself capable of performing major operations, which were, in fact, well beyond his ability. When I once assisted him with a fractured neck of the femur, he operated for hours. When he finally finished, the procedure had not been done correctly and an orthopaedic surgeon had to be called in to redo the operation soon afterwards.

The last straw was his attempt, with me as his only assistant, to perform an abdominoperineal resection, a surgical procedure for rectal cancer that involves the removal of the rectum. The first part of the operation is to mobilise the anus and the lower rectum via the perineum, which entails separating them from the surrounding tissues. An abdominal approach is then used to mobilise the upper part of the rectum and the lower part of the colon.

After more than two hours of dissecting, which was little more than scratching around, my partner was completely lost and still struggling to perform the first part of the procedure. I could see he had no clue of how badly the operation was going.

Both the anaesthetist and I became greatly concerned for the patient's life. I took the matter into my own hands: I left the operating room and phoned Dick Langford, one of the best surgeons I had ever worked with. With great difficulty, I convinced him to come and help. He was reluctant to interfere, but my pleading finally convinced him of the seriousness of the situation.

I went back into the operating room to assist my partner and told him what I had done. On the surface he was annoyed, but deep down I think he was actually quite relieved. I could not believe that he hadn't realised he was risking the life of the patient. Dick duly arrived, took over the surgery and soon the operation had been expertly completed.

From that case onwards, I never allowed a patient of mine to be operated on by my partner, which increased the animosity between us and made my decision to break up the partnership more urgent.

The problem we faced was who would take over the lease of our surgery. Whereas our other partner had his own consulting rooms in Hatfield, in Salisbury we had three consulting rooms, a large waiting room, a reception area and a bookkeeper's room. We employed two sisters and a bookkeeper. To continue in the same rooms held a great advantage; the patients already knew the phone number and location. The expenses would, however, be too great for only one doctor. Although my partner, as the senior, would have loved to keep the rooms, he had a much smaller practice and therefore the probability of less future income. He decided to move, taking with him his nursing sister, who disliked me intensely. The feeling was mutual.

My accountant friend, Luther van Zyl, happened to be looking for bigger work premises, so he moved into the vacated sections I didn't need. Not only were my expenses reduced, but my best friend was now my work neighbour.

However, there were disadvantages to being on one's own, including always being on duty, twenty-four hours a day. The phone had to be attended to around the clock at home, whether it was a weekday, weekend or public holiday. Inez was not too happy with this arrangement, so we installed a telephone-answering machine as well as a radio-telephone in my car. That improved matters and we were able to go out at night again.

Things were going well. We had a large circle of good friends and, when I bought our large house, I could pay in cash as we had no debt. My father and mother could come and visit us – not only could I pay their expenses, but I could provide them with much-needed extra money as well.

Having my parents with us was such a joy. They too enjoyed it, especially my father. He would go for long walks to the park, accompany me on country calls and dote on his two granddaughters with his usual loving heart.

But our joy could not last forever. During one visit, my father suffered an intestinal obstruction. We operated on him as an emergency and had to remove several inches of his small bowel. The pathology report, however, was effectively a death sentence: it revealed a carcinoma of the colon with spread to the adjacent glands. In short, it was incurable.

After this fateful diagnosis, my father's health deteriorated rapidly. He had returned to his birthplace, Knysna, from Prince Albert in 1953. As mentioned earlier, Inez and I, along with our two daughters, visited him for the last time as a family in December 1957. Here, he could look over the lagoon, the town and the Heads and my last vision of him was at this spectacular location, an area he loved with such passion.

My beloved father died in July 1958 at the age of eighty-two. At this time, our newborn son, Adam, had developed a sepsis of the umbilical cord and was very ill. As a consequence, I was unable to attend my father's funeral. My brother Chris informed us that on this occasion telegrams of sympathy were read from the African National Congress (ANC), the Indian National Congress and many other prominent black groups. It is wonderful that his endeavours were remembered. I still think of him daily and cannot thank

God enough for my parents. I loved them both, but my Deddie was someone very special – indeed a saint.

During one of Chris's last interviews before he died, he was asked what his greatest regret in life was. He answered that he wished his parents could have lived to witness our achievements. My response would have been different. I would have liked to thank them for all the sacrifices they made, which contributed so much towards our achievements.

* * *

My one-man practice continued to flourish and our daughters were happy and doing well at Blackiston School. My mother came to live with us soon after my father's death. She was little trouble but remained very deaf.

One night, about a year later, she suffered a massive stroke. We thought we were going to lose her, but after several months in hospital she came home. She spoke with great difficulty, was very weak on the right-hand side and struggled to walk. Since all the bedrooms were upstairs, this created another difficulty for her.

Chris was now at Groote Schuur Hospital practising cardiac surgery and on one of his trips overseas he promised my mother that, on his return, he would come and fetch her. She became obsessed with this promise and continually nagged us to send her back to South Africa. Chris's desire to take her back was, however, less enthusiastic when it came time to do so. Eventually he and Louwtjie agreed and she went to live with them. I promised, however, that I would continue to share the responsibility of caring for her.

I still loved being a GP, but wanted to specialise before becoming too old. The routine of my practice – consulting with patients, 80 per cent of whom had nothing really wrong with them, and travelling on house calls at all hours of the day and night – was fine, but I could not see myself doing it for the rest of my professional life.

From 1960 I started looking for a partner to introduce slowly to my practice, who could later take over from me. Such an opportunity soon came my way: the superintendent of Salisbury General Hospital at that time, Basil Laidlaw, knew of my search and called me to his office when I was on my hospital rounds one day.

There was a patient in the hospital who happened to be a doctor from Northern Rhodesia. He was looking for a practice in Salisbury, so I went to see him straight away. He was in his early forties, presentable and appeared very eager. After he was discharged, he came to see me. His medical knowledge was impressive and he had solid credentials: not only did he know many of the doctors that I had known at Groote Schuur Hospital, but he had a sound knowledge of its wards and theatres.

When I discussed my terms and the goodwill that went with it, he had no hesitation in accepting my offer. He promised to make all the financial and other arrangements and we settled on a date – a month from then – when he would join me. I was elated and went home to tell Inez.

But something troubled me. The sum I had quoted him was far too high and the terms unrealistic, but this didn't appear to concern him. It seemed to me that it was just too easy for him to pack up so quickly in Northern Rhodesia. Feeling uneasy, I went to see the hospital superintendent and told him what had happened. He went white in the face and pulled out a letter from one of his files. It was from the Northern Rhodesian police, warning hospitals that there was a bogus doctor who had practised there without any qualifications, and saying there was a warrant out for his arrest.

The description of the man left no doubt that this was my partner-to-be. He was duly arrested. I lost a partner but had learnt a valuable lesson: to make sure that any new future partner had a genuine medical qualification. But I wondered how he could have known so much about medicine, drugs, operations and Groote Schuur Hospital. After his arrest, I soon discovered that he had, in fact, been employed as a pharmaceutical agent and therefore had good training on many aspects of medicine. His area of business had included Groote Schuur Hospital. He certainly knew his medicine, but I doubt he would have been able to practise it during his three-year jail sentence.

Soon Dr Dolf Smith, who had practised in Mazabuku in then Northern Rhodesia, joined me. He was Afrikaans-speaking, always immaculately dressed and could have made a fortune as a storyteller. I, in turn, applied for a registrar's post with Professor James Louw, head of the Department of Obstetrics and Gynaecology at Groote Schuur Hospital. This was my first choice. But as there would be no vacancy in the department for a year, I applied for a registrar's post in surgery with Professor Jannie Louw and was offered an appointment that started on 1 July 1963.

I had two months to finalise my affairs and find accommodation and a school in Cape Town for Naudéne and Marie. I was so eager to leave that I literally gave my practice to Dolf Smith, to whom we also rented our home.

On 20 June, nine-and-a-half years after arriving in Southern Rhodesia – nine years longer than initially intended – with our car packed with three children, we left Number 5 Ross Avenue, Salisbury, for our three-day journey to Inez's parents' farm. Inez was very sad and cried all the way to Beit Bridge, but we were all excited about starting a new chapter in our lives. Little did we know that within four years I would obtain a master's degree in surgery, spend almost a year in America and have a date with history that would change my life completely.

But, looking back after nearly sixty years as a doctor, there is no doubt that the time spent in Southern Rhodesia was the happiest period of my life.

Registrar and Researcher

O N MY RETURN TO GROOTE SCHUUR HOSPITAL IN THE MIDDLE of 1963, I started work as a surgical registrar under Professor Jannie Louw, the head of the Department of Surgery.

In accordance with the separatist laws of the country at the time, Ward B1 was allocated exclusively to white patients while Ward B4 was for coloureds, Indians and blacks. Each ward had two wings, one for males and the other for females.

As the most junior of all the registrars, I was permitted to see patients but if I diagnosed, for example, an acute appendicitis, I had to ask another registrar whether he agreed with my diagnosis or not. This was totally demeaning. I was now thirty-five years old, with at least six years more experience than my supposed senior. But whether I liked it or not, I had to start again from the bottom.

Chris had, by this point, created a fair amount of fame and publicity for himself as a cardiac surgeon, something that he was an absolute master at. Professor Jannie Louw had just separated Siamese twins, and he too was in the newspapers, which featured photographs of his 'miracle healing hands'. They both enjoyed the limelight but, even though Professor Louw was his senior, Chris for the most part overshadowed him. As a result, the two had a very uneasy relationship and, from that time on, watched each other like hawks.

Chris was attempting cardiac procedures which, at that time, had never been performed before. During his earlier research, while working as a regis-trar under Professor Louw, Chris was the first to develop an experimental model which made it possible to understand the pathogenesis of *intestinal atresia* – a malformation where there is narrowing or absence of part of the small intestine. This research was actually quite spectacular. He would anaesthetise pregnant dogs and remove the puppies from the mother's uterus, still attached by their umbilical cords. He then opened their abdo-mens, identified their small intestines and tied off the blood vessels to small sections of their small intestines. This resulted in a reduction of the supply of blood to the heart – a condition known as *ischaemia*. The puppies' abdomens were then closed and they were returned to their mother's uterus. The mother was allowed to continue with her pregnancy but, once the puppies were born, they were sacrificed. When their small intestines were inspected, it was seen that the sections where the blood supply had been interrupted were diagnostic of small-bowel atresia.

This work was well received internationally, but a dispute arose between Chris and Professor Louw as to who had originally conceived the idea. I have no doubt in my mind that it was Chris, and he therefore deserved all the praise for this research.

Chris certainly loved the limelight. The Russians, around this time, had performed a transplant of a puppy's head onto the neck of an adult dog. Chris repeated this operation and the puppy's head survived – it even lapped up milk and tried to bark. When the press discovered this, it was widely publicised and raised an unbelievable storm of protest and criticism from animal welfare societies and animal lovers. Chris realised that he had gone too far and terminated the experiment.

But this event succeeded in giving Chris the accolades he desired – he always said that 'bad publicity is better than no publicity'. The young cardiac surgeon was now a well-known name and he subsequently ensured that his pioneering work in congenital heart surgery was both well publicised and praised. Such praise was well deserved and his contribution immense.

* * *

I had been working in Ward B4 for about a month when Professor Louw called me out for a right rollicking, even though the matter had nothing to do with me, as I eventually pointed out to him. The reason for his behaviour remains a mystery to me, but what was very clear was that the professor was out to get me. He moved me to Ward B1 and told the other surgeons that he wanted to keep an eye on me. In his eyes, I was arrogant and self-important and needed to be cut down to size.

Professor Jannie Louw always called me, at the advanced age of thirty-five, 'my boy', and often accused me of stealing his patients and being after his job. To me, this was the most absurd assertion: how could I, a junior registrar with less than six months' experience, have any possible notion of replacing him?

Sunday was reserved for Jannie Louw's grand ward round. I hated it. Hard-boiled eggs were generally served while we were doing the round and, as in my childhood, I couldn't tolerate the smell of the eggs, nor could I handle the sight of the yellow gums that greeted me.

One of Louw's staff had an uncanny sense of knowing when he would arrive from the medical school to do his rounds. He'd be waiting at the window and when Professor Louw duly arrived, he would rush down to open the door for him and carry his briefcase. I was certainly not going to demean myself with such stupidity.

After the Sunday ward round, it was my duty to give Professor Louw a list of the patients and operations that were to be performed during the following week. Operating times for the professor were all-day Wednesday and on Friday mornings. As head of the department, it was his prerogative to choose the operations he wanted to perform. Those that remained would be passed on to the other surgeons. He naturally chose the most interesting procedures for himself, but it was, for him, a very difficult process: he wanted to perform all the operations himself; it was an agony to give surgeries to others. Many changes had to be made to the list before a final schedule could ever be compiled.

When I arrived in Ward B1, the senior registrar was 'Muscles' MacKenzie. Contrary to his nickname, he was a very thin fellow. He had just written his final FRCS exam in London and had enjoyed the rare distinction of passing with the highest marks out of hundreds of other doctors from the United Kingdom and other parts of the world.

Shortly after my arrival in the ward, however, there was a falling-out between Professor Louw and Muscles. For reasons that remain unknown to me, he was banned from performing his duties, and I was appointed as the senior registrar within a year of joining the department.

Over a period of eighteen months, I was on duty every day and every second night – for thirty-six-hour sessions – looking after the wards and assisting Professor Louw. On some mornings, I literally crawled out of bed. To put it mildly, this period of my life was bloody awful. Every night of the week I had to return to the wards at around 9 p.m., do the round and then phone Professor Louw to inform him of the condition of every patient. Every night!

One of the biggest contradictions of being a registrar was that, during the day, you were the surgeon who could not be trusted with performing an operation, but, when the sun set, you immediately transformed into a highly qualified surgeon capable of executing the most complicated of operations.

This was the first and only time in our married life that my relationship with Inez took strain. Fortunately, the situation would be short-lived.

* * *

During 1965 I went to the research laboratory to work towards my Master in Surgery (MCh) thesis. The laboratory was situated next to the mortuary and there was a very amusing, oft-repeated story that involved the later 'famous' Hamilton Naki.

When Hami arrived at the laboratory, he was a young man from the Transkei with, not surprisingly, very little appreciation for European traditions. It was his daily task to unlock the main doors between the medical school and the laboratory and its adjacent post-mortem room.

The story starts one early morning in mid-winter, when Hami entered the darkened premises. He unlocked the door leading to the post-mortem room and, when he turned around to return to the laboratory, he saw two long-bearded men in black, standing in the passage with candles in hand, peering at him.

Hami took off as fast as he could to get as far away as possible from these ghostly apparitions. Needless to say, he only returned to work several days later.

But Hami hadn't seen any ghosts: during the night, a Jewish man had died and his body had been brought to the post-mortem room. The two men dressed in black with candles in hand were from the *chevra kadisha*: they were Jewish undertakers.

* * *

My first research project was a study on intra- and extracellular potassium. As I was by no means a biochemist, I found this research extremely difficult, and writing it up for a thesis impossible. But, with the help of the professor of medicine, we were able to compile an article that was subsequently well received overseas.

My study showed that the electrolytic imbalance in the blood, often as a result of low potassium occurring during and after bypass, was the cause of arrhythmia – a disorder of the heart rate or rhythm – and even cardiac arrest. I received expert assistance from Tessa Marks, a technician in this professor's department, who performed all the electrolyte analysis and knew more about my research than I did. Tessa and her husband later became, and remain, our great friends.

I still do not understand what I did, but, as a result of my work, the levels of potassium in the blood were subsequently monitored during and immediately after open-heart surgery.

On completion of this project, and still with no material for my thesis, I decided to conduct research in the field of heart valve disease, and specifically that of the mitral valve. Following the replacement of a human valve with a prosthetic valve, there was an alarmingly high incidence of clots forming on the valve. This could result in small clots coming loose into the bloodstream, leading to strokes, gangrene of the legs and other ischaemic complications.[1]

I attempted to establish an experimental model, similar to humans, by removing the mitral valves of dogs and replacing them with prosthetic valves.[2] I performed these operations daily for a few months and achieved very good results, and even long-term survivals. I named the surviving dogs after my professors and their wives. I had a 'Professor Brock' and a 'Professor Louw' and used the names of some of their spouses. One of the bitches came on heat and we cross-bred her with 'Professor Brock'. Not surprisingly, the puppies were born normally – without artificial valves.

In the process, I received my own early public recognition when I was visited by members of the South African Broadcasting Corporation (SABC), who recorded the puppies' heartbeats. This was aired on the radio and, I must admit, I enjoyed the publicity.

I finally had enough material for my thesis, and I submitted this research for my master's degree, which was approved by Professor Velva ('Val') Schrire, my brother Chris, and a very famous American cardiac surgeon from the world-renowned Mayo Clinic, John Kirklin.

And so, in 1966, three years after returning from Salisbury, having completed my final written and oral examinations, I was granted my MCh degree.

* * *

I slowly planned my future. My last six months of training in surgery at Groote Schuur were spent practising general surgery, again with Professor Louw – as if he hadn't had enough of me!

My relationship with him during this period had progressively worsened. I was now thirty-eight, with a wife and two teenage daughters, and I refused to be intimidated by him. I had already given him eighteen months of day-and-night, slave-like duty as one of his registrars.

Professor Louw remained extremely jealous of Chris and tried to take this out on him, but Chris was equal, if not superior, in fighting back. Consequently, I became Professor Jannie Louw's lightning conductor, and he would often vent his spleen on me in the most childish and ridiculous manner. On one occasion, while scrubbing before commencing surgery, Professor Louw entered the room and, to my surprise, verbally attacked me. He was furious: 'You want my job!' he shouted. 'You're just like your brother ... I'll show you!' He ranted for about five minutes, but I didn't say anything; I just kept scrubbing. I would usually open the case for him and, when he had completed the major part of the surgery, he would scrub out and I would close the patient. On this occasion, as soon as he said, 'Close the case,' I said to him, 'Professor, I want to talk to you afterwards.'

That afternoon, I went to his office and confronted him. 'Professor Louw,' I said, 'I'm ashamed of you – that a man in your position can carry on like this in front of the nursing staff. I'm sure they're ashamed of you too. But I promise you, if you say anything that would make my wife and children ashamed of me, I'll beat you up. I'm warning you.'

From that moment, he changed. We remained enemies, but I must admit that he took it relatively well. However, whatever shares I *had* built up with him by that point now took a distinct dip.

* * *

Despite the very unpleasant goings-on with Professor Louw, I became interested in cardio-vascular surgery, a specialisation involving surgery to the body's arteries and consisting mainly of the repair of aneurysms and the bypassing of obstructions. We followed the British school of practising as cardio-thoracic surgeons. Whereas cardiac surgery explicitly addresses the heart, cardio-thoracic surgery includes the heart and all the other major chest organs, such as the lungs and the oesophagus.

During the early sixties, the names of two American cardiac surgeons, Denton Cooley and Michael DeBakey, had become prominent, and articles about them appeared in the popular medical magazines. I had read about these two doctors as part of my research for my MCh. It became obvious to me that to work with either DeBakey or Cooley would be ideal for my future surgical career. They both practised as cardio-vascular surgeons, and I saw an opportunity to become one of the first South Africans to specialise in this field. In the United States I could train in vascular surgery – my first choice, and also in cardiac surgery – my second. Another reason for my not wanting to pursue cardio-thoracic surgery in Cape Town was that I knew I would find it difficult, if not impossible, to work with Chris.

I decided there and then that I would apply to Dr Michael DeBakey for a post as a Fellow at Baylor Medical Center and the Methodist Hospital in Houston, Texas. Shortly afterwards he advised me that they would be pleased to have me, and that I could start on 1 July. He also offered me a salary of $4 250 a year.

Only then did I inform Professor Louw of my decision. I understood that there was an unwritten rule that if you wanted to further your training overseas you had to do it through him and obtain his blessing. This made you beholden to him. If or when you decided to return, you would have his favour and a better chance of senior appointment. When I told Professor Louw of my intentions, he became very angry.

I was concerned as I still had to write my final exams, a process that Professor Louw also controlled. He could so easily have used his influence with the other examiners to fail me, but, to his credit, he helped me during my examination preparations. Not only did he not fail me, but he did everything possible to see that I passed. For this, I will always be in his debt. His actions towards me *afterwards*, however, caused much hardship, both for me and for my family.

My three years of training at Groote Schuur Hospital on a salary of R300 a month had resulted in our being short on finances. The little money I had saved while living and working in Southern Rhodesia had been blocked by the government, which wanted to prevent money from leaving the country, so I couldn't gain full access to it. But I still had two months' official leave due to me and had planned on using its payout to assist Inez and the family financially for the first few months I was away. Jannie Louw, I believe, evoked a provincial regulation and blocked this payment – an entirely inappropriate response, in my opinion, for a man in his position. I never received a cent.

I was left in the unfortunate position of having only enough money to buy a one-way ticket to the United States. The little money I had saved in South Africa would be used to support my wife and three children while I was overseas. It was frightening that I would only be able to afford a return ticket with my overseas earnings.

Under such circumstances I left for Houston, from Johannesburg's Jan Smuts Airport on 3 July 1966, with no money to return to South Africa and without Professor Jannie Louw's blessing.[3] He never forgave me for this.

12

Training in Houston

IN HOUSTON, TEXAS, I WORKED UNDER TWO OF THE WORLD'S leading cardio-vascular surgeons and was introduced to extraordinary characters in the medical field. I also met wonderful people, who took care of me while I was separated from my family.

I was to visit these shores again a year after the first human heart transplant, and many more times in later life, when I attended medical conferences. Later, I would travel to the United States while attempting to further critical illness insurance. Nothing has ever changed my love of the American people or my enduring admiration for their country.

* * *

When I arrived at Heathrow, London, having completed the first leg of my journey to Houston, I had to change flights. In the ensuing rush to make the interconnecting flight to Chicago on time, I realised that I'd left all my documents, including my master's degree, my health certificates and the X-rays of my chest, on the aeroplane that had flown me from South Africa. Fortunately, after a mad rush around the airport, I retrieved them before catching my flight to the United States. It was not an auspicious start.

My first shock was on arrival at O'Hare International Airport in Chicago, where I had to change planes again. I was absolutely bewildered: I had never witnessed so many planes and such hordes of people at any airport. As a result, I felt extremely insecure and expected the worst.

I had timed my arrival very badly. It was 4 July – Independence Day – and it seemed to me that everyone in the nation was flying. With so many planes lining up and waiting to take off, I was sure that there was going to be a crash – involving my plane! I had to change flights yet again in Dallas, but finally we were heading for my final destination, Houston. It was at this point that I had a chilling realisation: I was on my own. This was a frightening experience, and I still cannot understand how I could have arrived in a foreign country without having made any domestic arrangements beforehand. This fact dawned on me only when we were making our final descent. I had to commence work the next day at the Methodist Hospital, but had no

115

accommodation – I didn't even have a place to sleep that night – and I didn't know a single person in the United States.

After the aeroplane had landed and I was descending the aircraft's steps, a furnace hit me. The air was hot, humid and reeking of oil – Houston in the height of summer. As I stepped into the cool, air-conditioned airport, which revived me somewhat, I heard an announcement over the public announcement system. It was difficult to understand the strange Texan accent, but I thought I picked up the name *Barnard*. Listening carefully, I realised that it *was* my name. The announcer requested that I report to the information desk. I immediately thought of Inez and the children, who were visiting the Kruger National Park at the time. My anxiety levels, which were already higher than normal, suddenly escalated at the thought that something might be wrong at home.

On nervously approaching the desk, I observed a single individual standing there, a short, plump gentleman with a reddish face and a big friendly smile. He had a clerical collar around his neck. When he saw me, he walked towards me and asked, 'Are you Dr Barnard?' I was almost speechless that he knew my name.

'Yes,' I replied.

'Dr Barnard,' he said, 'I am the Reverend Tom Sumners. My wife and I would be pleased if you would spend your first night in the USA at our house.'

I am not ashamed to say that my relief at having somewhere to stay and people to talk to was so great that tears started running down my cheeks. I had no idea how this wonderful couple had known about me, but I soon found out. A few weeks prior to my leaving South Africa, we had had a patient, Miss Sussie Kagelhoffer, who was a retired school principal. During a conversation with her, I had told her about my plans. She had said that, during a visit to the Holy Land the previous year, she had met a very pleasant American couple who lived in Houston. She wrote to them and told them about me: she was the reason I had a roof over my head that night.

Tom and Doris Sumners not only became my dearest friends, but introduced me to many of their friends as well. I also worshipped with them in their church on Sundays when I wasn't on duty. They became my American parents, and when Inez came to visit me for a few weeks over the Christmas holidays, they treated her with the same love and affection.

The next morning, Mrs Sumners dropped me off at the Methodist Hospital, one of a group of hospitals of the Baylor College of Medicine, at

7 a.m. She would look for accommodation for me near the hospital, as I had no car and would never have been able to afford one. She would fetch me again that evening.

I managed to find the theatre, where a tough-looking nurse asked me who I was, glanced at some papers and tersely told me that I was four days late. She pointed to the changing room and ordered me to report to Theatre 7. I found the necessary theatre clothes, went to Theatre 7 and was told to scrub. Gowned and gloved, I took my position at the operating table as the third assistant.

The operation was already in progress and, without being introduced, I was handed a very large retractor to open the field of operation.[1] This was known by us as an *idiot stick* because you could stand holding it and do nothing else for hours during, as in this case, a difficult abdominal aortic aneurysm repair. If anything irritated the surgeon or an unexpected complication arose, it was usually the fault of the idiot-stick holder.

When one starts off as a junior surgeon, one's place at the operating table is on the left, where one either holds an idiot stick or assists the surgeon. With years of assisting and gaining in seniority, one is at last able to claim the right-hand side as senior surgeon. From left to right is not more than a yard, but it takes one at least three years to get there. Standing on the left-hand side of the operating table on my first day at the Methodist Hospital in Houston, I was reminded of a saying we have in our profession: 'The longest distance in the world is from the left- to the right-hand side of the operating table.'

When the aneurysm was exposed and isolated, in walked the big man. I could feel the whole atmosphere tense. He wore thick spectacles, his accent was awful and, to me, his surgery seemed hesitant. I would come to learn that he fought with his assistants all the time. Halfway through operations, he would be called out for important overseas calls, leaving us standing there with folded hands for half an hour or longer. He would then return to complete the graft and leave, allowing us to finish the operation.

When he left after that first operation, he took off his mask and I saw why he was called *Black Mike*. Dr Michael DeBakey had a dark complexion, with a crooked nose and a thin, angular face. This was the man that I, at great personal sacrifice, had come to see and work with. He was, in my opinion, technically a poor surgeon, although this may well be a biased perspective as I didn't like him much. I did, however, think that his eyesight was failing him, judging by the thick lenses he needed to wear when performing surgery.

Patients came from all over the world. To me, the indications for surgery were often unjustified. DeBakey was, however, incredibly hard-working – he had to be, with all the theatres working flat out from 7 a.m. until all the cases were done. He often went home at midnight and started his ward rounds at five o'clock the next morning.

DeBakey would always complain about the theatre lights and blamed his assistants for standing in his light. Early on, he accused me of the same crime. My response to him was, 'Professor, I have just travelled over 6 000 miles to work with you and assist you, and if I stand in your light it is just unfortunate, because I insist on seeing what you are doing.' As a person, I thought he was selfish and unpleasant; he was generally not a nice man. If I'd thought Jannie Louw and Chris were difficult to work with, DeBakey was worse.

His second in command was Ed Garrett, one of the best – if not *the* best – surgeons I ever worked with, and a very, very superior human being. We became great friends.

To those of us from Groote Schuur Hospital, post-operative care was as important as surgery, and Professor Louw, to his credit, had drilled this into us. DeBakey ran a good intensive care unit (ICU) but, with the exception of Ed Garrett, I wasn't particularly impressed by him or his unit.

There are perhaps two more contributing factors to my experience of working under DeBakey. I had found rooms in Dryden Avenue, a twenty-minute walk from the Methodist Hospital. This cost me $100 and left me with only $200 to buy food and to save for Inez's visit in December and my aeroplane ticket back home.

I couldn't afford much in the way of food. At the hospital, coffee was free of charge. For energy, I drank as many cups of well-sugared coffee as possible. Owing to this overindulgence, I have never put sugar in my coffee or tea since leaving Houston. I was able to afford one proper meal a week and soon discovered that chilli beans or chicken was the most affordable. Given the repetition of this diet, chicken has never been a favourite of mine since. But I still enjoy chilli beans! At the flat, I could satisfy my hunger with white bread and Coca-Cola. The gas expanded my stomach and gave me a sensation of fullness, but it didn't last long. When pharmaceutical companies occasionally invited me out, I used to eat all except the kitchen sink. The Sumners, of course, and their friends, invited me out to restaurants, but such outings were few and far between and, in the process, I lost a lot of weight. I soon realised that a lack of food caused chronic tiredness and severe constipation. Somehow I managed to keep body and soul together.

From my first savings, I bought a small portable radio for $5, which proved to be a great companion as I could now listen to music. Next, I bought a cheap, second-hand television. This changed my life, but there was one problem: my flat was situated beneath the flight path to and from Houston's airport. Whenever an aircraft flew overhead, it caused interference to the television screen, which would then scroll over for thirty or so seconds. Since aeroplanes took off from or landed at the airport at regular intervals, it was very difficult, if not impossible, to watch television.

During the Labour Day weekend of September 1966, I hitched a lift to Richmond, Virginia, where Chris was working with another famous surgeon, Dr Richard Lower. The latter was well known at the time for his research on kidney and heart transplantations with the world-renowned Dr Norman Shumway.

Near New Orleans, we were stopped by the police for speeding, and my travelling companion was arrested. Being from New York, and a Yankee at that, was perhaps a greater offence than the speeding. We were taken to the local prison, where he was placed in jail. But, being in the Deep South, when they discovered I was from South Africa I was treated like royalty and given food and Coca-Cola. Racial bigotry was still very much alive in the southern parts of the USA – clearly the Civil War had not been forgotten.

It was a thirty-six-hour journey to Richmond, and I spent a night with Chris at his apartment. For some or other reason, however, my visit was not convenient for him. He was very distant and his mind was elsewhere for the entire time I was there. In fact, I was largely ignored, despite having made the effort to travel a considerable distance to visit him. I was, obviously, both offended and disappointed by his lack of enthusiasm to see me.

I had to leave the next day by Greyhound bus for the two-day journey back to Houston. A bus is not, at the best of times, the most comfortable way to travel, especially during the hottest periods and in the hottest parts of the USA. It was even worse over a holiday weekend, when the bus was packed with all shapes, sizes and smells. It was, to say the least, a most unpleasant experience.

I arrived back in Houston during the early hours of the following morning. Washed and shaved, I was holding my idiot stick at 7 a.m. Dr DeBakey had just returned from a visit to South Africa, where he had met Inez at a reception and discovered that she and the children were unable to be with me. I think it was the first time he realised that I was there.

After more than two months, he finally took notice of me and asked me to come to his office. To my utter amazement, he offered me financial assist-ance to bring my family to Houston and a permanent appointment in his department.

I was very grateful, but preferred to tolerate the separation from my family – in spite of the loneliness and difficulties – rather than work in his department for one day longer than I needed to. I went back to theatre and, when DeBakey came in, he said to me, 'Dr Barnard, I have bad news for you. Your prime minister was assassinated today.' I continued to assist him, but that news was the last thing I had expected to hear.

This was how I learnt of the death of the great architect of 'separate development', Dr Hendrik Verwoerd. Later in life, I would sit in the opposi-tion benches in parliament opposite the seat where Verwoerd was stabbed to death by the deranged parliamentary messenger Dimitri Tsafendas.

I learnt very little else from DeBakey during my time in his department, but I was able to make some important observations, which were new to me. Their exposure of the aorta was very slick and much faster than ours, and they used plastic grafts to re-establish an unobstructed flow in the aorta or arteries. We still performed endarterectomies, whereby we removed the fatty deposits narrowing the artery.

During my time in Houston, I witnessed the world's first successful implantation of the clinical Left Ventricular Assist Device (LVAD) – a mechanical pump that helps to maintain the pumping ability of the heart – in a paracorporeal position.[2] DeBakey had selected a Mexican woman for the operation and I can clearly recall that she was a hairdresser by pro-fession. I was in theatre, all masked, gowned and wearing sterile clothes, but, given the large crowd of onlookers, I was all the way back in the third row. To see anything one had to be standing next to the operating table.

I saw nothing, and after a few attempts to improve my position in the surgical scrum, I left to enjoy a cup of coffee. I can't remember much more of this theatrical event than that the patient survived. In my opinion, she survived in spite of the artificial heart, not because of it.

A great frustration of mine while working under Dr DeBakey was that there was no teaching. We assisted with one case after another but were given no opportunity to operate. This disgruntlement led to our group of Fellows arranging a meeting with DeBakey to air our concerns and he agreed to meet with us. Unfortunately, the discussion yielded no positive results, but he did say something that I will never forget, and which has been of great significance in my own career. When we complained about the lack of teaching, he conceded: 'You can watch a man play a piano for twenty years and still not be able to play a single note.' As DeBakey himself was admitting, only with a hands-on approach would we learn how to operate.

I was scheduled to work under DeBakey for only three months. Thereafter, I could apply to work with him again or to three other firms – one being that of Dr Denton Cooley, the other glamour-boy of cardiac surgery at the time. The choice was easier when Ed Garrett, who could no longer take the unpleasant Dr DeBakey or what was going on at the hospital, resigned during my third month with the famous surgeon. I duly applied to work under Dr Denton Cooley and, much to my relief, I was accepted.

* * *

I joined the other famous American surgeon on 1 October 1966 at the Texas Children's Hospital.

As with Chris and Professor Louw, there existed great competition between Cooley and DeBakey, and this too was well publicised. According to one story, Dr DeBakey once pulled into a non-parking bay at the university. The parking attendant approached the famous doctor to inform him that this wasn't allowed. DeBakey looked at him indignantly and snapped, 'Do you know who I am?' The man replied by saying, 'Sir, I don't give a damn. Even if you're Dr Denton Cooley, you are not allowed to park here.'

My time with Denton Cooley was a far happier and productive period. Unlike my experience under Michael DeBakey, I was given patient responsibility. Three Americans and I were selected to be in charge of his patients, both pre- and post-operatively, and we were given preference to assist during operations. We were on duty one night in four and one weekend in four.

Having little else to do outside my work, and without a car, it suited me to spend such long hours at the hospital. I spent a lot of time in the wards with the patients, who had fruit sweets and other edibles that they readily shared with me. This was a welcome addition to my sparse diet and I was able to save money as a result of needing to buy less food.

One night, I was asked by a patient whether I was a doctor. I was surprised by the question and asked him why he had asked. His reply amazed me. 'But you visit us,' he said. He could not believe that a doctor could spend so much time with his patients!

One of the three selected American doctors was Jim Bozeman, a red-headed, hot-tempered surgeon from Lafayette, Louisiana. Jim was married with two young children and he and his wife, Betty, befriended me. I frequently enjoyed most welcome meals with them and, after too much bourbon and many Bloody Marys, often spent the night on their sofa.

He could put away a fair amount and, when his wife objected, he always replied that 'it makes you see double and makes you feel single'. Jim was from the Deep South, deeply conservative and a bit of a racist. His chief hatred was 'the goddamned Yankees'. Otherwise, their friendship towards me meant almost as much as that of the Sumners.

Denton Cooley performed a fair amount of congenital heart surgery, and I immediately took to it. His surgical skills and technique were exceptional, but he concentrated on speed and numbers. He operated from four operating rooms and we sometimes did sixteen cases a day, one after the other.

His bypass methods were intended for ease and speed but were very dangerous if the procedure was lengthy and complicated. He did not cool the patient or the heart, and after he had cross-clamped the aorta, the heart had no blood supply to its muscle. This created ideal conditions: with a non-beating heart and no blood in the operation field, even the most intricate operations could be performed with ease.

Cooley could, therefore, perform his operations much faster than others. However, the lack of oxygen to the heart muscle meant that it was less forgiving when the blood supply was restored, with the extreme risk of severe complications, including life-threatening arrhythmias and, worse still, a 'stone heart'. As the name implies, the heart would become as hard as stone and would never be able to beat again, let alone sustain life-supporting circulation.

Fortunately we didn't see many of these conditions, but the arrhythmias kept us going all night in the ICU and, by the time I left, I had become an expert in the diagnosis and treatment of such complications.

What I found even more alarming was that many visiting surgeons would view his skills and fast operations and then return home and attempt to do the same. But they lacked his skills and, with longer ischaemic times, their operative mortalities would be significant. I would, later on in my career, see examples of this in a few countries, including Spain and Romania.

Technically Cooley was superb. He would be surrounded by doctors from all over the world and they'd leave with signed photos saying 'To my esteemed colleague'. His famous saying was, 'Don't call me Denton, just call me G.O.D. – Good Old Denton.'

Because I was relatively senior in age Cooley treated me with a fair amount of respect. He was, however, prone to making goading comments. Frequently these concerned the number of operations that he managed to get through on a daily basis compared to the number of surgeries we performed – which was, at most, four. On one occasion during surgery, he said to me, 'So, Marius, how does it feel watching me doing so many cases a day when your little old unit in Africa can only manage two or three?' I was very annoyed and reacted: 'You remind me of a story I once heard. During the Second World War, a big American battleship was passing through the North Sea during a great storm with mountainous waves. A small British destroyer passed by, being tossed around and battling to cope with the huge swells. The battleship flashed an encoded signal to the destroyer – "Hi, how's the second-biggest navy in the world?" The British immediately responded, "Fine, how's the world's second best?"'

Cooley stopped operating for about ten seconds, which for him was an eternity. He stared at me and I thought he was going to hit me. But he then simply lowered his head and carried on with his procedure, not before muttering, 'You son of a bitch.'

Cooley was very often sarcastic. When, for example, I asked him what the indication was for a patient's surgery, he would say, 'He can lie down,' or 'He's in Houston.' He was, otherwise, nice to me, but could be very contemptuous of others.

Once, on completing an operation, before releasing the aortic clamp to restore blood flow to the heart, his anaesthetist injected a cocktail of drugs through one of the numerous drips. Once the clamp was released, the heart started to beat immediately. An admiring observer asked what was used in the solution. Cooley's immediate reply was 'intravenous Vaseline'. I could not believe my eyes when this reply was scribbled into a notebook. I sincerely hope it was never used!

Inez and I wrote to each other once a week. Since Cooley liked to 'knock' people, he said to me at the operating table one day, 'Wouldn't you like to be important?' I replied by saying, 'Dr Cooley, you're a big surgeon and people might think you're important, but every week the postman comes to my little apartment with a letter from my family in South Africa. So he is more important to me than you are.' To his credit, he took it well.

Cooley allowed me to get away with more things than other doctors would have, and of great significance to me was that he allowed me to give my opinion. I was reappointed to Cooley for another three months.

My life had certainly become more pleasant and I was greatly looking forward to Inez's three-week visit over Christmas and the New Year. When she arrived, the Sumners adopted her and Jim and Betty Bozeman were very kind and generous. Inez and I went on a ten-day tour with the little money I had saved, travelling mostly by Greyhound. We visited New Orleans, went by riverboat up the Mississippi and had a one-course meal at a garden restaurant, the Court of Two Sisters. I will never forget that evening. We drank mint juleps and then went to the Preservation Hall, a bare venue with hard wooden seats, where five or six octogenarian jazz musicians – all greats from yesteryear – held us in awe with their amazing playing. The evening was just magic.

Our visit to New Orleans was followed by a trip to Miami. Interestingly enough, this was on the invitation of the patient who had asked me whether I was a doctor. From there, we headed for Las Vegas. We hated it and expected the devil to jump out at any time from behind the one-armed bandits.

What a contrast our next visit would be, when we looked down on one of the most remarkable views in the world. It literally took my breath away. The cliffs of the Grand Canyon, eroded out of the Colorado River raging below, revealed millions of years of the earth's existence and made us aware of just how insignificant we were. We could not get enough of it. Our pledge to see it again came true many years later, and it certainly didn't disappoint us the second time around. We had changed during the forty years since our last visit, but the canyon and the river were just the same – another grand display of the wonders of God's creation.

The rest of the holiday was spent on a Greyhound bus travelling through New Mexico and southern Texas. With the exception of our visit to the Alamo, it was not very exciting. I knew the history of the area well, having been an avid reader of cowboy books and the early history of America in my youth. Here, I saw where the Mexicans had besieged the Texans, including one of my childhood heroes, Davy Crockett. I can still sing the song, 'Davy, Davy Crockett, king of the wild frontier'.

Inez's return home ended my happiest time in Houston, and all too soon I was back at work. I was very busy, but after Inez left I missed her and the children to such an extent that I decided to go home at the end of my second three-month period. When I informed Cooley, he offered me a more senior post with a much higher salary. But the call of Africa was too strong. I had high hopes for my future. An appointment at Groote Schuur Hospital in the Department of Surgery as a vascular surgeon was the first prize. I had concentrated on and intensely studied this exciting new development in the treatment of vascular diseases and had scrubbed in to as many cases as possible.

I confidently wrote to Professor Louw about such an interest and the experience I had gained. I believed that, on my return, I would be one of the best-trained vascular surgeons in South Africa. But Professor Jannie Louw had a long and vindictive memory and refused to offer me any such appointment. Chris tried to change Professor Louw's mind, but without success. So I had to face the reality of returning to South Africa without a job.

Realising my financial plight and responsibilities, Chris offered me a position as a consultant in cardiac surgery, a speciality that I had never intended to enter into permanently.

Home Again

O N RETURNING FROM HOUSTON, IT WAS WONDERFUL TO BE reunited with my family after nearly a year of absence. But we had numerous problems. I didn't like the house in Pinelands, which we had bought two years previously, particularly given the smells that we had to endure from the nearby Bisto Factory and Maitland abattoir. If I had to work with human flesh all day, the animal smells at night were the last thing I needed. In addition, the house was far from the schools my children attended.

We, therefore, needed to find a new house near to both the hospitals where I was to work, Groote Schuur Hospital and the Red Cross War Memorial Children's Hospital, and to my children's schools. My daughters, Naudéne and Marie, were enrolled at Rustenburg School for Girls and my son, Adam, at Rondebosch Boys' Preparatory School. We soon found an ideal home in Newlands, with an added bonus that it was five minutes away from the Newlands train station and the Newlands Cricket Ground.[1] More importantly, it was only a short walk away from the Newlands Rugby Stadium.

We were fortunate in that we sold our Pinelands house at a profit so, together with money from the sale of our house in Salisbury, we were able to buy the Newlands house in cash. I had, and still have, a loathing for debt. All of the houses we have bought in the fifty-nine years of our marriage – nine in all – have been paid for in cash. The same applies to the cars.

We now had a beautiful and conveniently situated home, and the children were at excellent schools. I was appointed both lecturer in the Department of Cardiac Surgery (an appointment at the University of Cape Town's Faculty of Medicine) and cardiac surgeon at Groote Schuur Hospital. My employer was the Cape Provincial Council, an elected body formed to take care of provincial matters for each of the then four provinces. As these were government appointments, my 'masters' were, therefore, members of the National Party – a group of politicians about whom I didn't have a particularly good feeling. It was a strange appointment that would later give me more trouble than I could ever have wished for.

But I had other problems to deal with. My one year of cardiac research in the mid-sixties under Chris's supervision had resulted in many clashes, some of which had been terribly acrimonious. This had convinced me of two things: firstly, that I never wanted to be a cardiac surgeon, and, secondly, that I never again wanted to work in the same department as Chris.

Yet here I was, working in his department once more. I have to admit that I owed the appointment to him, despite the fact that his difficult relationship with the head of surgery had probably been the source of Louw's attitude towards me. I often wonder how the rest of my life might have panned out had Chris not felt some compassion for me. I have to acknowledge that he must also have had doubts about appointing me, knowing in his heart of hearts that I would be trouble for him. Our youth together had not been rich in brotherly love and our two years together in one room as medical students were based on, to say the least, a hostile truce.

Socially, we were not even friends, and the joint care of our aged mother exposed our wives to unpleasant relations and resentment. This was certainly not an ideal recipe for a happy, professional relationship, and the thirteen years I spent in his department would not improve matters. If the roles had been reversed and I was the head of the department, knowing my relationship with my brother, I wonder if I would have appointed him in *my* department?

Another problem was that I was, in all honesty, very poorly trained as a cardiac surgeon, and I had done only six months of research in replacing mitral valves in dogs. During my year in Houston, I had assisted in many open-heart operations relating to both congenital and acquired heart conditions, but I had never performed any operations myself. So, as things stood at that point, I must have been the first consultant cardiac surgeon in a teaching hospital who, up until then, had never performed a single open-heart operation on a human.

I had wanted to be a vascular surgeon. I had been prepared to make so many sacrifices to achieve that objective. But now my future lay in cardiac surgery – something I had vowed never to do. I had, at great cost to myself, collected hundreds of slides that recorded operations and techniques on different types of vascular surgery to provide presentations to medical colleagues once back home. They would assist me in describing these new techniques, how we could implement them and, where possible, how to make improvements. I now realised that these slides would be worthless but kept them in hope. I reluctantly threw them away many, many years later.

* * *

Chris, as head of the Department of Cardiac Surgery, was supported by three surgeons. The first, Dr Rodney Hewitson, was a very senior and experienced surgeon. There is no doubt that he was, by far, the best surgeon in our unit. He held a part-time appointment, being in private practice too, and was in charge of thoracic surgery. Rodney was a man of few words, deeply religious and indispensable to Chris in the operating room.

Chris relied heavily on Rodney as his first assistant during operations. Fortunately, Chris respected him greatly and behaved himself when they operated together. He never blamed Rodney, as he did other assistants, when things went wrong during operations. Rodney was an immense help to us all and was a great surgeon to work with. Unfortunately, he was a poor communicator and had little in the way of leadership skills. He had vast experience, which he could have shared with us, but was regrettably unable to do so.

The second surgeon in the department was Terry O'Donovan, a consultant. He came with good previous experience, having worked in New Zealand with Sir Barratt-Boyes, a world-renowned paediatric cardiac surgeon. Terry was a pleasant man to work with but was a mediocre surgeon. I was the department's inexperienced third.

The team was completed by three registrars: Dr Bertie ('Bossie') Bosman, who, after many years as a GP in Barkly East, had come to Groote Schuur to specialise; Dr François Hitchcock, a competent and dedicated surgeon from Pretoria who showed signs of a great future; and Dr Coert Venter, who had trained in cardiac surgery in Pretoria before coming to Groote Schuur.

I didn't get on with Coert Venter from the first minute our paths crossed. He was aggressive, but never in front of his seniors. His greatest ambition was to operate at all costs. His surgery was rough and untidy; to him, operating was a drug, with the patient being a necessary evil. Little did I know that in less than six months, this surgical team would have a date with destiny!

Two other departments made it possible for us to perform excellent cardiac surgery. One was the Department of Cardiology, headed by the brilliant Professor Val Schrire, a pioneer of cardiology and an excellent diagnostician, long before the introduction of the modern technological aids we have today. By taking a simple history of a patient, listening to the sounds of the heart with his stethoscope and assessing a few of the special investigations – typically X-rays of the chest and ECG – he could diagnose even the most difficult and intricate cardiac conditions.

His clinical ability was amazing and he ran an excellent unit with great support from a very talented team comprising Wally Beck, Richard Fraser, Hymie Joffe and a few others. Our success as a surgical unit could never have been achieved without Val Schrire and his team. The untimely death of Professor Schrire a few years after I joined the team was a great loss. He was in the prime of his life and would have made an even greater contribution to cardiology had he lived longer.

It was sad, however, that after the first human heart transplant, due to Val's discontent with Chris's behaviour, of which he strongly disapproved, his and Chris's relationship deteriorated to such an extent that they seldom spoke to one another. On Val's passing, Wally Beck took over and, to Beck's credit, the unit never lowered its extremely high standard.

The other department we relied on very heavily was the Department of Anaesthetics. Here, again, we had excellent support. At Groote Schuur Hospital, Dr Joseph ('Ozzie') Ozinsky was the senior anaesthetist, an extremely competent, skilled and experienced doctor. Many desperate emergency operations were successfully performed due to Ozzie's unflappable competence.

At the Red Cross Children's Hospital, an old classmate of mine, Professor Tom Voss, was a member of the anaesthetics team. He was slow but meticulous, and highly skilled. Just how he and his colleagues managed to anaesthetise newborn infants and keep them alive, I never quite understood. When he left for Australia, Petro Malherbe and the eccentric Chris Swart took over.

Well-trained theatre staff supported us. Sisters Peggy Jordaan and Pittie Rautenbach provided excellent support at Groote Schuur Hospital, while at the Red Cross Children's Hospital we could rely on the experience of Sisters Mostert and Merman. At both hospitals, there were ICUs with highly competent and dedicated nursing staff. Day and night, they cared for our patients. Once the patients were well enough, they were transferred to the wards to be cared for by our well-trained sisters and nurses.

Lastly, there were the 'pump' technicians, who were responsible for managing the heart–lung machine that kept the patient alive while we operated. This is an extremely important function and the technicians never really received the recognition they deserved. I salute them and thank them for all they did for the patients and our unit.

When I arrived at Groote Schuur Hospital, Carl Goosen was the senior pump technician, but he left within a few months. A very inexperienced

Johan van Heerden, who started his training with me in the dog laboratory during my master's research, and Dene Friedmann took over. Despite their initial insecurity, they soon accepted their responsibilities and became invaluable and essential members of our team. The team was later strengthened by the arrival of the experienced Alistair Hope.

At Groote Schuur Hospital there were separate ICUs – one for whites and the other for coloureds, Indians and blacks – in accordance with the laws of our country. In this specific case, they were divided in terms of the then infamous Separate Amenities Act,[2] which had the added implication that no black nurses were allowed to train in the Western Cape or be appointed there. Only whites, coloureds and Indians were afforded this opportunity. I was most unhappy with this situation, as was Chris, who introduced the treatment of mixed races into the units under his charge from the first opportunity.

At the Red Cross Children's Hospital, patients were also separated in the wards on the basis of their race, but, as there was only one small ICU with four beds, Chris had all post-operative cases attended to in this unit, irrespective of the patient's skin colour. Although this was met with strong opposition, he refused to give in and won the fight.

In the single, non-segregated ICU it was amazing to see parents, who would never ordinarily allow their young, blonde white daughter to be nursed in the same ward as a black boy from the Transkei, praying with the black parents of the boy in the next-door bed. We have a great Afrikaans saying, 'Nood leer bid', meaning that desperation makes you pray. Nowhere was this better illustrated than in our racially mixed ICU. Even more amazing was seeing white and black parents mixing socially after their children had been transferred back to their separate wards. They would enquire about the progress of the other's child and even visit them. Once discharged, however, each returned to his or her own corner of apartheid South Africa. It is frightening to recall that this was happening in South Africa less than half a century ago.

* * *

With an increasing number of cases on our waiting list and a demanding Professor Schrire wanting us to attend to more cases, we were totally restricted by a lack of theatre time. With no theatres of our own, we made use of those allocated for general surgery.

We were allocated enough theatre time to do four cases on Mondays and four on Thursdays at Groote Schuur, and three at the Red Cross on Tuesdays. The Department of Anaesthetics, headed by Professor Arthur Bull, a strong ally of Professor Louw, was not particularly helpful and allocated capable but limited anaesthetic support.

Coming from Houston, where Michael DeBakey and Denton Cooley had at least eight theatres available, ICUs of thirty beds, and anaesthetists and staff capable of performing sixteen to twenty operations per day, I found our unit inadequate. The government and the provincial council had no interest in us, our funding was pathetic and few people even knew of our existence

In Houston, operations started promptly at 7 a.m. This meant that the surgeon would make his incision at that time, the patient already having been anaesthetised and draped in sterile gowns for surgery. By contrast, our anaesthetist would stroll in at 8 a.m. and we were lucky if we could start operating at 9 a.m. – two hours wasted. Such tardiness was not the fault of the government.

There were significant differences in the 'vintage' of the heart–lung machine that we used. In Houston, the pump technician used disposable plastic tubes, connections and an oxygenator. Within a few minutes, a modern Sarns – or roller pump – was then used to circulate the blood to and from the patient.

Our monster-like oxygenator was called a *helix reservoir* and had to be prepared long before each operation. The first pump that we used, known as the *finger pump*, had been a gift from Professor Owen Wangensteen to Chris when he had returned to Groote Schuur Hospital in 1958 after completing advanced studies in Minneapolis. Its name was appropriate because the action that enabled the blood to flow to the patient was achieved by way of finger-like metal protrusions, which propelled the blood forward via plastic tubes.

When using this pump, the occlusion had to be just right: too little and the blood flow to the patient would be inadequate; too tight and the metal fingers would chew up the plastic tube, which would then explode, covering the entire theatre in blood. This, in fact, happened at the start of the transplant of our second patient, Dr Philip Blaiberg, the impact of which I describe later.

In our ICUs, the situation was no better, as we had no ventilators and were compelled to make use of an oxygen tent. A mixture of oxygen and water vapour was pumped into the semi-transparent yellow-plastic tent to produce a fine mist. This, however, could result in dramatic post-operative complications. Many black people from the rural areas had little – if any – experience of modern technology. In spite of our warning them about what to expect after operations, many became totally uncontrollable and disorientated when they woke up in these misty yellow tents, thinking they had woken up in hell. They would pull out all their drains and plastic tubing and fight to get out of bed. Unfortunately, a few would have such severe post-surgery stress that they ended up in Valkenberg, the local mental institution close to Groote Schuur, where they recovered before being sent back to their homes.

Such was the technological state of the equipment and resources at the time, a far cry from the advanced medical machinery and theatre space of my colleagues in Houston. Yet it was in these conditions that I began work as a cardiac surgeon in Groote Schuur's Department of Cardiac Surgery in Cape Town.

Cardiac Surgeon

O N 1 APRIL 1967, I STARTED MY CAREER AS A CARDIAC SURGEON at the princely salary of R600 per month. With this, I had to support a wife and three school-going children. Fortunately, I still had some money coming in from my hard-earned income in Salisbury, but as this money was frozen we received only interest, and rent money from our house.

My first few months in Chris's department at Groote Schuur Hospital were utter hell, and I began to think of making a move to Durban, where Professor Ben le Roux was establishing a good cardiac unit at Wentworth Hospital. Inez, who had always loved Cape Town, was happily settled, however, and was near to her farming parents, brothers and sisters in Worcester. Inez and the children frequently spent weekends there or with her sister on a farm at nearby Franschhoek. The children were well settled and happy at school and it would have been highly disruptive to move them yet again. So I persevered at Groote Schuur.

During my first few weeks at the hospital, I had to assist Chris. Unfortunately, in the team context, this arrangement didn't work. I found his behaviour unacceptable and, however hard we tried, our efforts were never considered good enough. My resentment was obvious, especially in front of the rest of the staff. A few words of fighting-back became untenable to Chris and I was subsequently banned from assisting him. In retrospect, I don't blame him.

From that day on, Chris operated in what was termed the 'A' theatre, and I operated in the 'B' theatre. We became the kings of our respective theatres and this suited us both. This arrangement also applied at the Red Cross Children's Hospital. For the rest of my thirteen years with Chris, I never assisted him again, and he certainly didn't help me either. Although we had the occasional clash in the ICU, my life became more tolerable.

Chris had asked me to carry out research on heart transplants using dogs, and I soon realised why. It was part of his meticulous preparation for performing the world's first human-to-human heart transplant. While I was in Houston during the second half of 1966, Chris, as I have already mentioned, was working with Dr Richard Lower in Richmond, Virginia.

Chris had obviously followed the work on heart and kidney transplantations by Dr Lower and Dr Norman Shumway at Palo Alto, California, in the articles that they had published in medical journals. When Chris returned from Virginia, while I was still in Houston, I am convinced that his mind was already made up to perform a heart transplant. With his meticulous attention to detail, coupled with his uncanny ability to use others, he set about with the necessary preparations for doing just that.

I could never understand why the first human heart transplants were performed in South Africa. In Europe and the United States, cardiac surgeons had far better equipment than we had and their surgical ability was certainly not inferior to ours. Looking back now, I am certain that the major reason for our performing the first ever human heart transplant was Chris Barnard.

There are many false stories suggesting that there was a race between us and other surgeons, from the United States and England in particular, to perform the first heart transplant. This is utter nonsense, as any capable cardiac surgeon could have performed this transplant years earlier. The ability to perform successful cardiac surgery on patients with either acquired or congenital heart disease was already well established, while kidney and liver transplants had facilitated widespread medical recognition of rejection and the requirement to use immunosuppressive drugs during post-operative treatment.

Although we were far behind our foreign counterparts when it came to research and experimentation, I believe that the motivation to save the life of our patient was foremost in our minds. With no other treatment available, this was our indication to operate on the patient, not a race against other surgeons in the world.

* * *

Most of our patients were first seen and investigated by members of the Department of Cardiology. On Saturday mornings, we met in their unit, where they presented the cases for the following week. The patients were then transferred to our wards a day or two before their operations so that we could make our own assessment of their suitability for surgery. At the end of the Saturday-morning meeting, we had what was known as a 'post-mortem meeting', where we discussed any deaths following surgery in the previous week. We never, however, discussed the deaths in the cardiology unit.

The cardiologists could become very critical and self-righteous, and often made us feel responsible for our patients' deaths. They, of course, never accepted their own mistakes. These meetings could become unpleasant, but they kept us on our toes. I think the fear of being tried and found guilty for the death of a patient contributed to ensuring that our unit had post-operative results to match those anywhere else in the world.

I enjoyed cardiac surgery, particularly congenital cardiac surgery. In addition, I continued my research on heart transplantation in the dog laboratory, where I soon renewed my working relationships with the laboratory's cleaning staff, messengers and dog-kennel cleaners.

There was Victor Pick – a huge, humble giant. He was the self-appointed head of the cleaners but was also well trained in basic surgery. He not only prepared the dogs for surgery but opened their chests, exposed arteries and veins and assisted me in general.

Also present was the now well-known and highly controversial Hamilton Naki. He was our reluctant anaesthetist – we all understood he had other interests around the medical school and hospital. Hamilton could administer the basic anaesthetic and intubate animals, but he was lazy and his concentration and dedication poor.

There was John Rousseau, who attended to and fed the dogs. He was a pleasant, hard-working man who was a clarinettist in a Christmas band and very fond of his *dop*. He was always willing to help and in his spare time would earn extra money by working in our garden and doing other jobs.

Other staff included Lindela Mntonintshi and Prescott Madlingozi, among others. At the time, Prescott was the captain of the black South African rugby team, the Leopards, playing the position of hooker. I'll never forget him telling me of one occasion when his team played against a strong white team and how the big *boere* scrummed him into the ground.

Most of my responsibilities were a challenge and enjoyable. Why, then, was I so miserable and anxious to leave? Chris's moods were unpleasant and he had the unfortunate habit of venting his spleen on innocent staff. He was most unreasonable at times, but was unaware of the hurt he caused. His demands on the time of his residents were also unreasonable and resulted in a hard-working but unhappy team. In the operating theatre, he was a cumbersome, plodding surgeon with a very marked tremor. I was always amazed that he managed to place the needle in the right spot, yet somehow he always did.

In Chris's presence, there was, therefore, a degree of tension, even fear.

He operated very slowly but his work was meticulous. He handled the tissues with the greatest of care, making sure that the heart muscle was protected against rough handling and making doubly sure that the risk of post-operative bleeding was reduced. Although he appeared to struggle – and he often did – his results were excellent and world-class due to his great knowledge and understanding of cardiac surgery.

Like most surgeons, he was seldom happy with the theatre lights, which made him irritable. I must confess that I had the same problems when I operated. Chris's assistants often had to move the lights during operations but, however hard they tried, their efforts were seldom good enough.

Similarly, in the ICU, my brother also had his moments. The on-duty registrar and nurses were on high alert when he was around and would often feel the full force of his wrath. Again, his results were exceptional, and we all strived to emulate him. Most importantly, the patients never complained about him.

Chris never spent long hours in the ICU and was seldom, if ever, on night duty. As head of the department this, of course, was his right. But he did do his ward rounds at 8 a.m. daily. His uncanny knack for spotting complications before we could was amazing – I always said he would have made an excellent detective. No criminal would ever have escaped his ability to find any clue at the scene of the crime.

There were large flowsheets pinned on a board next to the bed of each ICU patient, which recorded, at hourly intervals, the patient's vital signs – the pulse rate, blood pressure, respiration rate and urinary output, for example. Blood loss, measured in bottles connected to the drainage tubes, and the patient's very important electrolyte levels were some of the parameters constantly monitored. Such recordings of the patient's progress and any changes alerted one very early to the possibility of complications setting in.

Chris's attention to the flowsheet each morning occasionally produced some humorous moments. One morning, he arrived in a foul mood. A registrar from Portugal, whose English was very poor, was on duty. Chris immediately observed signs of possible complications, which had been missed by the registrar. If not responded to, they could lead to the patient's death. Chris exploded, giving the registrar not only a lengthy lecture on the mistakes he'd made, but also a vivid description of his stupidity and his lack of responsibility. He told the registrar that if the patient died it would be due to him, and him alone.

When, after more than ten minutes of ranting, Chris finally stopped to take a deep breath, the registrar had a chance to get a word in. In broken English and with a blank face, he said, 'Please repeat, Professor. I did not understand.' This reply stopped Chris in his tracks. He gaped at the registrar and stormed out of the ward without saying another word.

* * *

My nine months' training under Denton Cooley and Michael DeBakey proved valuable, as I was able to share my experiences there with Groote Schuur Hospital's cardiac unit. While in Houston, I had assisted with operations performed in an attempt to increase the blood supply to the heart muscle. These operations were some of the pioneering attempts to treat angina and prevent heart attacks. Angina is a pain under and just to the left of the breastbone, and can radiate up into the neck and lower jaw and down the inside of the left arm as far as the baby and ring fingers. It is caused by insufficient blood to the heart muscle due to obstruction in the coronary arteries by fatty deposits lining the artery.[1] A heart attack – known medically as a *myocardial infarction* – means death of, or damage to, the heart muscle due to a reduced blood supply to the heart.

One of the operations I observed was called the *Beck procedure*. It was rough, even barbaric. If I tried it today, I would be charged with malpractice and, if the patient died – which was frequent – of murder. It was believed that if you scrubbed the skin of the heart with sterile, rough sandpaper until it was raw and oozing with blood, adhesions would form between the skin and the sac that surrounds the heart – the pericardium – and sheets of fat known as *omentum*, which were brought from the abdomen. These adhesions, it was thought, would result in new arteries developing between the pericardium, the omentum and the heart muscle. This procedure, however, proved to be a dismal failure.

The second operation was known as the *Vineberg procedure*.[2] The two mammary arteries running behind the sternum were dissected free and pulled into a tunnel that we had made into the heart muscle. The branches of these arteries were intended to form a surgical connection with the arteries in the heart muscle. Although in some cases this happened, it was insufficient to bring relief. In my own hands, these operations were failures with a high operative death rate. I performed only a few!

But I was able to make one successful contribution, which I'd acquired while in Houston, to heart surgery at Groote Schuur Hospital. Following cardiac surgery, arrhythmias were a serious and often fatal complication. I saw many such complications when I was working with Dr Denton Cooley, who was very successful in treating his patients with intravenous ligno-caine.[3] Once back at Groote Schuur Hospital, when I suggested using this drug on one of our patients, Chris initially vetoed it. But, after this treatment clearly demonstrated its efficacy in a few other cases of ours, he reluctantly accepted it.

* * *

When I started performing congenital heart surgery at the Red Cross War Memorial Children's Hospital, I found my niche. I love children. Nothing in medicine, with the exception of attending to the birth of a baby, can compare with the admission of a desperately ill 'blue baby', or any other child with a congenital heart condition, who, having arrived in the arms of anxious parents a week or two previously, could now be seen thriving, leaving the hospital with happy and grateful parents.

After more than twenty-nine years since performing my last cardiac operation, if there is anything I miss, it is these children and the fact that I was able to repair their hearts and provide them with a healthy future.

My love for children and the surgery I performed on young children at the Red Cross led me to write an article for the *Cape Times*, in which I appealed to the public to come forward and support them.[4] At the time, many of these young patients never received visits from their parents or relatives, and there was a dearth of toys, audio-visual stimulation and recreational facilities. I was subsequently approached to support an initiative that resulted in my becoming the founder member and first patron of the Friends of the Children's Hospital Association (FOCHA). Later on I discuss this wonderful organisation and the very important role it continues to fulfil today at this world-famous hospital.

I recently had the pleasure of receiving a letter from a patient I operated on at the Red Cross during my time there. Although I have received many such letters over the years from grateful South African patients, this one is special because she suffered from a very complicated lesion. The operation was a great success, leading to a long and happy life with good health. Cindy le Roux's letter follows below.

Hi Dr Barnard

Thank you so much for taking the time to reply to me. My husband and myself were living in the UK for about nine years and I had both my girls over there. It was only when I fell pregnant with my first child that the alarm bells were raised due to my heart surgery. I saw a number of cardiologists and one of them asked to use me as a case study (I think mainly because I was only 6½ months old when I had the operation and I had no complications my whole life).

My mom tried for years to obtain my medical papers from the Red Cross but they had apparently destroyed the records due to the age of them. I explained to the doctors in the UK what my mom was told when I was a baby and after a lengthy echo the diagnosis was as follows: 'Complete A-V septal defect with total anomalous drainage of the pulmonary veins – completely corrected'.

I must pass on my compliments to you as the professionals only had great things to say about your surgery on me and couldn't believe that I was still alive and was able to go through two pregnancies. I have often had anesthetists, nurses and doctors tell me what a lucky women I am to still be alive.

Thank you once again for your expertise and brilliant work. We are back in SA now and I am pregnant with my third child and obviously being watched very closely.

I did a search on the internet and found some information on 'en. wikipedia.org' which mentioned that you worked for Scottish Widows. I also tried to contact 3 of Chris's sons via Facebook but they never replied. I wasn't sure if they thought I was a con artist. I told my family that I was determined to contact you this year and thank you. Anyway, keep well and all the best for the New Year.

Warmest regards
Cindy le Roux

* * *

During my time at the Red Cross, Sir Barratt-Boyes of Auckland, New Zealand, achieved excellent results in repairing lesions in children less than one year of age by using what is called the *hypothermic technique*. This technique involves placing an anaesthetised infant in an ice bath to shut off the circulation system before operating.

Our little patient, once anaesthetised, would be cooled by ice cubes that were placed in his or her axilla, or armpits, and on the groin. These are the regions where the blood flow is most superficial. The patient would then be cooled down to 28 °C and, when put onto cardio-pulmonary bypass, further cooled to 8 °C. The heart–lung machine would then be stopped and the operation performed with no circulation and a bloodless heart. This technique made it much easier to perform the procedure, even on a heart not much bigger than a matchbox.

With no heartbeat and no respiration, the patient would basically be dead. When the defect had been corrected, the heart–lung machine would be started and the patient warmed to 37 °C. The heart usually started beating spontaneously; if not, it was defibrillated. The chest would be closed and soon an awake baby would be returned to the ICU.

This may sound impossible, but we knew that the still-developing brain tissue of an infant could withstand a lack of oxygen when cooled to 8 °C for periods of up to an hour or even longer. This enabled us to perform a complete repair of the lesion rather than doing palliative surgery, thereby precluding the need for further operations.[5]

The hypothermic technique opened exciting possibilities for cardiac surgery on infants at the time. Certain congenital heart lesions are incompatible with life, and infants with these conditions had to be operated on within days, if not hours, after birth to prevent death.[6] This technique made it possible to operate on infants with these defects, and others, successfully – I even enjoyed success with neonates less than one day old.

Chris was at the forefront of the development of congenital cardiac surgery. Due to the hysteria surrounding the world's first heart transplants, the pioneering work he did on other heart lesions is often forgotten. It might not be known that he was one of the first surgeons to operate successfully on complicated procedures such as *transposition of the great vessels*, a congenital heart defect in which the two major vessels that carry blood away from the heart – the aorta and the pulmonary artery – are switched, as well as *tricuspid atresia*, a form of congenital heart disease whereby there is a complete absence of the heart's tricuspid valve. Chris's patients survived, but unfortunately these operations did not stand the test of time, as newer and better procedures were subsequently developed in the United States of America and elsewhere.

There is no doubt, however, that by his example and leadership, our results were excellent, especially with tetralogy of Fallot, the most common cause of 'blue baby' syndrome and the probable cause of my brother Abraham's death.[7] In this regard, I published a paper with Chris on the results that we achieved with 100 consecutive cases and no post-operative deaths. When he presented the paper at a medical conference in London, not only were the results questioned by jealous British cardiac surgeons, but there were even attempts made to discredit him.

At the Red Cross, as at Groote Schuur, Chris's depth of knowledge of cardiac surgery and his ability to induce his team to deliver their best efforts resulted in the achievement of the highest standards and excellent results. His staff had to accept his rigid, non-compromising leadership but, as I have said, his patients and their relatives never had reason to complain because our results were excellent. I had many problems with Chris, but his contribution to cardiac surgery is far greater than that for which he is remembered.

Pioneering Heart Surgery

A SUCCESSFUL HEART TRANSPLANT CANNOT BE ACCOMPLISHED by one doctor alone. Chris recognised this and was able to build up an ideal team by inviting specialists from many departments of Groote Schuur Hospital and the University of Cape Town's medical school to participate in what would be the first successful human heart transplant.

Professor Val Schrire and Wally Beck from the Department of Cardiology took part, as well as Arden Forder from Bacteriology, Ozzie Ozinsky from Anaesthetics and Professor J.G. Thompson from Pathology. In addition, pulmonary physician A.D. Ferguson participated, while M.C. Botha from the blood transfusion service acted as immunologist. Other doctors as well as senior nurses and support staff were also of assistance.

Chris went to work by arranging lunchtime meetings every Wednesday, during which this team of highly skilled doctors discussed the problems associated with performing a human heart transplant, particularly the dangers of rejection and infection. Immunosuppression, tissue typing and many other vital aspects associated with this procedure were discussed in detail. While this was going on, our routine work – operating and caring for our patients – still had to be done.

I was at this stage very anxious to perform my own open-heart operation. After six weeks, I asked Chris why I was only assisting and not getting my own cases. His excuse was that he could not be seen to be favouring his brother. But, after two more months, my name at last appeared on the operating list. A white male, aged forty-two, needed a replacement of the mitral valve. This was, at the best of times, a difficult operation, but particularly so in this case, as the valve, which had calcified, was as hard as a rock and the left atrium was very small. It would not only be a battle to see the valve, but excising and replacing it would be a nightmare.

And so it proved to be. I sweated and struggled, but eventually completed the operation. I will always be grateful to Dr Rodney Hewitson, without whose patient guidance and help the patient would not have survived. I would have loved to have him assist me as often as possible, but Chris had first claim on him – I don't think he assisted me more than five times in thirteen years.

* * *

On Wednesdays, when I had no clinical responsibilities at Groote Schuur Hospital, I would go to the dog laboratory to perform heart transplants on dogs. To term this *research* is actually something of a joke. The edition of the *South African Medical Journal* that was published immediately after the first human heart transplant in December 1967 included numerous articles about the techniques of heart transplantation, immunology, prevention of infection and other similar subjects. Not a single article appeared about our heart transplant research – and for good reason: it did not exist, and therefore could make no contribution to the success of the first human heart transplant. I mention this because all the fabrications written about our research using dogs were, in fact, a lot of thumb-sucking. Our experiments involving dogs were actually surgical exercises that served only to help me become more proficient in performing cardiac surgery.

The dogs we used came from the pound. They were ill, starved and usually had some form of skin disease. We called all these experiments *acute* because the dogs were allowed to die within a few hours after the operation – much to my relief, as I could not stand seeing those loving, trusting animals suffering unnecessarily. When I was conducting mitral valve research, many of the animals survived and I found what we were doing to be cruel and unacceptable.

On only one occasion while I was working there did Chris enter the laboratory, to show us how the transplant should be performed. He was assisted by Victor Pick and Hamilton Naki was the anaesthetist. I was an interested spectator because I knew exactly what was going to happen: soon Chris was engaged in open warfare with both of them, as well as with poor Johan van Heerden, who managed the pump. After much trouble and strife, he aborted his exhibition and the operation was terminated. The only good that came out of this experience was that Chris never showed himself there again. So much for our great research team.

When the *South African Medical Journal*, which is published monthly, heard that the first human heart transplant had taken place, they decided to delay the release of their December issue, asking us if we would write articles relating to this historic event. This we did, and the edition was published later in the month but dated 2 December 1967. It includes an article that I wrote on the technique we used to prepare the heart–lung machine for the first human heart transplant. Today, this article has historic importance because it records the methods and procedures applied in the use of this equipment.

* * *

During the Wednesday lunchtime discussions, I sensed no wild enthusiasm from any of the attendees other than Chris. He was fiercely determined to press on, and most of us reluctantly followed. What became obvious was that there was no reason why we could *not* do a human heart transplant. We only had to apply what we had learnt over the past years about cardiac surgery and renal transplants, the latter having been done with increasing success for years at many medical centres around the world. Our preparation was methodical, and the actual operation was only seriously considered when everything possible was in place. Not once during these meetings was it ever mentioned that we should expedite our efforts because there was a race on between Norman Shumway, Adrian Kantrowitz and others to perform the first heart transplant. This only came later, and was the fabrication of desperate newspapers and other reporters.

I must emphasise that the surgical technique required to perform a heart transplant was not a problem. For years, we had carried out far more complicated surgical procedures with great success. We had no experience, however, with its post-operative treatment and dealing with complications.

As always, Chris had the solution. The first kidney transplant in South Africa had been performed in Johannesburg in 1966. Cape Town was lagging behind and still had to do its first kidney transplant. Chris decided that the cardiac team would go over the heads of the urologists and perform such a transplant. Although there was strong opposition from other departments, especially the Department of Urology, Chris went ahead and performed a kidney transplant in September 1967 on Edith Black.

This valuable experience gave us insight into the realities of obtaining permission from the relatives of a prospective donor, as well as other related considerations, such as *barrier nursing*, a method whereby all measures are taken to prevent infection. In the process, we experienced complications arising from rejection, infection and kidney failure, but gained invaluable experience. Edith survived for fifteen years. Our cardiac unit probably had one of the best survival rates of kidney transplantation in the world. But then, we only did one!

After the kidney transplant there was no stopping Chris. All he could talk about was the heart transplant. This suited me, as he became less involved with clinical responsibilities. I had an increased workload and was getting enough surgical experience to become confident and competent with all the procedures that would be required for the human heart transplant.

The procurement of donor hearts is, in my opinion, one of the most sensitive and difficult essentials of heart transplantation. How do you tell a mother or father that their young son of twenty-one years of age, who was involved in an accident, has died, and then immediately ask if his heart can be used as a donor for a heart transplant? I must confess, I could never bring myself to do this, as I found such situations emotionally unbearable.

Most well-educated people had never even heard about this procedure at the time, so to have to explain the procedure to simple, uneducated, God-fearing folk was an extremely difficult task. They couldn't understand how their now-dead relative's heart could be used for a heart transplant, or that this heart could continue to function normally in someone else's body. Strangely enough, after much explanation, most of these wonderful, trusting people accepted our request.

It was already agreed that the transplant team could have nothing to do with the management of the prospective donor prior to the operation; the team could become involved with the donor only once the neurosurgeons had declared him or her dead.

This responsibility rested with the Department of Neurosurgery, our main source of suitable donors since they dealt with fatal head injuries that often resulted in brain death. The department's neurosurgeons were never very keen to help us – in fact, some of them were aggressively obstructive. I wrote to the head of the department, a brilliant neurosurgeon, and complained about this situation, but nothing changed.

We had to be very careful to abide by the rules because the press were very suspicious. They were always looking for sensational news, especially in South Africa, as a result of the prevailing racial sensitivities, which were exacerbated by the apartheid society within which we lived. We were concerned that the press would use the fact that we would perform more transplants on white patients than on black patients, and this we did. But there was nothing sinister about it. About 10 per cent of our population was white, but 90 per cent of the patients needing heart transplants were white, given the very high incidence of coronary artery disease within this population group.[1] As 80 per cent of our population was black, 80 per cent of our donors would be black. In addition, the strict post-transplant care and treatment that was required was almost impossible for underprivileged patients living miles away from Groote Schuur Hospital in poverty, with a lack of proper sanitation and nutrition. It was, therefore, hardly surprising that heart recipients would be largely white and that heart donors would be largely black. It was as simple as that.

After the first transplant, our sensitivities and concerns in this regard proved to be justified. Several cartoons appeared showing blood dripping from our fingers with comments that we were only, and purposely, using blacks as donors. I dismissed this sensational rubbish, saying that, when I operated on patients and cut through the skin, I only saw red and no other colour. All of our patients were, first and foremost, considered to be cardiac patients; they were not classified, nor were they discriminated against, according to their race.

It was universally accepted at the time that a person was dead when his heart had stopped beating, not when he was brain dead. This was a major problem for us. Brain death was not commonly understood, nor was it cast in legislation. The definition of *death* at that time was therefore rather vague, and the fear of litigation was of great concern to the medical profession, especially in the United States. The removal of a healthy, beating heart from a transplant donor could have been construed as surgical malpractice – even murder – and controversy over this raged for a long time. Owing to the misunderstood concept of brain death, after the first heart transplant critics of South Africa alleged that we were removing the hearts of living people; a few even construed us as being murderers. We thus had to devise what we considered to be the appropriate protocol for managing donors prior to heart transplants. Since there was no legal definition for brain death at the time, we applied the clinical definition of the term. A prospective donor had to be comatose, non-responsive to painful stimuli, and unable to breathe and maintain, without artificial assistance, a life-supporting circulation. They also had to have a flat electroencephalograph (EEG). Only when all of these criteria were met was a neurosurgeon able to declare the patient dead. It was at this point that we could take over.

Eventually the United States passed legislation that included *brain death* in the legal definition of *death*, and South Africa adopted a similar legal definition soon afterwards.[2] This provided for the way in which heart transplant teams should manage the donor in the transplant process.[3]

During November, we at last found a potential donor, a young coloured male who had fallen from a truck on a farm near Caledon and suffered a fatal head injury. By coincidence, he was referred to Groote Schuur Hospital by Dr Fritz Mangold, a friend of mine and Chris's. I knew him from my first year at medical school.

We went through the long process of waiting for the neurosurgeon to declare the patient brain dead. Our team members had, by now, all been alerted that we may have found a suitable donor and, within thirty minutes of being notified of this possibility, both patient and donor were in adjoining but separate theatres.

Terry O'Donovan and I prepared the donor while Rodney Hewitson and François Hitchcock attended to the prospective recipient. Chris was walking around like a caged lion and we were immediately at loggerheads. I insisted that we remove the heart immediately rather than wait until it had stopped. Since the donor had already been declared brain dead, I saw no reason why we should wait until the heart had stopped. My rationale was that, the longer we waited, the greater would be the possibility of ischaemic damage to the heart muscle, thereby making it unsuitable for a successful transplant. I was insistent that our responsibility lay with the living recipient, not our dead donor.

As the surgeon in charge, however, Chris had his way and overruled me. As we waited and waited, the donor's blood pressure slowly dropped, the pulse rate slowed and the ECG showed a severely ischaemic heart. My argument proved to be correct. Chris, at last, realised that we had waited too long and that the heart was no longer suitable for a successful transplant. The operation was thus aborted.

The potential recipient, Louis Washkansky, was then taken back to the ward. As it was 2 a.m., we all went home to get as much sleep as possible before returning at seven o'clock the following morning. I really felt terribly sorry for Mr Washkansky, who was desperately ill at the time. On the night that we had the first potential donor, he was placed in theatre, only to be informed three hours later that the operation could not go ahead due to the problems we had experienced with the donor.

This attempt at the first human heart transplant was not well publicised, but ill-informed people recently referred to it on a local television programme in which the late Dirk de Villiers, a film director, was involved. De Villiers, who professed to be a great confidant of Chris, suggested, among other unfounded assertions, that the operation was aborted due to some or other unexplained 'sabotage', which prevented Chris from performing the transplant. The only people who could have sabotaged the operation were members of the donor team, and I can quite confidently state that this ridiculous assertion has not the slightest vestige of the truth.

* * *

Louis Washkansky was a fifty-five-year-old retired businessman in total cardiac failure. He was going to die within a few weeks, if not days. At that stage, there was no other medical or surgical treatment available to save his life, so he readily agreed to have the operation, despite the fact that no human-to-human heart transplantation had been done before then. He really had very little choice because, without such an attempt, he faced certain death.

Being of advanced years, he was a high-risk case for a successful transplant, but especially so because he had other complications, including diabetes. The latter disease was a definite contraindication for heart trans-plantation as the risk of infection resulting from immunosuppression would be very high. However, we were adamant about operating on a patient where alternative treatments were not possible to avoid subsequent criticism on this basis.

A few weeks later, on 2 December 1967 – a Saturday night – Inez and I were hosting a party at home with friends in celebration of our sixteenth wedding anniversary. I was already well wined and dined when the phone rang. I was expecting it to be a relative or friend, phoning to wish us happiness. It was indeed a relative, but there were no congratulations. My brother Chris simply told me to come to theatre immediately.

A young seventeen-year-old girl, Denise Darvall, had been knocked down and killed by a passing car while crossing the road in Observatory, a few miles from Groote Schuur Hospital. She had been declared brain dead as a result of a severe head injury, her parents had given permission for her to be a donor and both she and Mr Washkansky were already in the operating rooms. I didn't tell Inez or my friends why I was going to the hospital; I told them only that there was an emergency. I excused myself and rushed to Groote Schuur, where the first person I saw was Chris – already changed into his theatre clothes.

We had a few words with each other. I so wish I could remember what we said but our exchange has, unfortunately, faded completely from memory. I changed, and a few minutes later, scrubbed, masked and sterile, I took my place in theatre. The donor was prepared and the team was waiting for her heart to stop.

We had already planned to put the donor on the heart–lung machine as soon as the heart stopped and to then cool her body down to 28 °C. We stood waiting for an hour, but the donor heart kept on beating while the blood pressure slowly dropped. I was not prepared to wait for too long and again lose our opportunity to perform the transplant. Our duty was to the recipient, I felt, and not to the clinically dead donor-patient. If the donor heart was damaged through our waiting too long, Mr Washkansky would, in all likelihood, die. But my argument was again resisted.

We did wait for the heart to stop. It is interesting to note that Chris describes our disagreement over the timing of the removal of the heart in his first book, *One Life*. He argues that we had to wait for it to stop beating or we would otherwise have been severely criticised by the press, the public and politicians, some of whom would have accused us of being, at best, unethical, at worst, murderers. My argument that our responsibility lay with the recipient has been omitted. My insistence that the recipient should take precedence finally won the day, however, and from then on we removed a beating heart from all of our donors.

With the cessation of the donor's heart, we opened the chest and prepared the heart for transplantation. Mr Washkansky was anaesthetised by Ozzie Ozinsky, and Rodney Hewitson opened the chest. Dr Cecil Moss, an anaesthetist and a former Springbok rugby wing, performed a key role in monitoring the functioning of the donor heart. Dene Friedmann was the pump technician.

Chris then entered the donor theatre and, on my insistence, he removed the heart. I was adamant about his removing the heart for our first case because I felt that, given Chris's nature, he needed to have sufficient confidence that the donor heart had been correctly prepared by him. Similarly, he could then, with confidence, proceed to the recipient theatre and remove the badly damaged heart.

Chris performed the heart transplant, connecting left atrium of donor to left atrium of recipient, then right atrium to right atrium, pulmonary artery to pulmonary artery and, lastly, aorta to aorta. When the aortic clamp was removed, blood from the recipient perfused the donor heart and, after a minute or two, it started beating spontaneously.[4] Chris's only reaction was, '*Dit werk*' – 'It works.' But this came as no surprise. We all knew it would.

When bypass was discontinued, the transplanted heart took over the circulation, with a normal blood pressure and an adequate cardiac output.

We could complete the operation with the confidence that it had been, as we had expected, successful.

The patient was transferred to our rather inadequate isolation transplant unit, a two-bed ward that we had had to adapt by thorough cleaning to ensure that it remained sterile. To this end, strict rules had been applied to prevent the doctors and nurses from bringing infections into the unit.

The transplant of a heart into a human had, in fact, been done once before. This historical event, which was never well publicised, has since faded into obscurity. In January 1964, Dr James Hardy from Jackson, Mississippi, performed the first heart transplant into a human by using the heart of a chimpanzee. The *xenograft* method, which involves the surgical graft of tissue between a donor and a recipient of different species, failed, of course: the human body's immunosuppressive response to a species other than its own is immediate.[5] The transplanted heart rapidly deteriorates and certain death results in a few hours to a day or two, at most. After Hardy had transplanted the chimpanzee's heart, it beat in the human chest for seventy minutes before stopping.

Many years after our operation and during one of my later insurance talks in Alabama, I enquired about Dr Hardy. I was told that he was still alive but, before I could visit him, he died. Fortunately, in the interim I had been able to contact him telephonically, and I had expressed my recognition of the significance of his operation. Whenever I spoke about the first human heart transplant during my talks, I always gave Dr Hardy the recognition I believe he deserved for his courageous attempt to save his patient despite the known risks and the small chance of success. For this, he expressed his great appreciation. So, although we were projected as brave people who took such bold steps in history, it was a myth: such an operation had already been done before, albeit with a non-human donor heart. If anybody was brave, it was Dr Hardy.

* * *

As we had known, the surgical technique of performing a heart transplant was no more difficult than other cardiac operations. We were fully aware that our chance of a successful transplant was virtually 100 per cent, but that our problems would then start as we moved into uncharted waters. The patient had to be heavily immunosuppressed with the increased risk of infection, and we needed to ensure that we could immediately detect the first signs of rejection. Our experience with the kidney transplant was invaluable, but this was a heart and not a kidney, and there were definite differences in the management of these organs. In this regard, we relied very heavily on the help of Professor Schrire and others.

The patient was, by this point, in the transplant unit in the care of the registrar on duty, Bossie Bosman, and the specially selected nurses. We surgeons then went home, exhausted. I collapsed into bed on that Sunday morning when the sun was just appearing on the horizon.

At approximately midday, Inez woke me to say that we had to go to the hospital, as the *Cape Times* wanted a photograph of the so-called heart transplant team. But I didn't have the slightest intention of making this effort. It was Sunday 3 December and my two daughters were singing in the Rustenburg Girls School choir at their annual Christmas carol service that evening. I had no intention of missing this event, an uplifting occasion that I enjoyed immensely.

I had no knowledge of what was happening at Groote Schuur Hospital. The hospital superintendent was in total ignorance until he was phoned and informed of the operation after its completion. Someone, of course, had phoned the news media. I have no doubt it was Chris. While I was sleeping or enjoying the carols, the news of the world's first human heart transplant spread like wildfire, first through South Africa and then to all four corners of the globe.

I had some inkling of this when a few of my friends, who had partied with me the previous evening, phoned me to find out what it was all about as some of the national news reports carried our transplant story. That Monday morning, while parking in my usual spot in front of Groote Schuur Hospital, I was amazed to see a crowd of reporters and cameramen. From that moment onwards, a media frenzy ensued.

We were totally unprepared for this eventuality and had to handle it without, of course, having had any previous experience. We received no assistance from the hospital or the provincial administrators. I was fortunately able to continue with our routine surgery and patient care, but Chris took to this new celebrity status like a duck to water.

The first photograph published of the heart transplant team duly appeared that morning in the *Cape Times*. I was amazed to see faces of 'members of the team' that I had never seen before, and have not seen since. The team had more than doubled. My face was not in the photograph, my preference having been to attend my children's carol service.

16

Guardians of Lies

'A liar begins with making falsehood appear like truth, and ends with making truth itself appear like falsehood.' — WILLIAM SHENSTONE

I N THAT FIRST PHOTOGRAPH OF THE HEART TRANSPLANT TEAM that appeared on the front page of the *Cape Times* on Monday 4 December, there were two faces missing: mine and Hamilton Naki's. Mine did not appear because, as mentioned in the previous chapter, I had been at my children's carol service. Naki's missing face was attributable to the fact that, when the photograph had been taken that Sunday afternoon, he had not the slightest knowledge that a heart transplant had taken place. While it was being performed the previous night, he had been fast asleep in his bed, many miles away from Groote Schuur Hospital.

The true role of the now-deceased Hamilton Naki must be clarified.[1] Over the past several years, statements and articles have appeared in the press and on television, both locally and internationally, alleging that Naki played an important role in the first human heart transplant but that he had never been recognised for it. According to these ridiculous untruths, Naki removed the heart of the donor, washed it in fluid for hours, passed it over a glass screen to Chris and assisted Chris with the transplant. In addition, not only did he supposedly show Chris how to do the first heart transplant, but he demonstrated to overseas doctors how to perform heart transplants too. Many more laughable contentions were made, including the assertion that the transplant took forty-six hours.

All of these allegations are reputed to have been Naki's responses to interviews. In his defence, I did not see him making these claims on television myself; I was only told that he had made them. I never heard him denying them either.

The controversy started when Naki was interviewed by the British newspaper the *Guardian* in London in 2003. When *The Economist* first ran its story in 2005 on Naki's alleged role in the transplant, it was immediately published verbatim on the African Technology Development Forum website without the author having checked the facts with those present in the operating theatre on the night of the heart transplant.[2] Of course, the race card had been played. A similar article appeared on the *New African* website perpetuating the same myth: 'Last year, the British daily, the *Guardian*, interviewed Naki and aptly summed his amazing tale thus: "Two men transplanted the first human heart. One ended up rich and famous – the other had to pretend to be a gardener. Until now!"'[3]

When Naki died, the *New York Times* published an obituary on its website: 'In a painstaking operation lasting many hours, Mr. Naki's team removed Ms. Darvall's heart, washing it repeatedly to cleanse it of her blood before introducing some of Mr. Washkansky's.'[4] With blood all over his face, Naki allegedly passed the donor heart to Chris. Did this great surgeon not know that he was required to wear a mask?

Such statements and articles allege that, because Naki was black and living in apartheid South Africa, his true role would never have received proper recognition. According to such articles, he had to use a separate entrance to the hospital and was not allowed access to our research laboratories and operating theatres. All of this, of course, is utter nonsense.

Can anyone honestly believe that rumour-mongering news media could be so desperate as to dream up such misinformation more than thirty years after the first human-to-human heart transplant and be prepared to discredit our achievements? If it were true, we would never have been able to hide it from the press: they would have had the story out the next day, not decades later. I find it interesting that Naki kept it a secret until after Chris's death. What I cannot understand is why this blatant lie is still being perpetuated by certain elements in the media.

It is very sad that Naki allowed himself to be used by unscrupulous reporters and others to spread this misinformation around the world, but it is also exasperating that he never once repudiated this misinformation.

It was said that he once had dinner with all the medical dignitaries involved. If so, I was not invited. I also recall Chris's wife, Louwtjie, asking me, 'Just who is Hamilton Naki?'

The first that I heard about Naki's involvement in heart transplantations was in the local Sunday newspaper, *Rapport*, in an article quoting a well-known local film director. In this report, he cites Chris as having said that Naki was perhaps a better surgeon than him and that he had taught Chris how to perform a heart transplant. Of course, this type of statement was often made by Chris, but more as a joke than anything else. Chris's intent,

I am certain, was to draw publicity and was never intended to have been taken seriously.

My response is that if Naki taught Chris how to do the first human heart transplant, who taught him? Naki had never left South Africa and had therefore not been exposed to international cardiac surgery developments; he had not received formal medical or surgical training; and he was not involved in the build-up to the first heart transplant at Groote Schuur Hospital. Except for Chris, I was the only one who performed heart transplants, which I did in the experimental theatre, and I definitely never taught Naki to, or ever saw him, perform a heart transplant. Nor did he teach me.

I cannot understand how educated people, who called me after the *Rapport* article was published, could have believed that what was being written was true. And how could people, given the highly technical nature of cardiac operations performed at Groote Schuur Hospital at the time, imagine that the heart transplant could have been performed by an unqualified and unregistered person?

My medical associates and I have, for many years now, tried to rebut the articles that reflect such false allegations. We even wrote to the *Guardian* stating the facts of the matter but, till today, this newspaper has ignored us and our letter has never been published. I cannot understand why, because this would finally dispel this myth and, after all, the press prides itself on only reporting the truth. So why this gross exception?

When the local South African television programme *Kwêla* recently approached me on this topic, I readily agreed to participate but insisted that I should be given the opportunity to state the facts live on television. I never heard from them again. *Special Assignment*, a local SABC production, ran a documentary on this theme in June 2009.[5] The timing of this programme, which dispelled the Hamilton Naki myth, coincided with the local launch of the controversial documentary *Hidden Heart*. It should have been titled *Blatant Lies*.

The *Special Assignment* programme included interviews with certain members of the original heart transplant team: Dene Friedmann, the pump technician, and one of the nurses, Tollie Lambrechts. When asked to recall the night of 2 December 1967, Lambrechts stated the following: 'Mr Hamilton Naki was definitely not in the operating room on that night. Professor Barnard's brother, Marius Barnard, was the doctor in the donor theatre with his assistants. Professor [Chris] Barnard went there to take the heart out himself and he brought it here and he transplanted it here in this theatre.'

Others, including Hennie Joubert, the curator of Groote Schuur Hospital's heart museum and UCT's *Emeritus* Professor of Surgery, and Rosemary Hickman, who supervised surgery on animals with Naki during this period, could also not support the myth of Naki's involvement in any human heart transplantation.

It is unthinkable that Friedmann, Lamprechts, Joubert and Hickman could all have been involved in a grand 'apartheid cover-up'. This is simply because Friedmann, Lambrechts and the other people interviewed reported the facts. Significantly, very few of those who participated in this transplantation supported the Nationalist government – in fact, with a few exceptions, it was reviled. Should there have been such an alleged cover-up, this would certainly have been subsequently revealed by a critical press.

In concluding, this programme states that 'the *New York Times*, *The Economist* and the *Guardian*' – all complicit in the publication of articles alleging Naki's participation in human heart transplants – 'later retracted their stories'.

The launch of *Hidden Heart* was also reported on the *Guardian*'s website. It is noteworthy that the following was stated: 'After Naki's death, *The Economist* published an obituary saying Naki assisted in the transplant, but later published an amendment saying it had been assured by surgeons at Groote Schuur Hospital that Naki was nowhere near the operating theatre at the time.'[6]

In 2002, Hamilton was awarded the Order of Mapungubwe, South Africa's highest honour, by former President Thabo Mbeki. This was soon followed by an Honorary Master's degree in Medicine by his one-time employer, the University of Cape Town. But this could only have been in recognition for his surgical work performed on animals after the first human heart transplant, because he never, to my knowledge, ever performed operations on humans and was certainly never involved in human heart transplants.

I have no problem with Naki having received such awards. After the first heart transplant, I never returned to the experimental labs, but I have been told that his subsequent contributions, especially with liver transplant research on animals, were comparable to that of a trained surgeon and that he performed them well. If this is what his awards were for, I can only be pleased for him. If, however, they were awarded in recognition of his supposed involvement in the first human heart transplant, then I have to object, and in no uncertain terms.

My greatest sadness is that such fallacies, some still perpetuated today, have demeaned the name of Chris Barnard and his cardiac unit at Groote Schuur Hospital, and the magnificent contribution that we made to cardiac surgery. When such scurrilous articles were published, the Shumways and Cooleys and their cardiac units as well as other medical professions must have thought that we were the biggest medical joke.

Let me state categorically that Hamilton Naki never operated during, nor assisted with, human heart transplants at Groote Schuur Hospital. His alleged involvement in such operations, including the first human-to-human transplant, is a total fabrication of the truth.

As mentioned at the beginning of this chapter, Naki was fast asleep in bed a few miles away from Groote Schuur Hospital during the first human heart transplant, and he was not present for any of the others that followed. If he was actively party to these false reports, I am afraid to say he must have gone to his grave knowing in his heart that he had lied to his colleagues, the world and ultimately himself.

The truth could easily be verified by the reporters who wrote this unbelievable nonsense about Hamilton Naki if they would just take the trouble to confirm these stories with me or any of the eight living members of the team, all of whom who were in the operating theatre that historic night.

* * *

The distortion of Hamilton Naki's role was not the only instance of misinformation around the first heart transplants. In 2006 a book appeared called *Every Second Counts*, by Don McRae.[7] I had already had some dealings with McRae. He had interviewed me a few years earlier, saying that he wanted to write my biography, but this came to nought.

McRae's book advances the complete misperception that there existed a race between the world's surgeons to perform the first heart transplant, and his account is filled with errors. He writes the following about our preparation a month prior to the first heart transplant: 'By mid-November 1967, the unlikely Cape Town team had transplanted forty-eight hearts in dogs – 250 less than [Norman] Shumway and 210 less than [Adrian] Kantrowitz in New York'. This is not true. Not only did we have no record of the numbers, but we did not perform more than twenty heart transplants on dogs, if that. I performed at least 90 per cent of these operations. 'Unlike the Americans,' he continues, 'who could restore their transplant-dogs to full health for a year and more, the South Africans' longest survivor died after ten days.' Our dogs, in fact, survived no longer than ten hours. Our primary objective was to hone our surgical techniques and procedures; the dog fatalities were of secondary importance.

Our first attempt to perform the first heart transplant, McRae writes, was aborted because the donor's heart was either damaged or was not receiving enough oxygen-rich blood. He alleges that 'both Chris and Marius wavered. It was as if the courage suddenly drained out of them and that, perhaps, they were not quite yet ready to risk the wrath of the world.'

What 'wrath of the world'? The simple fact of the matter is that the heart became ischaemic and was therefore no longer suitable as a donor heart. In addition, I had no say in halting the transplant: it was Chris's decision entirely as leader of the team.

McRae then describes Chris and me in the scrub room prior to the first heart transplant, suggesting that Chris 'thought of all the dogs he had lost after transplanting their hearts' and how unsuccessful these transplants had been relative to the successes achieved by other notable surgeons at the time. The truth is that Chris performed no more than five dog transplants. How this could have troubled Chris – and how McRae knew Chris's thoughts at that moment – therefore remains a mystery.

Regrettably, McRae plays the apartheid card when he recounts how impressed I was with Chris when he succeeded in preventing the implementation of a policy dictating that cardiac surgery could be performed only on white people. This is just not the case. Although the government had many faults – and I have elaborated on several of these in this book – they never once prescribed to us what the race, sex or religion of our patients should be. I cannot understand on what basis McRae makes this statement.

There is one error in McRae's book that comes from an interview I gave him three years before his book was published. I was aware of the book he was writing, but our understanding was that the interview was not for that but for my biography. I'd had unpleasant experiences with the news media before, however, and had seen my words distorted, sensationalised and used without my permission. As a result, I'd learnt, whenever I gave information that was meant to be treated as confidential, to insert a single untruth which I would correct once my permission had been duly given. If this was then ever published, I would be able to trace the source.

For this reason I told McRae that, during the first transplant, we had not waited until the donor heart had stopped beating before removing it, but used an injection of potassium to arrest it. This, of course, is contrary to what actually happened, which I described in the previous chapter and which Chris recounts in his first book: we waited until the heart had stopped beating – period. But McRae quoted me without asking, and so the untruth was published.

McRae did, however, make many more mistakes on his own. When discussing the second heart transplant, he introduces Dr Raymond 'Bill' Hoffenberg into the donor team, saying that he was involved in confirming the brain death of the donor. Professor Jannie Louw, who never had anything to do with heart surgery or heart transplants, then puzzlingly joins Dr Hoffenberg. Professor Louw would rather have been seen dead than have been part of the team.

Bill Hoffenberg was a brilliant staff member from the Department of Medicine, but he was an endocrinologist, not a neurologist. He was therefore in no position to deliberate over or pronounce on the confirmation of brain death of any donor. It is my belief that McRae placed Hoffenberg in the Department of Neurology so that he could use Hoffenberg's unjust political banning to emphasise how awful the government of the day was.

Chris went overseas after the second heart transplant and, McRae alleges, left me in charge of the cardiac unit in his absence. Describing Chris's response to my objections, he writes, 'Anyway, Marius, I'm leaving Blaiberg in good hands – yours.' Yet again, this is simply not true – Chris asked Professor Val Schrire to be in charge while he was away.

I was disappointed by the degree of the inaccuracies and untruths contained in McRae's account of the first human heart transplants and the people involved in them. The public deserves to know the facts.

17

Transplant Aftermath

THE HEART TRANSPLANT CHANGED OUR LIVES COMPLETELY. I still cannot understand why it became such an epoch-making event, capturing the attention of the whole world. But there can be no doubt that it changed things forever.

On that momentous Saturday night, we went into the theatre as a team of doctors, nurses and pump technicians to perform an operation. We were hard-working and well-trained doctors, but, prior to this occasion, very few people knew about us or really wanted to know about us. Fewer still cared about our opinions. Twenty-four hours later, our names were spread all over the world. Our views were now sought on all subjects: at first, heart transplantation and cardiac surgery, then South African politics, followed by religion, sports and many others.

The heart transplant was certainly no great medical breakthrough. Kidney and liver transplants in humans, in particular, had already established the clinical feasibility of performing successful human organ transplantation. Immunosuppression, rejection and especially the complications associated with the high incidence of infection had already been well documented. If you were to ask who performed the first kidney transplant, nobody would know – and who really cares? Who did the first heart transplant? Even today, many will answer, 'Professor Chris Barnard'. Why the difference? Because it was the heart.

Throughout the centuries man has looked at the heart as the site of religion, love and nearly all human emotions. It is obvious that if you say to the one you love, 'My heart belongs to you', it has a special meaning as an expression of true love as compared to, say, 'My kidney belongs to you', or, 'My large bowel is true'. Not only would the reaction be different, but you would probably be rewarded with a slap in the face.

To emphasise this point, the Bible refers to the heart more than 700 times – 743 times, to be exact. The kidney, the next most frequently mentioned organ, is cited thirty times, and the liver a mere thirteen.

* * *

For the first few days after the transplant, Washkansky did very well. After two days, he was able to get out of bed. But our unit would never be the same again. The news media descended on us like vultures, feasting on each and every little morsel of news, true or untrue, and using every means, fair or foul, to obtain it. They reported on our success and rejoiced in our inexperience, frailty and failures. We even found one reporter masquerading as a doctor in the isolation unit in order to get an exclusive report. His camera was concealed under sterile clothing. He didn't succeed in getting his report: on being discovered, he was forcibly removed not only from the unit but from the hospital. What is sickening is that his possible scoop was worth more to him than the patient's well-being, which would have been compromised by the increased risk of infection as a result of his undercover presence.

The pro-government press immediately saw the strength of the heart transplant story and government officials and members of the National Party recognised the possibility of very favourable propaganda. At this stage, South Africa was the leper of the world due to its racially discriminating policies; the transplant was manna from heaven for a government desperately seeking something positive.

The local Cape Town daily newspaper, *Die Burger*, had a field day in this respect, portraying us as heroes carrying the good news from South Africa to the world. This included a cartoon depicting a conference hall at the United Nations, where the Cape Town heart transplant team is sitting right in the centre, smiling. All around us are other delegates from Africa looking miserable and unhappy.

Within a few days, we received visits from Dr Carel de Wet, the minister of health, and Dr L.A.P.A. Munnik, an old classmate of mine who was the member of the executive council (MEC) for Hospital Services. They arrived in our ward with photographers accompanying them. These were image-polishing exercises more than anything else: the government realised that the transplant could be used as a means of trying to improve its deservedly poor international image. In many respects these efforts succeeded. Poor Chris, who was always ready to please, would be increasingly drawn into this distasteful plan.

The members of our unit now had new and unexpected demands on our time. Our routine work continued, with the additional burden of looking after our transplant patient and, of course, the news media lurking in the background. The hospital authorities, who had actually had no knowledge of the heart transplant until it had been completed, could not, and did not, help in any way. But they provided great verbal support during press interviews. They were so 'proud' of us and what a 'great' team we were, and they 'promised' help, for which, of course, it was a bit late in the day.

Chris, as the leader of the team, received most of the publicity – as was his right – and took over dealing with the press. Most of the major role players in the team – Dr Hewitson, Professor Schrire and Dr Ozinsky – avoided the press like the plague. Others would love to have been part of it but, being junior staff members, were largely ignored. There is no doubt, though, that the direction of publicity towards some and not others was a cause of great tension. Professor Schrire wanted nothing to do with it, and his disenchantment with Chris's behaviour very soon resulted in a cooling-down of his relationship with Chris.

Dr M.C. Botha had very little clinical involvement before, during or after the transplant. His office was at the medical school, a short walking distance from Groote Schuur Hospital, but every morning he would now walk from the school to the front entrance of the hospital. He even responded to questions from the press about the patient's condition.

He would sit next to Chris at most media conferences. He was now regarded as a world authority on immunology and was purported to have played a leading role in tissue-typing donor and recipient in establishing whether there was a compatible match. It is true that his department did perform the tissue-matching for heart transplants, but we were seldom influenced by their data, as it was often only available either while a transplant was in progress or after it had been completed.

In one later case, the transplant was already well advanced when Dr Botha advised us that the match was so poor that under no circumstances should we even think of performing the transplant, as there would be severe rejection. This patient became one of our longest survivors. Despite this, Botha was a very capable specialist. A sociable man, he was a good friend of Chris's and didn't harm anyone.

Chris, at first, could not get enough of the publicity. Strange characters, journalists and others entered his life as great benefactors and loyal friends, but most of these so-called friends had a very bad influence on him. He craved praise and adoration but was, regrettably, blind to the consequences. This later led to unhappy and disastrous events that would come back to haunt him.

* * *

Chris had his first taste of world fame soon after the transplant. He was asked to appear on the *Today Show* in Washington, D.C. This meant he had to be away for a few days. If anything went wrong with our patient during that time, he could be severely criticised. The transplant was already being criticised as a publicity stunt, one doomed to failure because we should never have done it due to our 'lack of experience' and 'lack of previous experimental success'.

Chris discussed his forthcoming television appearance with me. Although we never saw eye to eye, he seemed to need my blessing when he wanted to do something he was not sure about. If I agreed to a suggestion or recommendation, all was well. But if I disagreed, acrimony prevailed. I agreed to his appearance on the *Today Show*, very strongly in fact, and I knew how much he wanted me to.

His visit to the United States was a great success. Although untrained for high-powered television interviews with highly experienced interviewers, Chris had an inborn ability to interview well and a knack for giving answers that the viewers wanted to hear. He was innocent and unsophisticated and his youthful good looks and toothy smile benefited him greatly. He was now 'made'. Chris requested a meeting with President Lyndon Johnson while in Washington. At his insistence, it was accepted, but the enthusiasm demonstrated by Chris was unfortunately not matched by that of the American president, who didn't seem particularly interested in Chris or the transplant.

Good reviews from all quarters resulted in invitations pouring in to appear on talk shows, give radio interviews, attend medical meetings and meet famous people. When Chris arrived home, however, he quickly came back to reality.

* * *

Mr Washkansky soon started showing signs of infection and was not at all well. Infection was one of the most serious complications in an immuno-suppressed patient, exacerbated by the fact that he was diabetic. In spite of the best possible treatment, his condition deteriorated rapidly and he died on the eighteenth post-operative day.

We were shattered. Our team had been so hopeful, as our patient had done extremely well up to this point. His death was a severe blow to all of us. While we received many condolences, I'm sure that some of our critics rejoiced in this failure, and the media had a field day bringing up and reporting our supposed lack of experience and insufficient research.

Being of the Jewish faith, Mr Washkansky was buried the next day. We were asked to be pall-bearers. Chris refused because he felt that his presence would have created a press circus. M.C. Botha and I had to face having cameras shoved in our faces while carrying the coffin. I was exhausted and emotionally drained. But the press had its photo; my face was featured on the front page of local and overseas newspapers.

After the death of Louis Washkansky, we had time to reflect. One thing we learnt for certain from our experience was that a heart transplant was not only feasible but had a great chance of success. Given a suitable recipient, there was a definite possibility for long-term survival.

We were by this point convinced that our current transplant unit was totally inadequate and that it was virtually impossible for us to ensure that it would remain an infection-free, sterile unit. The unit was a two-bed room in our surgical wards C2 and C3 on the third floor of Groote Schuur Hospital with a thoroughfare between the two other surgical wards, C1 and C5. We managed to find a much better facility in the new outpatients' block and prepared it for subsequent transplantations.

We had time to discuss the pressure of all the publicity and how to cope with it. We could not believe it when we received an offer of one million US dollars for one special photograph: that of the donor heart being placed into the chest of Mr Washkansky lying on the operating table without a heart.

We naturally rejected the offer but could never have claimed this reward anyway: we had not taken any photographs of the historic procedure on that Saturday night, as we hadn't thought it would be sufficiently newsworthy.

I remember discussing the publicity with Chris after the transplant. When I asked him whether he had ever expected all the publicity, his answer mirrored my sentiments on the matter. We did know that this would be a 'first in the world' but we thought that it would be reported on the local radio only – we had no television in South Africa at the time – and head-lined in the local press, as we had experienced after the kidney transplant.

That it was performed on the southern tip of 'darkest Africa', and not in the United States, the United Kingdom or Europe, came as a total surprise to the world, and, when reporters saw the unsophisticated, simple young surgeons who had carried out this operation, the requirements needed for international headlines were fulfilled.

Many people around the world – even cardiac surgeons – couldn't believe that modern hospitals such as Groote Schuur existed in South Africa, and that advanced medical techniques and patient care of the highest international standards were being applied. I remember subsequently being told by a visiting French doctor that he had expected the hospital situation to have been similar to those conditions in which Dr Albert Schweitzer had operated in West Africa. He had expected to see mud huts in Cape Town with goats, sheep and cows grazing around Groote Schuur Hospital, but had been greatly impressed when he witnessed this hospital for himself and the world-class standards that were being upheld, despite our rather outdated equipment.

I received far more publicity than I ever deserved, or was hungry for. The reasons for this were many: Chris was unable to cope with all the requests for interviews and other media gatherings; Dr Hewitson and Professor Schrire not only were reluctant to become involved but were not good media material; and, most importantly, I was Chris's brother, with the Barnard surname, and was therefore an acceptable substitute when he was not available.

The press found it interesting not only that we were brothers but also that we were on the same surgical team. A representative from *TIME* magazine, Peter Hawthorne – one of the better and more respected newsmen – interviewed me for hours. Of course, he also interviewed Chris and the families of the recipient and donor and, within a few weeks, the first book about the transplant, *The Transplanted Heart*, was published.[1] It included much of the material I had given him. Chris was very upset about the book, as he was already looking for a ghostwriter to write his story. I had no such ambitions and thought that Peter gave a very honest and factual account of what happened. We are still friends today.

The press hounded me for personal details about Inez and the children, and for any little bit of insignificant information. There were invitations to speak at functions and to dine at ambassadorial tables. These were heady days and I must admit that, initially, I enjoyed the limelight. I could, however, see the danger signals flashing.

One such dinner I remember attending was at Groote Schuur, the prime minister's residence, and I had to hire a tuxedo for the occasion.[2] We were met by our very charming hosts, John Vorster and his wife, Tienie. I recall very little about the evening except that we ate tahr meat.[3] When we eventually stood up to leave, to the amazement of my colleagues I said to Mr Vorster, 'Mr Prime Minister, I found you quite pleasant, so the next time I vote against you, the mark will not be so deliberate as before, but I'll still vote against you.' Unsurprisingly, this elicited no response; he simply walked away. Chris was incensed and considered my remarks totally uncalled for. But I actually enjoyed making them.

Chris was changing in front of my eyes. Though never having been a concerned dresser before, he now wore tight-fitting white polo-neck jerseys, white shoes and specially cut trousers, and the grey in his hair disappeared overnight. The saddest part, however, was that my brother underwent a total personality change. He was no longer the casual, unsophisticated country boy whom I knew so well, but had become a self-opinionated and intolerant person. He changed his friends and the new ones were people who used and abused him. As long as he was praised, he remained totally oblivious to this.

The team he so lavishly praised just after the transplant disappeared, and the word *I* replaced *we* and *them*. His real friends and those people to whom he owed a lot – Hewitson, Schrire and others – were slowly pushed aside. These unfortunate transformations obviously caused problems at home.

Louwtjie, his first wife, was a good and faithful partner. She had supported Chris during his struggling days when he was on his way up. She was not only the mother of his two children, but had worked during the day at the OK Stores branch in Adderley Street as their nurse when money was short. She sewed and darned and made clothes for her children and was a vital partner in their struggle to survive financially. She also cared for my mother when she spent six-month periods with her and Chris.

Louwtjie certainly had no intention of changing and found Chris's new-found fame and publicity unwelcome and tiresome. Knowing Louwtjie, I have no doubt that she was not shy to voice her feelings to Chris on many occasions. She was now a middle-aged housewife, while Chris, in his new position on the world stage, soon showed a preference for younger female company.

Ongoing Heart Operations

TOWARDS THE END OF DECEMBER 1967, CHRIS COULD TALK ONLY of doing another transplant. On 2 January 1968, his wish was fulfilled when Dr Philip Blaiberg, a retired Cape Town dentist, became our second recipient of a donor heart. The donor was twenty-four-year-old Clive Haupt.

During this operation, things went horribly wrong as soon as the patient went on bypass. That night, there was either a flaw in the tubing of our heart–lung machine, which, by way of its finger-like metal protrusions, propelled blood through plastic tubing to the patient, or the occlusion was too tight. We had fortunately been on bypass for a short period only when the tube was ripped to shreds. The surgeons, staff and instruments were showered in blood. There was blood everywhere – even on the walls and ceiling.

But cool heads and experience prevailed. While Chris and Rodney Hewitson kept circulation going by manual cardiac massage, Johan van Heerden, our pump technician, replaced the shredded tubing and, within a few minutes, we were able to continue with bypass. It took much longer to wipe away the blood from the surgeons and instruments.

From this point on the transplant went smoothly and was without further complications. The transplanted heart took over with perfect circulation and Dr Blaiberg was transferred to our improved transplant unit.

We were shocked to discover that a very senior staff member had smuggled a camera into the theatre and had secretly tried to take photographs for a journalist friend without our permission. Although he did not succeed, we realised that we could trust no one.

After completing the transplant and with brand-new publicity at his disposal, Chris jetted off on a visit to Europe with the status normally accorded to royalty. He took with him Doctors M.C. Botha and Bossie Bosman, neither of whom posed any threat in the publicity stakes.

This trip was a major publicity success. Chris received an audience with the Pope, met great leaders and addressed prestigious medical seminars. But in the press there appeared headline articles about Chris meeting the famous Italian film stars Sophia Loren and Gina Lollobrigida, and of a possible romance with the latter. In addition, there were photographs of the great surgeon dancing cheek to cheek with a young starlet in a German nightclub.

Knowing the new Chris, I realised that from this point forward there would be trouble both between him and Louwtjie and for us in the unit. Chris's involvement with Sophia Loren and another well-publicised rumour that he had slept with Gina Lollobrigida must have been the straw that broke the camel's back for Louwtjie.

When Chris arrived at the hospital in the mornings that followed his trips, his moods became darker and his behaviour increasingly unreasonable and irrational. During one of his attacks on me, he made the ridiculous assertion that he could have done the transplants on his own and he threatened to sack the whole team. Somewhere, something had to give – and it did.

After one of his overseas trips, he arrived at work one morning looking forlorn and unkempt. Later in his office after surgery, he told me that when he had arrived at his home at Zeekoevlei the previous day, he had found all of his belongings neatly packed in suitcases outside the front door – with the door locked.

Pleading to be allowed back home didn't help, and Chris had to find alternative accommodation with a friend. He bought a flat in a trendy Clifton apartment block and divorce soon followed. At the time, this didn't worry him much. What was intolerable to him, however, was that he had to pay Louwtjie maintenance. This remained a sore point for him. Bearing in mind how lavishly he treated his next two wives, his views on this seem unfair and cruel and did not fit the image he projected to the outside world.

Someone now had to take over the responsibility of the cardiac unit when Chris was abroad. This, of course, required that it be a surgeon on the permanent staff. Rodney Hewitson and Terry O'Donovan, both senior to me, were in private practice and had only part-time appointments at Groote Schuur Hospital. They assisted with operations but had no post-operative duties. This left only me, so Chris asked me to assume his duties at both Groote Schuur Hospital and the Red Cross War Memorial Children's Hospital.

I had experienced a miraculous first year as a cardiac surgeon, having been personally involved in the first heart transplant. Initially, I had been upset when Professor Louw had refused to appoint me to his unit on my return from Houston. But, unintentional as it was, he actually did me a great favour: the heart transplant afforded me international recognition and the opportunity to become the senior surgeon in charge of the remarkable cardiac unit while Chris was away. I could now also spend much of my time fulfilling my first love: performing paediatric cardiac surgery at the Red Cross. The transplant had another welcome plus for me: my monthly salary of R600 was increased to R900 and I was promoted to the ranks of Senior Lecturer and Senior Surgeon.

Chris, by this point, had become one of the best-known names in the world, if not *the* best-known. Awards and honours rained down on him: immediately after the transplant, the University of Cape Town conferred upon him an honorary Doctorate of Science, and he received the Freedom of the City of Cape Town. His team, however, was not invited to any of these award ceremonies. While he basked in the glory, we were bending over the patient in the operating theatre.

* * *

As can be expected, Chris considered the heart transplant programme as his private property and we were expected to help, but not to touch, when it came to the transplant itself. As head of surgery, this was his right. But, unfortunately for him, he had many invitations to go on overseas visits and considered these to be his private property too, again as was his right. He somehow managed to time his visits well, always returning in time for the next transplant.

But sooner rather than later he misjudged his timing. On this occasion, he was on the luxury liner the *Queen Mary* with his second wife, Barbara, when the eighth heart transplant patient acquired a suitable donor. Since I was next in line, it fell to me to head the procedure.

The transplant took place on a Sunday night in January 1972 and, as always, the team ensured that this procedure was a 'walk in the park' for me. It was certainly much easier than the experimental dog transplants. Doctors Rodney Hewitson and Ozzie Ozinsky, Sister Pittie Rautenbach, the pump technicians and the others were the perfect team to assist me.

The patient did very well and was soon up and about and able to return home within a few weeks. Unfortunately he suffered a massive pulmonary embolus a few months later and died. The transplant received a fair amount of publicity. Being Chris's brother, I suspect, was the part that made it newsworthy to the press; the event was even reported in *Life* magazine.[1]

Under the banner 'Another Dr. Barnard transplants a human heart', I was quoted as saying, 'We're no longer in the hit-or-miss era of heart transplants. Not long from now, we'll be getting 70 to 80% success [rates] – two or three years [of] survival. That's not bad for a dying patient, you know.' My future prediction proved to be correct even if somewhat conservative at the time. I went on to describe the pleasure I took in being able to perform this procedure: 'There's nothing more lucrative than the work I have here. I'll show you what I mean. Three months ago, a little girl from Milan came in. She was so sick we couldn't touch her. The medical boys got her into shape for corrective surgery, and I operated. This morning she sat up in bed, eating breakfast. The shortness of breath is gone. The swelling has disappeared. Her eyes are bright. I thought, if only everyone could see the beauty in this. I wonder if Chris can still see it? That's what worries me about him. Can he still see it?'

Chris was not too pleased that I had gone ahead and performed the operation without him. He even admitted to me later that when he had heard about the transplant while on board the ship, he had felt frustrated and a bit jealous – an amazing admission from him!

I performed about six or seven more transplants after this when Chris was absent. When I am asked by inquisitive people how many transplants I did, my straight-faced answer is always: 'Less than a hundred. I do not tell lies!'

But as my relationship with Chris deteriorated, I became more of a hindrance than a help to him and the discord between us became counterproductive to the unit. One of us had to go. Since Chris was leader of the team, it wasn't going to be him, so I was slowly moved out of the programme.

Of the heart transplants that I performed, there is one that I remember well, as it has particular significance for me personally. On 5 January 1979, the team and I successfully performed a 'piggyback' heart transplant on a fourteen-year-old boy, Paul Thesen, from Knysna. Paul was the youngest person to undergo heart transplantation at the time and became the world's youngest surviving recipient.

Paul underwent a second heart transplant in 1983 and, by 1996, the *Journal of Heart and Lung Transplantation* reported his progress in an article titled 'Don't Ever Give Up' accordingly: 'Our present longest surviving heart transplant recipient is Mr. Paul Thesen, who underwent heterotopic heart transplantation in January 1979 at the age of fourteen years for idiopathic cardiomyopathy.'[2]

During the heterotopic procedure, the patient's own heart is not removed when implanting the donor heart. The new heart is positioned so that the chambers and blood vessels of both hearts can be connected to form what is effectively a 'double heart'.

You will recall that my late father, during his early years, was employed at the Thesen wood factory in Knysna. I can think of no better way of showing my appreciation to his former employer than restoring the health of one of his descendants. I am very pleased to report that Paul continues to enjoy an active and healthy life. Thirty-two years after his first heart transplant, he is currently the world's longest-surviving transplant recipient.[3] I am extremely proud to have played a part in his recovery and am delighted that he continues to enjoy long-term health and prosperity.

I had the recent pleasure of meeting up with Paul while he was visiting Cape Town for a check-up at Groote Schuur Hospital. He remains indeed in excellent health. This opportunity coincidentally occurred after the manuscript of this book had been accepted and on the same day that we met with our publisher. After many decades of absence from Groote Schuur Hospital, I arranged, with my editor, to meet Paul at the Heart of Cape Town Museum. For me it was a most emotional and nostalgic visit, especially when revisiting the operating theatres in which the first heart transplant had taken place. My son, Adam, arranged a press conference and the local television station e.tv interviewed me and aired a short piece of my interview with Paul on prime-time television two days later.

I was delighted that this story enjoyed a front-page picture and article in both *Die Burger* and the *Cape Argus*, as it illustrates the importance of the first heart transplant, the ongoing successes that the doctors and staff of Groote Schuur Hospital's cardiac unit have achieved, and the enduring memory of my late brother.

* * *

Dr Bertie – or Bossie, as we knew him – Bosman was a registrar in our department at Groote Schuur Hospital at the time of the first human heart transplant. I first met Bossie when he was a family physician at Barkly East in the Eastern Cape where he served the farming community. While based there, Bossie brought a patient with a very large ischiorectal abscess to Professor Louw at Groote Schuur. I have a feeling that the experience of seeing us at work must have stimulated his interest in becoming a surgeon.

A tall, big man with protuberant eyes, Bossie was a conscientious, hard-working doctor. Along with François Hitchcock and Coert Venter, he was one of our three registrars responsible for the care of our first transplant patients. When Chris went overseas after the Blaiberg transplant he, much to the disgust of the other two registrars, took Bossie with him. For some or other reason, Bossie, on his return, took it as his life's mission to look after Blaiberg. He withdrew from all other responsibilities and was obsessed with Blaiberg's welfare. It is largely due to his personal devotion that Blaiberg became the world's longest-surviving heart transplant patient at that stage.[4]

The Blaiberg family was very grateful for his efforts and treated him with the greatest kindness. But Bossie was falling behind as first Venter, then Hitchcock, and soon Hannes Meyer, who joined us after the Blaiberg transplant, passed their MMed degrees in cardio-thoracic surgery. By contrast, Bossie seemed to have no direction and was getting nowhere.

When John Ackerman, who was in charge of renal transplantation at the time, left to go overseas, Bossie was appointed to continue with the kidney transplant programme.

Blaiberg's death eighteen months after his heart transplant was a terrible blow to him. The kidney transplant programme gave Bossie some prestige, but both Professor Louw and Chris, his two departmental heads, gave him neither help nor encouragement towards obtaining his specialist degree, a qualification that was essential for him to be appointed as a surgeon.

I noticed that Bossie had now become increasingly withdrawn; he walked around with a long, unhappy face. Unbelievable as it sounds, it came as a complete surprise to us when he took his own life.

I still harbour some guilt of not being sufficiently sensitive to his downward spiral of depression. If just one of us had stopped to listen to him crying for help, or had given him time and encouragement to study and sit for his specialist degree, I feel certain he would not have been driven to self-destruction. He was a good man and deserved better.

Bossie was not the only sacrifice to the transplant programme.

* * *

During one of his frequent trips overseas, Chris was given a pair of chimpanzees. Both primates were crated to South Africa and installed in our new animal house, a gift from the Chamber of Mines following the first heart transplant to replace the totally inadequate unit that was situated next to the mortuary.

A male and a female chimp – a devoted couple – were both frightened and scared in their new 'home', which they shared with baboons and pigs. Animal hearts were used to study the preservation of hearts for longer periods after harvesting so that they could be transported by plane and transplanted hours later at other units. In this way, more donor hearts could be used.

Pigs were used particularly for the liver transplant programme, which was now in full swing and headed by the now Professor of Surgery, John Terblanche. I took no part in any of these programmes as I was too busy with my clinical duties. I did not perform any other 'experiments' in the research laboratory after our first transplant. The whole idea of experimenting with animals had become unacceptable to me, especially when using dogs. Those loving animals would wag their tails in affection and trust when they were brought in to our theatre. They would lick the hand that inserted the fatal injection into their veins. I still have a feeling of guilt for my part in experimental surgery and hope that in dog-heaven they will forgive me.

But to Chris, the two new primates were a gift from heaven, as they offered him the opportunity to transplant a chimpanzee heart into a human patient. Chris must have known that the chances of success were basically nil, but performing a xenograft would arguably bide time until a human heart became available.[5] Deep down, however, I believe he pursued this option against all the facts at his disposal.

He just needed the right situation to use the chimpanzee heart. This eventuality occurred when one of our patients could not come off bypass. I have to admit that every possible attempt was made for the bypass to be discontinued, but this failed. So, the call went out for the transplant team to assemble. The male chimp was anaesthetised and smuggled via the back door into the theatre, where his heart was removed and transplanted. The xenograft was a dismal failure, as we knew it would be.

As discussed earlier, this operation was first performed by Dr James Hardy from Mississippi, and it too had failed. Other surgeons at overseas centres had even tried sheep's hearts knowing full well that there was no chance of success. I had in earlier days done a few experiments by perfusing a dog's heart with human blood. Within seconds, the dog's heart would slow, the contractions would become weaker and the heart would become as hard as a rock and stop. There was no evidence whatsoever that we would have achieved a better result clinically, and Chris knew it.

His undertaking of a chimpanzee heart transplant resulted in a fierce argument between the two of us. I opposed it completely and refused to have anything to do with the procedure. When the team was called for the operation, I was not needed and I was grateful for this. Surprise, surprise: the press heard all about this event and it made bold headlines.

Chris argued that his patient would have died anyway. That was an absolute fact, but I believed that this was not a justifiable reason for performing a lengthy and expensive – in time and material – operation, knowing full well that it would fail.

There was one further pathetic casualty that tore the hearts out of most of the staff responsible for the housing of the animals. The female chimpanzee went into total mourning for her mate, on which we had experimented. She cried for him and stopped eating. Her grief was intense, real and uncannily human-like. She was soon given away to a zoo, but this was not the end of the episode.

Shortly afterwards another patient of ours could not be weaned off the heart–lung machine. I remember this patient, a lady from Italy, well, as I had assisted with her first operation. Surgery had not been a lasting success, and she had had to return to be reoperated on. Chris performed this operation and, when she failed to come off the heart–lung machine, a baboon heart was transplanted into her. To my utter surprise, the patient survived a bit longer than the patient who had undergone the previous xenograft, but there was, of course, no chance of lasting success.

Again, I was not called on to assist. I remained silent on this issue, but this only served to irritate and annoy Chris further. The press, however, had another medical circus to report.

19

Initial Transplantation Results

THE INDICATION FOR HEART TRANSPLANTATION HAS NOT CHANGED since the motivation and performance of the first transplant. This implies that when a patient is at risk of dying due to irreversible damage to the heart muscle, resulting in end-stage congestive cardiac failure (CCF), a heart transplant is indicated as there are no other forms of medical or surgical treatment available to save the patient's life.

In spite of there being far superior treatment for CCF available today, many patients can still only achieve long-term survival by the removal of their diseased heart and its replacement with a healthy donor heart. Modern improvements in immunosuppression and enhanced experience in donor-heart preservation, surgical techniques and post-operative care have provided far better results than we attained at the time.

Two and a half years after we performed the first human heart transplant, all but twenty-one of one hundred and fifty transplant patients worldwide died. This was certainly a grim record and one, unless improved upon, would have brought an end to heart transplantations as a viable procedure.

After the initial frenzy surrounding the first heart transplant, a total of ninety-one more operations were performed worldwide in 1968. This number was largely due to its publicity and efforts by crazy surgeons from certain quarters who had a misguided belief in their own abilities and joined the publicity train with scant concern for their patients. They were either too inexperienced, or didn't have the proper facilities to care for their patients after the operation. The number dropped to forty-seven in 1969, however, and by the middle of 1970, only nine transplants were performed.

In the United States, the initial results were very poor. In 1968, a transplant team at the University of Texas Southwestern Medical Center in Dallas saw its first heart transplant recipient die after one and a half hours; the second lived for five days. The patient of a single transplant performed at the Albert Merritt Billings Hospital of the University of Chicago died after five hours. The only transplant patient at the Edward Hines Jr Veterans Affairs Hospital in Illinois survived for four hours, and a single transplantee at Allegheny General Hospital in Pittsburgh lived for two days.

In Houston, thirty-three transplant operations were performed on thirty-two recipients. Everything is bigger in Texas. I was quoted at the time in an article published in the *Chicago News* that 'things were going too heavy at one stage'.[1] And they certainly were.

At St Luke's Episcopal Hospital in Houston, Texas, Dr Denton Cooley performed twenty-one operations on twenty patients. One patient had a second transplant after the first was rejected. None of them survived. Good Old Denton. At the nearby Methodist Hospital, Dr DeBakey performed twelve transplants, of which only two transplantees survived.

At Stanford University Medical Center in Palo Alto, California, leading cardiac surgeon Dr Norman Shumway performed a similar number of operations as Dr Cooley. Seven of his patients survived. Despite such limited survival rates, Shumway's results – as could be expected – were far better than those of his fellow American counterparts. Ours, however, proved to be even better.

In Europe and from behind the Iron Curtain, the results were equally dismal. As recorded in the Organ Transplant Registry in Chicago, Illinois, eleven transplant teams all produced poor results. A single recipient in Czechoslovakia lived for five hours, while the only transplantee in Russia survived for one day. I couldn't have been a very good teacher to Professor Wisnefski, as this operation followed soon after our meeting in Holland, as will be described later.

Three transplant teams in France each performed a single transplant, but none of the patients survived for longer than two days. In Spain, a single person to receive a new heart lived for two days. Of the two operations performed in Germany, both patients died in one day and another transplantee died the day of the operation.

The only Polish transplantee died on the operating table, whereas in Turkey one patient survived for fourteen hours and the other one for a day. In India, two transplants were performed by the same surgical team. One survived for three hours and the other fourteen hours.

In South America, this trend continued. A single recipient in Venezuela survived for six hours and in Argentina another single patient lasted for fifteen hours only. Australia also registered no successes, its only transplantee surviving fourteen hours.

Within this period, our results proved to be much better than those from overseas. By today's standards they would be considered acceptable. Of the five patients who underwent transplants, three were still alive one year later. Our second patient survived eighteen months, as did our fourth. Our fifth patient survived for fifteen years, and our eighth patient for twenty-one years. Again, one can see Chris's hand in this.

The reason for the reduced number of heart transplants worldwide in 1969 and 1970 is that, due to poor survival rates, the initial enthusiasm of surgeons waned and a hostile press discouraged 'chancers'.

I stated in a newspaper article at the time that some of the inexperienced or ill-equipped surgeons 'should never do another heart transplant' because some of them were not capable of performing this procedure.[2] But as the 'Mickey Mouses' – 'transplant murderers', in fact – of cardiac surgery dropped out, so the more experienced and better-equipped units run by the likes of Norman Shumway and a few others in the United States, and units in the United Kingdom and France, as well as our own cardiac unit at Groote Schuur Hospital, reported improving survival rates.

Despite the poor results achieved abroad, I was emphatic that heart transplants should continue provided that surgical teams were qualified to perform the surgery. With the advent of improved immunosuppression, heart transplantation became routine surgery and more acceptable as a viable procedure. This, in turn, produced favourable survival statistics and the achievement of excellent results.

Recent transplantation results in the United States are sensational and prove just how far we have come since those early days. The authoritative American Heart Association quotes impressive figures that reflect not only the numbers of transplantees, but the relatively high survival rates that have since been achieved.

In 2008, for example, over 2 000 heart transplants were performed. By the middle of June 2009, the one-year survival rate was 88 per cent for males and 77 per cent for females. The five-year survival rate for males was 73 per cent and 67 per cent for females, with more than 50 per cent attaining survival expectancy in excess of ten years. With more recent advances in the prevention of rejection, such results can only improve.

* * *

The success of organ transplantation greatly depends on the correct use of immunosuppressive drugs. Without the development and utilisation of such drugs, we would not be able to perform heart transplants, nor any other major organ transplant.

As discussed earlier, prior to our first successful heart transplant in 1967, we had gained invaluable experience in the use of anti-rejection drugs during kidney transplants, as well as the corresponding management of patients in preventing infection. After our first heart transplant, many of the successive international attempts failed largely due to the rejection factor. These failures contributed to the sharp decrease in the performance of heart transplants in 1969 and 1970. Only when the issue of tissue rejection was better understood and when more sophisticated drugs were developed to control this problem did the number increase again.

Immunosuppressant therapy works by curbing the production and activity of lymphocytes. It has been used since the middle of the twentieth century to prevent the rejection of transplanted organs by the body's natural defence system. The advent of immunosuppressant therapy undoubtedly enabled surgeons from the mid-1950s onwards to perform organ transplantations with more confidence. Yet drug-induced immunosuppression has its drawbacks. While the anti-immune drugs may raise the chances for the survival of a transplanted organ, they render the patient more vulnerable to other infections. These drugs can be highly toxic and can cause malignancies in the patient, and the organ may be rejected in spite of immunosuppressive therapy.

Cyclosporine, isolated from the fungus *Tolypocladium inflatum*, played an enormous role in the continuation of heart transplantation. First discovered in 1971 in Basel, Switzerland, by the scientist Jean Borel, it is a very strong immunosuppressant with the added benefit of fewer side effects. Organ rejection and patient deaths fell dramatically with the clinical introduction of cyclosporine in 1984.

* * *

The exceptionally good heart transplantation results produced in recent years are achieved, and surpassed, by other forms of transplantation, especially kidney transplants. But the problem we had from the time of the first organ transplants remains a problem today, namely the lack of donors.

In the case of kidney transplants, there is the great advantage that living donors can be used. Where cadavers are used, two kidneys become available immediately. As far as heart transplants are concerned, such options are obviously not possible. I have heard that in some countries where they execute murderers, the organs of the cadavers are harvested for transplant use. In spite of it having been reported that we used this source in the early days, I can categorically state that we never even gave it a thought.

177

The numbers of donors can today be increased by protecting transplantable organs from irreversible damage over longer periods of time. This is achieved by cooling them after they have been harvested. In addition, organs can now be transported from one city or country to another within a very short space of time, resulting in more donors and better matching to patients waiting in the transplant pool.

But all over the world today, patients whose lives could be saved by transplants die while waiting for a suitable donor. The shortage of donors is progressively worsening due to the ever-increasing numbers of recipients on the waiting list. There is, of course, a simple solution if law makers just had the courage to change legislation in this regard.

Currently, permission must be given by the relatives of a potential donor before an organ can be used. When I was in parliament in the 1980s, the Human Tissue Act was passed and subsequently became law.[3] I proposed that we amend it by inserting a clause stating that every patient admitted to hospital should be considered a potential donor unless the patient or his or her relatives signed a form to forbid the use of the patient's organs. This would no longer place the onus on the transplant team to obtain permission, but rather on the patient's relatives to refuse. I was shouted down on the basis of totally unfounded arguments that we, as doctors, would abuse this, that grounds for litigation would emerge and, of course, that it would attract bad press. Up till today, organs that can save lives are committed to the grave or are cremated. What a waste.

20

A Famous Political Patient

DURING THE ONGOING POLITICAL TURMOIL IN SOUTH AFRICA in the 1970s, Robert Sobukwe, the founder of the Pan Africanist Congress (PAC), was placed under house arrest in Kimberley. Sobukwe was considered a greater threat to the Nationalist government than Nelson Mandela and the ANC because the PAC was closely aligned with the Black Consciousness Movement.

In 1977, we heard that we were receiving a new patient – Robert Mangaliso Sobukwe. He had complained of persistent symptoms that required referral to a specialist unit. The minister of justice and police, Jimmy Kruger, wanted him to go to a Johannesburg hospital, but Sobukwe requested transfer to Groote Schuur Hospital in Cape Town. After some delay, his wish was granted.

He arrived with a host of security police. Dr Joe de Nobrega, registrar in thoracic surgery at Groote Schuur Hospital at the time, played a very important role here. Joe, who had previously played striker for the local soccer club, Cape Town City, was a superb doctor and remains a great friend of mine. He immediately took a personal interest in the well-being of his new patient.

We cared for Sobukwe, but he was really a 'thoracic case'. Dr Rodney Hewitson performed tests that revealed a carcinoma of the lung.[1] During a subsequent operation to remove the affected lung, Dr Hewitson found that the cancer had spread, invading the pleura – the thin covering that protects and cushions the lungs – and the chest wall. He performed a pneumonectomy – an operation to remove the lung – and this was followed by three weeks of recovery to allow the wound to heal. After that Sobukwe was required to undergo radiotherapy treatment.

Sobukwe went through a difficult, slow and painful recovery. We considered him to be a very special person who stood up for his beliefs, and we nursed him in a single, private bed at Groote Schuur Hospital in Ward B11 – one normally reserved for whites. Two security policemen were posted at the door at all times. Sobukwe found this amusing and even joked about it with the medical staff.

Shortly after Sobukwe's surgery, Chris returned from an overseas trip. When he discovered Sobukwe in our ward, his immediate reaction was to evict the security police, insisting that this patient was his responsibility and that he would not tolerate anything that could compromise his recovery from major surgery. The men were dumbstruck. They promptly removed themselves, going to their vehicle in the hospital parking area – and stayed there.

Chris was keen to talk to Sobukwe, mainly to make sure that the patient was satisfied with his management. He showed particular empathy towards this great man, instructing his ward staff that his patient should be made as comfortable as possible during his painful recovery.

A French television team had arrived in Cape Town to interview Chris in his hospital setting and, on an impulse, Chris conceived the idea of including Sobukwe in his interview. He broached this with the patient, who promptly shut down the discussion in a polite but final manner. The way in which Sobukwe handled the persuasive and difficult Chris was impressive. The session ended with Sobukwe smiling broadly and Chris storming out of the ward.

I went to visit Sobukwe frequently as a result of my political views. He knew about me and we enjoyed many conversations. He was a deeply religious man and his wife, Veronica, who was the sweetest lady, used to visit him twice daily. They could always be seen reading the Bible together.

Sobukwe was mesmerising. When you were with him, you could sense that you were in the presence of a truly great man. It was evident that he harboured no bitterness or hatred, and that he was a leader of men. I was with him on the morning of 12 September 1977 before he went into theatre. Just before he entered theatre, the *Cape Times* arrived with the banner screaming out, 'Biko Dead'. So we whisked that newspaper away immediately and hid it.

The government then decided to send Sobukwe back to Kimberley, despite the fact that he was still waiting to undergo radiotherapy. When a team of pistol-brandishing policemen arrived at the hospital, they accosted both Sobukwe and his wife, who tearfully requested that Sobukwe stay on under Chris's supervision at Groote Schuur.

Joe, however, then offered Sobukwe accommodation, which he accepted. He and his wife spent two happy and relaxing weeks at Joe's home prior to the commencement of his therapy. Joe even provided daily morning coffee for the security police that were posted outside his front door. After the therapy Joe took him and his wife back to Kimberley, where Sobukwe died shortly afterwards. Joe attended Sobukwe's funeral at his birthplace, Graaff-Reinet, in the Eastern Cape. It was at Sobukwe's funeral that the crowd wanted to attack the leader of the Inkatha Freedom Party, Mangosuthu Buthelezi, and where Helen Suzman allegedly played an important part in protecting him.

My experience of Robert Sobukwe, and one endorsed by Joe de Nobrega and other members of our staff, is that his death was a huge loss and tragedy for South Africa. We needed a leader like him.

* * *

Steve Biko, the prominent voice of Black Consciousness during the same period, was serving time in detention. He was influenced by Sobukwe, with whom he shared common political ideologies and aspirations. Biko was permanently silenced by the apartheid government as a result of his convictions.

When Biko died, the same minister of justice and police, Jimmy Kruger, infamously said, '*Dit laat my koud*' – 'It leaves me cold' – and I was one of the first people to respond. I stated in a newspaper article that I had never heard a worse, or more callous, statement. I went on to say that 'whatever a man is, he's a human being and his people love him. No man's death will ever leave me cold.'

Jimmy Kruger and I had another encounter many years later when I was an MP. It was at a cocktail party given by the Italian Trade Commissioner. Bishop Desmond Tutu, as was his church appointment at the time, and his wife, Leah, were there when I arrived. A few minutes after my arrival, Jimmy Kruger walked through the front door. When Bishop Tutu realised that he was in the same room as Kruger, he and his wife promptly left. They justifiably couldn't stand him, nor could they bear the indignity of being in his presence.

A press photographer asked Jimmy Kruger, myself and another person if he could take a photo of the three of us. When he had taken the picture, he enquired of us, 'Can I ask you your name?' Jimmy Kruger pointed towards me and said, 'This is Dr Marius Barnard.' The indignant photographer responded by flatly stating, 'Of course, I know that, but who are you?'

So I got my own back, and this rather insignificant event made me feel rather good.

21

Fame and Travels

AFTER THE FIRST HEART TRANSPLANT AND THE EXTENSIVE PUB-
licity that our unit received, cardiac patients from all over the world
became aware of our landmark achievements and good results. Many felt
that they would have a better chance of surgical success and survival in
our unit.

We received letters from all over the globe. I even received a letter
addressed to my office titled 'The Professor of Heart Failure, South Africa'.
I'm still not sure why this person picked me for this honour. Letters poured
in from Greece and Italy, where Chris was now very popular. They also
arrived from other European countries, the Far East, the United States and
England; some even came from behind the Iron Curtain.

Invitations came in from all over the world requesting us to speak at
meetings, to appear on radio and to give television interviews. In addition to
the genuine interest expressed in the transplant, some people saw an opportunity to promote themselves or to make money through the publicity
they could achieve. There were, of course, many other worthy invitations,
including requests to assist charitable organisations and provide support to
medical congresses.

Chris, as the leader of the team, was by far the most sought after, and
he certainly used his position to the fullest. We could only read about his
television interviews, debates with people like Peter Hain, the UK-based
staunch anti-apartheid campaigner, and his involvement in other 'more
social' activities. While Chris was away, we kept the unit going and continued
to look after what he termed 'his transplant patients'.

But every dog has his day, and in February 1969 a visit to Europe was
arranged for me through the Cape Town–based manager of the Dutch airline KLM. My airfare was paid for, as were my accommodation and travel
expenses. I had to give talks on heart transplantations and visit hospitals at
the various centres I visited. Press interviews, I discovered to my distaste,
were always part of the deal.

My tour included a talk at the University of Oxford and visits to Leiden,
Paris, Nancy, Marseille, Madrid, Barcelona and Rome. It was an amazing trip

for me, as I had been overseas only twice before. On such occasions, this had always been at my own expense and, since I was short of money, I was forced to stay in the cheapest accommodation, enduring sparse meals and travelling economy class. I was now considered important: a first-class ticket to Amsterdam, the best hotels and big, black chauffeur-driven limousines to whisk me around – I had come a long way from the missionary's parsonage at Beaufort West!

For a few welcome weeks there were no long hours bent over the operating table, and no post-operative complications, bleeding, cardiac arrests or death. I now had some understanding of why Chris very seldom refused an opportunity to leave the reality of cardiac surgery for the fleshpots of overseas to experience the most addictive 'drug' of all – applause and adoration. I think very few people in his position and from his background could have resisted such opportunities. Unfortunately, it changed him, his values, his integrity and his personality, and contributed greatly to his final, lonely days on earth.

The whole trip was a great experience and an important learning curve of how to deal with so-called fame. After my arrival in England, I reached Oxford late in the afternoon, an hour before my talk was due to commence. I was exhausted, having travelled from Bethlehem, South Africa, where I had given a talk the previous afternoon, by private plane to Johannesburg. From Johannesburg I'd flown to Amsterdam, then London and finally by car with Bernie Gersh, who, at the time, was a Rhodes Scholar at Oxford.

I hardly had time to wash my face and enjoy a cup of English tea before being ushered into one of the university's lecture theatres. It was one of those old-fashioned halls, with the podium facing towards terraced seating that reached up to the ceiling. It was jam-packed, and there were many people standing as a result of the shortage of seats. This was my first experience of having to talk about heart transplantation to my peers and, as I soon realised, my superiors.

My visual material was unfortunately very poor. We used a thirty-five-millimetre slide projector and slides that belonged to Chris. He was always very reluctant to part with them but, fortunately, he had so many duplicates that he never noticed when I had carefully removed some of them while he was away on his overseas visits.

I was extremely nervous and felt so inferior that my hands shook and I started sweating. But as my talk progressed, it soon became obvious to me that my audience was listening intently, many were taking notes and some were even recording my talk with portable tape recorders. My confidence returned and then began to soar, and my talk improved. As I was coming to the end of my presentation, I recalled my youth and the books I had read about the famed University of Oxford. The movie *A Yank at Oxford* had moved me so deeply that I'd supported Oxford during the annual boat race and rugby 'intervarsity' against the University of Cambridge.

As I concluded my talk on transplantation, I asked the audience to bear with me for just a few more minutes. I then related very briefly to them how, and where, I grew up, my early introduction to their university and how, to me, it had become a symbol of education, the producer of high-quality graduates. I had aspired to being educated there, I said, but had never been able to. I closed by thanking them for making at least part of that dream a reality for me, and for the honour of being allowed to address them.

When I ended, I became very emotional because it was a very special moment of my life – a defining moment indeed. There were a few seconds of complete silence and then, to my utter amazement, the entire audience rose as one and gave me a standing ovation. I nearly fainted, as this was my first experience of such a show of appreciation. The emotions that it evoked were overwhelming.

While revising this chapter, I received wonderful news about my grandson Saul from his mother, my eldest daughter, Naudéne. He had just written his O-level examinations in England and had achieved amazing results, passing with an A+ in ten subjects, including science, chemistry, mathematics, physics, Latin and Mandarin. His ambition is to study at Oxford on completion of his A-levels. This, to me, is the fulfilment of a seed planted in my brain in dusty Beaufort West seventy-five years ago. It was impossible for me to achieve this dream so, although I am not sure that I will live long enough to see it come true, it will be amazing to have my ambition as a boy fulfilled by my grandson.

My next stop was Leiden, Holland, where I visited one of the country's leading hospitals. Here I was introduced to the head of one of their cardiac departments, a very charming Professor Brom. I visited their excellent immunology research unit, which proved to be light years ahead of our own. This was followed by a splendid dinner with Professor Brom and his very gracious wife at their home. I was now really mixing in the company of aristocrats!

I stayed at the Kasteel Oud Wassenaar Hotel and during the night was awoken from my slumber by a distant passing train. The sound was remarkably similar to one that I had experienced in my youth. In an instant I was back home in Beaufort West, lying in my bed and listening to a train cross-ing the railway bridge that spanned the Gamka River a mile or so away.

During the second day, I received a request through an official from the Russian Embassy to visit their chief army surgeon, Professor Wisnefski. He was also in charge of military cardiac surgery and was keen to meet me to hear about our experiences of heart transplantations. A meeting was hastily arranged and I met him in his suite at the Ambassador Hotel in The Hague. He was a short, round, bald-headed man, similar in appearance to the Russian spies depicted on American television and in the James Bond movie *From Russia with Love*.

There was a slide projector available and, sitting on the floor, I went through my talk with him. He couldn't understand English, but fortunately we had a translator. It is possible that our meeting was even taped by his security agents. The professor, who was very formal, asked a few questions and then thanked me, after which I made my exit.

The next day, the newspapers carried a report on our meeting under the headline 'International discussion between heart surgeons in Hague hotel'.[1] Another proclaimed that, as a result of our meeting, peace now existed between Russia and South Africa!

I never saw the professor again but, soon afterwards, there was a news report that he had performed the first human heart transplant in Soviet Russia. The patient, however, had died soon afterwards. I hope that his meeting with me didn't earn him a one-way trip to Siberia.

My visit to France was interesting but it saddened me, as I realised that, while we might have been first to do heart transplants, we were very far behind with regard to facilities, especially in the field of immunological research. Visits to the Pasteur Institute in Paris, Lyon and Marseille only depressed me further.

Madrid was something different, not from a medical or scientific per-spective but from a social and entertainment point of view, because in this city I moved up a few steps on the societal ladder, associating with men of power and nobility. I arrived in Madrid from Marseille in a small jet. I was, as usual, informally dressed and sitting in the front row. After we'd taxied to a stop, my seat companion noticed a small group of people on the apron with television cameras and photographers. As we started disembarking, he remarked to me that 'there must be a bigwig on the plane'. I will never forget his look of amazement when he saw all the cameras turning on me as I descended the steps. He obviously found it difficult to believe that the man sitting next to him was the 'bigwig'.

I was met by my host, who introduced himself as the Marquis of Villa-verde, or Cristóbal Martínez-Bordiú y Ortega. I soon resorted to calling him *Chris*. He was a cardiac surgeon practising in Madrid, but his real claim to fame was that he was married to María del Carmen Franco y Polo, or Carmen, the only child of the Spanish head of state, General Francisco Franco. I would meet her that night – a classic Spanish beauty, refined and sophisticated and the mother of six daughters and one son.

The Marquis was a tall, good-looking Spaniard. A better host I could not have dreamt for. I was whisked to my hotel in a chauffeur-driven Mercedes and immediately noticed that we were signalled through heavy traffic by the traffic police. I discovered that we were being transported in one of the head of state's official cars. That night, I had a magnificent dinner with the Marquis and the delectable Carmen along with other members of their 'high society'. My hotel accommodation was not the single room to which I was accus-tomed, but instead an expansive suite – my first experience of such luxury.

The following day was spent visiting one of the university hospitals, meeting cardiac surgeons, cardiologists and medical staff. I soon struck up good friendships with a few doctors, who divulged some startling stories about the Marquis. Evidently his ability as a cardiac surgeon left a lot to be desired – his training was apparently poor and his surgical ability limited. His position, it was said, was largely due to his 'connections' rather than his operating skills. A few uncomplimentary jokes about him then followed: 'What is the difference between the Chris of South Africa and the Chris of Spain?' The answer: 'The Chris of South Africa is a surgeon who wants to be a playboy and the Chris of Spain is a playboy who wants to be a surgeon.' I soon discovered how close to the truth this joke actually came.

My visit to Madrid was predominantly of a social nature and included eating Spanish omelettes in old Madrid, watching a bullfight, which I hated (I hoped that the bull would kill the matador, and not vice versa), and seeing the paintings by Rubens of fat ladies with large breasts at the Prado Museum. But most amazing of all was the flamenco dancing. The vibrant music and rhythm was captivating, as were the beautiful female dancers, with their shapely bodies and exquisite movements.

During my stay, the Marquis insisted that we go hunting. I am a strong supporter of the anti-hunting group and agreed to participate in this savage sport only because the hunt would take place inside in the palace grounds. Having been waved through by sentries at the guard posts, our black Mercedes came to a stop in front of the palace, where another Mercedes was waiting. It was open-styled and longer than usual, with four uniquely designed seats, two in front for the driver and gun handler and two raised swivel seats at the back.

We were soon off in the unusual car, Chris and I enthroned on the back seats. The vehicle hurtled through one gate and then another before bursting into the hunting grounds. We were each handed a loaded gun and very soon full-scale war broke out. My trigger-happy companion shot at anything that moved, whether birds, rabbits or deer. I remember an inquisitive rabbit losing its head when the full blast of a shotgun ended its life. After about an hour, and with my host disappointed that I had hardly shot at anything, the *Blitzkrieg* ended.

On our way back to my hotel, I asked Chris where his father-in-law had obtained this amazing hunting car – a veritable killing-machine. He rather reluctantly told me that it had been a present to General Franco from Adolf Hitler.

The next day, we were back on the swivel chairs, looking for a suitable animal for me to annihilate. Our road led us past a golf course. On one fairway there was a lone golfer with a row of armed soldiers lining either side of the fairway and several more standing both in front of and behind him. 'Would you like to meet my father-in-law?' Chris asked. I did not hesitate to say yes, and proceeded to meet a frail old man – the most powerful man in Spain – with a golf club in his hand. This was the same man that was responsible for the deaths of hundreds of thousands of people.

As we drove away, my Mauser in my hands, Chris said, 'By the way, in Spain, it is against the law to kill the head of state.' Indeed, this was true. I could, there and then, have shot General Franco at point-blank range. For obvious reasons, I didn't use that opportunity. Finally, however, I shot an unsuspecting deer. Perhaps I shot the wrong animal.

My next stop was Barcelona, where I had to give a lecture to the faculty of one of the city's medical schools. It was just before lunchtime and extremely hot. I was tired and had to deliver my talk through an interpreter. This was the norm when I was in Spain – and in many other foreign countries – therefore my talks generally took double the usual length of time. The only advantage to these talks that it gave me the opportunity to think clearly and deliberate over what I wanted to say.

Right in the middle of the lecture hall's front row sat one of the fattest men I had ever seen in my life. I was hypnotised by him and quickly realised that he was fast asleep. He woke up only when the audience applauded at the end of my lecture. A lunch had been prepared in my honour, where one of the faculty members had to introduce me and say a few words about me. To my great surprise, the fat man was given that honour. While he was talking, my interpreter told me that he said that he had never heard such an exceptionally informative lecture before, that it was one of the most brilliant speeches he had ever heard and that it had been a great honour to have attended. I was totally deflated. Here I was feeling very important, and I had just been praised by a man who had slept through my entire talk. Fortunately I saw the funny side, but this experience taught me an important lesson, which I carried with me from that day onwards: one shouldn't take oneself too seriously.

My final destination was Rome, where I was met by a South African delegation from the Department of Information. They obviously had a keen interest in me, but I never discovered why. While in Rome I was taken out for excellent dinners at smart restaurants. One evening, I ordered *coniglio* from the menu and, to my horror, found that it contained rabbit meat. Although as children we had frequently eaten rabbits shot by my father during our hunting outings, I had later dissected one soaked in formaldehyde during my first-year zoology class at university and had not been able to stomach them since. So, the first bite of this dish in the Italian restaurant proved to be my last.

A few days later, I was home and back to reality, bending over the operating table at Groote Schuur Hospital and tending to my patients. I did not know then that I would meet up with my very good Spanish friend, Cristóbal Martínez-Bordiú y Ortega, again later.

* * *

A few years after the first heart transplant, I was invited to attend a conference in Athens, Greece, organised by the DeBakey Society, a society open to surgeons who trained under 'Black Mike' DeBakey at the Methodist Hospital in Houston. I was not an active member of this group, nor was I particularly fond of the man. I was, therefore, reluctant to attend, but a Greek friend of mine invited Inez and me to spend a few days with him in Corfu. I needed no further incentive to go, especially as our airfare would be paid for.

The conference was not very impressive, but I was invited to appear on a live television show with a few other so-called celebrities, including Dr DeBakey himself. What gave me some degree of satisfaction was that the interviewer hardly gave DeBakey any attention at all – most of the interview was with me. Come question time, and the audience directed most of their questions towards me; the man who had taken no notice of me at the Methodist Hospital a few years earlier was now the one being ignored. Thinking back, it was really of no significance, but I felt good about it because I was now in the limelight – DeBakey could no longer accuse me of standing in his light!

A trip was arranged for the delegates to an exotic Greek island, and Inez accompanied us. The island itself was rather dry and of very little interest; the reason we went there was to see the tomb and embalmed body of a sainted religious leader. Our host was a gentleman by the name of Professor Ballas. It was fortunate for him that he didn't live in South Africa, because *ballas* in Afrikaans means *scrotum*. I could naturally not resist addressing him at all times as Professor Ballas, in spite of his pleading to call him by his Christian name.

After we had travelled through the countryside for a while – a part devoid of any suggestion of financial productivity – I said, 'Professor Ballas, what do you export from Greece?' After a few seconds of deep thought, he replied, 'Greeks.' Later, when visiting Chicago and Melbourne, I realised just how right he was.

Our visit to the beautiful island of Corfu was highlighted by an invitation to a party given by friends of our hosts. We had noticed a large yacht moored a short distance offshore and were told that they were filming the movie *The Greek Tycoon*, based on the lives of the Greek shipping tycoon Aristotle Onassis and Jackie Kennedy, who subsequently married Onassis.

We arrived at a well-attended party in 'Greek time' – just before midnight – to be greeted by our bombed-out hosts. They were so full of drugs that I don't think they could register our presence, or even cared. Quite a few of the other guests were in a similar state, if not worse. To us, this was a new experience. From my youth in Beaufort West, however, I could easily recognise the strange smell of marijuana wafting through the stately room.

One of the lucid couples excitedly told us that the great Anthony Quinn and Jacqueline Bisset – the lead actors of *The Greek Tycoon* – would be attending the party. I have to be honest that the news of who the leading lady was excited me more than the imminent appearance of Anthony Quinn. The great moment arrived a few minutes later, when Quinn, along with his entourage, made his grand entrance. I must confess that, to me, he was certainly not the 'Zorba' of that memorable movie. In fact, I thought he was rather ugly. He immediately approached a table laden with food and grabbed a leg of lamb.

As Zorba the Greek, he paced around for a minute or two to make sure the few in the room who could register knew that he was there before sinking his teeth into a mouthful of lamb. With great, theatrical bravado, he tore it off the bone. The meat reluctantly gave way but, unfortunately for Zorba, so did one of his prominent top incisors. He now looked absolutely ridiculous, the large gap between his teeth visible to all. Within a few seconds, Zorba the Greek had become Anthony the Quintessential Buffoon. He promptly gapped the party.

After Quinn's unrehearsed Oscar-winning performance, I wanted to leave, but was getting rather worried – where was the leading lady? I asked someone if and when she would be arriving, and was told that she was already in attendance. I was then shown where she was sitting.

Miss Bisset was certainly attractive, but without all the make-up of a cinema set, she didn't appear to be as special as I'd expected. In fact, I felt that Inez could easily have given her a run for her money. On my way out, I stopped at where she was sitting, introduced myself and informed her that my friends in South Africa would be very impressed if I told them that I had kissed her. Before she could react, I kissed her on her mouth and left.

When I arrived home, I bragged to all my friends that I had kissed the beautiful, famous actress Jacqueline Bisset. I doubt, however, that she told anyone about my kiss, or that she even remembered it.

* * *

During 1969, I was invited to visit a few centres in Brazil and Argentina to give talks. My status, however, didn't get me into first-class or business-class seats. I was happily installed in my economy-class seat on South African Airways to Rio de Janeiro when a flight attendant asked me to accompany him to the first-class section. Here I found my brother Chris, on his way to New York via Rio. I was permitted to sit next to him for a short while, and was taken by surprise when he told me that he, at the ripe old age of forty-eight, had become engaged to a local nineteen-year-old heiress, Barbara Zoellner.

I knew that he was very active among the ladies and frequently stopped over in Johannesburg on his way home from overseas. That he had a serious relationship with a society teenage beauty was, however, news to me.

The next I heard about the romance was what I read in the newspapers: that he was married to Barbara. Inez and I were only allowed to meet her then. Everybody said she was beautiful and I could see why, but my country upbringing did not respond to that kind of beauty. She was friendly, but at times rather distant and reserved. Barbara was very shy and must have found her new status as Chris's wife attractive. I doubted that their relationship would last long, however, once she got to know the real Chris.

Chris was without doubt very much in love with her, but he was restless and still attracted to other women, especially when they threw themselves at him – and that they certainly did. Chris was a master charmer. In addition, he was good-looking and famous. How could a female resist him when he turned on his charm?

Chris and Barbara moved into a magnificent house in the wealthy suburb of Constantia in Cape Town and, while living there, their two sons were born. Inez and I were hardly ever invited to their house and they never had time to see us. Except for the fact that we worked together and were brothers, we had nothing in common. We had different values and moved in different circles. Inez, although very fond of Chris, became bored with his constant talk of himself. Barbara never showed any inclination towards becoming friendly and, to be honest, Inez was just as guilty.

Sooner or later, we knew, there would be trouble. Barbara became extremely jealous of Chris and Chris persisted with his wandering eye until there was a final explosion between them. Although never on brotherly or sisterly terms with Barbara, we respected her. She was a fine woman and I believe that Chris didn't deserve her. I read about most of these goings-on in the press as I was by that time no longer at Groote Schuur Hospital. Chris was very distraught and didn't want the divorce, which was being highly publicised.

He later told me that he, the world-famous scientist and surgeon, had even summoned the help of a witch doctor to try to win her back. Not surprisingly, this failed.

After their divorce in 1982, Barbara subsequently remarried and moved to Johannesburg. I never saw her again, but she consulted my son-in-law, Darryl Kalil, for a cardiac condition while he was practising at Johannesburg's Milpark Hospital. I was, coincidentally, practising cardiac surgery at the same hospital during this period.

Much later, when I was admitted to the Park Lane Hospital in Johannesburg for my prostatic cancer surgery, our paths almost crossed again. As I was being accompanied to my ward, the sister in charge informed me that I had missed Barbara by one day. She had been discharged from the same ward after having had breast surgery for cancer. I never had any form of contact with her again. Barbara tragically died of breast cancer in 1998.

22

The Romanian Experience

*'When I operate here [in South Africa], I am only saving one life. But
when I go with my team to a country such as Romania, I am teaching
these people how to save lives – and surely by doing so, I achieve far more
than by remaining here.'* — MARIUS BARNARD[1]

M Y LIFE HAS BEEN FILLED WITH SO MANY EXPERIENCES THAT I
could never have dreamt of. The time I spent in Romania is one
of them. Prior to my first visit, Romania was, from my fairly limited perspective, simply a communist country somewhere in Eastern Europe. My
knowledge of the place was restricted to what I had learnt from my geography teacher at school. For some reason the name *Ploeşti* stuck in my
mind, probably due to its being in the news during the Second World War,
when South African airmen were conducting bombing raids to disrupt
Hitler's oil supplies. My most vivid impression of Romania, however, was
the horrific Count Dracula, whose evil deeds had petrified us in our youth
during our Saturday-afternoon outings to the local cinema. Little did I
know then that Romania would become an integral part of my life, that
I would sleep in the run-down, polluted city of Ploeşti, and that I would
visit Dracula's castle and observe the skeletons of his supposed victims.

Today, my knowledge of Romania is far more extensive. The original
inhabitants of Romania were the Dacians. In the eleventh century, they were
conquered by the Romans, who ruled them for approximately two hundred
years. The country was then occupied by the Goths and later became part
of the Ottoman Empire. This included Transylvania. Such geographical
'musical chairs' continued, and Transylvania then became part of the
Austro–Hungarian Empire. But after the Second World War it was ceded
back, and the state of Romania was established.

I visited this country seven times over a period of twenty-five years,
during which time I experienced its beauty and met its warm, friendly people.
I have been privileged to have made a contribution to the treatment of
their then desperate cardiac patients, as well as to the improvement of the
standards of cardiac surgery and the results achieved by their surgeons. If

I were to name my greatest achievement in life, it would probably be the influence I had on the treatment of cardiac patients and cardiac surgery in Romania.

While in Romania I also, however, experienced the devastating effects that communism had on its people and the society within which they lived. What I observed in that country makes it impossible for me to understand how we still have a communist party in South Africa today, one that forms an integral part of our ruling party, and that there are people who advocate such policies.

After the Second World War, Soviet influence dominated Romania and the king subsequently abdicated in 1947. With the Communist Party firmly in control, the Romanian People's Republic was formed and a new constitution, similar to that of Soviet Russia, was adopted. In 1967, the year of the first human heart transplant, Nicolae Ceauşescu became president. After ten years of rule by this madman and his wife, Helena – who in my opinion was considerably worse than him – I arrived in Romania.

How did I, of all people, find myself in Romania, when South Africa was then a sworn enemy of communism? Our government had passed the highly restrictive Suppression of Communism Act in 1950, which banned all forms of communist activity. The answer: the heart transplant, cardiac surgery and the destruction of medical standards by the great leader Ceauşescu and communism! While the communist leaders preached equality, they stole not only possessions from the people, but also their minds, souls and health.

The mass-media hysteria caused by the world's first human heart transplant raged not only in South Africa but in all corners of the globe, including behind the Iron Curtain and in Romania. It was especially noted by those families who had loved ones with heart lesions and who, living in Romania, had very little hope of help.

In Romania at that time there were only two units that performed cardiac surgery, the Fundeni clinic in Bucharest, which produced very poor results, and the unit at Tirgu Mureş, which fared significantly better. Only the most uncomplicated operations could be performed. The state had to grant patients special permission to be operated on elsewhere in Europe or in the United States, but consent was very seldom granted, unless you were highly ranked in the party. I must concede that being connected to an influential official of the governing party in South Africa at the time could also get one into Groote Schuur Hospital, or the Red Cross Children's Hospital!

No one could access his or her own passport, as it was held by the state.

The rulers were most reluctant for anyone to leave that communist utopia to receive treatment elsewhere because, when they did, they did not want to return to the oppression and poverty. If rare permission was granted, one had to buy dollars from the state, but at a greatly inflated rate. Few could afford this, but relatives in the United States and elsewhere in Europe were able to assist the few lucky ones. The others had to sit back and watch the suffering of their loved ones, without hope, until they died.

In the meantime, we, the 'miracle workers', were receiving requests from all over the world to provide assistance, particularly with complicated cases that were considered too high a risk to be performed in their own countries. Others simply felt that they would obtain the best treatment from Groote Schuur or the Red Cross. From all over the globe they came, especially · from Italy, Greece, Mauritius and parts of Africa, but also from the United Kingdom, the United States, Australia and France, whose facilities, surgeons and results were just as good as ours, if not better.

Our government, as I have mentioned, saw the publicity advantages of this situation and allowed us to operate on these overseas patients free of charge. Romanian parents, husbands and wives must have heard or read about this opportunity. The first to get in touch with us was a woman by the name of Cecilia Anghelescu-Sămărghitan. Her son, Horia, was born with a cyanotic heart condition; he was a 'blue baby'. He had survived but was eventually assessed at the Fundeni clinic in Bucharest by a cardiologist, Dr Daniel Constantinescu. Horia had the congenital lesion tetralogy of Fallot. He could not be operated on in Romania and a visit to Germany had brought no hope. In desperation, his mother appealed to us.

I received her letter and sent his details to our cardiologists. Although Horia had a severe obstruction to the outflow of blood to his lungs, he was considered suitable for surgery. Despite every setback possible, his mother finally obtained permission from the authorities – she must have had connections in high places – and had enough money for their airfare. ·

She arrived with Horia at Groote Schuur Hospital one afternoon in September 1969. After a long and exhausting journey, he was in an extreme condition. His blue complexion was now almost black, and it was decided to investigate him immediately, with the possibility of emergency surgery.

The diagnosis of severe tetralogy of Fallot was confirmed. But then Horia had a cardiac arrest in the cardiology theatre. With great skill, the cardiology team resuscitated him, our theatre was prepared and the patient was rushed from the cardiac clinic to the operating theatre. He was immediately anaesthetised and connected to the heart–lung machine. A successful correction of his cardiac defects was performed and Horia left theatre pink, stable and with an excellent chance of recovery. Within ten days he was discharged from hospital and three weeks later Horia and his mother were back in Romania.

This caused quite a sensation, and the Romanian news media disseminated Horia's experience, especially the positive outcome, to the Romanians and Europe.

I saw Horia regularly on my subsequent trips – the last one being in 2002, when, thirty-five years later, he was alive and well with a beautiful daughter but, tragically, a young wife dying of cancer. His mother, who had been told before she left Romania that it would be better and cheaper for her son to die in Romania than bring his ashes back, subsequently authored a book, *The Heart of My Child*. It was written in Romanian and later translated into German. She sent me one of the original copies, which I have on my bookshelf in my home today.

* * *

The publicity surrounding Horia's successful treatment brought a flood of letters and medical reports to our cardiac unit from Romania. Most of the medical reports came from Dr Daniel Constantinescu.

In early 1970 we admitted our second Romanian patient, a four-year-old girl named Sabina Popa. She had a single ventricle – an inoperable condition at that time. We performed a palliative Blalock–Taussig shunt on her but didn't expect her to survive for very long.[2] She is still alive and well years later, however – a miracle. She has never forgotten us, and each Christmas and Easter I receive a card from her.

At one stage, we had more than fifty Romanian patients on our waiting list. It was impossible for us to perform so many operations, as we simply didn't have the capacity to do so. We could operate on a few, but some of the Romanian children died while waiting to be called to Cape Town. I was sometimes blamed when they died and, on one occasion, received a photograph of a young boy in his coffin, the mother blaming me for his death.

The cardiac unit became unwilling to accept these patients – and quite rightly so. We had more than enough of our own patients to deal with. Even our government, via their hospital official, became less enthusiastic for us to treat them. In our correspondence, Dr Constantinescu complained bitterly about the poor results achieved by his cardiac surgeons. They had a high mortality rate with the simplest of congenital lesions, even when closing atrial septal defects (ASDs), where, in good hands, this rate should have been zero.[3]

With a handful of close associates, I soon started planning a visit to Romania to operate there and to improve their standards by teaching their surgeons our surgical techniques and post-operative care. But we had no idea how I could succeed in entering this country. As a South African, I was not allowed into communist Romania, and the airfares and other expenses posed a challenge. Neither the Romanians nor our South African authorities, from whom I never received financial support, would pay. The opportunity arose in April 1977 and it was completely by chance.

Having trained in Houston with Dr Michael DeBakey, I was, as mentioned earlier, invited to a conference in Athens in his honour. To justify my expenses, I had to present a paper on heart transplants. At this meeting, a Romanian surgeon delivered a poor paper in bad English. He presented the results achieved at the Fundeni clinic – I think only he understood what he was trying to say.

The surgeon in question was a Professor Pop da Popa, head of cardiac surgery at the Fundeni clinic. His full title was Professor Doctor Docent Pop da Popa, which was the custom in Romania. (I would also be given this meaningless title at a later stage.) I went to introduce myself to him. He was most charming and you could not help liking him. His disposition towards Inez was that of a real gentleman. We soon discussed the possibility of my coming to work in Romania. His invitation was warm and sincere and he said that I should proceed directly to his country after the Athens conference. But I didn't have a visa. Worse, my passport listed a number of countries for which it was not valid, Romania being one of them. At the time, there was a United Nations Resolution proclaiming apartheid a crime against humanity and Romania, ironically, was one of its signatories! We had no air tickets and no money to buy them. Yet none of these problems was a concern to the Prof. Dr Doc. The very next day, he presented us with two return tickets on TAROM, Romania's national airline, and told us that visas would be provided on our arrival in Bucharest.

Two days later, on 22 June 1977, Inez and I were seated in a noisy and uncomfortable Russian-built Tupolev jet, making our final approach to Otopeni Airport in Bucharest. Inez and I suddenly had our doubts. Communist country, no visas – what would happen if no one met us at the airport?

We needn't have worried. We were not allowed off the plane until all the other passengers had disembarked. When we came to the exit door, there stood our reception committee – approximately ten to twelve people, all of the men smartly attired in suits and ties. I had my casual clothes on and felt underdressed, not to say a trifle embarrassed. The ladies were all beautifully turned out, almost every one of them carrying a bunch of flowers.

I was relieved to see one face that I knew – Professor Doctor Docent Pop da Popa. He came to the steps of the plane and, as a South African, I encountered a new experience: he grabbed me in a bear hug and planted a kiss on each cheek. I was then introduced to Daniel and Anca Constantinescu, Dora Petrila and some of the doctors with whom I would closely work. Others I would never see again.

Later, I discovered that the group had included a few Communist Party officials, and even a man from the Romanian secret police, Securitate. They asked me for our visa-less passports and luggage tickets. I was reluctant to part with our passports – our umbilical cord to the West – but had no other choice. With much bowing and excited chatter in a language we couldn't understand, we were led to a small reception room – it must have been their imitation of a VIP room – while a man disappeared in a different direction with our passports. Fortunately, at least half of my new friends could speak English, and I was soon in conversation with Daniel, who was asking about my programme and informing me of other matters that I needed to know about.

We accepted their invitation of a cup of coffee. Another new experience: a small cup of black coffee – lukewarm, nauseatingly sweet and so strong that your heart rate immediately doubled! After a few more minutes, our passports were returned to us. We were told that our luggage was already in the car and that we would be taken to our hotel.

When we entered the arrivals hall it was packed with people who, when they saw us, started applauding and rushed forward to meet us. That day more men than I could have counted kissed me on both cheeks. My ribs felt thoroughly bruised afterwards. Flowers, envelopes of all sizes and small parcels were heaped on me. Who were these people? I could recognise a few – patients on whom we had operated back home in South Africa. These wonderful, warm people, who had so little, came forward to say thank you and had brought us presents to show their appreciation. The others were prospective patients and relatives, who brought me their medical reports, desperately hoping that I could help them.

I will never forget their faces: one group smiling, laughing and happy –

those that I had treated – and the others anxious, with no smiles, no laughter and begging for help. Some had come from hundreds of miles away with great expectation and hope – I was that hope.

I was eventually pushed through the crowd and into a car, with medical reports still being pushed through the windows, and then taken to our hotel. We were given time to freshen up before going down to lunch with a group of people, some of whom I had by now already met: Pop da Popa, Daniel and Anca, Dora, and a few others who were new to us.

Most people at the table could not speak a word of English. Like the later lunches and meetings I attended, the language barrier made things difficult. While you were talking to the few that could speak English, the others sat there with blank faces, staring into the distance. An interpreter then had to be used to emphasise to them that I recognised that they too were important to me.

During our first Romanian lunch, we discovered that most Romanian meals consist of six to eight small courses. The first – during breakfast, lunch and dinner – was a small glass of *tuică*, a ferocious plum brandy that we were instructed to down in one gulp. It immediately left my mouth and chest on fire. I soon recovered from the lightning bolt, and the after-effect was rather pleasant. One night, however, I found these effects too much to bear, so I threw the remainder onto the hot coals of the fireplace, which resulted in a massive, conspicuous explosion!

Then followed pickled vegetables, cheese, salami, talamati, warm vegetables, fish and some form of meat, usually chicken or pork, all swallowed down with reasonably pleasant, though very strong, white and red wine. Then came pudding, sweets and the ever-present strong black coffee.

During our first meal on Romanian soil, a trio playing violin, piano-accordion and a guitar-like string instrument entertained us. The music was foreign to me, sad and haunting but so beautiful. As I was the 'man of the moment', the musicians were very enthusiastic towards me and the violin was shoved close to my ear for my enjoyment.

After the meal – and more male kissing – we had a period of rest before the evening's entertainment. When we entered our room, it was decorated with pleading letters for help, medical reports, X-rays and even photographs of patients of all ages, sexes and sizes. I realised then that I had a significant problem. There was no way I could see all of these patients, let alone help them. My misgivings came all too true later and it turned into a personal nightmare.

The next morning, Daniel fetched me and we went to the Fundeni clinic for my first visit. When I entered the reception hall, I received a repeat performance of what had occurred at the airport the previous day. Milling crowds, hugging, male kisses, medical reports and the pleading words I could not understand. But, by this stage, I could guess what they wanted.

I was escorted to Prof. Dr Docent Pop da Popa's office, given a white coat and taken to see the hospital's wards and operating theatres. Accompanied by twenty to thirty doctors, nurses and hospital officials, there was not much I could immediately make out that was problematic.

The theatres looked adequate and I took it for granted that they had the proper instruments. The ICU had beds and a flock of nurses – but no patients. The wards had many beds, but again I saw no patients. I found this very strange, but did not comment on it during my all-too-brief inspection. I felt satisfied that the facilities were adequate – a grave mistake!

Back in the office, I started seeing patients and drinking the sweet, strong coffee. There was a range of old and new patients, and I soon discovered that their angio reports and angiograms (or *angios*, as we call them) were rather inadequate.[4] Whereas we normally used one reel for each patient, in Romania they had six to eight patients on one reel of film. Before I could make a comprehensive diagnosis of one patient from the film strip, the angiogram of another patient would appear. This, of course, prevented us from having sufficient information on each patient and it severely limited the extent to which we could make an accurate diagnosis. I later discovered that, due to a lack of funding, this was an attempt to increase the number of cases that they could investigate. How lucky we at Groote Schuur were by comparison.

After too many patients' pleading, tears and emotional pressure, I asked the hospital authorities not to send in any more. They placed two security guards at the door and we started discussing the future. The screaming of a female voice and a scuffling outside the office startled me. The next thing, the door was forced open and a frail mother with her young child in her arms brushed past the guards towards me.

When they tried to stop her, she screamed, 'My baby, my baby!' and threw the child onto my lap while her sobbing and screaming continued. The very frightened little girl flung her arms around my neck and clung on for dear life when the guards tried to remove her from me.

This was too much to bear, and I said I wanted to speak to the mother. Daniel knew the case and, after listening to the hysterical mother and to Daniel's explanation of the findings of the angio, it was obvious that this little girl was a typical tetralogy of Fallot – and one very suitable for surgery. I now felt responsible and promised the mother that I would do everything in my power, on my return to South Africa, to arrange for her daughter to come to the Red Cross Children's Hospital for surgery.

To experience the plight of people begging for the chance of a relative to be provided with life-preserving treatment is incredibly difficult. It had a profound effect on me. We tend to take treatment for granted and are often so ungrateful for the medical attention available to us.

After the woman left, we resumed our discussion and decided that, if I could arrange for finances to get a team of four to Athens at our expense, the Romanians would find funds to pay for our transport from Athens to Bucharest and back, as well as provide accommodation.

Inez and I then spent a few very pleasant days with Daniel and Anca, travelling by car through Transylvania to Moldavia. We drove through Sibiu and Braşov, with their beautiful scenery and quaint villages, and saw peasant settlements with hand-operated wells, public benches in the streets in front of most houses, where the villagers could sit and talk, and many other sights we had never witnessed before.

In Moldavia we visited two of the painted churches. These buildings were centuries old and had figures of biblical scenes painted on the walls, both inside and outside the church. The paintings were magnificent, but more remarkable was that those on the outer walls had withstood centuries of severe cold, snow and winds as well as the hot summer sun.

We arrived back in Bucharest in one piece, to our relief. We had discovered that Romanian drivers are fearless, reckless and risk life and limb by taking chances, and we had witnessed a few examples of the resultant carnage on their roads. In Bucharest we had a farewell dinner with many glasses of *tuică* and wine, and repeated ovations of '*La multo anni enima*' ('Many years to your heart'). This was to prove very appropriate, considering my future plans for their cardiac patients.

The following letter, written to me by Daniel Constantinescu in 2004, captures our most unique experience and describes the rich cultural history and diversity of Romania.

Dear Marius

I am late, again; writing these notes was a hard exercise in recollection as I was trying to put together facts and events which happened twenty-seven years ago. It was made easier by the well-known tendency of the old age to remember better the remote past than the recent one … Are you ready?

Inez and you arrived in Bucharest flying from Athens on June, 22 1977. Because there were no official relations between our countries, you were my personal guests. It was for the first time when Anca and I had the chance to meet the two of you. We knew each other (more or less) through patients and letters. (The secret police knew that too!)

After showing you around Bucharest and a short visit to the Fundeni Hospital – which was to become the place of your 'miracles' – we embarked on a trip to the north of the country to see the monasteries of Bucovina (part of which was snatched away by the Soviet Union in 1940 and now is still a part of Ukraine).

Romania has had a long Christian tradition; the apostle Andrew is considered our country's evangelist. There are documents mentioning Christianity according to the Nicean orthodoxy in the 4th century.

One early morning, the Constantinescus drove north [in the] family's Peugeot 404 after picking up the Barnards from their place of residence – Hotel Dorobanti. After less than 2 hours, we reached Sinaia, the most beautiful mountain resort of our country, situated at the foot of the Bucegi mountains at 860 m. altitude. We had a 'Romanian breakfast' at my cousin's Chetia, which astonished Marius and Inez by its abundance and by the fact that beer, vino and *tuică* [were] served. Coffee was not forgotten …

Then, we continued driving up the mountain to Predeal (1100 m.) and then started our descent to Transylvania, to the city of Braşov. In Romania, the Carpathian Mountains make a bend, changing N-S direction to E-W, thus separating to the east the province of Moldavia, to the south Muntenia and inside the loop, Transylvania. Crossing the mountains are rivers carving spectacular defiles [gorges] along which roads and railroads make possible the communication among provinces.

From Braşov, our beautiful Saxon city, we drove north, along the west side of the Oriental Carpathians, separating Transylvania from Moldova. After about 200 km, we passed Lacul Rosu [Red Lake], a very beautiful high-altitude tectonic lake, and through spectacular Bicaz River Gorges and we were in Moldavia.

Our first stop was north at the Agapia monastery, built in 1644 and restored in the 19th century. The interior was painted by the greatest Romanian painter, N. Grigorescu (1860). Agapia is a rich monastery – has multiple guest rooms in a building surrounding the church and a section reserved for very special guests.

As the Mother Superior, Mother Eustochia (Ana Ciucan), a very intelligent, cultivated and well-travelled nun, was my patient, Marius and Inez were lodged in the Royal Suite, unchanged since Romanian kings Carol and Ferdinand visited the place. There were marvellous carpets, old furniture and embroideries.

We had breakfast in the Royal Suite and dinner with other guests, Mother Eustochia and older nuns in 'trapeza' (monastery's dining room), served by novices and young nuns. The conversation was lively, interesting and cautious – secret police [were] everywhere ...

Next day we traveled north again, to Bucovina to visit the monastery of Voronet. This is an incredible work of art; built in 1488 by the Moldavian ruler Stephen the Great, was painted by a local artist in 1535 and dedicated to St George. Exterior mural painting showing scenes from the Gospel, Revelations and apocryphal stories is in Carpatho-Byzantine style. Scenes of 'Communion of the Apostles', 'Washing of the disciples' feet', 'Adam's deed' – depicting the mythical story about Adam signing a pact with the devil – and the most famous 'Last judgment' make Voronet the finest of all painted monasteries. The dominant colour of the paintings is blue, of a special kind, known as 'Voronet blue'. These magnificent paintings and their endurance throughout almost 500 years made some specialists consider Voronet as the 'Oriental Sistine Chapel'.

From Voronet, we headed N-W to the monastery of Moldovita, built by Petru Rares, the son of Stephen the Great, in 1532 and painted in 1535 by Toma of Suceava, a well-travelled local painter. We spent the night at Moldovita in the guest section of the monastery (Arhondaric) and Mother Superior gave us information regarding the history and the architecture of the church and offered a very courteous and friendly reception.

Next day, we travelled east, to Suceava, the former capital of Moldavia in Stephen the Great's time. We visited the city, the historic and cultural places and at the end of the day we attended a dinner offered by the mayor of the city in the honor of Dr and Mrs Barnard. The mayor's wife, Aurelia Siminiceanu, was later operated on in Cape Town by Dr Marius Barnard for a valvular disease.

Our return to Bucharest by car next day, approximately 520 km, was an opportunity to talk freely, without fearing the secret police and to establish closer professional and family ties. Upon return to Bucharest, two events are worth mentioning:

The reception at Hotel Dorobanti offered by Marius's patients. Very emotional meeting. May have been 80–100 people. During the dinner, a young man in his twenties stood up crying and asked what could he do to save the life of his twenty-three-year-old wife, Mariana Tota, suffering of severe mitral disease with cardiac failure. Marius was deeply impressed by his story and with tears in his eyes promised to come back and take care of his wife, even if it was to come only for her. The meeting ended in deep silence.

The other event was the invitation by the Minister of Health, Mr Nicolescu, to a 'get acquainted' meeting with Marius. This meeting set the stage for Marius's future visits and work in Romania.

With love,
Daniel

I can never explain adequately how blessed I was to visit these historic places and to meet such wonderful people.

* * *

Once back in South Africa, I carefully planned our return visit. I told nobody; those I did approach were sworn to secrecy. Olympic Airways readily gave me four return tickets to Athens. All I had to do in return was to see their employees in the Greek capital that had or complained of heart problems. The morning after my arrival in Athens would be set aside for this. My dear friend Heinz Kretzchmar supplied disposable tubing, oxygenators and syringes.

My next step was to track down an anaesthetist. After some persuasion, our chief cardiac anaesthetist, Dr Ozzie Ozinsky, agreed to go. Alistair Hope, our pump technician, who was an excellent perfusionist, also accepted the challenge eagerly.

I wanted another cardiac surgeon to assist me with surgery but approached only one, who, I think out of jealousy, refused. I eventually took Dr Charl Frank, a general surgeon and a good friend of mine. He had no cardiac surgery experience but would prove to be an invaluable member of our team, not so much during surgery but in keeping me calm, as well as joining me at public-relations functions.

All of this took me a few months to arrange. In the meantime, the little girl who had been thrown at me by her mother arrived at the Red Cross Hospital in an extreme purple-blue condition due to the poor oxygenation of her blood. She duly had her operation. One of the greatest miracles of a complete repair of a tetralogy of Fallot is that the patient arrives in theatre with purple-blue lips, tongue, conjunctiva and fingernails, but leaves with skin and membranes fully oxygenated and a beautiful pink colour.

When I arrived to see the little girl the next morning, she was lying in her bed staring into a mirror the nurses had brought her with a big smile on her face. It was the first time she had seen herself with a normal pink complexion. What a great reward for a surgeon!

Towards the last week of November 1977, my team and I arrived in Bucharest. As before, there was the waiting reception committee, but with them now was a beautiful young girl in a long pink dress, holding a bunch of flowers. She was now a normal-coloured, shy young lady who had come to say thank you to me for helping her to live a normal, healthy and happy life.

Incidents like this made all the hard work, frustrations and disappointments of a cardiac surgeon's life more than worthwhile. I often wonder where this girl is. I hope she is married with her own children. I wonder if she still remembers me.

Again we experienced the male bear-hugs and kisses, and our passports being taken away – much to the amazement of the other three members of the team. Again the same small, uncomfortable VIP room, black coffee and a large reception committee with more letters, medical reports and X-rays. Then it was on to the same hotel for lunch.

On arrival in Bucharest, I, as the team's cardiac surgeon, was immediately made the senior of our group despite the relative seniority of some of my assistants on the trip. Ozzie was by far my senior at Groote Schuur Hospital: he had a more senior post, longer service and was, in my opinion, far better qualified and experienced than me.

Being in charge of our team brought certain privileges. In my hotel, for example, I had a bigger room. We discovered that even in the toilet there was a class distinction: I had soft, two-ply toilet rolls whereas the other three had thick, rough, sandpaper-like toilet paper. This not only came as a big surprise to us, but gave us lots to laugh about – everyone was equal under communism, but not our bottoms!

That same afternoon, our team visited the Fundeni clinic, where we were soon separated: Ozzie went with the anaesthetists to examine their

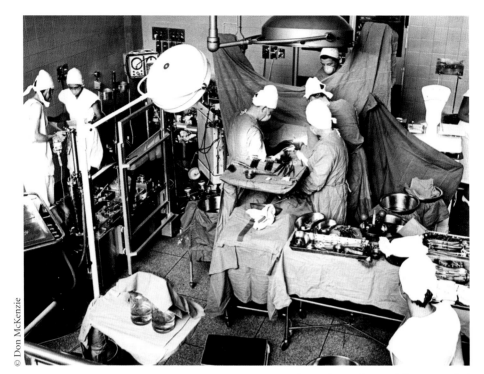

Operating at Groote Schuur Hospital

The world's first human heart transplant team. I am seated in the front row, third from the left.
Half of the people I had never seen before this photo was taken, nor have I see them since

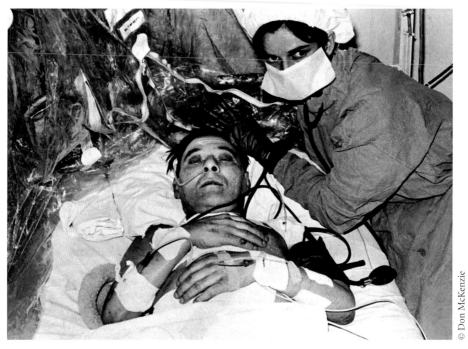

The world's first human heart transplant patient, Louis Washkansky, recovering in Groote Schuur Hospital's intensive care unit, December 1967

A cartoon that appeared after the first heart transplant depicting the team at the United Nations

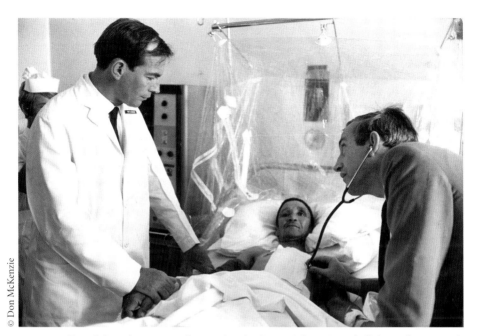

Examining a heart transplant patient in Groote Schuur Hospital's intensive care unit with my brother Chris (left)

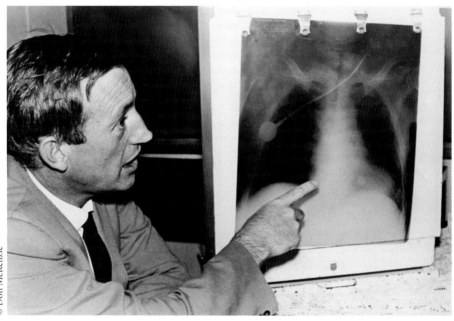

Inspecting an X-ray of the chest and heart of a heart transplant patient. The heart itself is clearly discernible

Sharing heart transplant details with Soviet Russia's chief army surgeon, Professor Wisnefski, in his hotel room surrounded by his security staff, The Hague, 1969

My mother on her eighty-fifth birthday, surrounded by family, Groote Schuur Hospital heart transplant recipients and their wives. Clockwise from back left: Mrs Smith, Mr Petrus Smith (our third recipient), me, Mrs Washkansky (widow of the first recipient, Louis), Dr Philip Blaiberg (our second recipient), Mrs Blaiberg, my elder daughter Naudéne, my younger daughter Marie, my mother, Inez, and my son Adam

Chief Mangosuthu Buthelezi with Inez and me after he and I were named
Newsmakers of the Year in 1973 by the South African Society of Journalists

Addressing university students in the politically turbulent 1970s

Inez and me in Venice, 1977, during a break from the medical conference I was attending

Surrounded by happy, healthy youngsters after I had operated on them in Bucharest, Romania, in the late 1970s. The cherubic-looking child in the centre was named Marius. The ever-present Professor Dr Pop da Popa is standing on the right

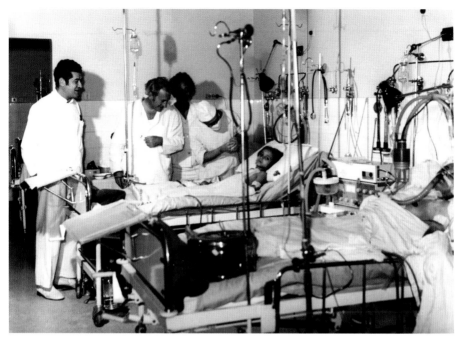

In the intensive care unit after a successful operation, surrounded by more medical staff than there were patients, Bucharest, *c.* 1977. Prof. Pop da Popa is on my right, looking on

A cartoon by Fred Mouton that appeared in *Rapport* in April 1980. Translated, the words attributed to me read, 'Roll them in, Van [Van Zyl Slabbert, then leader of the Progressive Federal Party]. If we transplant a million hearts, we'll rule the country!'

A cartoon published in February 1981 after my maiden speech as a member of parliament, which focused on environmental affairs and the necessity to legislate against the pollution of the sea

Examining a young Mauritian girl in the early 1980s

equipment, Alistair did the same with the pump technicians, and Charl and myself went into the wards to see the patients that had been admitted for surgery. They certainly expected us to work thirty-six hours a day, for there were at least sixty to eighty possible cases.

To the hospital staff's disappointment, I selected only one patient for surgery the next day. It was an uncomplicated closure of an ASD in a young boy with another important, non-medical indication: his name was Marius. We also started preliminary selection of other patients for the next few days.

That evening, the four of us met to discuss what we had found and what our chances were for a successful, up-to-standard first two weeks. I was not prepared to risk unnecessarily the lives of the patients we were operating on. If this became the case, we would swallow our pride and return home immediately.

Anaesthesia, especially in cardiac surgery, was of the utmost importance. I was extremely fortunate to have the best cardiac surgery anaesthetist in South Africa with me, and Ozzie Ozinsky's report on the hospital's resources was encouraging. Although many of the drugs, monitoring devices and other modern equipment that we took for granted were not available, he was confident about his role. Ozzie was always a very gentle, unflappable person, but this hid his steel-like determination, great experience and outstanding ability. What a valuable contribution he made.

Alistair's report, however, was not as favourable. We had brought enough disposable material for their first few cases – oxygenators and tubing, and the clinic's pump was a modern Sarns type, so there was no problem there. But Alistair, with his gentle, near-apologetic voice, warned me that we would have to be very careful, as he had a suspicion that the medical staff reused their oxygenators to save money. They were apparently washed and then sterilised before reuse. In spite of these sterilisation attempts, however, there was always risk of infection from other patients' blood. This suspicion was never proved, but it could explain the clinic's very high mortality rate, even for conditions such as ASD. During my stay, I never accused the staff of this murderous deed, but repeatedly told them of the dangers involved in this money-saving procedure.

We were ready, but we were too confident – little did I know what was waiting for us. We had arranged that Ozzie would start the anaesthetic with the help of Dr Dora Petrila and their other anaesthetists, Alistair would prepare the heart–lung machine, and two of their senior surgeons would open the chest.

I went into the scrub room and scrubbed my arms, hands and nails for eight minutes. A nurse was in attendance to help gown and glove me. The gloves were not the usual thin, disposable plastic gloves but thick ones that must have been sterilised many times after previous usage. They had six or more patches, which had been used to close up the holes made during previous operations. They reminded me of the bicycle tyre tubes that we patched many times when we were young.

When I walked into the operating room, the procedure was already well on its way, but I had to fight my way through a crowd of staff and onlookers, attempting with difficulty to remain sterilised. There must have been five anaesthetists helping Ozzie, who, when I spoke to him, just rolled his eyes up to the heavens. Alistair was also surrounded by a horde of helpers. There were at least three scrub nurses and then the onlookers as well. I could not believe that so little attention was being paid to ensuring sterilisation.

The next thing that hit me was the unbearable heat. There were no windows and the theatre was heated. There was no way they could turn the heat down. I had to operate in this sauna, my head and face covered with a cap and mask, my hands gloved and the rest of my body draped in a gown.

One of the nurses was specially assigned to mop the perspiration from my brow every few minutes. This was necessary to prevent it from dripping into the wound of the patient. At the end of the operation I could have poured a cupful of sweat out of my rubber boots. I lost quite a bit of weight in the process!

Everything went smoothly: the patient was cannulated – which involved inserting plastic tubing into the heart's main arteries and veins, thereby providing blood supply to and from the heart–lung machine – and put on bypass. When the heart was emptied of blood, however, air was sucked into one venous cannula and an airlock resulted. Given this situation, it was virtually impossible for Alistair to maintain an adequate bypass. This was not a new experience for me. All I had to do was to tie a ligature tightly around the cannula where it entered the atrium to prevent the air from being sucked in.

'Tie,' I said to the scrub nurse, asking her for the ligature that I needed. At that, one of my Romanian assistants grabbed a large pair of scissors and cut the offending cannula in two. I was so startled that for a few seconds I couldn't respond. Due to one cannula still being in the heart, a sort of bypass was still maintained. I calmly asked for another cannula, which they fortunately had, removed the offending cannula from the atrium and replaced it with the new one.

With the patient now 'recannulated' and connected to the heart–lung machine, we were again on full bypass within a few minutes. We were able to close the hole in the septum and complete the operation. Soon we were off bypass and Ozzie reported a stable patient. The latter was then sent to the ICU and made an uncomplicated recovery. But I had learnt my lesson. It was very difficult – if not impossible – to operate in a foreign language. My assistants and the nurses hardly understood a single word of my English instructions.

Why did the assistant cut the cannula in two? Because the word *tie*, which I had used in respect to the ligature, sounded just like a Romanian word meaning *cut*. He had simply carried out my instruction with good intentions. This could, however, have yielded catastrophic results.

Another problem was accessing the appropriate instruments for the operations I was performing. The theatre nurse helping me was very keen and efficient, but she too didn't understand a single word of English. When asking for a scalpel, forceps would be slapped into my hand and then, after a few more requests and translations from all around, the scalpel would finally arrive. By this stage I would have refused the forceps, needle holder and a variety of other unwanted but eagerly offered instruments. These delays didn't help my already impatient nature. We soon arranged for a doctor or nurse with a good working knowledge of English to position him- or herself next to Ozzie. This helped, but there was still the inevitable delay, solved at times by grabbing the needed instrument off the tray myself.

I quickly discovered that the instruments were not of the standard I required. The needle holders didn't grip the needles firmly, the scissors were blunt and many were better suited to a butcher's shop than an operating theatre. There was one particular pair of scissors I will never forget. They were too large for cardiac surgery and too heavy for me to handle. When they appeared in my hand, I refused them. Soon they were in my hand again. I then passed them over the anaesthetic screen to the interpreter. After five minutes, they were passed back to me. I finally got rid of them by dropping the offending scissors at my feet and firmly standing on them.

When I made my first visit to the ICU immediately after the first operation, I realised that my problems were not yet over. There were hordes of nurses, residents and unknowns running in different directions and without any evident purpose. Their monitoring equipment was totally inadequate to cope with the demands of modern cardiac surgery. Fortunately, my first patient was stable and gave no problems. I knew we were in trouble, however, and that to achieve favourable results I would need more, if not better, equipment.

The first thing I did was to select one doctor – a qualified anaesthetist – to take permanent care of the ICU. This was highly beneficial to me, as I then had to give orders to only one person and, after a few days, he could gain enough experience to fulfil his responsibilities to us adequately. His name was Emil and he proved to be an excellent choice. I demanded that he stay on duty twenty-four hours a day for the first seven days. To this, he readily agreed.

The second thing I did was to demand more and better equipment. This, I was told, would be impossible, so I gave them my ultimatum: I wanted to see the minister of health, otherwise no further surgery would be performed, and I would return home to tell the world what was going on in Romania! After many arguments, they agreed to try to secure an appointment with the minister the next day. Somewhere, enough pressure was applied and I saw him after the following day's surgery.

Accompanied by Pop da Popa and Daniel, I was taken to his ministry and, with much bowing and saluting by security guards, ushered into a room with a long table. The minister in question was well represented by an entourage of dour-looking officials. A secretary took notes, but I was later told that somewhere a tape recorder had been switched on.

I must confess that the minister was very kind and understanding, and he explained his problems to me, including a lack of money, the prevalence of infectious diseases such as tuberculosis, demanding staff, poor facilities and shortages of drugs – to mention but a few. I had heard this all before back home – there was always enough money for war-making, but never enough for health-making. I assured him that his problems were real and ended our conversation by curtly informing him that the next time one of the mothers of a child in Romania with an operable condition came to me, I would send her to him so that he, and not I, could tell her that her child would die because there was not enough money available to treat him or her.

He had no answer, but we left on favourable terms, and after this meeting there was an honest attempt made to improve the equipment and standards.

* * *

Shortly afterwards, we were hit with a totally unexpected situation. Our arrival in Romania and our reasons for being there were reported in the local news media, picked up overseas and relayed back to South Africa: a South African team was working in communist Romania. In South Africa, this was difficult to comprehend.

We were blissfully unaware of the commotion that this caused in South Africa. The MEC of Hospitals, Groote Schuur Hospital's superintendent and Chris were asked by the press to provide a statement about our visit to Romania. They all had one thing in common: they had absolutely no knowledge of our trip.

In Cape Town, the Director for Hospital Services and Groote Schuur's superintendent publically threatened that they would 'deal with me' on my return. Chris also went public and stated that he did not approve of us working in Romania. According to him, we would achieve poor results and it would have been better to have brought their doctors to South Africa for training and their patients for treatment.

Although we were oblivious to all this publicity and controversy, for me it had a bright side. A reporter from *Die Burger*, the Nationalist government's mouthpiece, phoned me from Bucharest's airport. He had thought he could achieve a scoop and had arrived in Romania without a visa, having flown from South Africa via London. Of course, the authorities didn't allow him into the country, but he was given permission to get in touch with me.

He pleaded with me, asking me to use my influence to get him into the country. This kind of influence I did not have and, even if I had, I certainly would not have helped him. I had many scores to settle with *Die Burger*, both politically and for the bad publicity they often gave me. Within a few hours, the reporter was back in London.

I was informed that the communist authorities were far from happy about the publicity we had created. There was nothing they could do, though, as I was there only because President Ceauşescu had given his personal permission. He was apparently kept regularly informed of what we did inside, as well as outside, the hospital. I was later told that our rooms had been bugged and that we were kept under twenty-four-hour surveillance. How true this is, I've never found out. We were always warned to be careful of what we said while in conversation with our friends. Even at dinners, it was joked that there might be a bug in the flowers on the table. The fear and intimidation of the Romanian people by the authorities was frightening. The only time we could speak freely was when in the privacy of a car.

But all this passed us by. We had enough trouble of our own in the hospital, theatre and ICU. We had started by operating on one patient a day, but now stepped it up to two and began to take on more complicated cases. Selecting cases took a new twist. Romania's blood transfusion service was very poor. Since we needed approximately four units for each patient, the blood transfusion service found it impossible – unbelievable as it may sound – to provide enough blood for two patients unless they were from the same blood group. We could therefore operate on only two (sometimes more) patients a day provided that their blood groups matched.

Each day we would very carefully choose the patients we would operate on the following day. A source of great irritation to me, however, was that on arriving at the hospital the next morning, two different cases would, to my utter surprise, appear on the operating table. When I took strong exception to this, I was informed that the hospital staff could not find sufficient quantities of compatible blood for those patients that I had selected the previous day. I was powerless to do anything about this situation.

But by now I had established a few close friends and it didn't take me long to discover what I had suspected. Among the waiting patients were those who had high positions, or connections and influence, within the communist elite or army. It soon became evident that what Daniel had told me during my first trip was true – in communist countries everyone is equal, some just more so than others.

As the first week progressed, I came under increasing pressure. Not only was every case a fight for the patients' survival – protecting them against the doctors, nurses and stupidity – but wherever I went I was subjected to begging from patients, relatives and strangers to operate on a particular person. On ward rounds, I could see their pleading faces and then the disappointment when they failed to make the list for the next day. Later, this would become desperation as they realised that their chances of treatment were diminishing as my time in their country was drawing to a close.

There was one boy who, every morning, would sit on the floor at the lift door as I went up to theatre. He begged for help and, when I came down, he would still be sitting there pleading. One adult female even fell to the floor at my feet and started kissing my shoes. As their desperate plight increased, so my state of mind deteriorated. I developed skin rashes on my hands and arms, which I scratched until they bled. I could not sleep. This hardly improved my temper, and I became impossible to work with and was very hard on the doctors and medical staff. Soon I had earned myself a nickname – *Dracula* (meaning *Devil*). Some of my friends in South Africa might think that this is an appropriate nickname for me – even today!

Most of the patients I have long forgotten, but a few I can remember clearly. One was a beautiful black-haired, blue-eyed twenty-one-year-old female student. She had severe aortic incompetence and was in urgent need of an aortic valve replacement. The night before the operation, Alistair came to me and said that I should make sure that there were sufficient aortic valves available. I discovered that there were no valves in the hospital. How they could have allowed me to go ahead with the operation without a valve is impossible to fathom.

Fortunately we had connections (so to speak) in Denmark, and a few days later aortic valves became available. We operated on her and the initial result was good, but on the third post-operative night, the young woman developed a temperature that soon climbed alarmingly to over 40 °C. Despite all attempts to help her, she died the next morning. I was destroyed.

She had obviously had a fulminating septicaemia, which often results in fatal complications.[5] The cause of this severe septicaemia is infected blood. The Romanian blood transfusion system could not even ensure that our patients were given sterile blood. After this unfortunate event, I became so obsessed with caring for our patients that I stayed in the hospital twenty-four hours a day. They gave me a room and I operated, ate and slept there at all times. I had many experiences during this time – too many to discuss in detail – but I shall relate one.

After seven days with very little rest, but with all the post-operative patients of the week stable and well on the road to recovery, I left the hospital. Emil, who had been on duty for many days, was also allowed some time off. When I walked into the ICU the next morning, there was a group of total strangers on duty – I had never seen one of them before. One of our patients who had been well the previous night was now in an extremely poor condition – poor circulation, low blood pressure and a rapid pulse. It took no genius to establish the cause: after a few seconds, I discovered that the drip she required was not running into her vein – it had become disconnected. A wet sheet and mattress indicated where the life-supporting drugs had ended up.

I became a screaming madman and demanded to know who was in charge. When a short middle-aged gentleman stepped forward, I told him, among other things, that if the patient had died I would have thrown him out the window of the ICU, which was a few floors up. This he was not prepared to take. 'Do you know who you are speaking to?' he remonstrated indignantly. 'I am the father of anaesthesia in Romania.' My answer, I suspect, did not endear myself to him any further. 'You have one more contribution to make,' I said. 'Resign immediately.' It is not surprising that I never saw this 'father of anaesthesia' again. Just as well, for his negligence in failing to notice the disconnected drip that night could have cost a patient's life.

Having emerged from my self-imposed quarantine in the hospital, I was obliged to enter the social frenzy again. There were dinners at night, where I met and immediately disliked all the 'higher-ups' of communist society, who lived, ate and drank well. Nothing was spared.

But with dear friends such as Daniel and Anca Constantinescu, Dora Petrila, and their relatives and friends, I met the most wonderful, warm and brave people. They despised the system and we had numerous long discussions about their oppression, lack of freedom and the prevalence of long queues for basic foodstuffs such as meat, fruit and cheese. The communist domination and doctrine had made them not only poor with regard to possessions, but poor in hope and spirit. With these people I developed enduring friendships and they were a great inspiration to me, even during my darkest moments.

On the Sunday morning after my meeting with Romania's 'father of anaesthesia', my medical team and I had to attend a function. We had received an invitation by the mayor of Bucharest to go to a lunch that had been arranged in our honour. After completing my rounds, we set off into the country, taken by car to Snagov. It was beautiful countryside far away from drab, boring Bucharest. The house we went to was situated on a large estate, well forested and very spacious. It must have belonged to aristocrats or royalty in days gone by.

The reception room was large and heated. The furniture, chandeliers and paintings were all antiques and I wondered from whom the communists had stolen them, lock, stock and barrel. Our team was introduced to men in well-tailored suits and women beautifully dressed in long, flowing dresses. We were offered the customary *tuică* and wine, followed by plates and plates of food. French champagne and caviar were freely available – all this on a Sunday morning!

Tired to the point of exhaustion and with no food in my stomach, the alcohol and the warmth of the room soon took effect. Music was produced by a band and the gathering started dancing around a tiled heater that was placed right in the middle of the room. I felt an uncontrollable need to sleep: the guest of honour lay himself down on the carpet next to the heater and fell into a deep slumber. While the music played and the talking and laughter increased in volume, I slept right through the party that had been held in my honour.

I was later told that the other guests were not too impressed by my manners. I agreed with them, but this did not worry me in the slightest. I was there to operate on their patients, not to impress the people who were responsible for the inadequate hospital facilities and the unnecessary suffering and deaths of their people.

The next day, we started our last week in Bucharest. We were now becoming a more efficient team and our Romanian colleagues were not only supportive but showed admiration for our work. They could see the favourable results that were being achieved, even with an increasing number of complicated cases – with survival outcomes – that they had never dared to operate on at the Fundeni clinic. We even operated on young children.

Years later, well after we had left this country, I was told that many of our patients developed infective hepatitis. Back home, blood was used in single units from one donor. But in Romania and many other countries in the world at that time, blood was pooled by blood type and the patient received blood from multiple donors. This greatly increased the risk of contracting diseases, especially hepatitis. This increased risk was amplified by the fact that, unlike in South Africa, where blood was donated without financial compensation, in Romania and other countries donors were paid for their blood. This became a great incentive for drug addicts and criminals to donate their blood, but one that increased the risk of infected blood and other associated complications.

* * *

Having completed our first two weeks under trying conditions, with failures but also with very good results, our team was satisfied that we had provided a good service to our patients, and were very grateful for this opportunity.

Ozzie had made a great impression on everybody. With his unflappable, quiet confidence, his contribution as a teacher to the anaesthetists and ICU staff was tremendous. I was very grateful to him. Alistair Hope was another quiet man, but a master pump technician – he never failed to run a perfect bypass. He was also invaluable in a totally non-technical sphere. He regularly associated with the non-doctor staff – technicians and nurses – and he picked up invaluable inside information from them.

This was of great help to me because it was sourced from some of the local doctors, who would not have divulged to me at that stage. So, in a sense, I also had a spy.

Being close friends with a few of the Romanian hospital staff, I would later learn a lot about the head of their cardiac unit, Professor Pop da Popa. Although a charming, friendly and hospitable man, I soon learnt that, as a member of the Communist Party, he had been specially picked over the heads of others that were perhaps more competent than he was. Many held him – rightly or wrongly – responsible for the poor facilities and, worse still, for the hospital's inadequate results.

But we achieved another very important success – the respect and support of the majority of the staff, who, at the beginning of our visit, had been suspicious of us and not too friendly. This proved invaluable to us later.

On the Saturday morning, our team of four were again seated in a rattling, vibrating Tupolev, this time heading to Oradea for a weekend at a hot-water spa in Felix. We were apprehensive on our flight because, according to our friends, the aircraft in which we were travelling had a reputation for falling out of the sky. I had, of course, travelled in this type of aircraft before, but our friends' prior warnings made us feel somewhat edgy that day.

Fortunately, we had a safe journey. The pilot welcomed us personally over the intercom and thanked us for what we were doing, while the flight attendants did everything possible to make our journey a pleasant one. We were given royal treatment in a communist country. This did not take away the fact that the engines were extremely noisy, the huge plane shook and vibrated excessively and the seats were extremely uncomfortable.

After arriving in Oradea, we were welcomed by the usual row of officials and taken in black Dacias to a large church. By now, I knew the significance of this specific vehicle. Built under licence of Renault, the Dacia was virtually the only make of car in Romania, and it was most commonly grey in colour. There were a few black ones, but these had special privileges. They had right of way, were waved through roadblocks and at petrol stations they had a special pump and could get petrol – as much as was needed – immediately. Not for them the long wait in mile-long queues, sometimes for hours or even days. Such were the perks of the high-ranking party members and other officials. So much for everyone being equal 'comrades'!

We were driven to a large Orthodox church and entertained for an hour by a famous organist on the biggest organ in Romania. Bach, Handel, Mozart and Romanian works that we had never heard before filled the church. It was magic! But why the church-organ recital? Because these wonderful, caring people had read somewhere that my mother used to play the organ in my father's church. This was their way of showing their appreciation to me.

After a short while, we arrived at the hot-water spa in Felix. There were seven large hotels, all with hundreds of rooms. We were amazed by their size. Here, the Romanians could come, at basically no cost, to soothe their aches and pains and to try to forget the hardships they had to endure daily. They were great believers in the remedial benefits of these spas. Each hotel was built in a square with a large indoor swimming pool with steaming-hot thermal water built in the centre. There was always a small passage that led through the wall outside, which allowed one to swim into an outdoor pool filled with even hotter water.

As it was winter, the outside pools were surrounded by snow. To us, it was a great novelty to leave the steaming water, roll in the snow and, when we started feeling the cold, to jump back in. One could not stay in the hot water for too long, and soon we were led into cubicles where we were given massages. It was wonderfully relaxing and I could feel all the tension of the previous two weeks oozing out of my body.

I must confess that when the masseur's probing fingers massaged my upper leg and groin, a very delicate, 'special' sensation was produced. As we had been away from home for two weeks, I considered myself lucky that it was not a female massaging me. I was attended to instead by a blind man who must have been the best masseur in Romania.

After a very pleasant thirty minutes, and feeling at peace with the world, I left the cubicle to get dressed. There, I found Charl Frank, who was already dressed and drinking a cold beer. I told him about my experience and that I was very glad that my masseur was a male. He told me that his had been a female. 'How did you cope when she came to your groin?' I asked. He answered that he had concentrated on the saddest moment of his life – his grandmother's funeral!

That night, we attended a great reception with Romanian music, dancing and food. The dancers were all in folk-dress and a group of four gypsies played and sang their sad music using instruments we had never seen or heard before, in particular the Russian harp. The music was beautiful and haunting. Wine flowed freely and we mixed with doctors from Russia and Hungary who had come to meet us and listen to my talk the next morning. All this was new and exciting and we had a wonderful day forgetting, for a few hours, about sick and dying patients begging for life, distraught and demanding relatives, and the severity and austerity of an unjust regime.

* * *

That Sunday we set off by car to Tirgu Mureş in Transylvania, where we were to spend our final week in Romania with Dr Radu Deac and his team. I had met Radu when he had come to watch us operate in Bucharest, and interacted with him during discussions about our forthcoming visit to his unit. Radu spoke English very well, having completed much of his training in England, and he impressed me greatly.

We were due to begin work with Radu Deac and his team the following day, but we first had to stop at a town called Cluj-Napoca. My hosts had organised a meeting for me and I was also invited to an opera. At the meeting, which was attended by doctors and nurses, a professor – a delightful man – introduced me in the now-familiar communist fashion as Professor Docent Doctor Comrade Marius Barnard. When he used the word *Comrade*, he immediately recognised his mistake and, with laughter from the audience, he repeated the title but left out the *Comrade* part!

I was very tired and wanted to leave as soon as possible, but my hosts were insistent that I attend the opera. My favourite opera, Puccini's *La Bohème*, was being performed. The first act has the famous aria 'Your tiny hand is frozen'. During his performance, the tenor swept his arms wide and knocked over a bottle of wine from a nearby table. I have to say that he would have been a tremendous cricketer, because he managed, without changing a single word in the song, to catch the bottle before it reached the ground and place it back on the table, as if this were a rehearsed part of the act. It was an excellent performance, but I had to leave early so missed the final act, where the obese, usually buxom heroine dies of tuberculosis.

On our way back to Tirgu Mureş, we were accompanied by a very high official in their Department of Health – another Dr Popa. Once in the car, the Romanians complained bitterly about the lack of food, oppression of speech and other related issues in Romania. The official in the back seat responded after a while with something significant that I think applies to South Africa today. 'My country's bread might be bad,' he said, 'but it's my country's bread.' The lesson he was trying to convey is that although the situation might not be to one's liking, one has to do something about it rather than just complain.

We went straight to the hospital, where we met Dr Deac and his team.

Here, to our great relief, we found things to be much better than we had experienced at the Fundeni clinic. The patients were well investigated and Radu ran an excellent unit with dedicated and well-trained doctors and staff. We went to bed that night tired but at ease.

The next morning, we were again taken to the hospital. Radu and his team were already operating and preparing the patient for bypass. Once scrubbed, gowned and gloved, I entered the operating theatre. I will never forget my first sight of Radu, his assistants, Ozzie Ozinsky and Alistair Hope. They were all dressed in light-blue gowns and were framed by a large window, through which I could make out in the distance a field with trees covered by a thick blanket of snow – magic. It was like operating in fairyland; all we needed was Father Christmas and 'Jingle Bells'!

The first case we attended to with Radu was a valve replacement. All went smoothly and the patient did very well. The ICU had a sufficient number of monitors and the conduct of the staff was excellent.

Much later, during my second or third visit to Romania, Radu told me that when he first saw me in Bucharest and witnessed my insistence for more equipment, he and his staff had phoned around to all the nearby hospitals and commandeered all of their available equipment.

Radu would not allow more than one case a day and we did a few tetralogies of Fallot and an ASD closure. I recall that we had only one failure – a high-risk aortic valve replacement. All too soon, the week was over.

We had the usual dinners and social contact at night but all were very subdued. I think that this was because Radu sensed my aversion to communist officials and spared me that ordeal. The following Sunday we travelled by car through the beautiful snow-covered and quaint Eastern European cities of Transylvania, Braşov and Sibiu, and then on to grey, depressing Bucharest. The next morning, we were on our way back to Cape Town.

I will always be indebted to Ozzie, Alistair and Charl, not only for their professional skill and for never letting me down, but also for their moral support and encouragement under the most demanding of circumstances.

* * *

Our visit to Bucharest made a significant impression on the Fundeni clinic's doctors and medical staff. During 1977, there had been a disastrous earthquake. The country had been dismantled, its national economy in crisis. The Fundeni clinic looked terribly run-down, with large cracks in the walls.

The anaesthetist, Dora Petrila, later related the sight of our team arriving at Otopeni Airport as being 'four tall and elegant gentlemen, good-looking, well-dressed, casual, and smiling. It was the smell of the free, uninhibited and undefeated spirit of man, like Prometheus bringing fire to the earth people.' She went on to praise our equipment, devices, disposables and even our operating gowns, coloured overshoes and face masks. She also lamented the inadequacy of the hospital's electricity and its water supplies. This had caused numerous problems during surgery to which we were not accustomed in South Africa. To the medical staff at the Fundeni clinic, our presence, resources and skills threw into stark relief the deficiencies of the 'Ceaușescu age', which was characterised by a lack of everything, from basic necessities to luxuries.

But Dora recognised that over this period, which would be extended later in Romania, we 'brought and taught brilliant surgical techniques, the best habits of anaesthesia, the best ideas in the diagnosis of heart diseases' and that we 'inspired the strong desire to transform the Romanian school of surgery into a modern one'.

What was important was that, over and above the capabilities and medical training we provided, we were able to shine a light of hope in the darkness created by Ceaușescu's communist regime. The whole scene was depressing, dark and grey, and this significantly influenced the moods of the locals during this period. I once remarked, 'You Romanians, you never smile. You dress yourself in grey and black. Where are the colours, for God's sake? I can't see colours in your streets.'

We knew that we were being watched by the regime from the time we set foot in the country, and we remained uncomfortable at all times during our stay. We made sure that we never gave offence. To make matters worse, our trip had not been sanctioned by the South African Nationalist government either, so it was very much a case of escaping from one security apparatus to enter another, both expounding radically differing ideologies but sharing the common attributes of oppression and wickedness.

Despite this difficult situation, we pursued our objectives vigorously, not only to provide medical care to the desperate and guidance to the country's medical fraternity, but because, from a humanitarian perspective, it was the right thing to do.

* * *

On my arrival back in South Africa, Inez warned me that trouble awaited me at Groote Schuur Hospital. While we were in Romania, our visit had been frowned upon by our political masters and the head of my department. Chris went very public about my sins and I didn't have to wait long for the acrimony to present itself.

Hardly had I finished my first operation when I received the letter to which I was now well accustomed. It was hand delivered, and I had to sign for receipt of it. It summoned me to the hospital's superintendent the next day. I must admit that I was worried. My relationship with the hospital authorities and Chris was at rock-bottom, and I was certain that my days at Groote Schuur Hospital were numbered. I didn't think I had done anything wrong: I had taken official leave and what I had done was in my own free time. I had had no obligation to tell them where I was going. It was really their problem, not mine.

My meeting with the hospital's superintendent the next morning was short and to the point. After generalities, I was asked why I had not sought permission to go to Romania. I pointed out that there was no need to ask; if I had and had been refused, I would still have gone. It was at this stage in the meeting that all my sins of the previous few years were pointed out to me.[6]

I told the superintendant quite candidly how I felt, conceded that I was still an employee of the hospital (and the province) and that they could do with me as they saw fit, but that I was my own man and would in the future do just what I wanted to do. Our conversation came to an abrupt end.

Although he publicly criticised me in the press for this visit, Chris gave me the silent treatment and never referred to it. But I did notice that he reduced the number of operations that I had normally been allowed to do. As I was still very tired from my efforts abroad, however, he unknowingly did me a favour. Soon, Chris was away on his overseas trips again and I was once again left in charge of the cardiac unit. This enabled me to perform the same number of operations as before. My relationship with Chris, however, was coming to a crossroads.

I started giving interviews about why I had gone to Romania and what I had done there. I appeared on a local television chat show with the well-known writer P.G. du Plessis. Chris went public again, on this occasion criticising me and suggesting that operating in a foreign country would contribute to the lowering of standards there and result in unnecessarily high mortalities. This, of course, was entirely the opposite of what was actually occurring in Romania.

Because this spat was taking place in the public domain, I, of course, was compelled to defend myself. I stated that, if asked to go to Romania again, I would, and that nothing would stop me. Chris and I now enjoyed a no-greet, no-speak relationship, and my only relief from this unpleasantness was when Chris was overseas. But I was already planning a follow-up trip to the Fundeni clinic and Tirgu Mureş.

It had become a passion of mine to help Romanian patients, especially those with no hope of surgery, by teaching their doctors and staff how to treat successfully the hundreds of children and adults with operable heart lesions.

For me to be able to operate effectively on infants in Romania, I needed an experienced paediatric cardiologist to assist me. At the Red Cross Hospital, we had just such a person in Dr Hymie Joffe. I needed an equally experienced theatre nurse and obtained the services of one of the best, Sister Pittie Rautenbach. It took both of them only a few seconds to accept my invitation.

Heinz Kretzchmar again willingly supplied instruments and disposable gloves, tubes and oxygenators. But we still needed money for our air tickets! Fortunately, I was friendly with a German industrialist who was familiar with my work in Romania. Due to a life-threatening lung condition, he had actually come to South Africa on a previous occasion to see Rodney Hewitson and me. When I asked him for help, he was very generous and that problem was settled.

* * *

In spite of my deteriorating relationship with Chris, my response when he and his second wife, Barbara, were involved in a serious car accident proved that blood is thicker than water – and that I am my brother's keeper.

Chris and Barbara were married with two young sons when they went out for dinner one night in Sea Point. What happened next has never been clarified, but what is very clear is that, while crossing Main Road, they were knocked down by a passing truck and both Chris and Barbara sustained serious injuries. They were immediately transferred to Groote Schuur Hospital, where they were admitted. Chris had the more severe injuries, with suspected damage to one of his kidneys. Barbara suffered a fracture of her shoulder blade. It was not too serious, but very painful.

I was informed of the incident by telephone and immediately rushed to the hospital. When I arrived in the ward, Chris was surrounded by a scrum of medical personnel, what I call a *surge of surgeons*. Perhaps the word *vultures* would be a more apt description, as every surgeon was after my brother's flesh. When I saw the glint in the eyes of the more senior surgeons surrounding

Chris, I realised that his kidney was in serious danger of being claimed as a vital insert into the curriculum vitae of one of the surgeons.

It has always amazed me how doctors are so very keen to treat those whom they perceive to be important patients. Surgeons, in particular, delight in claiming that they have operated on VIPs. President Mandela, for example, has had his fair share of urologists, who have treated him from Robben Island to Houghton.

I was, of course, very junior at the time, but decided to be my brother's keeper – or, better still, the protector of his kidney. I demanded a 'wait and see' approach and said that I would be doing the 'wait and see'.

Chris had already had an intravenous pyelogram (IVP) that showed swelling of his kidney but no definite indications of a tear or rupture.[7] He had blood in his urine, and the most likely diagnosis was that he had severe bruising only. As it was well past midnight, I requested an easy chair and seated myself opposite Chris's bed. Slowly the group of very disappointed surgeons trooped out of the ward, leaving Chris in my care, but not before I'd received their strict instructions that, if there were signs of increased bleeding from the kidney, I was to get the theatre prepared and call them.

I spent the whole night with Chris. I do not think that he knew I was there, as he was heavily sedated, but not heavily enough to prevent him from listening to his ECG. When you fall asleep, your pulse rate slows and, as Chris heard his pulse rate drop, he immediately woke up. With a dazed expression, he watched the ECG intently. I am sure that as the rate dropped he thought he might be dying.

The night passed very slowly, as all nights do when one is on duty. I did not sleep, as I also observed Barbara, who was very uncomfortable and needed regular sedation. And then, of course, there was the press, who, as was their wont, tried to get a story by all means, fair or foul.

The next morning, a string of disappointed surgeons had to agree with me that Chris was stable, and that there was no need to add him to the 'VIP' lists on their CVs. I remained concerned about Chris's condition and stayed with him the whole day. When I left on the second morning, Chris was well enough to protect himself.

Barbara showed her gratitude a few months later by giving me a new suit. Since my clothes were always of a rather poor quality, it was actually a very appropriate gift.

* * *

In May 1978, my team and I returned to Bucharest and the Fundeni clinic.
I was overwhelmed, as I now found the cardiac wards overflowing with
patients and couldn't imagine how they thought that I would be able to
operate on all of them. As a result, we agreed to operate on two, possibly
three, patients a day.

Our schedule consisted of spending one week at the Fundeni clinic and
one week at the Tirgu Mureş hospital, and then repeating this process. I was
prepared for the week-long stresses of the Fundeni, but needed the sanity of
Radu Deac and his team in Tirgu Mureş to recuperate from the Fundeni.

We were able to perform more ASDs, pulmonary stenoses, and tetralogies
of Fallot on young children because, with Hymie Joffe in support, we had
expert cardiological back-up and confidence in each diagnosis. It was hard
work, but very rewarding.

I had a new experience at the Fundeni. During my first week at the
Fundeni, the president of Romania, Nicolae Ceauşescu, was attending a
state visit to England, which included a visit to the queen. Professor Pop da
Popa, with whom my professional relationship was never very favourable,
accompanied him as his physician and he put me in charge of the unit. So,
for one week I was appointed head of the cardiac unit at the Fundeni clinic.
I must admit that we did not miss him very much and, on most days, we
were able to perform three operations.

Pittie Rautenbach was also invaluable. Not only did she greatly help the
theatre nurses, but my instruments were now placed in my hand without a
round of interpretation. I also had time to make friends and gain their confidence. What a warm, generous and hospitable people these Romanians
were. Their love and devotion, and the sacrifices that they were prepared to
make for their families, and in particular their children, were a great lesson
to me. In spite of their hardships, long queues and lack of money and food,
they had a wicked sense of humour and shared many jokes with me about
their political system.

One joke I really enjoyed was about a man wanting to buy meat. He had
to stand in an hours-long queue. When he eventually reached the counter,
he looked up and saw no meat. 'Is there no meat?' he asked. 'No,' said the
man behind the counter, 'this is not the queue for no meat; the queue for no
meat is next door. This is the queue for no cheese.'

Another was of an old lady dressed in the usual black dress, standing
looking at a photograph through a shop window. The old lady was ordered
by a security officer to move on, but she curtly stated that she was looking

at a photograph. 'Do you not know who it is?' asked the security guard. She conceded that she didn't. 'It is Stalin,' responded the guard.

'Who is Stalin?' she enquired.

'He is the man who saved us from the dreadful Germans.'

She crossed herself and responded, 'Please can he not save us from the Russians too?'

I spent many evenings at my working colleagues' small flats, in small rooms and kitchens. I learnt a lot about Romanians, what communism had done to them and their bitter hatred for Ceauşescu and his fellow oppressors. That both he and his wife, Helena, would eventually be executed came as no surprise to me. It was what they deserved. Before entering Romania I had some vague leanings toward the teachings of Lenin, but my subsequent experiences in this country, and later those in Poland, cured that.

During our second working visit to Romania, we made a great contribution and performed many successful operations, but we had a few unfortunate deaths too. We made good friends and influenced the future lives of many people. A few of the doctors saw what our western democracy offered and the good results that were achievable. Many decided that they could no longer live and work under this rigid regime, where people had no future unless they were politically connected. Even then, it was a poor future. They started planning and plotting to leave Romania for the West. From that visit on, both Daniel and Martin Constantinescu (who was no relation to Daniel and Anca Constantinescu) decided to find their futures in the United States.

A year later, Daniel brought a well-connected patient for us to operate on in Cape Town. He saw how we worked at Groote Schuur and the Red Cross, as well as how we lived and played. He could not believe that one could walk into a butcher shop and, without queuing, buy as much meat as one wanted. This provided him with a final incentive to leave Romania to settle in the United States. He and Anca were sincere, hard-working doctors with two young sons. They were soon to sacrifice everything to take their sons to a better place.

* * *

Back home in South Africa, my success in Romania and my unhappiness with the way Chris was running the cardiac unit at Groote Schuur Hospital was heading for a finale. Chris was caught between two worlds: he wanted to be in charge of the unit, with all its glory, but he also wanted to be overseas with all of *its* glory.

I was more than happy to allow him that, on condition that our unit continued to make progress. Unfortunately, he resented my position at Groote Schuur Hospital, where an increasing number of patients were now being referred to me. He insisted that all the patients were his and that he should decide who would operate on them. This, I thought, was unreasonable and, in most cases, I would arrange for their operations to take place while he was away. But when Chris returned, there would be hell to pay.

Another factor working against me was that I was now also receiving overseas recognition and stealing what he considered his, and his alone: publicity and glory. Rightly or wrongly, I came to the conclusion that Chris, with his attitude, was blocking the progress of the unit. We were getting nowhere. Although we had sufficient facilities and staff to double the number of cases we were doing easily, for some or other reason he blocked our initiatives. I was especially supported in this regard by Dr Joe de Nobrega. With sufficient numbers of staff, I was frustrated by the fact that I was only performing two operations per week and that a highly competent surgeon in the form of Joe did one, sometimes no operations a week. As a result, we could not improve our skills; they were, in fact, being wasted.

Joe was an excellent surgeon who had an intense interest in his patients. As a result of this unpleasant situation, we made an appointment to see Chris one fateful afternoon. We marched down from Groote Schuur Hospital to his office at the medical school to present to him what I thought was a reasonable proposal.

We told him that he could get all the honour as head of the unit and that he could travel as much as he wanted to. Furthermore, we would guarantee him that we would not only maintain the standard of work, but also increase the volume of operations. This was all we wanted. We had another condition, however, and I was blunt about it. I told Chris that he was now a hindrance, not a help, and that he should remove himself from running the unit. He could still get all the credit, but he should just get out of our way.

Thinking back, I must have been very naive or just plain crazy to think that Chris would meekly accept my proposal. To his credit, he didn't rant or rave although, in retrospect, I have to admit that he had every justification to do so. Not surprisingly, he rejected the proposal in no uncertain terms and showed us the door.

That day was the final nail in my coffin at Groote Schuur Hospital. My dream of taking over from Chris in the future was blown out, like Elton John's well-known song 'Candle in the Wind'. My vision of building a

world-class unit, one that would provide the paediatric cardiac surgery that
I loved, with sufficient facilities and staff to operate on hundreds of patients
from all over the world, particularly those from poor countries with no
cardiac surgery facilities, was now shattered.

Looking back, I think I was unfair to Chris and that I could have tried to
achieve my aims and objectives in a more tactful way. But the opportunity
was lost forever and my dream was never realised.

In Chris's second book, *The Second Life*, he refers to me only twice,
but relates this unpleasant confrontation and, strangely enough, concedes
that I was right and that he should have listened to me and accepted my
offer. To my surprise, he admits that after I left Groote Schuur Hospital the
standards at the unit dropped when he was away. He actually warned me
about the inclusion of this content before this book was published, stating
that he had praised me but adding that he was 'not sure if this was deserved'.

It is now too late for tears, but I still regret his decision. It could have
been so different. Instead, Chris fought back in a cool and calculated way to
destroy me. My operations became less frequent and he gave those patients
who he knew wanted me to other surgeons. His next step was to demote me
at the Red Cross Children's Hospital cardiac unit. He informed me that he
was now in charge and would make all the decisions at this hospital.

At the time, the *Cape Times* wrote a critical but amusing article on
Chris's obsession with publicity. I read it in the ward and had a good laugh
because I thought it was very funny. Somebody told him about this – I
think it was the ward secretary – and Chris didn't take kindly to how I had
reacted.

He proceeded to report me to the head of the Department of Surgery –
to this day, I still don't know for what – and took away my responsibilities
at Groote Schuur Hospital during his absences. He proceeded to put Joe de
Nobrega in charge of the unit, but he still allowed me to run the Red Cross
unit when he was away. This might sound generous of him, but there was
really no one else who could take over from him – or me, for that matter.

Chris wrote a letter to me on 31 August 1978, which reveals much about
the circumstances and his attitude in this regard:

Dear Marius,

I heard that you had a good laugh at the editorial which appeared in
the *Cape Times* yesterday, 30th August 1978, after I left the B10 office and
then you even showed it to other members of my staff to read.

I thought I would draw your attention to another editorial which appeared today in the hope this would provide you much material for another laugh.

As to your statement late in the day that I am jealous of you, I find this difficult to understand as you have excelled in the field of cardiac surgery only in projects that I have initiated. A claim I believe you cannot make of me. Even your Romanian experience was started by me. The first Romanian patient was referred to me and I operated on him successfully.

I was the first one to be invited to visit Romania and to offer them assistance by our team. By the way, I have never heard you give me this credit.

A few weeks ago I was quite amused to hear you say that Angelo and Ari are your two best friends overseas.

I would not at all be surprised if your next project would be Kenya. I believe you have already initiated this by asking the doctor who accompanied the last child from Kenya to ask Mr Charles Njonjo to invite you to Kenya.

I am deeply distressed to inform you that I find your behaviour unacceptable and have put up with it long enough. I have therefore decided that from now on you will be treated as any other member of the staff and will judge you solely on your merit.

During my absence for the next two weeks overseas, Dr de Nobreiga [*sic*] and Dr Alan Wolpowitz will look after Groote Schuur Hospital and I will appreciate it if you will look after the Red Cross.

I don't want any changes in the organisation of the Unit made during my absence.

I hope you will find these arrangements acceptable, if not you can discuss it with Prof J Louw, the Head of the Department of Surgery who I will inform about my decision.

My best wishes
Chris

As a postscript, I must point out that Angelo and Ari were about the only people I knew in Italy and Greece respectively.

My demotion during Chris's absences also had a ridiculous side. Joe was most uncomfortable and ill at ease with this situation and, in practical terms, he allowed me to run the unit. During our Saturday meetings at the cardiac clinic, where we'd discuss cases we had operated on and select cases for the following week's list, things went on as if nothing had happened. Professor Wally Beck and his team still regarded me as the most senior cardiac surgeon and I was, therefore, still obliged to make all the final decisions. This situation didn't last long. With no admission from Chris about his ill-directed actions, he restored me to my previous position at Groote Schuur Hospital, but continued to work me out of the Red Cross.

My relationship with Professor Louw and the hospital authorities reached an all-time low. I was quoted in the newspapers – for a change correctly – that the University of Cape Town, while professing liberal principles, condoned a hospital where apartheid was being practised. I based this statement on the fact that the university's professors at Groote Schuur always started their ward rounds on white patients and conducted the rounds in the blacks ward afterwards. Operations would take place on white patients first, and only then would blacks be operated on. Furthermore, surgery on black patients would often be assigned to junior staff.

I recommended that we should take screwdrivers and remove all the *Whites Only* and *Non-Whites Only* signs from the hospital's entrances and benches. I received no response from the university, but Professor Louw called me to his office and read me the riot act. The little man was apoplectic. How could I accuse him of practising apartheid?

I simply pointed out to him that he should look at the signs at the front entrance of the hospital. To emphasise that what I thought was correct, I stood my ground, but I cannot remember what else was said. I was told afterwards by a member of Louw's staff that, from that day onwards, many ward rounds started in the non-white ward, with coloureds and blacks often finding themselves first on the operating list. One victory to me!

At the Red Cross Children's Hospital, I had another clash with its superintendent. The youngest son, Adam, of the well-known singing duo Des and Dawn Lindberg had a congenital heart lesion. Chris was going to operate, but the surgery was scheduled for when he was overseas. The operation would either have to wait until his return or I would perform it. The Lindbergs said that they were more than happy for me to go ahead.

The Lindbergs had absolutely no colour prejudice and, during Adam's recovery, they visited the non-white ward and socialised with patients and family. The *Cape Times* picked up the story and a photographer took a photo of – horror of horrors – Adam and a coloured patient sitting together on a swing in the garden.

When the hospital's superintendent heard about this, he blew a fuse and phoned the *Cape Times*. He demanded in the strongest terms that the photograph should not be published. My subsequent clash with him was both vocal and abusive, but I lost the battle. This photograph was never published. Looking back on this incident of some thirty years ago and considering what has subsequently happened in our country, it is difficult to believe that such racial madness was part of my working conditions and that hospitals, including ours, condoned such practices.

* * *

My third working trip to Romania came in 1981, when I was a member of parliament in South Africa. It was around this time that the Nationalists were very keen to justify their presence in Angola. They invited MPs from all political parties – including their wives – to go on tours with them. Although Inez went on an all-wives tour, I resisted this, as I didn't feel comfortable being associated with a bunch of nuts.

But I must admit I was inquisitive to see what was happening on 'the Border'. Given the armed conflict in Angola at the time, the border was strategically extended beyond those of South Africa to the northern borders of South West Africa (now Namibia) to repulse the Cuban-supported Angolan MPLA forces.[8] The deployment of young South African boys to fight this adversary beyond our geographical boundaries was a highly controversial issue.

I expressed my wish to go, but in my capacity as a doctor only, and with the sole purpose of inspecting the medical facilities provided for our young soldiers. Such a visit was arranged and, as the only MP, I made this tour accompanied by doctors and nurses – and with wounded soldiers on my return.

A week after I returned from what was an invitational tour by our Ministry of Defence, I was back in Romania, on my third working visit, but this time on the invitation of *their* minister of defence – our bitter communist enemy!

On this trip to Bucharest, only Inez accompanied me. I worked in the military hospital, and we were given full military honours and driven around in, of course, a black car. We were accommodated in a military hotel normally reserved for high-ranking officers only and every time we entered our hotel, the guards presented arms.

An entire wing was emptied for us. We had our own dining room and we were served by a young soldier. What we found difficult to understand was that, after he served us, he would walk backwards through the door. On the second day, I asked him what this was all about. I was amazed that his orders were that, to show respect, he was not permitted to turn his back on us. I told him that this was utter nonsense. He liked my idea, and observing his back when he left the room did not spoil our appetites.

My host was a previous acquaintance from my earlier years, Colonel Kinde, who by that stage had become General Kinde. He was very softly spoken and gentle. All his staff were majors and of higher rank. Their facilities were less than adequate and their results left much to be desired. We could operate on only one patient a day and I helped the general through these, taking over only when I saw mistakes being made. We took a long time to perform these operations, but because I selected relatively simple cases the results were good.

At night, there were official functions with what I presumed were high-ranking officials and other supposed dignitaries. There were many toasts and *tuicǎs* and I was even made an honorary member of the Romanian Military Medical Association. I wondered what General Magnus Malan, South Africa's then minister of defence, thought about this, as I had reliable information that there was great interest in South Africa of what I was doing.

Despite the prevalence of communist atheism, the Orthodox, Catholic and Lutheran churches were all well-supported at Christmas time. Inez and I actually attended a Christmas morning service in a Lutheran church. The sermon was in Hungarian and although we did not understand one word, the hymns and carols were familiar.

Our second weekend with General Kinde was over the New Year, and it was then that we experienced the power and influence of the military. Accompanied by the general and his overambitious wife, and followed by an entourage of four or five more black cars, all filled to capacity with generals, colonels, majors and other ranks, we set off for Braşov.

It being the middle of winter, the roads and mountainous regions were covered in layers of snow – not a usual sight for a boy from Beaufort West. These mountains form part of the Carpathian mountain range, with beautiful scenery of snow-topped trees and valleys. Nestled among the snow-covered slopes were the sad sights of run-down buildings and dilapidated skiing resorts with non-functioning ski-lifts. Despite these chilly, though spectacular, surroundings, we were lavishly entertained and spent our first night in military accommodation in Braşov.

After breakfast the next morning, we visited wine estates with excellent wines – especially the reds – and glass factories where they made the most beautiful crystal cut glass. Inez was kindly given some wine glasses, which we still use when entertaining visitors.

We visited several historical buildings, monuments and monasteries. Here, I had to sign the visitors' book. It was pointed out to me that it included the names of past dignitaries (or should I say villains) who had previously visited these establishments during the Second World War. I recognised a few, including Adolf Hitler's foreign minister, Joachim von Ribbentrop, and Franz von Papen, a previous Chancellor of Germany who was later appointed ambassador of Nazi Germany to Austria.

That night in Braşov was intended to be the highlight of our visit. And so it was. We were among the many guests at our military hosts' New Year's Ball. It appeared to me that they had spent all the year's savings on that evening. The tables were laden with food and there was Scottish whisky everywhere. The ladies were stately in their long evening dresses. There was a large band and we danced the New Year in. The band played Romanian music and, to our surprise, the western music played was from the war years and included songs that were popular when Inez and I were courting, such as 'Wish Me Luck as You Wave Me Goodbye', 'When Johnny Comes Marching Home', and others sung by the darling of the Allied forces at the time, Vera Lynn.

The band also played early rock 'n' roll songs that had emerged after the war years, which prompted memories of the time when I was practising as a GP in Salisbury and Inez was busy raising babies. So, on 1 January 1982, I kissed Inez 'Happy New Year' in Braşov, Romania.

* * *

Back in Bucharest, I had to resort to having discreet meetings with Daniel and Anca Constantinescu. In addition to having to endure many other forms of persecution, they were in disgrace and were not allowed to work. This was a major blow to us because they were our best friends and a great source of strength during trying times.

Daniel had committed one of the greatest crimes in communist Romania … no, nothing as trivial as stealing or even murder, nor had he attempted illegally to escape to the West. His only crime was that he had asked for official permission for him and his family to leave the country.

On the last Friday of this visit to Romania, after two weeks of trying to teach the local surgeons the proper steps and pitfalls associated with cardiac surgery, I allowed the general and his team to perform a straightforward mitral valve replacement on their own. I would wait in the office and they could call me if they thought this necessary. I had misgivings but was mindful of the fact that the following Monday I would be far away in Cape Town and not only would they then be on their own, but they would not even be able to call me.

Most Romanian surgeons, Dr Radu Deac being a notable exception, seemed to experience a feeling of power – a surgical high. When operating, the performance of the procedure was considered to be of the greatest importance, with the outcome being less significant. I had taught them that there were essential steps required during surgery for a successful operation. One of these steps – a vital one – didn't seem to impress them.

During surgery, we opened the heart to work inside it. At the end of the operation, there was always the risk that air could become entrapped inside the heart when it was closed. It was therefore absolutely essential for us to carry out 'manoeuvres' to expel this air before the heart–lung machine was started. If not, the air would be pumped to the brain after the first contractions of the heart, which would cause air embolisms that could result in strokes and even death.

The general and his team took more than three hours to complete the operation, and they didn't call me until the patient was wheeled into the ICU. I had a look at the patient and, though still unconscious, she appeared to be in good condition. This was not surprising so soon after the operation. I left on a round of farewells, but popped in during the late afternoon before going out for our final dinner.

The alarm bells started ringing. The patient was still deeply unconscious but she had dilated pupils. I prayed that my worst fear – that she had suffered the consequences of an air embolism, the most likely scenario – had not come true. At that stage, I could not be 100 per cent sure, as her signs could well have been attributed to the after-effects of the anaesthetic. On questioning the ICU staff and doctors, they all remained extremely satisfied with her condition. The next morning, before we drove to the airport, I went to see her again. A diagnosis could be confirmed: it was clinically clear that she had suffered permanent and irreversible brain damage and was brain dead. In as calm a voice as possible, I requested that all the senior staff come to the ICU, including the chief matron and superintendent – both generals.

Once assembled, I asked them to repeat after me: 'I killed this woman.'

What I said was translated into Romanian and, ashamed and in tears, these generals, majors and others had to dutifully repeat this. On that note, I left. I think this one line taught them more than what they had learnt during the entire two weeks spent in the operating room.

* * *

My fifth visit to Romania – the fourth to help with cardiac surgery – was in 1986. We went to Radu Deac's unit at Tirgu Mureş to help specifically with coronary artery surgery. I was accompanied by Rob Girdwood, my associate in private practice who was not only an excellent surgeon but highly skilled and experienced in performing this specialised form of surgery. By this time, Radu's unit boasted excellent facilities and had attained high levels of competence. I now led a life of luxury, hardly ever scrubbing and leaving most of the teaching to my very capable associate.

I have only two lasting memories of this visit. We were introduced to the Chief of the Romanian Air Force, whose wife had severe mitral stenosis and was a high-risk patient. Another patient who needed surgery was the brother of the minister of health. Both were operated on and both made uneventful recoveries.

With the powerful influence of these high-ranking men, we were showered with privileges that must have been the envy of the Romanian doctors. But they were permitted a brief taste of this as they were allowed to accompany us.

On our last weekend, we were whisked off by jet to Constanta, on the Black Sea, where we were lavishly entertained by our patient, the minister's brother. A visit to their hospital was followed by a short trip to the Danube Delta. There, a large ambulance boat awaited us and soon we had cast off for a night and a day on the delta.

After dinner that night, the television was switched on and we watched a Russian broadcast – the northernmost tributary of the delta snaked eastwards along the southern border of the Ukraine, at the time part of Soviet Russia. Although I couldn't understand what was being said, the imagery on the news was easily recognisable. Black people were running all over the place and were being chased and beaten by baton-wielding policemen. They wore the easily identifiable tunics of the South African Police, the law enforcers of the Nationalist government. My guests said nothing, but an uneasy silence prevailed.

The next day, we travelled around the delta. It was boring: canals and more canals on endless waterways through reed-covered marshes. Of the flocks of birds, we only saw a few pelicans, but I saw people living on the islands in poverty-stricken conditions; their hovels compared with the worst of our squatter camps. I was very relieved when we left.

On our return to Bucharest, we were very tired. All I wanted was a bed, as our flight out the next day departed at 10 a.m. But our rotund and robust general took over, having arranged a party for us that we were naturally obliged to attend.

I used every excuse, including the fact that we were leaving early the next day for Athens. This was no problem to him: he said he would simply delay the departure of this international flight. And this he did.

When we finally climbed aboard the next day, two hours late, all the passengers were in their seats, having been strapped in for two hours. If looks could kill, Rob Girdwood and I would have performed our last operations ever.

* * *

Although I would return only many years later, Romania remained a part of my life. I pored over regular medical reports from desperate patients requiring help, I received annual Christmas and Easter cards from Sabina Popa, and I joined in the attempts to get Daniel and his family out of the country. Despite great difficulties with the communist government, Daniel and Anca, along with their close relatives, were eventually given permission to emigrate to the United States in September 1983, after a four-year struggle. Since they were accorded 'refugee' status, it was more of an extradition than anything else.

As time passed, however, Romania faded from my life, although I observed the fall of communism at the end of 1989 from afar with keen interest and great happiness. One leader who seemed oblivious to what was going on around him was Nicolae Ceauşescu, who completely misjudged his power. Maybe, after so many years of completely arrogant dictatorship, he could not see that in spite of his power, which had spanned many years, he was despised by his people.

The uprising started in beautiful Timişoara. Even heavy-handed repression could not stop the popular movement. Ceauşescu's very own inner circle turned against him, and on 25 December that year, both he and his wife were captured, tried and executed. Ceauşescu was the only leader of the overthrown communist countries to be executed.

233

After several years, I was sure that I had been forgotten in Romania, with the exception of possibly a few people only. How wrong I was. In 1996, I received a letter from the University of Timişoara, signed by the head of its medical school, stating that I had been awarded an honorary Doctor of Medicine degree. It took me some time to arrange a visit, but with the help of friends and one Mr Micu, I once again returned to Romania. It is a strange coincidence that I should go to the same Timişoara where the uprising had begun, and a full ten years after my last visit to Dr Radu Deac. Little did I know when I had left Romania in 1986 that I would return to a country free of communism when Ceauşescu was long dead.

For all of my previous visits during the communist era, I had never once been required to obtain a visa. My passport had never been stamped, and there was no evidence that I had ever visited Romania. I now needed a visa and had to go through passport control and customs. There was no reception waiting for me on the tarmac. When I entered the arrival lounge, however, General Kinde was there, with a few of the doctors from the Fundeni clinic and Professor Pop da Popa, in attendance with television cameras and reporters. Two Rolls-Royces were awaiting us and I was driven off with Da Popa, with whom I had never been on the best of terms, to attend a television interview.

I soon discovered that the professor had now retired – well, that was his version. His enemies told me that he had been kicked out. He was standing as a candidate for the presidency of Romania and the election was due to take place within a few weeks. This explained our renewed bosom friend-ship. He used my presence to gain publicity for himself. He was thoroughly trounced, however, and never ran for the presidency again.

This was my first visit to a non-communist Romania. I looked for changes for the better, but was shocked as, to me, it appeared worse.

The next day, I arrived by plane at Timişoara. My host was the head of the medical school and also the head of cardiology. In addition, he was the minister of health. I visited the Department of Cardiology and found many patients in their wards. I was then taken to the Department of Cardiac Surgery. The cardiac unit was equipped with the most modern theatres and ICUs but, in spite of these impressive facilities and equipment, there were no patients in the wards.

Apparently, there had been a clash between the heads of cardiology and cardiac surgery over something that sounded very trivial. So the head of cardiology referred no patients for surgery. Medical politics, in my experience, are worse than party politics.

I received my Doctor of Medicine degree *honoris causa* from the University of Timişoara that morning. The ceremony was conducted solely in Romanian and the translator was our miracle, Sabina Popa, on whom we had operated nearly thirty years prior to this event. She was still alive, reasonably well and could now speak English.

In my speech, I accepted the award on behalf of the cardiac patients of Romania. Referring to my translator, I stated that this was probably the first and only time that the translation of my speech had ever been done by a person whose heart I had previously held in my hands.

* * *

In 2002, I received a second honorary Doctor of Medicine degree, this time from the University of Tirgu Mureş. I have no doubt that Radu Deac was responsible for this. In addition, I was awarded the Order of the Gold Cross by the Romanian government.

Six years after my last visit, Bucharest was totally different. My first night was spent in an extremely comfortable western-style hotel. We had dinner in a French restaurant, prior to which my hosts had fetched me in one of their modern 4×4s. The ladies were expensively dressed and it was obvious that some people were making fortunes. My host that evening was one of the richest men in the country and a former patient on whom I had successfully operated on for a tetralogy of Fallot.

The next day, I was honoured by the president of Romania in what had been the palace of the Romanian kings. The award was given with dignified formality. As I walked through the vast palace corridors and stood in the impressively large rooms with all their splendour, I thought back to my earlier visits, which had started more than twenty years previously.

In the same palace, the previous president had been informed about my movements during those visits. Without his permission, my entry into the country would have been denied. The treatment given to several well-connected patients that had come to Cape Town was largely as a result of his wife's interventions. He had had all the power and I had had none, but here I was now standing in this palace, with the country freed from his murderous oppression. Life is strange!

Things had changed for Radu. During communist times, he had not been highly ranked and had been forced to fight for every small improvement to his unit. Now he was the deputy minister of health and headed a modern cardiac unit, where many procedures to correct cardiac lesions could be performed, with world-class results.

After the ceremony, we travelled by car to Tirgu Mureş for a dinner reception given in my honour. This event coincided with the first Romanian transplant congress, attended by delegates from all over the world.

A few of the medical officials from Tirgu Mureş had arrived in Bucharest to attend my award ceremony, including their Director of Hospitals, who had an ambulance at his disposal. He offered me a lift in it to Tirgu Mureş. As we were running late, this would afford the obvious advantage of being able to speed through the traffic, lights flashing and siren blaring, to be in time for the dinner.

Radu, however, decided it would be better if I accompanied him personally. He waved the official off, stating that we would see him that night at the dinner. Well, we did see him again, but not at the function.

We were slowed down by a traffic jam several miles long. Our driver made slow headway by weaving and cutting in. We were told that there had been a serious accident – a petrol truck had hit another car on a narrow bridge. We discovered that the car had been occupied by the same official who offered me a lift, and that both he and the driver had been killed. The official was still sitting upright in his seat, but had died instantaneously. His whole face had been smashed to pieces, his brain spattered all over the car. Not surprisingly, the dinner that followed was rather subdued.

That night, I slept at Radu's house. With magnificent large rooms and modern bathrooms and kitchen appliances, it was a far cry from the pokey two-roomed unit of yesteryear! I later visited the military hospital as well as a new private unit in Bucharest, and I saw cardiac units that were better equipped than ours in South Africa. How things had changed since 1977 – the Romanians were getting ahead while we were lagging behind.

The next day, I received my second Doctor of Medicine degree *honoris causa* at a splendid and, for me, emotional ceremony. Also in attendance was the friendly South African ambassador, who had come all the way from Hungary with his charming wife to support me. I was greatly honoured and left two days later, most likely for the last time.

* * *

In reflecting on my travels to and work in Romania – a most significant, if not *the* most significant, chapter in my life – several issues stand out.

I was employed at the time at Groote Schuur Hospital by the provincial government. During all visits to Romania, I took official leave, to which I was entitled. I never received financial support from the Nationalist government of the day, nor from any other government-linked organisation. Neither I, nor the colleagues who accompanied me, ever received any payment, nor did we ask for any.

During our first visit to Romania, the Romanian health department had given us a small allowance for the duration of our stay in their official currency, the lei, which amounted to a total of less than $20. The official exchange rate at the time was twelve lei to the dollar; on the black market, however, this exchange resulted in several hundreds. One of my colleagues, who will remain anonymous, once informed me that if you wanted to change $100, you would end up being one of the most 'lei-ed' men in Romania.

In the interval between my 1977 and 1978 visits, I had been phoned by a South African brigadier who identified himself as working for the then notorious Bureau of State Security (BOSS). He told me they had noticed that I had visited Romania twice and he offered any help should I ever need it. When I asked him to furnish details, he became very vague. Having some knowledge of Chris's involvement with the Department of Information, I told him he was speaking to the wrong Barnard and that I certainly would not disgrace or demean myself by having anything to do with them. I never heard from this organisation again.

During my time in Romania, I was told and became aware of the fact that I was being tailed. I suspect this was because I shunned the communist 'higher-ups' and associated myself with non-party members and critics only. When in Tirgu Mureş, I once became fully aware of this aspect when a thin man with a yellow complexion was sitting on a bench outside the hotel where I was staying. When I came back from the hospital, he was still there. The next morning, I greeted him like a long-lost friend. He soon disappeared.

Dora Petrila's accounts of this period are significant in relating the political shenanigans that were going on behind our backs during our earlier visits. The Romanian Securitate had been watching our every step when we entered the country, as had the medical staff with which we engaged on a daily basis. They were forced to supply written reports of what we said and did. Some, like Dora, refused, and were accused of being 'resistant' to the regime.

The true role of Professor Doctor Pop da Popa also became apparent in such revelations. The 'charming and polite' Da Popa evidently had had a direct line to the Bucharest Communist Party and its first secretary. A few months before Ceauşescu's fall, Dora Petrila and several of her medical colleagues were summoned to Da Popa's office and accused by him of disloyalty and making utterances against the 'superior leadership' of the Communist Party. Dora was further informed that she was at the top of a list of dissidents. So, our Romanian medical colleagues were subjected to enormous intimidation while we were there and showed great courage under such harrowing circumstances.

This immensely rewarding and significant period of my life was furnished with lasting friendships. The letter below, sent from my dear friends, Dr Daniel Constantinescu and his lovely wife, Anca, for my eighty-second birthday, illustrates the bond that was first forged as medical colleagues more than thirty years ago and one that remains strong today.

Dear Marius,

For your (doesn't matter how many years) birthday we wish you happy birthday, happiness, health and strength. May God give you all these blessings! We every day remember you and what you did and what you represent for us, for Romanian cardiology and cardiac surgery, for the Romanian doctors and patients as well as for doctors and patients all over the world. Happy birthday! 'La Multi Ani'!

On our last trip to Romania in May–June this year we celebrated thirty-two years from your first visit to Romania in June 1977 with some people still around (some of them are gone ...).

Tomorrow we will celebrate your birthday with Miki and Viorel around some bottles of Sauvignon Blanc from Stellenbosch and we will sing traditional 'Multi ani traiasca' ('Live many years' – in Romanian) and of course, 'Happy birthday to you, dear Marius'.

Great love to you and Inez!

Daniel & Anca

Poland

'My experience in Poland and elsewhere is that God made all men equal.'
— MARIUS BARNARD[1]

M Y FIRST VISIT TO POLAND TOOK PLACE IN 1979. IT WAS ORGAN-ised by my very good friend Heinz Kretzchmar, who had arranged for me to speak at a medical conference in Szczecin. Heinz not only helped me financially by paying for the two tickets for my subsequent working visit to this country a year later, but as the managing director of a South African company called Medical Distributors he also provided us with essential surgical equipment, including plastic tubing and disposable oxygenators.[2]

Following the initial and cumbersome helix reservoir, the development of the disposable bubble oxygenator was of great assistance in the operating theatre. The bubble oxygenator came in a sterilised plastic bag and could be connected within a few minutes, unlike the helix reservoir, which took hours to prepare. One of the first bubble oxygenators was known as the *Rygg bag* and was manufactured by the Danish company Polystan, which had a great interest in supplying hospitals in Poland. As Polystan's agent in South Africa, Heinz had both arranged for me to speak at the medical conference in Szczecin and been able to supply us with the disposable oxygenators.

So, I found myself in Copenhagen in the company of Professor Rygg, the developer of the bubble oxygenator. On my first evening, after a splendid dinner, we left by boat for Gdańsk. No sooner had we left the harbour than we were invited by the boat's captain to join him in the casino. This was my first surprise of the trip – I never thought that such capitalist corruption would ever be permitted in Poland.

After a very uncomfortable night on the boat, which creaked and tossed endlessly, we arrived at the port. Soon we were on our way by car to Szczecin. During this journey, I had another new experience. Every few minutes, a car would drive past. Through the back window I would see a man gesturing to us by rubbing his thumb and index finger vigorously against one another. This puzzled me, but it was explained that these people wanted to exchange local money for US dollars, an illegal activity, hence the strange method of drawing our attention.

I soon made the discovery that everyone wanted dollars, which could buy them freedom by enabling them to leave Poland. This was highlighted that evening in Szczecin when, after the dinner, I entered a small room in the hotel where a band was playing and some couples were dancing. What was different was that for every male there were at least five females, who were young and, for the most part, good-looking. They pounced on every available male, including this old and tired surgeon. I was soon told by one of my hosts that these girls were selling themselves for dollars and that most of them were doctors, dentists, lawyers and other professionals. They all had one ambition: to get out of Poland. So much for communism.

Having always been a political animal, I quickly realised that, although the communists were in control, the Polish people hated them. Devoted to the Roman Catholic Church, the Poles revered the Black Madonna, but not the Communist Party or its leaders. They hated Russia, and the independent Solidarity trade union movement led by Lech Wałęsa was already gaining much support.

The conference itself was attended by very few Western European delegates; most were from Eastern Europe. Nearly all of the talks were given in Polish, a language that was 'double Dutch' to me. The day after the meeting, I had to fly back to South Africa via Warsaw, but there was a heavy fog so all flights were cancelled. I had commitments in South Africa and was desperate to get back on time. A West German pharmaceutical representative who had attended the conference came to my rescue: it was arranged that he would take me by car through East Germany to Berlin. My problem was that I had no visa and, being a South African, I wasn't allowed into East Germany.

After much discussion, I decided to take my chances. Very early that morning, I was picked up at the hotel by my German friend, who was protected against the cold by a thick, black cashmere coat and a big Mercedes-Benz. The Polish border presented no problem, but when we arrived at the East German border post our troubles started. Two surly officials in drab grey uniforms approached us and ordered the driver to get out of the car. Their machine guns did not help my growing anxiety. They then put my poor friend through an aggressive interrogation, looking through all of his papers, body-searching him, going through his car in the finest detail and then opening the car boot and his suitcase.

After scratching through his clothes, they tipped all the contents out onto the wet, muddy road and left him to pick them up. It was now my turn. I handed over my passport, which they carefully inspected with great suspicion. They then looked at me again, and then at the passport again, and finally one of them said to me: 'Was your first heart transplant patient Washkansky or Blaiberg?'

I was immediately invited into the building and offered coffee while we discussed heart transplantations. They told me I didn't need to worry about Checkpoint Charlie as they would phone ahead. This they did, because when I arrived in Berlin I was given VIP treatment while my now livid West German friend had to endure further humiliation and an even more intense car search. Such was the power at the time of having been involved in the first human heart transplant.

I will never forget the relief I felt when we crossed the final border into West Germany. We came to a small sentry post, where we showed our passports through the window to an indifferent official who, without even looking at our documents, waved us through.

I had only a few hours to wait before boarding my plane, but I used the time for a splendid meal of *Eisbein* and *Sauerkraut* washed down with a delicious German lager, as well as a short visit to the Berlin Wall.

* * *

Back home again, and with the help of Heinz Kretzchmar and Polystan, I arranged a working visit to Łódź, Poland, in 1980. During the visit I would assist with cardiac surgery on children. Although I had very little knowledge of the Polish facilities and medical expertise, I now felt confident, having worked in Romania, that I could cope with sub-standard conditions.

My choice of Dr Chris Swart, the paediatric anaesthetist from the Red Cross Children's Hospital, would turn out to be the key to our success. Dr Antonio Curcio, an Italian cardiac surgeon who had trained with us, and a pump technician from Denmark completed the rest of my team.

On our arrival, a Professor Moll, who had only one eye, having lost the other in an accident, introduced himself and we arranged a working session at his hospital in Łódź. I was reminded of the idiom, 'In the land of the blind, the one-eyed man is king.'

In Łódź, I discovered the same problems that I had already experienced in Romania: no money for proper facilities or surgical equipment. To make matters worse, however, we had to use instruments that were suitable for adults only. Operating on small children, and especially infants, is very different from operating on older people. The instruments must be smaller and the intravenous infusions administered in minute amounts. At the Red Cross Children's Hospital, we had what were known as *mini-droppers*, which served this purpose.

I asked for such a mini-dropper in the Łódź hospital, but the doctors said that they couldn't obtain any. So I told them that I would phone a contact in Holland and arrange to have them delivered in two days' time. They arrived within this period, and Chris Swart introduced the mini-dropper in all further operations. Frustrated by the attitude of the medical staff, I called them together and told them what could be achieved if they wanted it. But they responded, 'You can do it because you are Marius Barnard.'

'No,' I retorted, 'you are totally wrong. I don't do it because I'm Marius Barnard; I'm Marius Barnard because I do it.' That was the difference. I urged them to take responsibility and to do what was necessary for the health of their patients.

The Polish cardiologist, surgeons and staff were cooperative and eager to learn, but their training and experience were inadequate. Despite the fact that the facilities of their ICU were not up to the required standard, however, we performed about fifteen operations. I selected the cases very carefully and we achieved acceptable results.

My Polish hosts, like the Romanians, were very proud of their country. On my first weekend in the country we attended a meeting at the birthplace of Frédéric Chopin. Here, we visited a museum honouring him and saw his piano and other belongings.

On the second weekend, we were taken to Kraków, one of the oldest cities in Europe, with many interesting modern features and old historical sites. We arrived late on a Saturday night. The next morning I started a tour that I will always remember.

The first stop was the ancient Wawel Cathedral, which has been the traditional coronation site of Polish monarchs and their main burial site since the fourteenth century.[3] It has been significantly extended and altered over time as individual rulers have added multiple burial chapels. I marvelled as I walked through the surrounding grounds, taking in the cathedral's 1000-year history. Coincidentally, this is the same cathedral in which President Lech Kaczyński and his wife were buried after being killed in an aircraft crash in April 2010. I couldn't get nearer than fifty yards to the entrance due to the thousands upon thousands of worshippers. Their fanatical devotion was far greater than anything I had expected. I soon understood the reason for the number of devotees: the recently installed Pope had, until a few months previously, been the Bishop of Kraków.

My next stop on the tour had been arranged for the purpose of finding the graves of the twenty or so South African Air Force crewmen who had been shot down and killed while dropping relief supplies during the Warsaw uprising. I had been asked by the Polish Ex-Servicemen League in South Africa to take a video of their graves. Armed with my video camera, I set off in search of the graves in what was still called the British Empire cemetery. Whereas the Russian cemetery was ill-kept, with an overgrowth of weeds and destroyed memorial plaques, the British Empire cemetery was well maintained and spotless. I soon found the graves, which had crosses identifying the final resting places of the deceased. They were engraved with South Africa's previous coat-of-arms motto: 'Unity is strength – *Eendrag maak mag*'. I read the crewmen's names and ages. Two of them had been taken in their youth; they had been only eighteen years old. I could not understand why these young boys had needed to lose their lives in a senseless war. *What a waste*, I thought. *When will we ever learn?*

Close to the graves were two monuments depicting the tombs of the Pope's parents, who were buried near to the South African crewmen and whose graves were surrounded by a large gathering of people holding lit candles and praying. Unlike my fallen countrymen, I had experienced another thirty years of life, and I could not help wondering if their ultimate sacrifice had been remembered. Today, more than sixty years on, they lie buried in a foreign country. One wonders what they would have accomplished and experienced if war hadn't taken their lives.

My next stop on the tour was an experience worse than any horror I could ever have imagined. I hated it and was repulsed by everything I witnessed. At the time I was sorry I had gone, but later felt glad that I had. I think it might be beneficial to make it compulsory for every politician – or would-be politician – to see it. There, over a period of two hours, I saw evidence of what so-called educated and civilised people can do. The cruelty, inhumanity, fear and pain they inflicted on innocent people, for no reason other than that they had a different religion and belonged to a different ethnic group, sickened me. How decent, honest people – doctors, judges, lawyers – could blindly follow a depraved madman was beyond my comprehension. Yes, I visited Adolf Hitler's 'Final Solution' death camp, Auschwitz.

When I arrived, the camp was closed. The Russians were in charge, but somehow it was opened for me. Accompanied by only one guide, I entered through the well-known gate with its inscription 'Arbeid Adel', meaning 'Labour is Noble'. It should have read, 'Labour, Torture and Murder'.

I visited room after room of artificial limbs, dentures, hair now silver due to arsenic poisoning. I observed suitcases, still with their owners' names on them – Dr Cohen, Rotterdam; Lydia Abromiwitz, Antwerp – and rooms filled with more of the possessions of innocent, living people, before they were tortured, gassed, incinerated and buried.

I saw photographs of doctors who had taken the Hippocratic oath, selecting those fit for work and sending the 'useless' to the Nazis for immediate execution. I entered the gas chambers and incinerators and relived the agony of the millions of people who had been herded into them. I was shocked and felt brutalised because, although I had read and heard about this evil, I actually had to witness the scene to comprehend the full extent of the Holocaust.

I was only too happy to escape into the open; to see clouds and the blue sky and to smell fresh air. But there was one more structure, built after the release of the starved, skin-and-bone inmates who survived, to see. It was made of wood, and was the gallows where Rudolf Höss, the camp commander, had deservedly been hanged.

But my day was far from over. I was taken back to what is now Jagiellonian University in Kraków, one of the oldest universities in Europe, where I saw the literature and instruments of one of its pre-eminent alumni, Nicolaus Copernicus, the great fifteenth-century astronomer.

That night, I addressed their students' union. After my talk, the very large gathering of students kept me there for at least three more hours, asking questions about South Africa, apartheid and other political issues. It was obvious that their dreams were dominated by the hope of freedom and the end of communism. When I had to sign their Book of Speakers, I paged back and saw that I was part of an illustrious group that included John F. Kennedy and Nikita Khrushchev.

The next day, we stopped at Częstochowa. As we drew up to a small church, I noticed rows of seats, almost as far as one could see, below a small hill. The new Pope, on his first return to his native Poland since his election, had about a million people attending Mass. This church is famous as it houses the painting of the Black Madonna, which is both the country's holiest relic and one of its national symbols. Centuries earlier, during a

Protestant Hussite invasion against the Catholics, the church was ransacked and set on fire – hence the black Madonna.[4] When a Hussite soldier saw the wooden icon of the Madonna, he slashed it with his sword. Legend has it that blood ran out of the Madonna's cheek. I saw the blackened icon and the two cuts on the right cheek, but no blood was visible on the day I visited.

* * *

The team that accompanied me to Poland on that first working visit provided excellent support, none more so than the anaesthetist Chris Swart. At well over six feet he was a tall man, and he smoked about eighty cigarettes a day. Chris had long silver hair and a bushy silver beard, which reminded me of a painting of Moses. He could drink with the best of them, a fact that the Poles discovered with great interest, as they prided themselves on their ability to drink vodka. Chris matched them glass for glass. When they were already under the influence, he remained steady and coherent, and a few hours later he would be back at the hospital, ready to start surgery. The child-patient would be perfectly anaesthetised with minute needles placed into tiny arteries and veins. Chris was devoted to his patients, applied great skill and had a vast knowledge of intensive care for infants. A truly remarkable man, he was a gentle giant to whom I owe a lot.

During our last night at Łódź, the rector of the university hosted a dinner in our honour. The pre-dinner drinks consisted of vodka, and were followed by wine at the table, then cognac and more vodka afterwards – neat. The final outcome was that the rector passed out under the dining table and Chris, somehow, made his way back to the hospital, where he passed out in the bathroom. So we picked him up and he spent his last night in Poland sleeping on a bed in the ICU.

Earlier, Chris had received a medal from the Polish anaesthetic society. It was awarded in recognition of his contribution to helping me. But his interpretation was that he received it in recognition of his drinking for South Africa!

* * *

One of the very special experiences I had in Poland involved a Polish doctor and his son. Of the hundreds of patients I saw and operated on, I remember few. Fewer still stand out in my memory. I remember those that touched me in a unique way because of a personality that appealed to me; the post-operative death of an only child of elderly parents; the survival of a patient who had suffered four cardiac arrests and was post-operatively resuscitated after his heart had stopped for thirty minutes; and others like this.

But my short association with a Polish doctor and his two-year-old son, Jazk, will remain part of me forever. During my last week in Szczecin, I was asked to see a young boy. I found a very sick little man lying in his bed. He was 'blue', short of breath and poorly developed. Alongside him sat his father. If you want a definition of love and devotion – but also concern and anxiety – you had only to take a photograph of that father. His emotions were certainly justified because, after analysing the results of the angiogram, the diagnosis of transposition of the great arteries was clear. As I have mentioned, I've had a lasting suspicion that my brother Abraham died of the same congenital abnormality; thus I was especially interested in the condition, which is not compatible with life. Survival is, at best, a few years.

In a normal heart, oxygen-depleted blood is pumped from the right side of the heart through the pulmonary artery to the lungs, where it is oxygenated. The oxygen-rich blood then returns to the left side of the heart via the pulmonary veins, and is pumped by the left ventricle through the aorta to the rest of the body, including the heart muscle itself.

As mentioned earlier, transposition of the great vessels – or arteries – is a congenital heart defect in which the two major vessels that carry blood away from the heart, the aorta and the pulmonary artery, are switched. The implication is that there is too little oxygen in the blood pumped from the heart to the rest of the body. Low blood oxygen leads to cyanosis – the bluish-purple colour of the skin – shortness of breath and other fatal complications.

For the patient to survive, one had to impose some mixing of the oxygenated and oxygen-depleted blood between the right and left atria. A palliative operation was at first the only method of prolonging life. It involved cutting out most of the interatrial septum – the wall of tissue separating the left and right atria – to facilitate the mixing of the blood. But this was only a temporary solution.

One of the pioneering operations to achieve a complete repair successfully was developed by Chris. A complicated procedure that yielded poor results, it was soon abandoned after the Mustard procedure produced acceptable results in the 1960s.[5]

The Mustard procedure involved switching the atria so that the blood flow could be redirected to the appropriate large vessels. This was done by removing the atrial septum and, with a piece of pericardium from the patient, stitching it back in such a way that deoxygenated blood flowed to the lungs and the returning oxygenated blood to the rest of the body.

The procedure was just as complicated as it sounds, and it demanded dedicated skill and precision. This was a challenge I relished. But to perform this operation on my little Polish patient carried too high a risk. The hospital's facilities and support were, in my opinion, not up to the standards required for an acceptable chance of success. I expressed my view to my Polish colleagues and thought that this would be the end of the matter. As the patient's relatives were not allowed to have contact with me, I knew that my colleagues would have explained my decision to the father.

The following day, I was surprised to hear that the infant's father had been permitted to talk to me. That he was a doctor, I'm sure, played a major role in this regard. I found the father sitting next to his child in the same position that he had been in the day before. His face and demeanour reflected a beaten and destroyed man. He pleaded with me to operate on his son – his only son. I suggested to him that he take his child to a centre in Germany or France to have the procedure performed there. But, for him, that was not an option, as he did not know where he would get the money. I explained to him that alternative forms of treatment were not attainable and again expressed to him my concerns regarding the inadequate facilities and the associated risks, which I was not prepared to take.

The father looked me straight in the eye and said, 'Does this mean my only son must die?' This father pleading for the chance of life for his son touched every compassionate feeling in me. There and then, I decided to operate on the boy the next day and to accept the risk of a failure for me while providing the chance of life for his son.

That evening, I again visited the ward and found the father still sitting next to his son. I explained to him all the problems that his son would have to face during the operation and that the chances of success were minimal. With tears streaming from his eyes, he said, 'Doctor, tomorrow my son will be born again.'

The next morning, when I arrived in the theatre, Chris Swart had the patient anaesthetised and draped and I started the operation immediately. Everything went well and, after two and a half hours, I had completed the Mustard procedure. Bypass was stopped and the now normally functioning heart took over with a good blood pressure. Of course, at this stage, little Jazk was no longer cyanotic but a very healthy pink.

For two days, Jazk's post-operative course was, however, very stormy. But due to Chris Swart's excellent post-operative care, the child improved. When I left for South Africa a few days later, he was already in the recovery ward. Whatever happened to Jazk and his father I will never know. I pray that he is fine.

Unfortunately the long-term results of the Mustard procedure proved to be unfavourable and today a new procedure that yields much better results is used. I do hope that if young Jazk needed another operation, there would have been someone in his country capable of performing it. I will never forget this case. It exemplified a father's total love and dedication to his son. The fond memory of this will remain with me always.

The story of this experience was covered in one of our local news-papers.[6] The article describes how the operation we did on this young man was one of ten that we performed during our three weeks in Poland. These operations were filmed and watched by more than a hundred people in a separate room in the hospital – but not by Jazk's father.

On my return to South Africa, I had in my baggage a precious book – a gift from the young boy's parents. Written in it was the following inscription: 'For Professor Marius Barnard in memory of the day of creation of a new life for our son, Jazk. Deeply appreciative parents. Łódź 14.v.1980.'

* * *

My second visit to Poland in 1980 came to a close with a happy event: I succeeded in facilitating the reunion of two men who had been incarcerated in a German prisoner-of-war camp during the Second World War, where they had became friends.

During my visit, I was approached by a Polish surgeon, Dr Henryk Grabowski, who was trying to re-establish contact with a South African, known to him only as *Reineke*. Dr Grabowski told me that, in 1943, Reineke had been a South African pilot flying for the Royal Air Force when he was captured by the Germans and imprisoned in Stalag IIA at Neubrandenburg, Mecklenburg. His mother apparently worked in Bloemfontein and he had been living with her prior to his capture.

While this surgeon was treating the South African in the prison camp's surgical department, they became friends. During the pilot's stay as a patient, he showed great interest in medical problems and Dr Grabowski spent many hours teaching him about the principles of anatomy and physiology. Reineke wrote a fond letter in the surgeon's diary, stating, 'My stay with you was the one bright period in my unnatural confinement in Germany. I only hope that as free men sometime, somehow, we may meet again.'

I asked Dr Grabowski to write to me in Cape Town providing as many details as possible about his friend. When I returned to South Africa, an envelope was awaiting me that included a letter and a picture of the surgeon during his time as a prisoner of war.

The *Cape Times* found this story to be of sufficient interest to publish, and asked that anyone with information on 'Reineke of Stalag II' should get in touch with me via the newspaper and that, if the South African was still alive, it would be wonderful if the two wartime friends could be reunited.[7]

The very next morning, while I was still in bed, the phone rang. Reineke, who was now Dr Reineke, had been identified and given my contact details. Shortly afterwards, Dr Reineke called me and then contacted Dr Grabowski himself. The Polish surgeon flew out to South Africa, where I met up with him, and the friends were reunited. What started in the dreadful atmosphere of a German prisoner-of-war camp all those years ago had an unexpectedly happy ending in South Africa.

24

Not Just a Diseased Heart

O F THE MANY HUNDREDS OF PATIENTS THAT I DEALT WITH AS A GP and later as a surgeon, most have faded from my memory. There are some, however, that I will never forget. One such patient is Saul. He was present in my life for only two days, but he taught me an unforgettable truth about what my main purpose in life should be: to put the care of my patients above all things. In February 1975, when I was practising at both Groote Schuur Hospital and the Red Cross War Memorial Children's Hospital, I wrote an article for *Reader's Digest* magazine about him. The article was titled 'A Piece of Bread'.

It has been a difficult Wednesday for the surgeon. What should have been a routine operation in a theatre at the Red Cross War Memorial Children's Hospital turned into a nightmare of problems. The problem had been solved – but it had taken all day – and now he was tired, drained.

A quick cup of hot, sweet tea, a check on the patients in the Intensive Care Unit and then a ward round. He must not appear irritated, he must not appear upset – the children loved his visits because he always had a smile and a joke for them.

But tonight the smiles were tired and the jokes half-hearted. The round was brief and minutes later the surgeon was in his car crawling through the home-going suburban traffic towards Groote Schuur Hospital, two kilometres away on the mountain slope overlooking Cape Town's southern suburbs.

His body craved a relaxing meal in the cheerful company of his family. He thought of the book he was reading about the Karoo, the arid plain in central South Africa where he had grown up. He wanted to stretch out on his living-room couch and lose himself in the book. But he had to put these thoughts away – now he had to see the patients at Groote Schuur Hospital.

The Sister was brisk as she accompanied him on the ward round. All was in order, there were no special problems. The last patient to be seen was a young boy who was scheduled for surgery the next morning.

Saul had been admitted that day and as the surgeon approached his bed the boy was propped up by four pillows. Saul was sixteen years old, but weighed about thirty-five kilograms. He was short of breath, his body and liver were swollen and his heartbeat was too fast and irregular. Examination revealed a body of cardiac disease in its terminal phase, but although the body was old and sick the face was that of a boy.

When the surgeon spoke to him, Saul's face lit up. His smile was wide and his eyes bright and hopeful – for a moment all fear was lost.

Saul was one of twelve children of a desperately poor family. They lived in a *pondokkie* on the wind-blown Cape Flats; one of the thousands of such dwellings that scar the Cape Peninsula and which the authorities hope will eventually be replaced by adequate housing.

All his life Saul had known only sickness. As a toddler he had contracted rheumatic fever and this resulted in his diseased heart and dishevelled body. Due to his health his schooling had been very limited. Toys were something that existed in another world. He had been unable to play with the other children and ice-cream had never touched his lips.

His clothes were the rags his elder brothers no longer used and he shared his bed at night with six of his brothers and sisters. However, at times, his mother had given him an orange to suck on and this was a real luxury. He was one of life's castaways. The next day would be full of new experiences, but today he lay in the unaccustomed luxury of his clean hospital bed.

The surgeon's brown hair was greying prematurely and his lined face showed that life had left its mark on him. But his face was strong and confident and Saul felt a little less lonely. Without saying much the surgeon turned and left the ward. Driving home through the night he reflected on how God could have given Saul the body of an old man, but with a bright, open, intelligent young face.

He wondered whether the boy would be able to rise out of the depths into which he had been born. Science could save his life, but what would happen then? He was clearly bright. He had some education and the Sister had told him the boy could write and read a little.

The surgeon saw Saul the next day, but Saul did not see him. The boy was on the operating table, draped, anaesthetized and ready for the healing knife – another statistic in the workaday life of a great hospital.

The theatre team started their work with barely a word spoken. This was routine. Gross disease of the heart's mitral valve had been diagnosed and this ailment was now to be treated.

The procedure had been performed many times before. Saul's bloodstream was linked to the cardio-pulmonary bypass machine – in other words the heart was relieved of the task of pumping the blood through the body, thus enabling the surgeon to work on it – his left atrium opened and the diseased mitral valve replaced with an artificial one. Saul left the operating table in what appeared to be a good condition and his future seemed more assured. The surgeon forgot about Saul and turned his attention to other patients.

That night, as Saul lay in the Intensive Care Unit, it became clear that his condition was deteriorating rapidly and something had gone drastically wrong. The surgeon and his colleagues worried over the case as the seconds of Saul's life began to tick away. It was decided that more was wrong with the heart than the diseased mitral valve and the tricuspid and aortic valves should also have been replaced. Another operation would have to be carried out without delay.

Gently, the surgeon told Saul that he would be having another operation. The boy could not speak, but there was agitation and fear on his face. A tube, which had been inserted through his mouth into his trachea to assist with his breathing, prevented him from talking. Splints, which held his arms down so that the plastic tubes, inserted into his veins to supply fluid, nutrient and antibiotics and also to monitor the vital functions of his organs, could be kept in position, prevented him from moving his arms fully. Only his large dark brown eyes begged the surgeon for something. The surgeon smiled and turned to go to theatre to prepare for the operation. But something stopped him and he retraced his steps to the boy's side, leaned over and said, '*Wil jy iets sê, Saul?*' ('Do you want to say something, Saul?').

The boy nodded. A piece of paper and pencil were brought and with his trapped arms Saul weakly scrawled his message. His request was simple. The scratchy, almost illegible writing spelt out the words … '*Stukkie brood*' ('Piece of bread').

In the midst of his discomfort, agony and fear, the boy wanted the reassurance of the only luxury he knew – a simple piece of bread. Leaning over, the surgeon whispered to Saul that this was not possible because he could not eat before an operation and also he could not eat with a tube in his mouth. However, there would be plenty of bread – and more – later.

On his bed, Saul was taken back to theatre. That morning he had been anaesthetized in an ante-room next to the theatre. Now, due to his critical condition, he was to be anaesthetized in the operating room. As his bed was wheeled in Saul's eyes opened wide as he saw the big room, with its clean, sterile white tiles, full of strange people in green surgical gowns with masks on their faces, the big lights overhead and the weird, shiny machinery all round. Never before in his life had he seen anything like it. His eyes followed the surgeon, anaesthetist and sisters around the theatre. What must the boy be thinking? wondered the surgeon. What must he be making of all this?

The anaesthetist took over and Saul started to drift off. The operation began. The surgeon and his assistants worked confidently, with deft skill. They opened the heart again and replaced the tricuspid and aortic valves. As each valve costs R350 this boy, who never had anything, now had R1050 worth of valves in his heart.

As the hours ticked away the heart team joined their skills to save the life on the table. The heart sewn up, the moment of truth arrived. This is when the cardio-pulmonary bypass machine, which has been keeping the patient alive during the operation, is switched off and the heart has to take over the function of pumping its own blood through its own body. 'Switch off the pump,' the surgeon said confidently.

Almost immediately Saul's blood pressure dropped and it was clear the heart could not perform this vital function. The pump was re-started and the surgeon went back to work. 'Stop the pump,' he ordered again. Everyone was now alert, but after a few seconds the heart again became weaker and weaker and the blood pressure started dropping ominously.

The pump was again re-started and again the surgeon went back to work, trying everything possible to improve the heart action. After ten minutes the order was again given to stop the pump, but the heart action failed and the pump had to be re-started. The doctors were now reaching the stage where they had very little else to offer. It was decided to implant a pacemaker, a little device which is attached to the heart thus regulating the heartbeat automatically. When this was done the pump was once more stopped. The blood pressure immediately failed again and the pump was again switched on. For another hour everything was tried and the pump went off and on, off and on, but always Saul's repaired heart failed to do its job.

Now the surgeon was conscious of the looks towards him of his colleagues in the theatre. They knew, as he did, that the time was coming when he would not order the pump to be switched on again. This was the moment of failure and the heart would not be able to sustain the patient's life. One more try and then finally the surgeon said, 'Pump off.'

The heart kept beating for a few more minutes and the blood pressure gradually dropped. A few minutes later the anaesthetic machine was turned off and after a few more weak, futile irregular beats, Saul's heart stopped ... forever.

The surgeon turned away from the table and wearily removed his gown, mask and cap. Another line was added to his face. The theatre was quiet, nobody said a word. The surgeon tried to brace his shoulders, tried to think of something cheerful to say, but all he could think of was a sixteen-year-old boy lying dead on the operating table.

This young boy had been born in poverty knowing only sickness, over-crowding, hospital visits, shortness of breath and swelling of his body. He was brought to a modern hospital where he was tended by people whose training had gone on intensely for years. He had received the very best of everything. He was operated on with equipment costing thousands of rands and valves costing R1050 had been placed in his heart.

As the surgeon left the operating room his staff could hear him say softly, 'But in spite of all this we failed to give him a piece of bread.'[1]

* * *

Another one of my cardiac patients, whom I treated the following year while working at Groote Schuur Hospital, had a great impact on me. In December 1976, I wrote an article about him, also for the *Reader's Digest*. The article was titled 'Soul of his Feet'.

I got to know Mtutuzeli Nkosi[2] through the soles of his feet. On paper, he was case number: B7591476, sex: male, race: Bantu, age: 56, married, occupation: farm labourer, home: a village near Riversdale, 300 kilometres from Cape Town. But it was when I saw the tough, cracked, leathery soles that I was drawn to the man and the life that lay unrevealed behind his face.

Two years before, Mtutuzeli had started tiring more and more quickly. They saw each other, man to man, and the surgeon realized that a greater constriction than the fist-like grip tightening round his patient's heart held the humble black farm labourer captive when he hefted the heavy sacks of grain during harvest time. Eventually, weak and in pain, he dressed in his best clothes and, armed with four rands, set out to see a doctor in Riversdale. After waiting at the back of the consulting room for several hours, he was examined and told that there was 'too much water' in him. In exchange for his money, he was given a bottle of pills.

The pills helped, but when he had completed the dosage the sickness returned and his condition worsened until one morning he was too ill even to walk. This time, his employer's wife accompanied him to the doctor in Riversdale. Hazily, he recollects an injection, then the rush by ambulance to Cape Town's Groote Schuur Hospital.

Mtutuzeli had constrictive pericarditis, caused by tuberculosis bacteria invading the thin, pliable sac (the pericardium) enclosing his heart. It is an inflammatory process in which the sac thickens and its layers adhere to each other, causing the heart to be gripped tighter and tighter, impairing its function and bringing shortness of breath, swelling of the liver and legs and fluid in the abdomen. The fist-like grip of the shrinking sac can eventually lead to complete heart failure and death.

When he arrived in our ward, Mtutuzeli was in an advanced state of heart failure. Surgery was imperative. In the operating theatre, he was gently lifted onto the table by masked and gowned figures and anaesthetized. An incision was made from the notch above his breastbone to a few centimetres above the umbilicus. Then an electric saw whirred, the bone split, and a large, silvery retractor was used to separate the edges of the sternum. Mtutuzeli's pericardium now lay revealed.

A cross-incision was made, millimetre by millimetre, through the diseased sac. With scissors the flaps were lifted, and the cardiac muscle bulged through the small hole. Slowly the pericardium was stripped off, freeing the heart and allowing it to recapture its strong contractions. Finally, the operation over, the sternum was wired together and the skin was closed.

Soon Mtutuzeli was back in the ward. It was here, when I visited him to find out how his heart was mending, that I saw the soles of his feet.

Many years of working on the farm without shoes had made the skin thick and calloused. The rough, hot ground had hardened and cracked the soles so that their texture was like the surface of a brick. I was frequently at Mtutuzeli's bedside, more to find out who he *really* was than to check on his complication-free post-operative course.

Born in the Transkei, Mtutuzeli had never met his father and had seen his mother only a few times. He was cared for by his grandmother, sharing her precarious existence with six other children. These 'brothers' and 'sisters' were the grandmother's only means of economic survival. Small amounts of money were brought or sent by the parents in payment for Granny's care of the children. Looking after their own youngsters would have prevented the mothers from earning a living in the city.

Mtutuzeli's life was a struggle from the start. Food, warmth, clothing, happiness, even love were in short supply. His education was minimal, but he was brighter than his brothers and sisters and managed to learn elementary reading and writing. As he grew, the deposit of babies at Grandmother's hut continued, and Mtutuzeli realized that his only hope for a future lay in the outside world.

At about fourteen, he found his first job in East London. The pay was poor, but he had regular meals, a room to sleep in and a grand-sounding occupation: garden boy. The shout of 'Boy!' would bring him running, a big grin on his friendly face. On Sundays he would take a bus to the location and spend a blissful day with his friends, drinking beer and watching the women walk past.

This state of affairs would have continued for years but for an incident when the neighbours lost their maid. Mtutuzeli overheard part of a conversation between his madam and the other housewife: 'You cannot trust these girls any more. Imagine her leaving us after five years without even a month's notice. Only last month we increased her wages to R10.' He remembers thinking that R10 was an enormous salary, and that he could not understand why the maid had left such a wonderful job.

But as Mtutuzeli's boyhood rapidly progressed to manhood, he realized he could never have a home or a wife and family if he remained a garden boy. So he left, also without a month's notice, taking the road south to Cape Town where, he'd heard, jobs were plentiful and pay high.

After many years, as many jobs and a stay in jail for fighting, he found himself penniless, without food, possessing only the clothes he wore. In desperation, he looked for work on the farms and so began his life as a carrier of grain bags. The carrying and lifting of heavy bags onto the big trucks day after day – from sunrise to sunset during harvest time – was an energy-sapping task. His wages kept body and soul together, but only just.

His hut, built from discarded sheets of corrugated iron and wooden boxes, was hot in summer, cold and wet in winter. One room served as kitchen, sitting-room and bedroom. This room became two when he brought a wife back from his yearly visit to the Transkei. Six children later, it was still two rooms.

All the years on the farm, he remained a labourer known only to the white people as 'Friday'. (He had come to ask for work on a Friday, and his first name was too difficult to pronounce.) Although he had small pay increases, food also became more expensive. Towards the end of each month, there was no money and still many things to be bought. Slowly but surely, society encased him in a situation with no escape. Then the tuberculosis germ started squeezing his heart.

Now, in hospital, he was no longer 'Friday', but was addressed as Mr Nkosi by doctors and the hospital staff. His overcrowded, dank hut gave way to a bright, clean ward. Instead of tossing and turning on an uncomfortable coir mattress, he lay under crisp sheets in a real bed with a foam-rubber mattress. Food was in abundance and served on plates with knives and forks, and even a serviette. He had to ask another patient what to do with this last article.

His face would break into a happy smile at every kindness shown. He became stronger and began to walk. For the first time in his life, he had the wonderful experience of sitting in a hot bath. He had few requests, but the second day after his operation, he wanted to know how long he had to stay in hospital. The next day, apologizing for troubling us, he repeated this question. From then on it was asked more insistently until, after ten days, it seemed his only topic of conversation.

This puzzled me. I had spoken to him on many occasions, finding out about his work, his family and his way of life. I knew the deprivations he suffered. Here, he had comforts he had never known before. We could not wish for a more grateful patient, but it was obvious that he would leave the moment we told him he could.

Released from its restrictive pericardial prison, Mtutuzeli's heart responded to its freedom. The wound healed and the patient was soon ready to leave hospital. On his last morning, I found him sitting on a chair, dressed in an old but clean suit, eager to be on his way.

'Mtutuzeli,' I teased, 'why don't you like us?' His answer was soft but firm: 'Doctor, you know that I like all of you. You made my heart better. How can I not like you?'

'But Mtutuzeli,' I replied, 'every time I see you, all you say is, "When can I go home?" Today for the first time I see you really happy.'

'You don't understand, doctor,' he said. 'You have all been good to me, but this is not my home, you are not my family. All I want to do now that my heart is better, is to go where I belong, where I am loved, where I am needed.'

And so I said goodbye to Mtutuzeli Nkosi, case number: B7591476, sex: male, race: Bantu. I was pleased that we had been able to release his heart from its constriction. But I felt a great sadness about this simple man. I knew that as soon as he left the hospital our society would slowly grip him again and force him back into his daily struggle for existence.[3]

PART III

Politics

A top surgeon. A senior partner in a medical team that made history and won international acclaim for its pioneering heart transplant surgery. Why would Marius Barnard put all that behind him to enter the world of politics? Moreover, why, in doing so, would he choose to join a political group that had no hope of achieving political power?

The answer is simple: Barnard is a man of humility. He is not a power seeker. He was, and is, a humanitarian motivated by love for his fellow human beings and a loathing of injustice. The concept of apartheid and race discrimination that held his beloved South Africa in a vice grip for forty years and more was anathema to him. As a proud Afrikaner, he could not find empathy with the racist ideologies which the Afrikaner-dominated government espoused and which kept it in power for so long. He was not part of the apartheid tribe.

Marius was a welcome addition to the beleaguered Progressive Party – the small, official opposition in the South African parliament – and brought lustre to its ranks. He and I struck up an instant and lasting friendship for we found much in common. He shared all the ideals and principles of his colleagues – a commitment to a non-racial South Africa and an abhorrence of the apartheid system.

He was a popular member of the parliamentary caucus and his rigid opposition to all the draconian measures of the apartheid government incurred the constant wrath of the authorities. He brought with him many qualities, not the least of which was a delightful and mischievous sense of humour – a valuable and rare asset during the grim days of the anti-apartheid struggle.

He retains all these qualities today and his account of his years in politics is highly commended.

RAY SWART
DURBAN, KWAZULU-NATAL
AUGUST 2010

25

Racial Awakenings

'Fools' names, like fools' faces, are often seen in public places.'
— THOMAS FULLER

I GREW UP IN AN EXTREMELY POLITICISED SOCIETY. MOST RURAL towns of South Africa during my youth were both conservative and racially polarised. Many whites entertained a brand of racism that, although not yet cast in legislation, was widely practised and, in fact, condoned. Our town was no exception. I remember the church bell tolling at 9 p.m., warning all blacks that they had to be firmly ensconced in their location and not in the white Beaufort West town.

The white townsfolk of Beaufort West supported either the pro-Afrikaner Nationalists (typically referred to as *Nats*), or the governing pro-English South African Party (SAP). Neither embraced inclusiveness of all South Africans; both preserved and furthered white privilege, albeit by differing degrees. With the formation of the United Party (UP) from the SAP in 1934, many of us maintained our allegiance with the UP and were known as *bloedsappe*.[1]

As a youth, I was easily able to perceive the racial and cultural divides perpetuated by the Nats in our town and elsewhere. These divides were felt keenly by my father, whose views differed dramatically from those held by the majority of the other whites in Beaufort West. My father bore the brunt of discrimination for the entire period that he lived there.

During the war years, the Nats – from my youthful perspective – were not only anti-English, but very supportive of Nazi Germany. They were, therefore, vehemently against the South Africans fighting on the side of the Allied forces – which included my brother Dodsley.

My opinion of politics and politicians was shaped by a saying of my father's. When voicing his disgust at the political situation of the time, he would tell me, 'Politicians are the unemployed, or the unemployable.' In later life, I was to discover just how right he was.

My disdain for the Nats was heightened by the attitude of our neighbours. Our houses were separated only by Mortimer and Hill, the department store, and the house belonging to the parents of my lifelong friend Ray de Villiers. These neighbours were the family of our local MP, Eric Louw, who was later minister of foreign affairs in D.F. Malan's government. I disliked them, not only because of their political affiliation, but because Louw's two opinionated sons made no attempt whatsoever to socialise with the sons of a missionary. To add insult to injury, we were told that his American wife thought that we were 'too Afrikaans'.

My feelings were strengthened by my father's strict rule that *Die Burger* newspaper – the Nationalist mouthpiece in the Cape – was not allowed in our house. My father read only the Cape Town afternoon daily, the *Cape Argus*, an English newspaper that arrived by train at about midday, having gone to print the previous day. Often, my father had to wait at the shop next door when it was late in arriving.

One afternoon, he came home with the newspaper and told my mother of an altercation he had just witnessed. While he was waiting for his *Argus*, one of Beaufort West's highbrow white citizens – a wife of 'superior' social standing – was awaiting the arrival of her *Burger*. I overheard my father describing to my mother how a young coloured woman of about twenty-five years old had walked past them. The sight of this woman, who was smart and well dressed yet belonged to a 'lower' social category, was too much for the white woman, and she expressed her misgivings loudly.

'My, my,' she said to the woman. 'What is Beaufort West coming to? A young coloured woman should be working in her madam's house at this time of the day. And how can you afford such smart clothes if you do not work?'

'Madam,' the young woman replied, 'if you kept your husband out of our locations at night, I would not be able to afford these clothes!'

If there was a reply I never heard it, but I am sure that there was one husband in Beaufort West that night who had a very unhappy homecoming. And I am sure that his wife, from then on, suffered from a permanent headache.

* * *

Years later, many people found it strange that I had such strong anti-apartheid sentiments and was so outspoken about the Nationalist government's racial policies. I simply replied, 'I received it in my mother's milk.' And so I did. Neither of my parents ever demonstrated any form of racism. To them, all men and woman were equal in the sight of God. Thankfully, I inherited their belief.

On 26 May 1948, while I was in my fourth year of studying medicine at
the University of Cape Town, the National Party, under the leadership of
Dr D.F. Malan and with the support of most Afrikaners, defeated General
Jan Smuts's United Party to become the governing party of South Africa.
The Nationalists ruled the country until Nelson Mandela's ANC swept the
polls in the nation's first democratic election in 1994.

From the outset, the Nationalist government set about implementing its
policy of racial segregation, or apartheid, with a vengeance. Whites were kept
separate from blacks, Indians and coloureds in all areas of life, including
housing, marriage, schooling, hospitals, transport and entertainment. Legislation was passed to support apartheid policies: in 1949 the Immorality
Amendment Act and the Prohibition of Mixed Marriages Act were passed,
and in 1950 the Population Registration Act and the Group Areas Act were
legislated.

The government's obsession with race legislation had a direct impact on
me during my early medical career. Such racism had existed at UCT and
other South African universities prior to the commencement of my studies.
In the 1920s, no blacks, coloureds or Indians were permitted to enrol to
study medicine. In a document that describes the minutes of a 1927 medical
faculty meeting, it is written: 'At a special meeting in 1927 the UCT Medical
Faculty recommended that "it was not desirable that natives be admitted to
the existing medical classes at the University". The Medical School preferred,
in fact, that a separate medical school be established for black students and
that the standard should be the same as that at existing medical schools.'[2]
An African medical school, however, was deemed 'inadvisable' as it could not
offer the same facilities as the existing schools. While UCT admitted some
non-white students for the pre-clinical years of their medical training, black
students were not permitted entry to the hospital wards, so clinical training
was a problem. When UCT raised the matter with the Cape Hospital Board
in the 1930s, the board refused admission to black students. This situation
was accepted by the university without objection, and by 1937 non-white
students were still not allowed to undertake their clinical work in Cape
hospitals. The state of affairs changed, however, when the new hospital,
Groote Schuur, was opened.[3]

Coloured and Indian students were permitted in the 'non-European'
hospital wards from 1943, on condition that they had absolutely no contact
with white patients, even when conducting post-mortems.[4] Such racism persisted, and in 1944 there was a public outcry about the presence of black

students at an operation on a white child.[5] Letters were published in *Die Burger* and a question in this regard was raised in parliament. The furore abated after the students involved explained that they had not known that the child was white.

At the time of my enrolment at UCT's Faculty of Medicine in 1945, there were four non-white medical students in my class. They were required to leave the lecture theatre when a white patient was demonstrated on, they were not given access to the white wards, and they were not permitted to examine white patients.

For almost fifty years, South Africans were treated, and in many cases punished, on the basis of skin colour. Such was the horrendous ideology of apartheid, which spanned so many years of my life and the lives of my fellow South Africans.

I find it hard to comprehend today, more than sixty years later, that this was the political climate in which I grew up. That this extreme level of intolerance existed in our country for so many years is almost unimaginable, and I find explaining such racial discrimination to my grandchildren extremely difficult. This political landscape prevailed throughout most of my career as a practising medical doctor and cardiac surgeon. Given these circumstances, I was eventually compelled to oppose the Nationalist government during my time as a member of parliament in the 1980s.

Initiation

S OUTH AFRICA IN 1972 WAS EXTREMELY TURBULENT. BLACK TOWN-
ships were simmering with unrest and the government applied brutal
force to suppress the liberation struggle, aggravating the plight of those
who so desperately sought to unshackle themselves from the evils of apartheid. It was sickening to me that my fellow Afrikaners were responsible for
the misery of so many, that they so callously suppressed the freedom of the
majority of South Africans.

After one week of particularly brutal violence, I felt obliged to speak out
about the untenable situation. Through the *Cape Times*, I stated: 'I want my
fellow Afrikaners to think, and to think carefully, about what has happened
to our country this week.'

Students from English-speaking universities – notably my *alma mater*
UCT, the universities of the Witwatersrand and Natal, and Rhodes University – were vociferous in their disdain of National Party policies, constantly
organising rallies and mass protests. Vigils were often held in churches and
cathedrals, while leading anti-apartheid campaigners and students were
harassed by the police or thrown into detention. Many were placed under
house arrest or 'banned'.

My first real and active involvement in politics – or, rather, student politics – began during this year, when my eldest daughter, Naudéne, was in her
first year of studies at UCT. She came home one day flushed and angry but
very motivated. There had been student demonstrations against the abysmal
state of 'Bantu education' at many of the university campuses. Although
not part of any specific university political group, Naudéne had been an
interested bystander at one of the protest meetings, which generally took
place on the steps of Jameson Hall.

As virtually anything and everything against the Nats at the time was
considered illegal at best and subversive at worst, the meeting had been
broken up by the police, who had used their brutal strong-arm tactics – tear
gas, *sjamboks* and batons – to do so. Students had been beaten up and
dragged down the steps of Jameson Hall. Naudéne had been manhandled,
and this was enough to stimulate her into further action.

A massive protest meeting was arranged in the Cape Town City Hall and Naudéne, without my knowledge, nominated me as a speaker. As a member of the heart transplant team and being reasonably prominent at the time, I felt that I had to accept the request when it was put to me.

Two days before the meeting, I received the first of quite a few letters – for which I always had to sign – via the superintendent of Groote Schuur Hospital from my old classmate Dr L.A.P.A. Munnik, the MEC for Hospital Services in the Nationalist-dominated Cape Provincial Council – my employer.

It had come to his attention that I had accepted the invitation to speak at the protest meeting. The letter warned me that, as a provincial employee, and in accordance with the conditions of my contract, it was illegal for me to take part in any such political activities and that, were I to do so, my actions could lead to my dismissal.

Naturally I took this threat very seriously. At that stage, there were no available private practices for cardiac surgery, and although seeking an appointment overseas was a possibility, my financial position would not have allowed me to pursue this from a practical point of view. In any event, my children were at a point in their schooling where moving countries would have been too great an upheaval for them.

I had a choice: either risk it or back out. I asked myself what my father would have done. There was no doubt in my mind that he would have done the right thing. So I called Inez and the children together in our lounge and, after explaining my position to them, I told them that I had decided to go ahead and speak at the gathering. Inez and the children, without hesitation, supported me.

For the first time in my life, I addressed a students' protest meeting. Other speakers included Helen Suzman, Sonny Leon and student leaders from the 'chief hate of the Nats', the National Union of South African Students (NUSAS).[1] The City Hall was packed, with only standing room available.

The late Barry Streek, a distinguished political journalist – and at the time a prominent political activist – had helped me by providing statistics that indicated clearly the great discrimination between white and black education. But with regard to other burning student issues, I knew very little and had only a small contribution to make. I did, however, raise the important point that protests were justified and necessary and that we could make a significant contribution by becoming actively involved in improving so-called Bantu education. As an example, I quoted the contribution that the *Star* newspaper's Teach Each African Child (TEACH) programme had made by raising funds and supplying books and other teaching materials to black children.

As a result of my talk, the *Cape Argus* started its own TEACH fund and asked me to be their first patron. Educating South Africa's children of all races was – and still is – a matter of urgency, and TEACH allowed everybody to participate in a material way towards South Africa's future. By June 1973, the fund had collected over R75 000, which enabled the construction of four schools for black education.[2]

But I kept my trump card until the end. I pulled out Dr Munnik's letter and read out loud its threatening contents, which exemplified the provincial authorities' intolerance of any form of protest. Ending my talk, I appealed to my audience to work together to rid our country of these people and place it back into the hands of responsible leaders. I received a standing ovation and felt that, had I told my audience to go out onto the streets and break down parliament, it would have responded accordingly. The effect was electric. This was the kind of call these eager young students wanted to hear.

Of course, my speech was reported in the newspapers, which largely focused on how I had been threatened by the provincial authorities and that such threats would not stop me from taking action. All hell broke loose! Our phone started ringing day and night, and, since I was often at work, poor Inez had to answer most of these calls. There were a few messages of support, but they were for the most part anonymous phone calls of the most disgusting, vile, abusive and threatening nature. It was tragic to me that so many of them were from fellow Afrikaners. The callousness was unbelievable, and the calls revealed the hatred, intolerance and viciousness of our country during this period. Far from dissuading me of my political stance, they served only to strengthen my convictions.

I found the abuse very difficult to understand. One day I was a darling of the heart transplant team and one of South Africa's greatest sons; the next I was a despicable anti-white communist traitor!

An extreme right-wing organisation, the Scorpions, was operating in Cape Town at the time. Its primary activity was to target anti-government voices. A Methodist minister's house in the suburb of Mowbray had recently been bombed, and I was informed by an anonymous caller that my home would be next. This organisation was later suspected of firing a bullet through the front door of the home of Progressive Party politician Colin Eglin.

I must admit that I then took the route of the coward. I packed my wife and children into the car and quietly went to stay in a house in Hermanus for a few days.

My eldest brother, Johannes, from whom I was estranged, was strongly opposed to my political stance and attacked me in an article that appeared in *Die Burger*. Of course, the Nats of Beaufort West could not resist entering the fracas and had a field day – it was a perfect opportunity to continue the fight they had started with my father so many years earlier. It was even reported that some of the townsfolk suggested starting a collection for the purchase of a one-way ticket to rid South Africa of me. The mayor stated that he was ashamed that Chris and I had been born there. Naturally, I received much publicity in the process.

To his credit, Chris joined in this spat by publicly supporting me. He was so incensed that he vowed never to set foot in the place of his birth again. But Chris had the capacity to go back on his word when it suited him: very soon afterwards, he received the Freedom of the Town of Beaufort West and the Chris Barnard Museum was instituted in the old town hall. From then on he changed his opinion and repeatedly stated to the public that he was 'getting old' and wanted to go home. He would get this opportunity, but only many years later.

* * *

A day or two after the protest meeting at the Cape Town City Hall, I received a now easily recognisable letter from the superintendent of Groote Schuur Hospital. As usual, I had to sign for it. The letter was brief and to the point. I had addressed the meeting without official approval and, worse still, without taking heed of the consequences outlined in the initial letter that had been sent to me.

Chris went public in my defence, stating, 'If they sack my brother Marius, I'll close up shop and leave with him.' But, unfortunately, his support proved to be short-lived.

My defiance of the hospital authorities stung them and their retribution was swift. I was summoned to a meeting at the office of the director of hospital services. I had an idea of what it was going to be about, but when I arrived there late in the afternoon, I was met by an unexpected delegation.

The province was represented by three people: the MEC for health, Dr L.A.P.A. Munnik; the director of hospital services, Dr Loubser; and the superintendent of Groote Schuur Hospital. There were also, to my great surprise, three others present: UCT's principal and vice-chancellor, Sir Richard

Luyt; Professor Jannie Louw, head of the Department of Surgery; and Chris, head of the Department of Cardiac Surgery. I was certainly outranked, but felt confident that the latter three would support me. I soon discovered my error of judgement.

Munnik led the inquisition aggressively. He pointed out that I had acted against my conditions of service and that I had disregarded his letter prohibiting me from attending the protest as a speaker. He then read aloud a part of my speech that had been secretly taped. I had said, 'It is time that government comes back into the hands of responsible people.' My inquisitors thought that this was entirely unacceptable and that I should be punished.

I was rather proud of what I had said, but was asked what I intended to do about it. I replied that it had been my right and duty to speak at the meeting. I had indeed said what they had taped and played back to me. The decision had been mine, and what I had said I believed was true.

The threats started. I looked to my three supposed supporters for back-up, but they had forgotten how to speak. They just sat there looking disgusted at me. Dr Munnik finally asked me what I was going to do about it. 'Nothing,' I replied. The meeting ended abruptly.

It was already dark when I arrived home that evening. I had hardly sat down to explain to my anxious family what had happened when the telephone rang. It was Sir Richard Luyt, summoning me to his residence, where Jannie Louw and Chris were already gathered. I went to Luyt's house immediately with great hope of their support. On arrival, however, I was quickly disillusioned. Professor Louw and Chris started to attack me, telling me that my actions were harmful to the relations between the Department of Surgery and the Cape Provincial Administration (CPA). They had, to my utter amazement, been frightened by their political masters.

They finally threw me an olive branch: if I apologised to the provincial administrator, they would try to convince the authorities to forget about my transgression. I thanked them for their concern, but again refused the offer. This brought about another rapid end to another acrimonious meeting. Luyt kindly offered me legal support, should it be necessary, from the university's Faculty of Law.

And that is how the matter rested. I went on with my normal working life and the event was soon forgotten. Or so I thought.

A few weeks later, I received another familiar-looking letter from the hospital's superintendent. Dr Munnik had added his signature at the bottom. It stated that if I apologised to the administrator and promised never to make political statements or criticise the government again, they would take no further action against me.

I thought about this before I responded, as I still believed that I had done nothing wrong. I finally replied that if the administrator himself considered what I had done to be wrong, I would carefully consider his opinion and, if I agreed with him, I would apologise and sign his letter before returning it to him. This response, I believe, could have led to my dismissal. I would certainly have gone to court to fight my accusers. But those measures were never necessary, and I heard nothing further from them until months later, when I received yet another letter from the same MEC. Again, my misdeeds were outlined in the greatest detail, but I was told that no further action would be taken against me if I was a good boy.

This final letter did not, however, stop me from remaining involved in activities to help abolish the offensive regime. By now, I think my adversaries felt that if they tried to stop me there would be more trouble than I was worth.

The episode worsened my already strained relationships with Jannie Louw and Chris. I realised that I had no long-term future at Groote Schuur Hospital and that sooner or later I would have to resign, unless I was kicked out earlier.

The students took me into their hearts as one of their leaders. I was elected president of the UCT Students' Medical Council, a member of the Students' Staff organisation, and chairman of trustees of the National Union of South African Students' Education Secretariat (NUSED) Fund, as well as to several other posts.

Having created a political platform for myself, I became increasingly vocal, criticising the Nationalist government and expressing my absolute rejection of apartheid. Ignoring the political restraints instituted by my employers, I readily accepted invitations to attend protest meetings at universities across the country.

27

The Road to Parliament

A ROUND THE MIDDLE OF 1973, I RECEIVED AN INVITATION FROM an unexpected quarter. From out of the blue, John Wiley, the United Party member of parliament for Simon's Town at the time, asked me to have lunch with him. Over lunch, we were joined by two other MPs from the UP, Tony Hickman and Myburgh Streicher.

They were direct with me: if I joined their party, they would offer me a seat in parliament. Jack Basson, then MP for Sea Point, would not be seeking re-election in the upcoming general election – planned for 1974 – and I could take his place if I was interested. My precarious situation with the provincial authorities and Chris made their offer very tempting. After discussions with Inez, I became a member of the UP and heir to the Sea Point nomination.

I started meeting other party members and soon became a frequent visitor at the dinner table of the most gracious hosts, the party's leader, Sir De Villiers Graaff, and his very charming wife, Ina. I remember those evenings well. They were formal and dignified affairs, usually attended in black tie, at which important businessmen and ambassadors were often in attendance.

But something was not right for me. Politically, this was not my home. The United Party was so similar to the National Party with regard to its racial policies that I felt completely out of step with its members, who were also viciously contemptuous of the so-called liberal students – my political bedfellows.

During a meeting with Barry Streek and a few other student leaders, I received an offer from another party to stand for parliament. This invitation, which I subsequently declined, was for me to stand as the Groote Schuur constituency candidate for the Progressive Party, or the *Progs*, as we called them. This party was formed in 1959 after a group of liberal members of the United Party broke away to form a parliamentary opposition to apartheid. Their first leader was Dr Jan Steytler, at the time the Cape leader of the UP. Coincidentally, he had been my family's GP in Beaufort West when he was practising there as a family doctor.

Behind the split was the UP's inability to find a clear-cut alternative to the National Party's apartheid policy. The Progressive Party took its stand on constitutional reform, calling for an entrenched constitution incorporating a Bill of Rights, an independent judiciary and a federal constitution in which the powers of the provinces would be protected. It stood for an economy based upon the principles of free enterprise. It would be another thirty-five years before the founding members of the Progressive Party saw their ideals realised in South Africa's interim constitution.

In the 1961 election, only Helen Suzman kept her seat in parliament for the Progs. Thus began one of the great parliamentary performances of all time. Suzman sat alone for thirteen years, the sole principled opponent of racial discrimination in the entire South African parliament.

But now, as the 1974 election approached, it became unofficial public knowledge that I was going to be nominated by the UP for the Sea Point constituency. According to my conditions of service with the province, accepting a nomination to stand for parliament would mean resigning from my job – with immediate effect.

My opponent for this constituency would be Colin Eglin, then leader of the Progs, who had high hopes of winning further seats in parliament to enable more of their members to join Helen Suzman. They truly thought that Sea Point was winnable and, as I was seen as a real threat to such political aspirations, great pressure was placed on me to withdraw. Letters, phone calls, press articles and close friends tried to dissuade me. Even Inez opposed my running against Colin: not only was he a good friend but, deep down, Inez and I both felt closer to the Progs.

One evening while we were having supper, I received a telephone call that influenced me greatly and played a major part in my decision. The caller was Colin. What he said to me that night proved what a great man he is. If I was prepared to leave the UP, he said, he would withdraw his nomination and I could get Sea Point for the Progs. I was still formally nominated by the UP, but this had not yet been made public officially.

My final decision, however, was made easy for me. The Schlebusch Commission's report on student activities had been recently published, and its recommendations involved placing draconian restrictions on certain organisations' rights. Two years earlier, a National Party MP, Alwyn Schlebusch, had been appointed by the government to head the notorious Commission of Inquiry into Certain Organisations, commonly referred to as the *Schlebusch Commission*. The recommendations of this commission resulted in the passing of legislation that allowed the authorities to declare civil society organisations 'affected'. This meant that they could not receive foreign funding, and allowed the state to seize documents and any money the organisations already had.

Among the organisations declared 'affected' as a direct result of Schlebusch's recommendations were NUSAS and the Christian Institute of South Africa. The commission also attacked the South African Institute of Race Relations and the University Christian Movement.

Three commissioners of the report, John Wiley, Myburgh Streicher and Lionel Murray, were all members of the UP. Not only did they sign the Bill that followed, but they were very aggressive characters. I discovered that many UP members were in fact ardent Nats dressed in UP clothing, and none more so than my three recruiters, Wiley, Hickman and Streicher. Later years would prove me right: they all subsequently joined the National Party.

I could not support a party that, in participating in and endorsing the Schlebusch Commission, effectively backed the possible incarceration of leading human-rights activists such as Theo Kotze and Reverend Beyers Naudé, nor could I countenance any form of restriction being placed on the freedom of speech – especially that of the nation's youth.

My discontent was furthered by the United Party's handling of the Mahlabatini Declaration of Faith. The Transvaal leader of the UP during this period, Harry Schwarz, met with Mangosuthu Buthelezi and signed the Mahlabatini Declaration. They agreed on a five-point plan for racial peace in South Africa. The purpose of the declaration was to provide a blueprint for government by consent and racial peace in a multiracial society, stressing opportunity for all, consultation with all, the federal concept and a Bill of Rights.

This declaration, however, was more akin to the Progs' policy than that of the United Party and, despite being a co-signatory, the UP effectively rejected the accord. I felt that a golden opportunity for racial reconciliation had been missed.

In addition to the United Party's endorsement of the Schlebusch Commission and its stance on the Mahlabatini Declaration, I was less than enamoured with the way the party handled its nominations of candidates. Members in the greater Johannesburg region as well as party leaders in the Cape were inclined to side with their own, and both regions tended to fight at all costs to 'get their man in'.

My final moments with the UP took place at a house meeting in Sea

Point addressed by the leader of the party in the Cape, Myburgh Streicher, who made a right-wing speech and was warmly applauded afterwards. That was it! I had a letter of resignation in my pocket and I handed it to the chairman of the party and left. In February 1974, I revealed the reasons for my withdrawal as UP candidate in an interview given to the *Argus*.[1]

David de Villiers Graaff, the son of Sir 'Div', was nominated for Sea Point. He was rather anaemic and not a popular choice and, to my great delight, was defeated by Colin Eglin in the election that followed.

I am sure Colin thinks that he would have beaten me had I stood for the UP. I think otherwise – that the surname Barnard and not my political experience would have carried me through. What I later discovered was that Colin was a great leader and a much better politician than I could ever be. We have since become great friends. He spent more than thirty years in parliament and was one of the relatively small number of white South Africans who made a significant contribution to the establishment of the democratic country in which we live today.

After I had declined to stand as the Progressive's candidate for the constituency of Groote Schuur, the next choice was Professor Meyer Veldberg, then head of UCT's business school. After his refusal to stand, the nomination fell to Dr Frederik Van Zyl Slabbert, who accepted. His campaign was brilliant and he won easily. His rise in politics was meteoric and he became party leader in 1979, shortly after which our paths crossed.

After the 1974 election, six more Progressive Party members won seats in parliament. Soon afterwards, the party merged with a new breakaway group from the United Party – the Reform Party – to become, in 1975, the Progressive Reform Party (PRP). Another group of UP members left their party in 1977 to form the Committee for a United Opposition, which then joined the PRP to become the Progressive Federal Party (PFP), under the leadership of Colin Eglin.

For some reason that I have never understood, the United Party asked me to stand as its candidate in the Pinelands by-election a few months after my withdrawal from the UP. Their request came after the untimely death of the party's MP for Pinelands, Ossie Newton-Thompson, who was tragically killed in a plane crash in South West Africa – now Namibia – during the election campaign. Naturally, I happily refused the invitation.

I often wonder how South African opposition politics would have been impacted upon had I contested and won either the Sea Point or the Groote Schuur seat for the Progs in the 1974 general election. Should I have succeeded in Sea Point, this may well have diminished the magnificent role Colin Eglin played in politics for so many years afterwards. Alternatively, had I succeeded in winning Groote Schuur, this could have halted Frederik Van Zyl Slabbert's introduction to and rise in politics and possibly denied the country the outstanding contribution he made, as well as his subsequent dynamic leadership to the PFP. Clearly my decision not to stand in this general election ultimately proved to be the right one.

* * *

After I returned from a working trip to Asia early in 1980, Inez informed me that Van Zyl Slabbert, now leader of the PFP, wanted me to phone him. I duly contacted him and we arranged to have lunch in parliament. It was a Friday and we met in the large main dining room, which was dominated by a painting of a previous prime minister, Hendrik Verwoerd. It depicted him explaining to his Cabinet his views and future plans for his grand policy of 'separate development'.

By this time, Verwoerd had already been dead for fourteen years, but his policy – and its appalling impact on our black citizens in particular and our country in general – was alive and well and being enthusiastically implemented by his successors.

Van Zyl very soon came out with the reason for our lunch. Zach de Beer, a medical doctor who had qualified a year after me at UCT, but who at a very young age had gone into politics and parliament, was the current MP for Parktown, a constituency in Johannesburg that was very English, very affluent and one of the safest Prog seats. De Beer intended to resign and Van Zyl asked me whether I would accept the nomination to replace him. This, of course, was on condition that the Parktown constituency committee accepted me.

This offer was the last thing I had expected. After an excellent lunch – subsidised by the taxpayers – and good wine, I asked Van Zyl to give me the weekend so that I could discuss the matter with Inez and think it over. He was very keen for a quick decision – there were many other well-qualified and very able – if not better – aspirants for this position.

At home, Inez was as shocked as I had been when I told her what the lunch had been all about. To move to Johannesburg would not be a great problem: we were living in a small bungalow on Fourth Beach, Clifton, which would be suitable as a base when parliament was in session in Cape Town from the first week in February until its recess at the end of June.

Factors that made it easy to leave Cape Town for the remainder of the year were that all our children had by this stage left home. Two were already married. In addition, there were my ongoing problems with Chris and no future prospects at Groote Schuur Hospital.

I had always dreamt of running the cardiac unit at Groote Schuur, but I knew that, should Chris leave, the long knives of the provincial government and hospital authorities would be drawn and used against me. In any event, I felt that they wouldn't tolerate another Barnard.

Inez, in her usual measured way, made my decision easy by reminding me that I had always harboured ambitions of going to parliament, that I had turned down four opportunities over the last six years and that this would be my last chance: if I didn't accept now, I would never be asked again.

Early the following Monday morning, I contacted Van Zyl and said that, if the Progs and Parktown wanted me, I would gladly accept.

My proposed nomination to the Parktown constituency was kept a secret for various reasons, not the least of which was that I was still a provincial employee. I was also not a PFP member. I immediately applied for party membership and, on the same day, Inez and I became PFP members of the constituency of Sea Point thanks to the great help of an old friend, Percy Helman.

A trip to Johannesburg was immediately arranged, where a meeting with the constituency committee was held in Zach de Beer's house. They were all 'proper' English people; the only person I knew at this gathering was De Beer himself.

Parktown had four public representatives. The MEC, who was also a city councillor, was Sam Moss. I could sense that he was hardly thrilled by my presence; his resentment was evident. I could hardly blame him for this reaction, as he obviously felt that he should have been the future Parktown candidate. He was, however, rather blusterous and pompous and didn't appear to be much of a politician. He was also a previous member of the UP.

There were three other city councillors: Mrs Ray Graham, whom Inez and I soon named 'Mrs I', as she could only talk about herself; Lacon Stanton, who was rather weak; and Ian Davidson – young, bright and very sincere about his political beliefs. In him, I immediately saw someone who would be of great help to me and who would be a great asset to the future of the party. (My assessment of Davidson was completely correct. He is currently the Democratic Alliance's chief whip in parliament, having previously been its chief spokesman on finances.)

The other three public representatives for Parktown caused me problems but, as I had expected, they subsequently disappeared into political oblivion.

Taffy Lloyd was the chairman of the constituency committee, very bright and jovial, and a highly successful professional in his own right. The rest of the committee members were mostly elderly women.

We had a very uncomfortable meeting and I was asked a few questions, some of them irrelevant. One person asked whether, if I were accepted, I would move to Johannesburg and live in the constituency while continuing to practise as a cardiac surgeon. To this, of course, I readily replied in the affirmative. We left the gathering with a promise that the committee would hold a follow-up meeting to decide my political future.

On my way back to Cape Town, I reflected on the meeting. With my background, I could agree with them that I was not a very suitable candidate. I felt that they – and quite rightly so – saw me as an unwelcome intruder forced, from out of the blue, into their constituency by the party's leader. I knew, however, that I would have strong support from Zach de Beer, Taffy Lloyd and Ian Davidson.

* * *

A few days after I met with Van Zyl, he informed me that the Parktown constituency committee had, much to my surprise, accepted me. It was difficult to oppose the wishes of the leader of the party and, during my tenure as MP for Parktown, the undercurrent of resentment would be badly hidden. A few years later, it all boiled out into the open.

In March 1980, I resigned from Groote Schuur Hospital. The *Argus*, in an article titled 'Barnard Resigns', reported: 'World famous heart transplant surgeon Professor Marius Barnard is to resign from Groote Schuur Hospital. This was confirmed by the medical superintendent of the hospital, Dr H. Reeve-Sanders, who said she had received a letter from Professor Barnard in which he announced his intention to resign and asked her to accept his resignation.'[2]

My resignation was made very public in the local newspapers. Various reasons for leaving were cited, including my numerous clashes with the provincial administration and my 'sorties into politics from time to time'.[3] The member of the provincial council for Groote Schuur Hospital and chairman of the Teaching Hospitals' Board at the time, Mr F.M. Botha, was quoted in an article as stating, 'Dr Barnard is not the beginning and end of the world, let's make no mistake.'[4] I could not have expected a different response from this quarter, but I actually had to agree with him. Not all the comments were negative, however. Dr J.P. van Niekerk, deputy dean of the medical school at UCT, commented: 'It will be sad to see him go, Professor Barnard was a colourful character.' Just exactly what he was implying, I have no idea.[5] When asked to comment, Chris, in a rare moment of generosity stated: 'It's very difficult to get surgeons of his quality and therefore it will be very difficult to replace him.'[6]

At Groote Schuur Hospital, Chris was obviously sensing that something was going on. I knew the date that the PFP was going to make my candidacy public and arranged to vanish to a very small holiday resort at Keurbooms River, near Plettenberg Bay.

The press was eager to find out what my reasons were for leaving Groote Schuur, but I had quietly disappeared. One reporter, a man whom I disliked intensely, somehow found me at Keurbooms River. I sent him on his way, and in no uncertain terms. Once I was back in Cape Town, the press hounded me. I'm sure that they would have loved a family feud and bloodletting between the Barnard brothers.

My main reasons for leaving Groote Schuur Hospital were not only my enduring problems with the provincial and hospital authorities, but also my disappointment in Chris. This was not because of his lifestyle or his publicity addiction, but rather due to the restrictive, non-forward-moving and irrational ways in which he managed the cardiac unit. Another major reason for my disappointment was that he allowed the Nats to use him, both at home and internationally, for their foul plans and policies.

To Chris, my employers and my friends, confirmation of my departure from Groote Schuur Hospital and my nomination as the Parktown parliamentary candidate took the form of *Cape Argus* posters exhibited all over Cape Town, proclaiming, 'Marius Barnard to stand for Parliament'.

My replacement of Zach de Beer as nominated candidate for Parktown rattled a few cages among certain politicians in the constituency. One of its newspapers stated that my nomination had been 'almost entirely unfavourable'.[7] The Transvaal chairman of the New Republic Party, a remnant of the once-powerful United Party of General Smuts, was quoted in the same article as saying, 'I am most surprised that the PFP has seen fit to transplant its candidate for the Parktown parliamentary seat from the Cape' and that they were considering contesting the seat. They never did, which spoke volumes at the time about this rather insignificant group.

After the news that I had been nominated to stand for parliament became public knowledge, I quickly received another letter from the director of hospital services. The letter drew my attention to the rules and regulations of my employment with the provincial government. The salient point was that, according to such regulations, employees had to work for one month after resigning. But they wanted to exercise one last bit of authority and unpleasantness, and this legal requirement was waived: one day later, I received a call from Dr Hannah Reeve-Sanders saying that I had been relieved of my duties and was to leave immediately.

I had already removed most of my correspondence, books and other belongings from my office. What was left I packed in my car and, after three years as a registrar and thirteen as a cardiac surgeon – during which time I had given my all in time, dedication and a high standard of patient care – I left without even saying goodbye. I was treated badly and was given no farewell – not even a cup of tea. I did receive a short note from Dr Sanders to thank me for my services. There was no letter or any other form of recognition for my contribution from the head of the Department of Surgery, Professor Jannie Louw – but that was to be expected – or my other employer, the University of Cape Town. I have never been back to the cardiac unit at Groote Schuur Hospital, and only once have I returned to the Red Cross War Memorial Children's Hospital.

Chris met me in the corridor as I was leaving the hospital. His only comment was, 'I suppose you are going to blame me for why you left.' He never thanked me in person for any of my efforts nor for the support I had provided to his cardiac unit. Since that day, I can't have seen my brother more than five times before he died, although during the last few years of his life he phoned me frequently.

Except for the money I had paid into a pension fund plus 3 per cent interest – a grand sum of R71 000 – I departed with nothing. Should I have dropped dead at that stage, Inez would have had great difficulty in supporting herself with no income, no pension and only a bungalow at Clifton, which was worth little in those days.

And so, on 14 July 1980 – my son Adam's birthday – with our car packed to the brim, Inez and I left Cape Town to embark on a long journey to Johannesburg, where I was set to begin an entirely new career.

* * *

Fate had taken a turn in my favour. I had discovered prior to our move that Milpark Hospital, a private hospital with excellent facilities for cardiac surgery, had just opened its doors in a suburb in the Parktown constituency. I had promptly phoned its owner, Barney Hurwitz. After we had met, I had gone to look at the hospital's cardiac theatre, ICU, wards and equipment. Not only were the facilities as good, if not better, than those I was used to at Groote Schuur Hospital, but Milpark had a well-qualified nursing staff experienced in cardiac operations. The hospital also provided excellent post-operative care.

Barney Hurwitz not only allowed me to work in the hospital, but gave me consulting rooms and a house in the grounds of the hospital free of charge. I will always be indebted to him for his kindness in this respect.

I had been extremely fortunate in being able to persuade my anaesthetist at Red Cross War Memorial Children's Hospital, Chris Swart, to move to Johannesburg, and we found a full-time cardio-pulmonary technician, Ted Brayshaw. Rob Girdwood, who was practising in Johannesburg at the time, moved into the same rooms as me and we became associates.

With the excellent facilities at Milpark; a skilled and dedicated cardiac surgeon in Rob Girdwood; Chris Swart, who was the best paediatric cardiac anaesthetist, in my opinion, in South Africa at that time; Ted Brayshaw as the pump technician; and a committed, competent staff in the ICU, I felt confident that we could practise cardiac surgery of the highest standard. And we did.

With my political commitments I found it extremely difficult to give to my practice and patients the attention that they deserved. But in Rob Girdwood I had found a colleague who subscribed to the same standards I strived to achieve, and in Chris Swart a dedicated doctor who cared deeply for his patients. He was brilliant in the ICU and saved many of our patients' lives.

* * *

When Inez and I arrived in Parktown, a by-election date was set and my committee introduced me – a total novice – to the processes and procedures of running an election campaign. Each voter of our constituency had a ward within which they voted and a number on the voters' roll. All of these and other details, including address, phone number and previous voting record, were filled in on a card. Such administration had to be brought up to date continually. This included the removal of those people who were deceased, updating changes of addresses as required and making out new cards when constituents were registered for the first time.

We started house-to-house canvassing. I hated this, but Inez took to it like a duck to water, as she is partial to a good chat. I think she persuaded and changed the minds of many more voters than I was ever able to.

The sitting of a nomination court was gazetted for 28 July 1980. As the date for the sitting neared, there was much speculation about whether I would be opposed or not. We proceeded as if there were going to be an opposing candidate and as if we would have to fight a by-election. On the day before the court sat, most of the tree trunks and lamp posts of Parktown were plastered with my photograph.

As mentioned in Part 1 of this book, the Parktown constituency had close links to Inez's family and, more specifically, to her grandfather, Louw Geldenhuys, who had been an MP in this area some fifty years previously. It was therefore coincidental but, I felt, rather fitting that I was now stepping into the shoes previously filled by this great man.

I arrived at the court at the appointed time and place. We sat waiting and waiting until nominations closed at 11 a.m. At precisely this time, I was the only nomination. The presiding officer stood up and stated that, as Dr Marius Barnard was the only nomination, he was declared the legal representative of the constituency of Parktown.

From that second on, I was a member of parliament, with its privileges, salary, medical aid, free travel allowances and other lavish perks to which politicians are entitled. After congratulations from my new party and a celebratory lunch at Taffy Lloyd's house, I went home and continued my cardiac practice as if nothing had changed.

Inez and I now had the best of both worlds: we could live in our bungalow in Clifton during the first half of the year, when parliament was in session in Cape Town, and return to Johannesburg for the remainder of the year to perform constituency work, and where I could also practise cardiac surgery.

Chris's Politics

FROM THE EARLY 1960S, WHEN SOUTH AFRICA WAS EXPELLED FROM the Commonwealth and became a republic, the country's image abroad deteriorated rapidly as a result of the world's rejection of our political policies. Anti-apartheid activists from South Africa were successfully increasing overseas awareness of what was going on in our country, and their activity was becoming progressively more effective. It was beginning to 'hurt' sports-mad South Africa. Rugby and cricket enthusiasts were the worst hit, as we were no longer allowed to compete internationally.

The first human heart transplant afforded local and international recognition and the projection of a favourable image of our very high medical standards. Our government, as I remarked earlier, quickly recognised the great political mileage that they could gain from the transplant. For this, they needed Chris.

By the late 1960s, not only was Chris one of the best-known figures internationally, but he was an excellent speaker, a good debater and had a 'miracle-man' image all over the world. If the government could recruit him to their cause, they could use him in many guises for their own sinister purposes. They could not fail: Chris's personality made him a pushover for such a ploy.

One of Chris's most charming features was his willingness to please everyone. It was also his biggest weakness and resulted in numerous disastrous adventures. When one was in his company or when he was addressing an audience, Chris had an uncanny ability to sense what people wanted to hear or what they would approve of. He could, for example, be a liberal or a conservative at the appropriate time, when it suited him.

In public, Chris was a hesitant liberal, pointing out the evils of apartheid and creating and nursing this image of himself. In private, he certainly did not display the same sentiments and had many fierce arguments with me. He disliked the Progs with a passion. I never knew whether this was due to our policies or because they had asked me, and not him, to become one of their MPs.

The success of the Nats in luring Chris as an image-polisher was subtle, and very few of us were aware of it. What we did notice was that Chris was able to obtain as much leave as he wanted. We ordinary employees had to fill in leave application forms that had to be approved by the head of the department and then by the hospital's superintendent. Our leave was limited to three weeks per year.

Chris had no such restrictions. This was considered strange at the time but, on reflection, it could be justified, as he had so many invitations to speak at conferences and visit medical facilities. If the hospital authorities made an exception for him, it was their right and he, in fact, deserved it.

My first realisation of Chris's increasing political involvement was when he called me to his office and showed me a large pile of documents. He had been invited to a debate with one of the Nationalist government's most hated men abroad, Peter Hain, on a televised BBC broadcast.

Hain was a former South African who had become a political refugee in the United Kingdom. A so-called radical, he had fled South Africa to become a very vocal and successful anti-apartheid campaigner – and a thorn in the side of the Nats.

The documents that Chris showed me were lengthy – pages and pages on Hain, this 'enemy of South Africa', compiled by none other than the government's infamous and sinister Bureau of State Security. Chris had been given the file so that he could prepare himself adequately for the debate with Hain. I was shocked and refused to look at the documents. I left perplexed, but with a broader understanding of what was going on. I could not believe that Chris was allowing himself to be used by the Nats as a form of secret agent.

The debate between Chris and Hain was widely reported in South Africa, and the Nats loved it. According to their followers, Chris apparently did very well. I never heard what the anti-apartheid supporters felt, but I have no doubt that they believed their champion, Hain, to be the victor.

When I recently discussed this episode with former PFP MP Ray Swart, I was amazed to hear that he was well acquainted with the debate. He and a few others had intended to meet with Hain at around the same time, a plan that was well publicised. Chris had become aware of their intentions and had gone to see Swart and his colleagues in Durban to obtain more information about his television opponent. One thing about Chris was that he was always meticulously thorough.

In the aftermath, when Swart and his group were at the old Jan Smuts International Airport on their way to London, they received a call from a very angry Helen Suzman, who believed that, because Swart and his team had met with Chris before their departure to London, they were going to try to convince Hain not to support the sports boycott against South Africa. It will come as no surprise that their trip to London never took place.

* * *

By the mid-1970s, Chris was going on frequent high-profile visits overseas in order to improve South Africa's image abroad. Although for the most part I read about them in the newspapers, he told me about a few trips, including his visit to the Shah of Persia. This was a (well-disguised) attempt to break the sanctions imposed on South Africa at the time. It was construed by the government as an opportunity to influence the man on the Peacock Throne to keep oil flowing South Africa's way.

I was subsequently told that the trip was a success and that Chris had invited the Shah, who was in kidney failure at the time, to come to South Africa for a kidney transplant. The poor Shah, however, soon had bigger problems than kidney failure and never arrived.

Chris went on many other visits and soon new and ominous faces started to appear in the passages of Groote Schuur Hospital. Dr Eschel Rhoodie, his brother and others of the now-infamous Department of Information became regular visitors to Chris's office, which was close to mine.[1] Although Chris was certainly under no obligation to report his activities to me, I felt compelled to warn him of the dangers of consorting with these men.

After one of Eschel Rhoodie's visits, Chris accompanied him to the lift, which was about twenty yards down the corridor. After Rhoodie had disappeared in the lift, Chris returned to his office. I met him before he could enter, and I will never forget my words to him. 'Chris,' I warned, 'those who sup with the Devil need a long spoon.' He slammed the door in my face.

My suspicions were proved correct when the infamous Information Scandal, or *Muldergate*,[2] became public knowledge soon afterwards. In 1978, the Auditor-General tabled a report accusing the Department of Information of serious financial irregularities and the use of government funds without the knowledge or the approval of the treasury. During 1975, public money had been used to covertly fund a new English-language newspaper, the *Citizen*, to counter alleged liberal, anti-Nationalist press found in publications like the *Rand Daily Mail* and other English newspapers, including the *Cape Times* and the *Daily Dispatch*.

When this can of worms was finally opened, it became clear that the department – and more specifically the two Rhoodie brothers with Connie Mulder – had spearheaded this subterfuge using taxpayers' money. When the matter was raised in parliament, Mulder and the minister of finance, Dr Owen Horwood, as well as Prime Minister John Vorster, denied any knowledge of it. But increased public exposure exerted so much pressure on the prime minister that he was forced to resign from his position to take up a largely ceremonious post of state president.

The debacle thus forced the National Party caucus to elect a new party leader. Owing to the party's overwhelming majority in parliament, their leader would become the country's prime minister. The 1978 race for party leadership was largely waged between P.W. Botha and Connie Mulder, though Pik Botha also participated. Although Mulder, who was the National Party leader of the Transvaal, had the majority support of its members, his future in politics was now in doubt given his suspected involvement in the Information Scandal.

To me, they were all very poor future leaders. In any event, the battle for leadership was hotly contested. Chris was evidently backing Mulder: again from my office I saw a deputation waiting to see Chris, this time the same Eschel Rhoodie and Dominee Bingle, a pastor of the Reformed Church.[3] We Afrikaners are fiercely divided not only in politics, but also in our worship: we had three Afrikaans Reformed churches at the time, as we do today.

They had a meeting with Chris behind closed doors, which lasted for a very long time. When the delegation eventually left, it became clear to me what it had been all about. I could clearly hear Chris on the phone canvassing votes for Connie Mulder from members of the National Party caucus.

Chris's efforts didn't help, however, because soon afterwards Mulder had to resign in disgrace when the sorry affair of the Information Scandal entered the public domain. Sadly, P.W. Botha, as party leader, was duly elected and became the prime minister – and a very poor one at that.

Poor Chris. I think few people were as used and abused as he was. After this, his enthusiasm to act as an envoy to polish the tarnished image of the government waned.

I have no knowledge of what happened later, as I resigned from Groote Schuur Hospital soon afterwards, in 1980, but Chris told me over the phone in 1986 that he had been offered a post of ambassador and that his suggested preferences were London or Washington, D.C. He was very excited about this prospect; I am sure he saw himself as 'Mr Ambassador'. In fact, I believe that Chris, with his boyish charm and his excellent public-speaking ability, would have made an excellent foreign representative.

But the bubble soon burst. Chris's dreams were dashed when the best the government could offer him was Rome or Athens. He felt that those appointments were beneath his dignity, and he declined them.

29

Member of Parliament

'The end of apartheid is the beginning of our country. I would like to
make it clear that my Afrikaner Progressive Partyism is not disloyalty to
South Africa, is not working with the enemy, is not Marxism. I would
like to convince my fellow-Afrikaners I am at one with them on the basic
issue of love of this country.' — MARIUS BARNARD[1]

B ETWEEN 1980 AND 1989, I SERVED IN THE HOUSE OF ASSEMBLY
as a member of parliament. Over a period spanning nine years and one
month, I represented my party as its spokesman on health and saw out two
general elections and a referendum. I staved off a challenge in a nomination
battle for Parktown in 1987 and, with the subsequent disbanding of the
Progressive Federal Party two years later, served the remainder of my time
in parliament.

The first step in a new member of parliament's career is to be sworn in by
the Speaker. I had been elected in July 1980 and, given that the next session
of parliament was due to commence only in February of the following year,
I would have had to wait seven months on full salary with all the parliamentary privileges before being officially inducted into the legislature.

There was, however, a short sitting convened during September, and it
was during this period that I was sworn in. I'm sure that the Nats assumed
that I was going to be a conservative member of the PFP, based on the facts
that I was an Afrikaner and had originally hailed from rural Beaufort West.
Their eyes must have nearly popped out when they saw me being sworn in
flanked by liberal stalwarts Helen Suzman and Colin Eglin.

In 1981, the South African parliament was opened on the first Friday
in February with a twenty-one-gun salute and a short ceremony, which
was presided over by the prime minister. Official business started on the
following Monday, with a week-long no-confidence debate introduced by the
leader of the opposition. This provided the opposition with the opportunity
to take the government to task. During this occasion, a new member of
parliament used this opportunity to make his or her maiden speech. The

speech had to be made as soon as possible to enable the new member to participate freely in any ensuing debates. For some unknown reason, an MP's first speech was considered a very important event. I still cannot understand why. There was an unwritten understanding that it would not be interrupted by interjections, nor would there be any other attempts from the House to interrupt.

I chose to speak on environmental affairs and the necessity to legislate against the pollution of the sea. My speech was recognised in *Die Burger*, which depicted a cartoon of me titled 'The Doctor of the Sea'.

As spokesman for health, one of my responsibilities was to respond to questions from the press that related to our stance and policies on health matters. I soon discovered how the Nats survived on harassment and subtle persecution.

I received a letter from the South African Medical Council[2] to inform me that I had been reported to the council on the grounds that I was 'advertising' and that this contravened their rules. The complaint had been made by one of the council's members, Professor Guy de Klerk. According to him, my comments reported in the press constituted advertising. This was a ridiculous accusation but one that was, to me, not surprising from a National Party member of this council, one filled predominantly with members of this party.

My response was short and to the point. As an MP responsible to my party for health, it was my duty to speak about such matters and I would continue to do so. I never heard a word from the council again.

This was the same council that saw no reason to take any action against the doctors that attended to Steve Biko, and it was, with the exception of a few members, what I called the 'Nationalist Medical Council'. Its attempt to get me into trouble demonstrates just how silly responsible people can become when ideology becomes obsession.

* * *

Although I found parliament generally boring, one quite sensational event occurred in 1982, when a splinter group broke away from the National Party to form the Conservative Party (CP). This decision was taken largely in reaction to the government's constitutional proposals, which formed the basis of the newly introduced tricameral constitution, but the move also reflected the rise of extreme white conservatism and racism that was so prevalent during this bleak political period.

Under the leadership of Dr Andries Treurnicht, yet another former Dutch Reformed Church *dominee*, this ultra-right-wing party sought to entrench the already draconian and conservative laws of the country. Not surprisingly, they fared very well in the following election, taking many seats from the Nats but not enough to unseat the PFP as the official opposition. Prior to the CP's formation, Treurnicht was the Transvaal leader of the National Party. His advocacy of white hegemony and racial discrimination was both widely known and deeply disturbing.

I spoke out strongly against Treurnicht and his party's policies in early 1980, prior to my formal entry into politics. I was quoted by the *Sunday Times* as being 'the man who is certain to succeed Zac de Beer as MP for the [Parktown] constituency'.[3] The article went on to say that I regarded it as my mission to recruit Afrikaners to the Progressive Federal Party and that I pledged to fight racial discrimination on all levels.

At the 1980 press conference, which I gave in Johannesburg before flying out to Poland with my cardiac team, I listed particular issues for which I wanted to take up the political cudgel. These included addressing racial discrimination in the medical services, press freedom, the alienation of South Africa's black youth and foreign relations.

Having heard about the contents of a political speech made by Treurnicht in Benoni, I expressed my concern over the firm entrenchment of the racial policies of apartheid in South Africa, stating that it was difficult for me to believe that anyone could take the National Party seriously any longer. During the same speech of Treurnicht's, he declared that the infamous Immorality Act and Mixed Marriages Act would never be repealed and that the laws would be kept intact in all spheres of life. Clearly, nobody ever told him 'never say never'.

What Treurnicht said was complete 'double Dutch' to me. When he made further 'qualifying' statements, such as 'vertical differentiation', I rebuked him, saying that his advocacy of racial separation made me dizzy.

I admitted in the same press conference to being worried about the poor salaries being paid to coloured nurses in our hospitals. 'These girls have given us a devotion to duty which you cannot find anywhere else in the world,' I said, adding, 'then they, who treated us with such excellence, have to go home at the end of the month with less pay than whites. I call this hurtful discrimination.' This was entirely true and reflected the sorry state of white politics in our country at the time. I had always been particularly vociferous in my stance on racial equality in hospitals and was quoted as saying, 'If we have to start in one place to get rid of racial discrimination, we must start in medicine.'[4]

In 1982, the National Party had proposed a national referendum to gauge white public opinion and support for their planned tricameral system. They attempted to camouflage apartheid by establishing three separate Houses of Parliament: the House of Assembly for whites, the House of Representatives for coloureds and the House of Delegates for Indians. Each of the three chambers would determine laws relating to their own racial group. The government's intent was to establish an 'own-affairs' capability for the latter groups and to provide them with some form of political 'self-determination'. South African blacks, of course, had no such representation when this parliamentary system came into being in 1983.

There were many discussions held within the PFP about whether we should vote *yes* or *no* in this referendum. My view was that we should abstain. Firstly, I was not in favour of supporting any 'initiative' by the NP and, in my opinion, it was politically dishonest. Secondly, it would have been easy for the Nats to brand us as bedfellows of the Conservative Party, which was clearly not supportive of the ruling party's initiative. Thirdly, I knew that the black population would not only oppose this political dispensation, but actively engage against it.

Unfortunately, on Van Zyl's insistence, the PFP decided not to abstain but to vote *no*. Most of our party were actually not very enthusiastic about supporting the *no* vote either, so the majority of the meetings regarding the referendum were badly organised and, consequently, poorly attended.

During this time it was my responsibility to talk at meetings in mainly Afrikaans-speaking conservative areas, since that language is, of course, my mother tongue. These events, as can be expected, were never well attended and, at two of them, I was ignored completely: not one solitary seat in the hall was occupied.

Our organisers often totally misread these meetings. On one occasion, a referendum-related meeting was arranged by our party in Potchefstroom, where some idiot had hired a hall with about 400 seats. Because we were the organisers, we had to travel all the way from Johannesburg and arrive an hour early to arrange the hall and adorn it with slogans and other party paraphernalia. I had to then stand outside and wait for the time that the meeting was due to start.

With five minutes to go, we had an audience of four people. While I was standing outside praying for more people to attend, a married couple stopped at the hall and our numbers increased significantly from four to six. I watched them expectantly entering the hall. But as they went in, the husband looked up at our slogans and said to his wife, 'Good God, old woman, it's the Progs. We have enough problems with the Nats.' They left immediately, and I had the dubious honour of addressing an audience of four – and 396 empty seats.

To no one's surprise, the Nats easily garnered sufficient support from the white electorate to push the referendum through.

* * *

I wish I could say that my presence in parliament had an impact on my constituency or on South Africa, but in all honesty I can't. If I had to rate my overall contribution as a member of parliament, I think I would give myself a score of three out of ten at the most.

My constituents never really needed an MP. Many of them were affluent and, although largely Prog supporters, most didn't have a clue about our non-racial, non-discriminatory and one-man-one-vote policy. If they had, they would not have voted for me: often, while doing door-to-door canvassing in blocks of flats, they would tell me that they always voted for the Progs, but at the same time they made dreadfully racist remarks and begged me to do something about the 'K*****s' in the street down below.

I was bored to death sitting in parliament, having to listen to poor speeches by poor speakers on subjects I had no interest in – debates on farming subsidies, the railways, trade unions and others. There were, however, a few very good debaters in the House. The best, I thought, was Dr Ferdi Hartzenberg, a natural and passionate speaker. Although a member of the Conservative Party, he could give a rousing speech. Even if I didn't agree with what he was saying – which was most of the time – I could always listen to him attentively.

Amusingly, and much to my delight, he attacked the Nats mercilessly. This, of course, had the effect of dramatically raising the blood pressure of the party to which he had once belonged and, in the process, caused severe embarrassment to many of its members.

Our leader, Van Zyl Slabbert, was an excellent speaker. His speeches were well prepared, well thought-out and made perfect political sense. He tore the National Party's speeches and policies to shreds but, tragically, the Nationalists never listened to him.

I can't really judge the Nats objectively, and for good reason. Not only did I find their policies unconscionable, but I disliked most of their MPs. There were, however, a few exceptions, including Hendrik Schoeman, the minister of transport; Hans Rabie; and a handful more.

There were even members of my own party whom I found insincere and who played more for the press gallery than for the party – and their country.

But the worst speaker of all was P.W. Botha, a man of very little ability who, in spite of his mediocrity and due to perseverance and his many years in parliament, rose through the party ranks to become prime minister and later state president. His style of debate was that of a bully: attacking and aggressive. All of his Nat MPs had to sit through his belligerent and often finger-wagging tirades with expressions of adoration on their faces, laughing at his stupid jokes, with well-rehearsed 'hear! hear!s'.

To the amusement of the opposition and even to his own supporters, one of P.W. Botha's speeches was totally destroyed by a member of ours, Horace van Rensburg, or Horrible Horace, which was how he was referred to by the Nats. Horace, with his loud, clear, booming voice, was the best interjector in the House. In one of his supposedly important monologues, P.W. Botha followed the 'I have a dream' theme from Martin Luther King Jr's famous speech. In P.W.'s version, he had one important dream after another for South Africa. The Nats were looking up at him, starry-eyed and admiring, while the rest of the House remained deadly silent.

Immediately after he had trumpeted his last 'I have a dream', Horace's voice boomed out, resonating in every corner of the House, as he interjected in Afrikaans: '*Maar dit is maar net 'n Nat droom.*' Translated, this means, 'But it is only a Nat dream.' Unfortunately for the Nats, the word *nat* in Afrikaans has another meaning – *wet*.

The House collapsed in peals of laughter. Even his own party members couldn't contain themselves, and P.W.'s great policy statement was totally destroyed. Such moments were unfortunately very few and far between. If one considers what happened after the P.W. years and the subsequent demise of the NP, Horace was completely correct – it was only a wet dream.

We almost always came off second best during the no-confidence debate. Due to the Nats' having far more representatives, they had considerably more debating time – a ratio of at least two to one.

Van Zyl Slabbert's lead-in speech was always far better than anything the Nats could produce. One or two of their members, whose sole purpose was not to debate its merits but to ridicule our party, would follow his speech and launch a personal attack on Van Zyl with their usual nonsensical rubbish.

We soon, however, had an opportunity to come out on top. In 1986, Pik Botha had made a speech in which he admitted that, in the future, a black person could well become the president of South Africa. This was a certainty to our party, but to most Nats it was absolute sacrilege. During his final speech in the debate, P.W. Botha not only contradicted Pik, but severely took him to task, openly humiliating him. Pik just sat there like a naughty schoolboy, looking fearful and trembling.

When Van Zyl stood up for the closing speech of this no-confidence debate, the members of the PFP waited expectantly for him to destroy the Nats and cause further dissent. But, without informing our caucus or most of its senior members, he announced his resignation from parliament.

To me, his resignation was no surprise. I had watched Van Zyl's body language and noticed his dejection. He was fast losing interest, and was not his usual vibrant personality during this debate.

On the morning of Van Zyl's resignation, Alex Boraine had come to see me and said that he had a message for me from Van Zyl. I had immediately responded, 'Van Zyl is going to resign, isn't he?' Boraine had looked at me, surprised, and asked, 'How do you know?' I had replied that I could read it in his posture and his behaviour.

Van Zyl resigned from his position as parliamentarian because he felt that it was becoming an irrelevant institution in the context of South Africa's political problems. Although we empathised with his stance, for us the timing of his departure was unforgivable. Poor Colin Eglin had to take over the leadership again and was left to repair bridges. Alex Boraine followed Van Zyl out, but I think that Boraine would have stayed on had he been elected leader. I suspect that he must have realised that his opinion of his own ability to lead the Progs was not shared by the majority of the caucus.

Van Zyl Slabbert's resignation as PFP leader in 1986 was a great personal loss for me. It was due to him that I had entered parliament in the first place. He was a popular and outstanding leader, an exceptionally astute politician and a personal friend of mine. His departure strengthened my disillusion-ment with parliament and my desire to leave when the time was right.

Total Onslaught(er)

T HE 1987 GENERAL ELECTION WAS A DIFFICULT TIME, NOT ONLY
for me, but for our party as well. We lost many seats to the Nats and
suffered reduced majorities in those constituencies that we were able to win.
The Conservative Party, however, fared far better and became the official
opposition in parliament.

I must have set a political record during this year, for, within a few
months, I was opposed twice, not by the Nats but by members of my very
own party, the Progs.

The first few weeks of the new parliamentary session had passed when
one of the four constituency councillors, Ian Davidson, informed me by
telephone that fellow councillor Sam Moss was planning to oppose my
nomination, and that he had the support of two of the other councillors,
Lacon Stanton and Ray Graham.

As I mentioned earlier, from the first day of meeting them I had felt that
they didn't want me in Parktown. This animosity had grown over the years.
All three were insignificant politicians and I felt that their input was not
what the constituency needed. (Not that my input, to be honest, was either.)

But I would not leave on Sam and his henchmen's terms so, that very
night, I flew back to Johannesburg from Cape Town to plan my campaign
to defeat Sam. I wanted to get rid of him in the constituency. Ian Davidson
was totally supportive of my nomination and put a great deal of time, advice
and effort into my organising efforts.

At least 80 per cent of the constituency committee supported me, but Sam
discovered a technicality: that their election was not legal – the constituency
was required to elect a new committee, which would then decide who would
be their candidate.

My close friends and I organised to get my supporters to the meeting to
elect the committee. I went on to obtain significant support from the committee, and Sam was soundly thrashed. He realised that his political future
was over but tried, even then, to find fault with the election. He eventually
withdrew his name for the sake of 'party peace'. The fact was that he was a
beaten man. He soon resigned from the PFP and as a councillor.

As the general election neared, there was again speculation about my being opposed. We had a candidates' meeting on a Saturday morning, attended by prospective candidates, councillors and committee members. Here, we discussed strategy for the election.

An active participant at the meeting was Zoe Marchand, a Prog and past mayor of Sandton. She asked questions about our plans and, when she left the meeting, she went straight to the National Party officials and became their candidate for Parktown.

I could understand her reasons. She was very ambitious and must have felt rejected by the Progs, who never considered nominating her to higher office. The reason for her failure, however, was her political mediocrity. As an English-speaking and high-society lady with influential friends, to the Nats she was a very attractive option for a mainly English-speaking constituency. Above all, however, she was a well-known Prog who could embarrass us by leaving the party.

An election is never pleasant. I hated canvassing, especially the door-to-door duties. To get through the front door of potential voters was like trying to get into Fort Knox – aggressive dogs, security gates and multiple-padlocked doors. On several occasions, I was verbally abused and chased away.

But Killarney, previously zoned within Helen Suzman's Houghton constituency and later falling under Parktown, was a joy in which to canvass. Flat upon flat was opened by friendly old ladies, their husbands dead, their children overseas, and only too pleased to see another living creature – and offering cakes, chocolates and tea. Often, I had to give a free consultation.

'I always vote for Helen,' they would greet me. On election day, they would turn out in their hundreds to vote. God bless them, because Zoe Marchand was defeated, never to be heard of again politically.

* * *

Although during my parliamentary career my contribution was not as significant as I had hoped it would be, I can claim at least one success. Every year in the committee stage of the transport vote, our spokesperson was short of speakers. A ten-minute slot was easy to fill, and every year I used this opportunity, as party spokesman on health, to attack the authorisation of smoking on South African Airways (SAA) flights and to warn of its associated dangers to the heart and health in general.

Every year, the minister of transport, Hendrik Schoeman, in his usual frivolous style, shot down my argument by claiming that it would result in job losses on the tobacco farms. He accused me and the Progs of hating farmers. Every year, my plea fell on deaf ears.

Before the 1987 general election, Schoeman – a smoker himself, who exhibited all the health hazards of smoking, including severe emphysema – retired. His successor was Eli Louw. During Louw's vote, I made my same anti-tobacco speech and plea to ban smoking on the national carrier.

To my amazement, and to that of those Nat Cabinet ministers who smoked, he accepted my argument and banned smoking on our national airline. This was not really a political triumph, but a great breakthrough for the anti-smoking lobby. I was told that Louw made this decision without Cabinet approval and was in real trouble with his colleagues who smoked heavily – including F.W. de Klerk and Pik Botha.

When I now, many years later, hear the no-smoking announcement on SAA flights, I cannot help but believe that I played a small part in what is now a smoking ban in all public places.

* * *

My workload became increasingly heavy, particularly when parliament was in session. From the beginning of January to the end of June, parliament sat in Cape Town, so I commuted every week between our Clifton home in Cape Town and Johannesburg.

Monday was spent at parliament. On Monday evening I'd return to Johannesburg to do ward rounds and see my patients. On Tuesday, I'd operate and then fly back to Cape Town that night. During the day on Wednesday I'd be back in parliament. Then it was back to Johannesburg the same evening, ready to operate on Thursday and then return to Cape Town on Friday to spend the weekend with my family.

At the same time, I was giving medical insurance presentations for Crusader Life all over South Africa. As if I wasn't busy enough, I became a consultant for Golden Products between 1988 and 1989.

My attendance at parliament during this period was, therefore, poor, and my contribution was not what I had hoped it would be when I first entered politics. Very often, when there was a vote taking place, I didn't even know what we were voting for.

As part of their election campaign, the Nats ran a huge fear campaign, spearheaded by its minister of foreign affairs (who was 'never in favour of apartheid') and the minister of defence. These were the final days of the

Angolan conflict and the 'total onslaught' against the Republic of South Africa by *Die Rooi Gevaar* – 'The Red (Communist) Danger' – took precedence over all other regional and domestic activities. Our troops were engaged in Angola and South West Africa and our boys were fighting and dying on the Border. Pik Botha, ably assisted by his fellow propagandists, was making much use of this in every devious way possible. During the campaign, the Progs were identified as being 'in bed with the ANC'.

Two photographs published during the campaign were particularly effective. One was of Helen Suzman at one or other meeting, standing with her arm around Nelson Mandela's wife, Winnie, who was probably the most hated woman by white government supporters at the time. The other depicted one of our MPs, Pierre Cronje, attending a meeting and giving a rather half-hearted 'Black Power' salute. This was their 'evidence' of where the Progs' loyalty lay.

Our party, however, was becoming irrelevant and we were now outnumbered by the Conservative Party hardliners. Clive Derby-Lewis was one such character. He sat next to me in the House, separated only by a one-yard passage. His interjections, heard by only a few near to him, were so racist that I detested the man. It came as no surprise when he was charged and convicted as the co-murderer of black liberation leader Chris Hani.

With our poor showing in the 1987 election, the rise of the Conservative Party and my total disillusionment with parliament, my determination to leave became an obsession. There were increasing rumblings of discontent in the party, led by former MPs who had failed to retain their seats in the previous election.

Many members of the party felt that we could increase our support base by amalgamating with two minority groups led by two past members of the National Party, Denis Worrall and Wynand Malan. I didn't trust either of them and believed that all they were interested in, having been rejected by the Nats, was getting into parliament, which they would do by using the Progs as a vehicle. To me, they were not Progs at heart. How right I later turned out to be!

Of course, there had to be a scapegoat for our poor election results. Colin Eglin was blamed and his position as head of the party was made untenable. After all of his years of loyal service to the PFP, including his willingness to step in at short notice to lead the Progs when Van Zyl Slabbert resigned, his reward from the party was pressure to resign.

Colin duly did so and in 1988 Zach de Beer was chosen as the party's new leader, entering parliament by becoming a nominated member.[1] We had only one such member at the time, so poor old Professor Nic Olivier had to resign to make way for Zach. This was not well received, especially not by the professor's wife.

I will never forget how, when Zach was introduced as the man who was going to lead the Progs, John Malcomess mumbled, 'Not to lead the party, but to bury the party.' He was ultimately proved correct. Zach was a pleasant and honourable man but not a great leader and, as a politician, he was not in Colin Eglin's class.

Fortunately, Colin remained closely involved in party affairs and stayed in a position to continue making all major party decisions. By now, the idea of disbanding the PFP and joining up with other factions to form a new party was gaining momentum within the caucus. The majority of MPs were in favour of this option, but there was strong opposition by most of the senior 'old Progs', including party stalwarts Helen Suzman and Ray Swart.

The most vociferous opposition, however, came from Harry Schwarz. He was one of the members with whom I had never felt particularly comfortable. He always had a problem with something or other, or with something that one of the other members had said. Schwarz had the dubious distinction of making the most amazing speeches in parliament: for the first half he was a Prog, and the second half a Nat. It thus came as no surprise that the Nats later rewarded him with the ambassadorship to the United States. In his defence, Schwarz was one of the most hard-working MPs we had, could discuss every Bill and, as spokesman for finance, made a most brilliant contribution. He should really have been the spokesman of every department and, most importantly, the only member of his party. He was very much his own man and not a team player.

The move towards disbanding the party and amalgamating with the others was supported by the majority of the caucus. In April 1989, a meeting was held in Johannesburg to obtain final party approval. There were hundreds of delegates present and Colin Eglin, as chairman, presided.

When the vote was taken, hundreds of hands were raised: it appeared that everybody was in favour of the disbanding. When Colin asked whether there were 'any against', only one hand was raised – mine. Colin, not realising it was me, made a derogatory remark to 'dismiss the only stupid dissident'.

A newly formed party, the Democratic Party (DP) – or the 'Dead Party', as I termed it, because of its carrying of dead wood and probable demise – was subsequently formed. I was now the only surviving member of the once proud Progressive Federal Party, whose founding members had formed the party based on honourable ideals.

When I arrived at parliament a few days later, I found all my books, correspondence and belongings removed. I was relegated to a small office among the Nats. My seat in parliament was no longer mine and I was banished to the seat that was the furthest away from the Speaker's chair. I was now the only Independent in parliament and had committed political suicide.

Farewell to Politics

M Y FATHER WAS RIGHT: POLITICIANS ARE THE UNEMPLOYED or the unemployable. As an MP, I was the embodiment of that statement. Although my nine years in parliament made very little impact and my contribution was far smaller than I had initially hoped it would be, I did experience visits to parts of South Africa that saddened me and influenced me personally.

One of these was to the so-called Border. Here, I saw and spoke to bewildered eighteen-year-old boys, just out of school and far from home, preparing for war in the bush and practising with live bullets. I visited the wounded in field hospitals – some maimed for life.

At night, we had barbecues with brigadiers, generals and other senior officers, drinking 'Klippies and Coke' and the best South African wines. Talk about the 'wicked SWAPO', 'ultimate victory' and 'preparedness' grew louder.[1] As the alcohol flowed freely to the brain, jokes became increasingly crude and the laughter more boisterous – all while our young boys were fighting and dying in a foreign country for an unjust cause.

One slogan I saw was emblazoned on the instrument panel of a helicopter that flew me from one base in Namibia to another. It read 'Slam Sam', in reference to Sam Nujoma, the leader of SWAPO. Sam was so 'slammed' that he served as president of Namibia for fifteen years. The great 'victorious' officers eventually reaped their rewards and are now living on good pensions in splendid retirement.

I will never forget the fearful, anxious faces of those young boys and how they fought and were wounded, maimed and killed for a war that was lost before it even started. History will not forget the great follies of P.W. Botha, General Magnus Malan and the rest of the Cabinet during this awful period.

* * *

Other visits that I will never forget during this time were to homes for abandoned children as well as mentally and physically disabled children. I saw nuns at St Joseph's Home near Cape Town's airport giving love, care and devotion to the most severely disabled of children.

We cardiac surgeons had praise and honour heaped on us for our accomplishments, but compared to these nuns we were nothing. But then, of course, their life's work didn't sell newspapers – the news media could not create sensational news headlines and money out of the work of living saints.

I visited mental institutions, especially those in the Eastern Cape, where patients were often incarcerated for life and where the care facilities and living conditions left much to be desired. Again, I witnessed many hard-working and dedicated staff in thankless careers.

My prison visits were more than depressing. The prisons were over-crowded, young boys mixed with adults, who were angry, desperate and harbouring enormous hate for the whites – a perfect breeding ground for future criminals. I found it both strange and disturbing that white South Africans could sleep at night while this was going on a few miles from their large secured homes. I am sure that many criminals of today received their training in those prisons.

* * *

Before the 1989 election, the remnants of the once largest party, which under General Jan Smuts had led the country during the Second World War, had dwindled to just four MPs. The remaining PFP members formed part of the Democratic Party, and the legacy of the South African Party became history.

During January of that year, P.W. Botha suffered a stroke that left him partially paralysed. Botha officially resigned from the presidency during August 1989, and, after the Nats won the general election that took place a month later, F.W. de Klerk assumed the role of president.

The uniting of those parties in forming the DP ironically resulted in significantly better results being obtained in this election.[2] But despite their winning thirty-four seats, the Conservative Party, which opposed any form of power-sharing with other racial groups, strengthened their position as the official opposition, attaining forty-one.

My prediction of a break-up within the DP soon came true, however. Once back in parliament, a few members of Wynand Malan's party joined the ANC and Malan and Worrall themselves were looking for greener pastures.

Being an Independent had its advantages. There were no boring caucus meetings to attend, no chief whip breathing down your neck and you could come and go as you pleased.

On the last day of that session of parliament – a Friday – I attended its opening. After the parliamentary prayer, I walked out of this institution, and politics, for the last time. I never looked back.

* * *

Though not overly impressed with my own performance, I am very proud of the party to which I belonged. I supported their policies and principles then and today. I was proud to be in a caucus with such magnificent and progressive thinkers: Helen Suzman, whose contribution can never be appreciated enough; Colin Eglin, a man of principle and dedication and a willingness to continue fighting when all was lost; Ray Swart, who along with a supportive wife was a person not often spoken about, but who sacrificed his whole life for the progressive cause; and many others.

These were some of the few brave men and women who, in 1959, were principled enough to risk their parliamentary future to break away from the United Party. In forming the Progressive Party they entered a political wilderness with a policy that, at the time, made most white South Africans shudder. The party accepted the equality of South Africans, no matter what colour, religion, sex or creed. It advocated no racial discrimination, a universal franchise and a strong Bill of Rights to protect individuals against the state.

To the vast majority of white South Africans, this was a totally unacceptable perspective. Accusations of being in collusion with *Die Swart Gevaar* – 'The Black Danger' – and being 'soft on communism' were continually flung at us. When the PFP first advocated the release of Nelson Mandela and the unbanning of the ANC, the attack on the party became all the more vicious.

I still find it very strange today – after some seventeen years of democracy – that very few white South Africans supported our party's constitution during the apartheid years. That 'the great danger', Nelson Mandela, would become president for five years and the ANC the governing party today makes the rejection of our policies by the white electorate all the more difficult to understand.

And what are the cornerstones of our young democracy? No racial discrimination, one-man, one-vote and a strong Bill of Rights protecting individuals – all principles that we so strongly advocated. Even stranger and supremely ironic is that, although the once strong racist National Party is now an unpleasant memory of our country's past, some of its members have managed to worm their way into the ANC and their Cabinet.

After the Second World War, it was virtually impossible to find a German who admitted ever to having been a Nazi. After 1994, the Nats followed these Germans' dishonest example and, today, it is difficult to find anyone who will admit that he or she was a Nat or supported the National Party's policies. I can understand this: as the deeds for which they were responsible and their ramifications continue to unfold, I would be very ashamed to have supported this party.

When the National Party was eventually disbanded in 2005, it was one of the greatest days of my life. The party that had caused so much damage and untold suffering to all South Africans – black and white, young and old – was now finally history. I would really like this day declared a public holiday for all South Africans so that we may remember this party with all the bitterness and contempt it deserves.

And what of the Progs? How should we be judged? We had a just policy and pointed out all the injustices and cruelty towards the disenfranchised blacks during the apartheid era, but we were all comfortable in our white cocoons, protected, privileged and living in affluence and comfort.

I still, however, feel satisfied with the role we played in helping to shape the political destiny of South Africa. When history is one day recorded, it will recognise that we stood up and *were* counted. I remain exceptionally proud and deeply humbled to have been the last serving representative of this honourable party.

PART IV

Critical Illness Insurance

Good minds create ideas and dreams. Great minds take the ideas and dreams and make them real. Dr Marius Barnard is one of those great minds. Recognising his patients' need for a type of insurance product that provided financial protection on diagnosis of a critical condition, not death, he began to seek ways of making that insurance policy a reality.

Dr Barnard was met with resistance at every turn, and it became clear to him that, in order to make this insurance product come to life, he would have to educate himself on the duties of pricing actuaries, underwriters, legal reviewers and advisors. Combining the precision of a cardiac surgeon, the fire of a politician and the passion of a missionary's son, he did just that. He read and studied every item he could get his hands on to learn the insurance industry from the inside out. Now when someone challenged him on the development of his idea, he was armed with the knowledge to counter them in a way only Marius Barnard can do.

His hard work and tenacity finally paid off when the first critical illness insurance policy was introduced in South Africa. Then the work really began, and he became the ambassador of critical illness insurance, delivering the message across his home country.

On 6 August 1996, the chief marketing officer for my company walked into my office and handed me a folder with a picture of Dr Marius Barnard on the front cover. The folder also had the statement on the cover: 'Not because you are going to die but because you are going to live.' In that very instant, Dr Barnard's message changed my world forever.

I contacted him and asked if he would help me bring a product to the United States. He agreed and we developed a plan to introduce critical illness insurance to the US market through a nationwide tour. What a journey it was! He worked tirelessly, always challenging those around him to do more, think more, sell more and build new features into the product. He listened to excuses, new thoughts and ideas, criticisms and enthusiastic cheers, taking in every word. He spent sleepless nights sifting through that information and inventing ways to improve his concept.

He would meet me every morning before the talks and ask how many people had confirmed attendance. He would check the room to see if the chairs were arranged properly and make sure that there was space to bring in more chairs as the room filled to capacity. He would drill me as soon as the meeting was over about what my plans were for following up with the attendees to thank them and see if they understood the product and his message. He would have me move his slides around and revise his talk based on the reaction of the day. He would not eat (unless I tricked him with ice cream). He would pace and rub his hands. He always expressed his concerns to me after every talk about what and how he could do more. He was relentless. And he was a success, and he made me a success.

My travels with Dr Barnard enabled me to see the man the world saw: the hard-driving, passionate, 'no excuses', sometimes moody and temperamental person. But those travels also blessed me with the opportunity to get to know the man who had a twinkle in his eye, a deep love for his wife and family, a great sense of humour, a charm that could turn the world in a different direction and a practical joker with tricks that knew no bounds.

The practical jokes he pulled when we travelled together continue to bring me joy. He once, for example, took our laser pointer and hid behind a counter in an airport shop. I was looking for an antacid (due to the heartburn he gave me) and had no idea he was anywhere around. While I was trying to decide which one to choose, a red dot appeared on a particular brand. I immediately told the sales lady, 'I'll have the one with the red dot on it.' She looked at me totally confused and handed me the package just as Marius came out from hiding behind the counter, laser pointer in hand, smiling – and quite proud of himself.

Another time we checked into one of the hotels on our speaking tour and a professional baseball team was staying at the same hotel. There was a big sign in the lobby proclaiming, 'Please do not ask for autographs.' We went to the check-in counter and Marius proudly said to the young lady checking him in, 'I see you are expecting me this evening.' Her bewildered face was priceless.

There are so many things I could share about this great man and what he has meant in my life and in so many other lives around the world. My hope is that you will catch a glimpse of the man I came to know and cherish, and that you will gain an understanding of the part of his life that, in my humble opinion, gave the world his greatest gift of all: a product that protects a person's financial health while they are regaining their physical health. Dr Marius Barnard, thank you for your wonderful gift.

MARCIA JOHNSON
BIRMINGHAM, ALABAMA
AUGUST 2010

32

Departure Point

O N A COLD, BLUSTERY CAPE WINTER'S MORNING, INEZ AND I LEFT
our comfortable bungalow on Clifton's Fourth Beach, Cape Town,
to embark on a new career in politics. The move to Johannesburg would
prove to be another defining moment of my life: never in my wildest dreams
could I have imagined that, within a few months, a new insurance policy
would form an integral part of my daily life.

People often ask me how I, as a doctor, became involved in insurance.
This is difficult to explain. Perhaps the seed was sown by my parents, whose
lives were dominated by compassion and the desire to help their fellow
human beings.

As a boy of thirteen years, I was introduced to insurance by my father.
Up until that point, I had been unaware of its existence, let alone its importance. In Beaufort West at that time there was an Old Mutual insurance
office. Whereas youngsters like me had no appreciation for its manager's
occupation, what we certainly did appreciate was the fact that he had two
beautiful daughters, both of whom were much admired and desired by the
older boys. I was still too young to experience such feelings, but I frequently
heard the fantasy talk of my friends about what they would like to do with
these two beauties.

One autumn afternoon, on 13 April 1940, my father asked me to accompany him after school to the Old Mutual office in Donkin Street, a short
distance from our house. The manager sat behind a big desk looking very
stern. He quickly became friendly when my father explained the purpose
of our visit.

I didn't understand much of what was discussed by the two of them,
but, when we left an hour later, my father informed me that he had just
taken out a life insurance policy of £250 for me. My immediate reaction was
that I would be extremely rich when I died one day. In those days, £250 was
a fortune – it was approximately equal to my father's annual income. I still
have the policy document today, along with its policy number: 411124.

My father faithfully paid the annual premium of £4 6s until I started
earning an income in 1951, after which I took over the payment of the

premiums. The £4 became R8 when South Africa changed its currency from pounds to rands in the early 1960s.

Every year, just before my birthday, the account for R8 would arrive and I'd pay it without fail. It was part of the memory of my loving father, and every premium payment reminded me of him, his sacrifices for us and the day that we walked up the road to the Old Mutual office – and what I had considered to be an unbelievable wealth of £250.

My next encounter with an insurance agent occurred many years later, in 1951, soon after I had qualified as a doctor and started my residency at Groote Schuur Hospital. I have to be honest and admit that I felt flattered that I was considered economically important enough for such a high-powered financial advisor to visit me. I was earning only £20 a month. With this misguided financial ego, it didn't take much persuasion to become the proud owner of a life insurance policy of £2 000 from Sanlam. What wealth! At that stage, I knew only of life insurance; endowment and disability policies were for the future.

My third experience with an insurance agent took place when I went into private practice as a general practitioner in Salisbury in 1953. When it became known that there was a new doctor in town, I was overrun by life insurance agents from all of the companies in the city, including Sanlam, Old Mutual, Norwich and Southern Life, among others. Again, I was rather flattered and I listened to them all.

One agent, Oom Karl Herbst – a Sanlam representative – was very gentle and not disposed towards being pushy. We soon decided that I needed an endowment policy that would pay out the princely sum of £5 000 when I reached fifty years of age. Oom Karl and Tannie Bet's eldest daughter, Younsi, as a matter of interest, was my first introduction to congenital heart disease and cardiac surgery. She was about sixteen years old and suffered from a severe congenital heart abnormality, tetralogy of Fallot. I had not the faintest idea what this was all about then but, by a strange coincidence, Chris was in Minneapolis training under Dr Walton Lillehei at the time, furthering his career as a cardiac surgeon. I contacted him with great difficulty by telephone and sent him the medical investigations available on Younsi. They agreed to see her and she left Salisbury by plane for the United States, where they operated on her. Congenital cardiac surgery was still in its infancy back then, and she died on the operating table. We were all shattered after such great hope and expectation of success. Her ashes were all that returned, in a small wooden cask. We bonded with the Herbst family over this sad event and remained bosom friends with them until their deaths. That was not the end of my relationship with tetralogy of Fallot, however: I later performed many successful operations on patients with this condition, as described in Part II of this book.

Inez and I, in our innocent immaturity, thought that the endowment policy organised by Oom Karl when we were in Salisbury was a fortune. We actually discussed what we would do with the money when the policy paid out twenty years later – we'd go on an expensive holiday, buy a Bentley or purchase a luxury holiday home. We never considered a thing called *inflation*.

In 1953, we could buy a new car for £400 and a solid, big new house for £5 000. But when the policy finally matured, £5 000 couldn't have bought a one-bedroomed cabin. It could perhaps have bought a run-down second-hand car.

I soon instructed my receptionist in Salisbury that I would not see any more insurance agents because they became persistent nuisances who wasted my time. In addition, with three insurance policies to my name, I believed that I faced a financially secure future.

While working at Groote Schuur Hospital later, it became obvious to me that, due to certain circumstances, I would not work there until retirement age. As a consequence I consulted a financial advisor from Sanlam, who gave me excellent advice, and I took out a retirement annuity policy with a premium of R150 per month. That was all that I could afford, but what a wonderful investment it proved to be. From 1980, I paid the annual R1 800 premium and, when it matured in 1997, it was valued at R450 000. If only I could have afforded R18 000 a year from the start. But that is water under the bridge.

* * *

The concept of insurance has been around for a long time. It is possible that it was already known and practised in ancient times. It seems, though, that the first records date from the Middle Ages.

The first ever life insurance policy is said to have been issued in 1583, but the first time insurance was officially recognised and passed into law was in England in 1601. It was only in the second half of the seventeenth century, however, that the insurance business as we know it today began to find its feet.

For two centuries thereafter, the most common types of insurance were those that indemnified the insured against fire, or loss of ships and cargo at sea. These sectors of the industry probably evolved as a result of historical precedents – insurance against fire because of the devastation caused by the Great Fire of London in 1666, and marine insurance as a result of Britain's being a world leader in trade on the high seas at the time.

Each evolving step in the endeavours of mankind saw – and continues to see – a parallel transformation in the insurance industry. In the industrial age, the concept of insurance as it affected the ordinary man began to expand. Insurers started to specialise in areas beyond those of fire and shipping.

If one studies the history of medical insurance carefully, it is obvious that the necessity for the policy and its development were as a result of the medical conditions of the time, the knowledge of the diseases and the outcomes after treatment.

Up to the 1900s, the major causes of death were infectious diseases caused by bacteria and viruses. These diseases affected all age groups and often resulted in epidemics. Such epidemics, including smallpox, the bubonic plague, polio and other scourges, form a significant part of history. The Spanish flu epidemic of 1918, for example, killed more people than those that perished in the Second World War. The virus caused between 40 and 100 million deaths worldwide. Smallpox, which had ravaged mankind for some 800 years, was cured as a result of the pioneering efforts of Edward Jenner in the late 1700s, and the incidence of smallpox in Europe then began to disappear with the spread of vaccination. It took many more years, however, for doctors to start investigating the application of the principles behind vaccination against smallpox to other infectious diseases.

With the exception of Jenner's exceptional discovery of the smallpox vaccine, few, if any, cures were available and treatments were symptomatic – tepid sponging to reduce the fever, administering cough mixtures and providing nourishing broth, for example. The patient was confined to bed and there were effectively only two outcomes: death or complete recovery. By 1900, pneumonias and enteritis (diarrhoea) were some of the most common causes of death, while cancer, heart attacks and strokes were less prevalent. Accidental deaths were, unlike today, rare.

All ages were affected: life expectancy for males was forty-two and for females forty-eight. These statistics had major financial implications: if a thirty-six-year-old male developed pneumonia and recovered completely within a few days, he could go back to work and earn as before. Should he die, however, his income would stop, leaving his wife and dependants destitute.

For these reasons, the insurance industry developed life insurance, which, on the death of the policy holder, paid out the insured sum, relieving the financial uncertainty of those left behind. Life insurance remains a leading protection insurance policy today.

In 1929, Alexander Fleming discovered penicillin, the world's first antibiotic. Owing to his magnificent contribution and those of others, antibiotics provided the breakthrough for the cure of bacterial infections. Some years later, in the 1950s, Jonas Salk successfully developed the vaccine against the dreaded viral disease polio, which was then administered to entire populations. From this point, great strides were made in the combating of infectious diseases, which subsequently became preventable by the advanced development of vaccines and immunisations. Greater life expectancy was the inevitable result and, associated with this, the development of a healthier and more affluent society.

People in the workplace increasingly required more money to foot the bill of their material needs. Injuries at work and disability, however, emerged as the greatest financial threats to the well-being of the employee and his or her dependants. Again, insurance came to the rescue. Policies for income protection and permanent disability were introduced, providing money when it was needed most. These policies remain popular today, as they supply a monthly income to replace the loss of earnings under such circumstances.

Short-term insurance is easy to understand. One insures one's house to ensure financial protection if it burns down and one's car in case it is stolen or involved in a road accident. We all consider this form of insurance to be essential, and we take it out without hesitation. Long-term insurance includes a group of policies that cover life, disability, critical illness and long-term care insurance. What is important to realise is that these policies will not pay out unless the claimant has a medical condition and a doctor's certificate to confirm the diagnosis.

Life insurance pays out only on the diagnosis of death, and disability insurance on the diagnosis of a medical condition that makes it impossible for the claimant to work. It is therefore no wonder that these policies are collectively termed *protection insurance*: they protect people financially should their health fail.

* * *

The World Health Organization (WHO) defines health as a 'state of physical, mental and social well-being and not merely the absence of disease or infirmity'.[1] I believe that every practising doctor, especially the modern doctor, should have this definition displayed in large print on his or her wall. In addition to physical health, there are two other very important requirements for this definition of health to be met: mental and social well-being. The definition makes it absolutely clear that a person can be sick even when free of disease.

To prove this point, I use the example of a forty-five-year-old Zulu male. He has no physical disease and is strong; he is physically able to work in a mine and perform other forms of manual labour. He has, however, been unemployed for three years. He therefore has no income and cannot provide shelter or food for his family. As a result, he has become severely depressed, which has not only led to social dysfunctionality, but has perpetuated his inability to find employment. According to the above WHO definition, he is not healthy because he is socially and mentally ill.

For we cardiac surgeons at Groote Schuur Hospital, our patients' socio-economic problems were of very little concern to us. We were the 'miracle surgeons' who performed life-saving operations. When patients left hospital, they were on their own – it was a case of 'good luck to them'.

But when I arrived in Johannesburg in 1980 and entered into private practice, things changed dramatically. Most patients came to see me directly and I would refer them to a cardiologist. I discussed with patients and their families personal matters that I had previously never considered to be relevant. The questions asked by patients were predominantly related to their operations and to what I thought their chances of success were, but I also had to answer questions about how much the operation was going to cost, how long they would have to remain in hospital and, most importantly, when they would be able to return to work. My patients told me about their children and the cost of their school fees and mortgages, and it soon became obvious to me that they were often more concerned about their financial future than the immediate outcome of their surgery.

Thinking back, I can remember experiencing similar conversations when practising as a GP in Salisbury. There, I delivered my patients' babies, shared their childhood illnesses and cared for them. I attended the christenings of infants that I had delivered and witnessed my patients' twenty-first birth-days, weddings and wedding receptions, their fiftieth wedding anniversaries and funerals. What an enriching experience it was for me as their family doctor and friend – I was a part of the family. I am saddened that these old-fashioned 'family doctors' have long disappeared. The profession is greatly worse off without them.

During my subsequent thirteen years as a cardiac surgeon at Groote

Schuur Hospital, I had become, without even realising it, a technician, and no longer – in the fullest sense of its definition – a doctor. My close relationships with patients and their families were not what they had been before.

As soon as I entered into private practice in Johannesburg, this feeling of 'togetherness' returned. Owing to the crippling cost of surgery, especially the hospital fees and the costs required for survival after hospital treatment, it all came back to me: there is a significant financial side to critical illness treatment. More importantly, I became increasingly aware that, although the cost of medical treatment was frightening, the cost of survival was worse – and this at a time when the patients' poor health often prevented them from providing the necessary income for them and their family: the patients faced early retirement, losing their job, or having to rely on a partner to assist them with financial and recuperative support, to name just a few possibilities. As the patients' expenses would increase, so their income would diminish. These financial difficulties added considerably to the patients' plight.

* * *

We are all aware of the impact that changing lifestyles have had in recent times on the health and well-being of the present population. Smoking, alcohol abuse, obesity, lack of exercise, stress and ageing are responsible for a dramatic increase of two pathological conditions in humankind: atherosclerosis and cancer.

Atherosclerosis involves the build-up of fatty material along the interior walls of arteries. The fatty matter thickens and hardens, forming calcium deposits, and can eventually block the arteries, leading to angina, heart attacks or death. It is fascinating that only humans develop atherosclerosis, but it is hardly a surprise. Have you ever seen a pig smoke? Elephants don't devour mixed grills and hippos seldom consume large quantities of fish and chips.

Cancer is a disease of human cells. The affected cells grow uncontrollably and are spread locally and to other parts and organs of the body by the blood and lymphatic system. Caused by abnormalities in the genetic material of the transformed cells, cancer is often a result of the effects of carcinogens such as tobacco smoke, radiation, chemicals or infectious agents.

It was only after the Canadian Veterans Study pointed out the high incidence of lung cancer in smokers (subsequently confirmed by the United States Surgeon General's report in 1964) that the association between smoking and cancer was taken seriously.[2] Before this, we all smoked.

As a schoolboy, my preference was Camel. I was encouraged to smoke this brand of cigarette for many reasons, including peer pressure, but also as a result of my admiration for our family doctor. He was my hero: he had the biggest car in town, the prettiest wife and a large, modern house with a tennis court and swimming pool. He also smoked Camels. An advertisement in a magazine stating, 'More Doctors Smoke CAMELS than any other cigarette' was enough for me to try to feel important by copying my role model.

The challenges of degenerative diseases in more recent times were accepted by the medical profession and great advances have been made in their diagnosis and management. I was fortunate enough not only to experience this, but to play a small part in the successful treatment of such diseases from the time of my qualification as a doctor.

Throughout my medical career of more than fifty years, I have witnessed the most amazing developments in cardiac management with the advent of coronary care units (CCUs), angiography, the heart–lung machine, and so many other incredible aids. The same student who was warned not to touch a patient's heart during an operation because the patient would then die has removed a heart and replaced it with a donor heart. He has repaired the cardiac lesions of a one-day-old infant and replaced leaking heart valves.

Our patients now survive after suffering heart attacks – 50 per cent will live for thirteen years or more. Fifty per cent of cancer patients will survive for five years and longer, and more than 70 per cent of stroke victims will be alive a year later. And survival rates are improving: 70 per cent of patients with breast cancer and prostatic cancer will be cured. These statistics are impressive, and we of the medical profession are deservedly proud of our achievements. Many journal and conference papers today deal with the introduction and development of new procedures, resulting in better survival projections.

The incidence of degenerative diseases today, however, is frightening, in spite of all the exercise regimes, diets and 'this-is-good-for-you-and-that-is-bad-for-you' slogans. The protracted ageing of our population is another major reason for such high incidences. Humans now have a one-in-three chance of developing cancer, a one-in-four chance of suffering a heart attack, and an eight-in-one-hundred chance of having a stroke.

In the event of death, a patient will incur no further medical costs or living expenses. If a patient should survive, however, these costs not only remain, but often increase as a result of medical and other related expenses.

It is estimated, for example, that in the case of cancer one-third of the cost is medically related, while the remainder comprises indirect non-medical expenses. It is therefore important to emphasise that survival entails a price: not always does one experience a 'live-happily-ever-after' fairy tale. Many adjustments have to be made, including long recuperation periods, early retirement, a partner in business and nursing help. These are just some of the challenges that patients have to face, and often for many years.

* * *

While practising as a cardiac surgeon at Milpark Hospital, I became obsessed with the question of how to provide my patients with money in the event that they survived. I had experienced so many cases where money was needed, not only on the diagnosis of death, but on the diagnosis of a so-called dread disease like cancer, heart attack and stroke. One specific case, which affected me profoundly, illustrates the problem succinctly: it involved a patient who survived, but who 'died' financially.

A thirty-four-year-old divorcee consulted me – or, rather, came to see me, as I knew her and her family well. After a bitterly contested divorce, she had been given a poor settlement with insufficient money to support her and her two young children. With a twelve-year-old son and a ten-year-old daughter, she had to earn an income, and she had a steady job.

Her history and symptoms made the diagnosis more than obvious. She smoked around forty cigarettes per day, always felt tired, coughed, had a poor appetite and was losing weight. An X-ray of her chest and a lung biopsy confirmed the presence of a malignant cancer in her right lung. She was still operable but, with little chance of a cure, a right pneumonectomy was required. A week later, although short of breath, she was back home and, within a month, had returned to work.

I followed her progress with six-monthly check-ups over the next three years. It emerged that the cancer had not been cured but had spread – first to the left lung and then to the liver and bones. Palliative treatment was the only option left as her health continued to deteriorate.

About three years after the initial diagnosis and treatment, she came to see me again. This beautiful mother of two young children was now a walking skeleton. Gasping for breath and deathly pale with deeply sunken eyes, she was obviously terminally ill. I was amazed that she had managed to drag her frail, cancer-ridden body to my rooms at all.

I wondered why she had not stayed in her flat to spend as much time as possible with her two children, who were soon going to lose their mother. When I asked her why she had chosen to come to my rooms and not called me to see her at home, her answer was the very last thing I expected. 'Doctor,' she said, 'I have come from work.' Despite her extreme physical illness, she needed money at the end of every month to pay the rent and buy food and all the other essentials required for daily living.

She died a few weeks later. The case haunted me. She had taken out a life insurance policy that was certainly of great benefit to her children after her death, but it did absolutely nothing for her. *What about her?* I thought. We had provided her with an operation in an attempt to prolong her life in terms of quantity, but had failed to provide her with quality of life. Her insurance policy had failed her when she was in desperate need of money – she had not been able to claim a cent: she had to die before the money became available.

It had become acutely obvious to me that the survival of many of my patients gave rise to an immense financial crisis for them. They needed money from the moment I told them the worst news they would ever hear in their life: 'You have had a severe heart attack' or 'Your wife has had a stroke and will never walk or talk again' or 'Your child has leukaemia.'

When I found the solution to the problem, it was so simple that it is unbelievable that no one had thought of it earlier: an insurance policy that pays out on the diagnosis of the disease and not on death.

33

Formulating and
Launching the Concept

H AVING WORKED AS A MEDICAL DOCTOR FOR THIRTY YEARS, I had now identified the need for an insurance product that would provide immediate financial assistance to patients on the diagnosis of a life-threatening disease rather than on death or disability. The most common diseases requiring such financial support were heart attack, cancer and stroke, as approximately 80 per cent of people will be diagnosed with one of these conditions during their lifetimes.

The first step was to find an insurance company that would develop the 'dread disease' policy and market it. So I took the concept to Zach de Beer, then CEO of the large insurance company Southern Life.[1] Zach thought that it was a good idea and asked me to give him some time to take my suggested policy to his actuaries to establish whether it was feasible. He came back to me a week or two later and said that, although the medical doctors and actuaries of his company believed the proposed policy to have merit, the actuaries were doubtful that its implementation would be possible, as there weren't sufficient statistics on which premiums could correctly be based.

Although I was very disappointed by this response, I didn't drop the idea. I had very little knowledge about the life insurance industry and I wasn't sure how to take the concept further, but I decided to persevere.

Then, nearly three years later, in March 1983, two brothers, Alexander 'Don' and Bob Rowand, both active in the insurance industry in South Africa, contacted me. Soon, with an actuary from America in tow, Don came to see me in parliament. Don explained that they had just bought a small insurance company called Crusader Life and were keen to develop a niche product in the life insurance industry. They'd approached me, they said, because I was a health professional with the knowledge and experience they were seeking. In addition, they knew I'd be able to give advice that was credible. And, let's be honest, my surname helped.

As you can imagine, I was flabbergasted. Not only was I the man they were looking for, but they were exactly the people I'd been seeking for three years. I told them that they needed to look no further, as I had in mind just the product they wanted. I explained to them there and then that, in more than thirty years as a medical doctor, I had witnessed great changes in patient survival but that I had become very concerned about the financial plight of those patients that survived treatment. I explained my policy to them and suggested that we start with the four most common conditions: cancer, heart attack, stroke and coronary artery bypass graft (CABG).

Without reservation, they agreed to the idea and, by the time they had left my office that autumn afternoon, they were jubilant. Their enthusiasm matched my own: I had waited for so long, and it now seemed that my idea would at last find fruition.

But my work wasn't over yet. Little did I realise that this concept and its eventual implementation would occupy me until today, twenty-eight years later, and that the policy, conceived while I sat in the South African Houses of Parliament, would become one of the most successful insurance policies in the world.

* * *

I was appointed as the medical consultant to the Crusader Life team – for which I was paid a titular sum of R1 000. In establishing the policy document, it fell to me to define when such a policy would pay out. To this role I readily agreed.

To assist me in the formulation of my concept, I'd been given some examples of definitions brought to us from America by the actuary. The one defining a heart attack was an amazing four pages long and included complicated concepts such as *MUGA scanning, inverted T-waves,* and so on. Imagine some poor insurance advisor trying to sell this policy to a toughened Karoo farmer. When asking the advisor what exactly constitutes a heart attack, the advisor, not really understanding the concept himself, would reply that it had something to do with *MUGA scanning* and *inverted T-waves.* That farmer would in all likelihood tell the advisor to go to hell. For all the good such a policy would provide him, he'd rather buy a cow.

Definitions, I realised, needed to be as simple as possible for brokers, agents and independent financial advisors (IFAs) to understand, as these people would eventually be promoting the product to the prospective policy holder. It was also very important that the client be able to understand without the slightest difficulty what it was that he or she was purchasing.

Defining concepts was not easy. In an attempt to explore how I should go about the task, my thoughts returned to the first human heart transplant.

At that time, we had been in the unenviable position of having to explain to the public when a patient was dead. People were used to cowboy films, in which the crook was dead when the sheriff approached his prostrate body in the dusty main street, bent down and put his ear on the chest (in the wrong place) to listen to the crook's heart, felt his pulse and declared him dead. And so, as far as the public was concerned, the cessation of the heartbeat was the moment of death.

As a result, it was very difficult for people to understand how a dead person could become the donor of a heart, and how the recipient would survive when his or her diseased heart was replaced with the healthy heart of a dead donor. As I mentioned earlier, this caused great controversy in the press and other public media, and even among religious leaders and politicians. Many attempts were made to define 'the moment of death'. Our religious leaders outlined their definitions and the concept became even more difficult to understand. Lawyers then tried to define it, and that complicated things further. Finally, the politicians joined the fray. For a few months, *nobody* really knew when a person was dead.

I then remembered a question asked of Chris during an interview with the American television station NBC. 'Professor Barnard,' Chris had been asked, 'when is a person dead?' Chris had looked the camera straight in the eye and replied in his guttural Beaufort West accent, 'A person is dead when his doctor says he's dead.' This was my answer to the problem of formulating definitions in the policy.

I could use the basis of this simple approach in explaining, for example, when a person had suffered a heart attack. When a doctor informs his patient that he or she has had a heart attack, the diagnosis has been made on the following findings: typical chest pain, a rise in cardiac enzymes and new ECG changes. Similarly, I could make use of other appropriate definitions for the remaining three conditions defined in the policy.

These definitions were accepted by the brokers, who had great success in explaining what conditions the policy covered and that it paid out on the diagnosis of these conditions and not on death. Today, these definitions – although having been modified and improved upon – remain the cornerstone for hundreds of insurance providers all over the world.

* * *

Don Rowand and his team at Crusader Life wasted no time. The most important task was to find a *re-insurer*. At that time, the word *re-insurer* meant nothing to me. I subsequently established that, when somebody takes out an insurance policy, the insurance company will share the risk of a payout being made by passing some of that risk to a re-insurance company in return for a portion of the premium. If a claim is solicited and a payout made, the insurance company and the re-insurer will, therefore, at a percentage earlier determined, collectively share the amount of the claim.

Securing a re-insurer proved to be easier than the Crusader Life team had thought it would be. Unlike the actuaries who had been consulted three years previously, Liberty Life saw the merit in the concept and easily found the necessary statistics to be able to price the risks. Although I'm sure that Crusader Life used other re-insurance companies, Liberty Life, I believe, became the world's first re-insurer for critical illness insurance.

A marketing team was established and everyone at Crusader Life worked with great enthusiasm for the launch of the first 'dread disease' policy in the world. Parliament went into recess at the end of June and I returned to my cardiac practice and my constituency in Parktown. Soon afterwards, I was invited to lunch at Crusader House, where I met the team that would be responsible for marketing the new policy: Bob, Don's brother, whom I had met earlier in the year; and Brian Peters, a tall, jovial man who knew most brokers and agents and had wonderful working relationships with them. Brian and I later criss-crossed South Africa together for many years to introduce and market our product to IFAs and their clients. Dick Slingsby, another member of the team that I met that day at Crusader House, was responsible for corporate schemes.

Dick was a party animal and it was very pleasant to be around him. According to him, he sold millions of rands in premiums almost daily ... but we had our doubts. Although he seemed to know very little about 'dread disease' insurance, Dick was awarded the Insurance Man of the Year award by the Association of Professional Financial Planners for his role in developing this insurance policy. He did, however, mention Don and me in his acceptance speech.

After an excellent lunch and good wine at Crusader House, Don invited me to his office. He asked me to continue not only as the medical consultant for Crusader Life, but also as a director of the board. This would be a part-time job and therefore would not intrude on my roles as member of parliament and cardiac surgeon.

A director: Inez and I never in our wildest dreams thought that I would one day become a director of a company. I didn't even know what a director did. I did know, however, that a director earned a fee, and this in itself was good enough for me.

The launch date of our 'dread disease' insurance product was set for 6 August 1983, my eldest daughter Naudéne's birthday. Crusader Life had no career agents – or *tied agents* as they are called – only broker consultants that serviced agents of other companies, and particularly independent financial advisors. A tied agent, as the term implies, could sell only the policies of his or her company, whereas broker consultants and IFAs have the advantage of being able to sell policies from different companies.

Standard Bank Insurance Brokers was the first brokerage to launch our product. One of the largest banks in South Africa, it had a substantial broker force, with banks and offices in all the cities and most towns in South Africa. The policy they launched with us was our product, but they called it *living insurance*, a description that I considered very appropriate, as this product was geared towards the living, not the dead.

The policy was totally new and different from any other form of protection policy because of its payout on diagnosis of any of the four conditions defined in the policy, rather than on death or disability. The policy holder was not paid out based on the severity of the disease, but on its diagnosis only. If the policy holder met the conditions of the diagnosis, he or she could do with the money whatever he or she wanted.

As the launch date approached, Don asked me to give a talk to the managers and brokers of Standard Bank Insurance Brokers at its headquarters in downtown Johannesburg. This was a great challenge for me: I had delivered talks on cardiac surgery and made political speeches, but I had never spoken on the subject of insurance.

The afternoon started well when I was fetched from my consulting rooms by a beautiful blonde secretary. I met the 'higher-ups' of Standard Bank Insurance Brokers, as well as their marketing team and agents. I cannot remember much of what I said, but I explained how I had become aware of the financial plight of our patients, who no longer died as in the past but instead survived for many years.

As can be expected, the policy was completely new to my audience, and they had very little knowledge about medical conditions and the outcomes after treatment. My strategy was to dazzle and disturb them with medical facts and bloody slides of heart attacks, cancerous lungs, and amputations of gangrenous limbs, among other things, to prove the need for this product. I included statistics on incidence, survival and the cost of survival and how I had come to what I thought was the solution. I emphasised that the product covered four conditions – cancer, heart attack, stroke, and coronary artery bypass surgery – and that it paid out on the diagnosis of the condition. I also discussed the definitions.

And so 'dread disease' insurance was launched. Initially it was not well accepted, but slowly an increasing number of companies offered the product. Its name was, however, soon changed in the United Kingdom to *critical illness insurance* on the basis that 'dread disease' was not easily marketable. It also had the potential to be confused with a cancer insurance policy that had been discredited in the United States.

This was the start of a new career for me, and I began to travel the length and breadth of South Africa, launching, motivating to IFAs and developing the product further.

34

Spreading the Word

M Y ROLE IN PROMOTING OUR CRITICAL ILLNESS INSURANCE product grew rapidly. I was passionate about the policy: I sincerely believed that this was the protection policy that our patients needed. I was mindful of the fact that, if one were to ask a hundred people in the street what life insurance meant, more than 90 per cent would know that it pays out after death, but if one were to ask the same number of people what critical illness insurance entailed, it would be surprising if even one person had heard of it.

I travelled throughout South Africa addressing independent financial advisors, actuaries, agricultural societies, women's associations and other interested groups. I believed that all future patients should know about the product and be given the opportunity to buy it. Not all would, but I was desperate for them to be informed, at least, of what it could offer them and be given the opportunity to buy it.

So, I threw my heart and soul into promoting the product and travelled from Walvis Bay on the west coast of then South West Africa to Durban on the east coast of South Africa; from Louis Trichardt in the north of the country to Simon's Town in the far south.

It was a busy and, at times, exhausting period of my life, especially as I was still in private practice as a cardiac surgeon and a serving member of parliament. It was at this stage that I began to spend an increasing amount of time commuting between Johannesburg and Cape Town to satisfy both responsibilities.

In the meantime, I had become a spokesperson for Golden Products, a company that promoted and sold alternative medicine, and this position also required travelling and talks. Eventually the hectic schedule affected my own health. But that's a story for later.

* * *

While I continued with both my medical and political careers, things in the insurance world were moving faster than I, or anyone else at Crusader Life, had expected. After our initial launch, the agents received the product with great enthusiasm. It was new – no other company was promoting it – so not only could they introduce it to prospective policy holders, but they could go back to all of their old policy holders with this new concept of insurance.

The results were spectacular. Not every client bought the product, but everyone thought it was a great idea. We made many sales and the word spread.

Bowring Insurance, the insurance arm of First National Bank, was the next group to launch our product. They called it *Survival Life* – to my mind a very appropriate name because it described exactly the purpose of the policy. Again, I was asked to give my presentation, which was well received.

As a director, I attended board meetings whenever I could. This was a new experience for me, because my knowledge of the running of an insurance company was effectively zero. However, I very quickly learnt about re-insurance, underwriting, legal requirements and other intricate details. For me, the best part of those meetings was the excellent lunches served in the boardroom after the meetings.

* * *

When we first launched the 'dread disease' policy, major South African insurance giants such as Old Mutual, Sanlam, Liberty Life and Southern Life scoffed at the policy. They could see no future for Crusader Life or our product. We were told that our company was too small, that we had no financial strength, that the statistics were inadequate for proper pricing and that the premiums were too expensive. They found fault with the definitions and suggested that few claims, if any, would be paid … and these were only some of their criticisms!

But, like us, they were soon surprised by the sales results we achieved and the pressure on them from their agents, who wanted a 'dread disease' policy to sell. So they all joined in with a policy very similar to ours, which incorporated my definitions virtually word for word.

We were pleased that other companies had taken to this form of insurance, as we realised only too well that the greater the number of products that entered the market, the greater the likelihood that agents would offer them to their clients and the better such insurance would become known. We responded to the challenge and stayed at the forefront, with better policies that added more critical illnesses.

By 1986, illnesses covered included aortic aneurysm, heart valve surgery, organ transplantation and renal failure. Again, I had to write the definitions applicable to these conditions, but this proved to be of no difficulty. We could offer this improved product to all new and existing clients, but without increasing the premium. This 'something for nothing' was a great sales incentive. A few years later, paralysis, multiple sclerosis, Alzheimer's disease, blindness, deafness, coma, loss of speech, severe burns, loss of limbs, occupational HIV, motor neuron disease, benign brain tumour, Parkinson's disease and other conditions were added.

But at this point I discovered a new term: *new-business strain*. Crusader Life was a small, new company without large reserves of funds. When a policy was sold, the agent would collect a commission to the value of the first year's premium, if not more. In addition, there were considerable expenses in underwriting it,[1] paying the doctor if a medical report was required and generating policy documents and marketing material, as well as paying the staff, of course.

All of these expenses had to be met long before the monthly premiums would cover them. If the number of policies issued increased rapidly, as it did, it would be years before income exceeded expenses – and there were still claims to be paid.

For the nine years I was with Crusader Life, I was led to believe that our biggest problem was our success, and that this subsequently resulted in new-business strain. Although I never really understood how, I was told that any shortfalls incurred were financed by re-insurance. The dilemma of getting into trouble because you were doing too well was, and still is, a mystery to me. In my profession as a doctor, my patients never died when they were doing 'too well'; they left hospital. They died when they did *not* do 'too well'.

What I found difficult to understand was that, after our first policy was issued, and as the weeks became months, the marketing team and management were praying for a policy holder to submit a claim. Their prayer was soon answered when a claim for a heart attack was submitted. The claim was clearly correct according to our definitions and all the parameters for the diagnosis of a heart attack had been included. Everyone wanted the policy paid out immediately. According to marketing and management, this would be of great publicity value.

I, however, looked at the claim and found that there was indisputable evidence of non-disclosure. As the term suggests, *non-disclosure* is when material information for which an insurer has asked isn't provided, or is misrepresented. The medical report was correct in the diagnosis of a heart attack, but in the claimant's past history there was symptomatic evidence of angina and a previous heart attack. When I investigated the claim further, I discovered that the claimant was a top agent for one of our biggest supporting bank insurance companies.

As the medical consultant, I repudiated the claim – much to the horror of the marketing team. I thought that this decision was final but discovered a few weeks later that, in spite of my rejection of the claim, it was paid. I was disgusted and complained bitterly, only to be told that paying the claim was a cheap form of advertising and that my job was to stick to the developing and marketing of our products. I was to keep my nose out of all decisions taken by the managers. I was bitterly disappointed and very tempted to resign.

* * *

During a lunch with the Rowand brothers at the Johannesburg country club in 1986, I explained to them my vision of introducing the product to overseas markets. My reasons for this were many, not least that the 'dread disease' insurance policy we had developed would be new to all countries. I believed that we would have the same success on foreign shores as we had had in South Africa.

The political situation in our country at the time was, to say the least, unstable, and the future uncertain. We felt, therefore, that Crusader Life would experience a major financial boost if we could establish a company abroad, or link up with overseas insurance groups. We unanimously decided to investigate all avenues to achieve this.

My opportunity came the following year when I visited my son, Adam, in Sydney, Australia. Ian MacRitchie, one of Liberty Life's top agents who had South African experience of trauma insurance, had relocated to Sydney and was working for Sedgwick Insurance. During my visit, he introduced me to a few insurance companies.

One of the companies we visited showed great interest in our policy. I gave a presentation to their top management and marketing team and they were even more impressed. We agreed that Don Rowand, our CEO, would visit them.

A few months later, after this company had received most of the details of our product, its pricing, marketing material and policy details, Don left for Australia. When he returned, he reported that they had decided to market our product and that this would be handled as a joint venture with us. At last, we had our foot in the door of an overseas company. With great expectation, we waited for their launch.

A few weeks before the big day, they informed us that they had decided to break off their relationship with us because we were a South African company: their directors, shareholders and policy holders were not prepared to take the risk of being associated with us given both our government's racial policies and the international trade boycott against our country.

We were more than disappointed and felt betrayed, but this disappointment soon turned to gratitude: shortly after the Australian company broke their agreement with us, it was taken over by another group. A year or two later, the CEO of that group succeeded in stealing all of his company's reserve funds and fled the country. The company subsequently went into liquidation and the former CEO was eventually caught and jailed. Thinking back, we had a lucky escape. Perhaps their refusal to go into business with us was one of the very few good things that emerged from our government's policies.

Undeterred, we targeted the United Kingdom. We held discussions with some interested parties, but all of our initiatives fizzled out. Then we landed a big fish – one of the UK's more prominent insurance groups. Again, we gave them all of our product details, agreed to a joint venture and waited in anticipation for our big moment. Again, we were told that the company would not continue to work with us for the same political and trade reasons.

It later transpired that they were one of the first companies, if not *the* first, to launch a critical illness insurance policy that paid out on the diagnosis of the diseases covered in their policy. What further infuriated me was the fact that they used my definitions and our policy documents virtually word for word. Their policy initially took on very slowly in the UK and, as I pointed out in the previous chapter, it soon became known as *critical illness insurance*. I believed that this was – and is – a much better term than *dread disease* or *trauma insurance*, as it gives a clearer indication of what the policy covered.

Though disappointed by our lack of success abroad, we remained heartened by the success of the policy in South Africa and the subsequent changes that we had made to it due to increasing competition.

The first policy we had launched paid only 25 per cent of the insurable amount on the diagnosis of the disease; the rest paid out as an endowment, or as life insurance. The agents complained, however, that when they introduced this product to their clients, a major objection was that the clients already had too much life insurance.

In response to this, we developed a stand-alone policy that excluded life cover, paying out only on the diagnosis of the conditions covered. The maximum entry age was increased from fifty-five to sixty, and later to sixty-five. In addition, we increased the maximum insurable amount – some clients insured up to a million rand.

I now became more involved in evaluating claims and, with my medical knowledge, I disallowed many due to non-disclosure and anti-selection. *Anti-selection* is defined as the adverse impact on an insurer when risks are selected that have a greater chance of loss than that contemplated by the relevant insurance rate. Agents objected when we rejected claims on the basis of non-disclosure – for example family history, previous history of diseases covered, high blood pressure, obesity and raised cholesterol – and anti-selection. There was much complaining and threats that support would be removed.

To appease insurance groups and agents that supplied us with a lot of business, I was often overruled. As a result of this, I eventually submitted my resignation. I believed that this practice was unethical and would lead to disaster. My resignation, however, was not accepted. Instead, my salary was increased and I stayed on. I had clashes with my seniors over the matter and soon realised that, although one can certainly buy business, one has to pay for it at one stage or another.

* * *

In 1989, we made another attempt to penetrate the UK market. At last, we were successful: Barings Bank (as the major shareholder), Rupert Hambro's boutique bank and Crusader Life were licensed as the insurance company Pegasus in the United Kingdom.

I was very impressed with Barings and its significant banking history. As the oldest merchant bank in England, it had, over more than two centuries, provided the financial services necessary for the rapid growth of international trade. I had read of its facilitation of the purchase of Louisiana from Napoleon on behalf of the United States government in 1802, and that it had saved Canadian Pacific Railways (CPR) from bankruptcy in 1885. Surely a partner to dream of ... but how wrong I ultimately proved to be.[2]

There was great excitement in the boardroom in Anderson Street, Johannesburg, during this time in 1989. I was not, however, involved in the deal, nor in the launch of Pegasus's critical illness insurance policy in the United Kingdom, but we were told that a very successful insurance manager by the name of Dan Dane would head up Pegasus. The name *Dan Dane*, and all the great things he was going to do, made me fantasise about him –

that he was our cowboy hero sitting astride a white horse, wearing a wide-brimmed white hat.

A few months elapsed and I sensed that the initial high hopes of immediate success were not being fulfilled. It soon became apparent that things were going too slowly in the UK – we needed more sales. No longer an MP, I had more time on my hands and was spending most of it attending to cardiac surgery. In September that year, Don Rowand approached me with a request to visit England to conduct a nationwide trip there. This would include giving presentations to the tied agents of Pegasus as well as IFAs. It would certainly be a fresh challenge.

Accompanied by Brian Peters and a carousel full of slides, we jetted off from Johannesburg's airport one chilly evening. We travelled on British Airways and I enjoyed a new experience – travelling business class. I felt very special, very rich and very important.

During the night on the aeroplane, I woke up to the fact that I had absolutely no knowledge of insurance in the United Kingdom. They had a National Health system; the motivation and sales talks I gave in South Africa could be totally inappropriate. When we arrived at Heathrow, the broker manager of Pegasus, who was meant to meet us, didn't arrive. After almost an hour of waiting, he pitched up without offering an apology. This was not exactly an auspicious start. We were taken to the Cumberland Hotel in Oxford Street and, when I saw the hotel, the reception area and my room, my confidence about the venture returned.

We had to leave the hotel again almost immediately to have breakfast with Dan Dane. We met Dan, his wife and their teenage daughter in a very smart restaurant. The breakfast was good, but the conversation was dominated by Dan's wife talking constantly about how her daughter would one day become a famous plastic surgeon. She never mentioned the fact that the girl would first have to become a doctor.

I found it strange that neither critical illness insurance nor our programme for the next two weeks was discussed, but it was later revealed that our business was to commence the next day, a Monday. Dan would drive us down to Bristol, where Pegasus had its headquarters, and Don, who was already in London, would join us.

At eight o'clock the next morning, Dan arrived with Don in a brand-new Daimler – a company car, of course. I thought that it was rather expensive but assumed that this went with the perks commensurate with the position of manager in the UK insurance business.

During our two-hour journey to Bristol, Dan repeatedly called the branches on the car phone. Every time, he enquired, 'Anything new?' Although I couldn't hear the response, the talk was so brief that there was obviously 'nothing new'.

After meeting the management staff in Bristol, we had an expensive lunch. That afternoon I gave my first presentation in Bath, a pleasant coincidence, as thirty-seven years earlier I had been a senior surgical houseman in this city at St Martin's Hospital.

My presentation took place at a magnificent historical country house and was attended by about a hundred agents, who had come from all of the regions where Pegasus had offices. As my presentation progressed, I could see a few of the members of the audience turning pale, sweating and then fainting. This was completely new to me. When presenting in South Africa, I generally included about twelve really bloody slides of diseased hearts, cancerous lungs and operations. Back home, the audience loved this and could seldom get enough of the gory slides.

By contrast, English males (and it was never the females) reacted very differently: during that first forty-minute talk of mine in Bath, three men fainted and one had a fit. Nowhere else in the world would I observe this same reaction. I still don't know why the English reacted so differently. I have an opinion, but I'll keep it to myself.

It was not nice having to present with grown-up men lying on the floor in a dead faint. Soon after my first experience in Bath, I started to warn my audience that, should they start to feel faint, it was advisable that they put their heads between their legs rather than try to get up. But they did not listen, and attempted – unsuccessfully at that – to leave the room. As a general rule, after no more than two steps they would be lying on the floor.

In Manchester, I had to interrupt my talk to help a man who felt faint and fell flat on his face, cutting his lip and tongue in the process. He was rushed to casualty in an ambulance and, for the next month or two, I was petrified that he might sue me. It was at this point that I removed all but two of my gory slides from my presentations. Even then, I flashed them on the screen for a few seconds only.

In spite of the faints, however, my talks were well received. It fast became obvious that the agents had no idea about the need for critical illness insurance or how to market it.

Our next presentation was to take place at the new head office of Barings Bank in London, where Brian Peters and I would be presenting to the city's

'Fools' names, like fools' faces, are often seen in public places'

© *Die Burger*

'And *nothing* for these other two gentlemen?' Expressing my disgust at one of the founding
members of the newly formed Democratic Party, seen here consuming the 'Prog inheritance'
while 'starving out' the other two founders of this alliance. The cartoon appeared on 16 June
1989, after I declined to join the newly formed Democratic Party. I am labelled a
'PFP bittereinder' – a PFP diehard

Examining an elephant's heart in 1990 near Satara, Kruger National Park, with a veterinary doctor in attendance

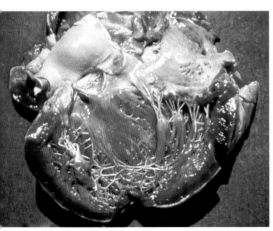

The normal, healthy heart of a twenty-four-year-old man tragically killed in a car accident

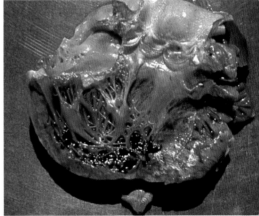

A severely diseased heart removed from one of our transplant patients

Peter Dodd and Marcia Johnson, who spent many days with me on critical illness insurance roadshows in the UK and the USA

Inez (centre) with Australian insurance colleague Howard Davy (right) and a friend

Family gathering for our fiftieth wedding anniversary in 2001 at Fernkloof, Hermanus

Inez, me and Chris's first wife, Louwtjie

'The Barnard Babes' (from left to right): Adam and Janneka's daughter, Alexandra Barnard; and Marie and Darryl's daughters, Melissa, Natalie and Hayley-Marie Kalil, *c.* 2001

Receiving the Order of the Gold Cross from the Romanian president, His Excellency Ion Iliescu, in the Royal Palace, Bucharest, 2002

With former Romanian medical colleagues and lifelong friends Daniel and Anca Constantinescu, celebrating their twenty-fifth anniversary of residency in the USA, 2003

Among one of God's visual wonders: the West Coast spring flowers, Kamieskroon, Northern Cape

'How Great Thou Art': the kaleidoscopic fall colours, New Hampshire, USA, with Inez and Marie in the foreground, 2005

Inez and me visiting the Great Wall of China in 2006 while on a critical illness
insurance tour in the Far East

My seventy-ninth birthday in Beijing, 3 November 2006, surrounded by Chinese beauties

Briefing the local media with Paul Thesen, the world's longest-surviving heart recipient, at the Heart of Cape Town Museum, Groote Schuur Hospital, in August 2010

Working with Simon Norval on this book at 'Berg 'n See', Hermanus, September 2010

top bankers, accountants and financial icons. Prior to the talk, its importance was repeatedly impressed upon us and we had to send our slides to the lecture auditorium the night before the presentation so that those in charge could make absolutely sure that everything was in order.

The next morning, I arrived at the tall building and mingled with the auspicious audience for about fifteen minutes before we started. I felt completely inferior: to them, I must have looked totally undressed. They were all attired in smart suits and black shoes – I was the only one with brown shoes and I felt completely naked, not to mention extremely embarrassed.

Brian Peters started his talk and the slides appeared on the screen. I soon sensed that he was struggling with them and thought that he must have slipped up in the order that he had arranged them in the carousel. Then my big moment came – Marius Barnard addressing big-business tycoons in the heart of financial Britain. Who could have ever dreamt of this?

My problems soon started: every second slide was out of order; my presentation and slides were mismatched. I stopped to try to get the projectionist to sort out the problems that I was encountering, but the projector was brand new and they evidently had no experience with it. I was told that it was 'all automatic' and that it would take them an hour or longer to correct the problem. So much for modern technology.

My slides were really the strength of my presentation, but I was powerless and had to deliver the talk without them. I battled on bravely, but it was a disaster. I felt cheated and defeated. Brown shoes, no slides – what else would go wrong? The audience was, however, very kind and sympathetic and praised my talk. I knew better. My first important talk in the UK was my worst.

I presented in Manchester, Birmingham, London and Brighton – with audiences of, at the most, about twelve agents, but sometimes only three. At one venue, nobody turned up.

Question time was an ordeal, as the attendees were largely aggressive and suspicious. They gave us the impression that they would not accept critical illness insurance as a necessary product to present to their clients.

Following my talks, there was, however, increased interest in critical illness insurance and, even more importantly, a steady stream of policies was issued. This was only among independent financial brokers; our tied sales team, recruited by Dan Dane at great expense, hardly sold one policy.

Dan had signed five-year contracts for offices in London, Bristol and Manchester. He had recruited nearly 100 sales persons, again at a high cost.

With rising expenses and very little income, Pegasus was soon in financial trouble, as the investors were reluctant to advance more funds.

The general opinion, it seemed to me, was that the board held Dan responsible. While I was doing my best to promote sales, there was great tension in the company – particularly between Dan and Don. The break-up came while I was giving my presentations. Soon Dan was gone, along with all of his agents, and we were left with a small broker consultant force of three and a single manager, who, being loyal to Dan, resigned too.

Pegasus had just three offices and a five-year lease on each remaining. The offices were now 90 per cent empty. In the Bristol office, there was an actuary, a secretary, an underwriter, a few other personnel and some equipment – the basic requisites to run a small insurance company. Despite the adverse circumstances, critical illness insurance remained a good product, and we still had the best product developer in the UK, our actuary, Geoff Brown.

Don took on the responsibility of saving the company from bankruptcy and stayed on as CEO of Pegasus. We realised that we needed to concentrate our energies on the independent financial advisors. This was not only cheaper, but would provide a more receptive market.

We divided our sales force into three regions: Central (London and surrounds), Western (based in Bristol) and Northern (Manchester, up to Scotland and Northern Ireland). We appointed a manager in each region and slowly built up our broker consultant team. I then returned to South Africa.

* * *

Meanwhile, at home, Crusader Life seemed to be doing well. We desperately needed greater financial strength, however. We appeared to have achieved this when we were bought in 1990 by Anglovaal, one of South Africa's major mining companies, which had insurance interests in the form, among others, of its ownership of a business called AA Life Insurance Company.

Initially, this was considered to be of great benefit, as we thought that Crusader Life would be given a financial injection that would remove its new-business strain. Unfortunately, this proved not to be the case. I believe that it was a mistake to have joined up with them. We continued to trade independently, but two of their senior executives were appointed to our board. I took an immediate dislike to both of them.

A short while later, we developed the first major medical expenses policy in South Africa. I warned that this policy was easy to manipulate. The claims subsequently became a nightmare, and it actually degenerated into a policy that made it profitable to get sick. It lent itself to total abuse of medical accounts, and some accounts that we received were clearly fraudulent.

I was asked to help to try to restrict the claims. This I could do, but it immediately led to threats from brokers that they would take their business elsewhere, and it made our sales team panic. I lost my popularity and, feeling that I was on my way out, I refused to carry on overseeing claims.

In September 1990, I left for the UK and, during my month of seminars, while travelling all over the country, I met our new broker sales manager, Andre Fouche, who accompanied me on most of the visits. Each region's manager was introduced to me and I presented to brokers and their clients as well as other groups consisting largely of accountants, bankers and lawyers.

I delivered presentations at most major and not-so-major centres. I was on the road daily and, on some days, due to short distances between venues, gave several presentations. The attendance numbers at these meetings varied: at some venues up to fifty people attended, but at two talks I had the depressing experience of a zero attendance.

Again, the brokers were aggressive and made many negative comments. They told me that the policy was flawed and too expensive, that the definitions were difficult to understand and that it would not pay out. However, our increasing sales proved otherwise, and with Pegasus's market penetration other competitors started to take us seriously.

At the same time, I had valuable support from Geoff Brown, who responded to each competitor's product by developing a superior product for Pegasus. From early on, we annually won awards for the best product, marketing material and broker service. But again, new-business strain reared its ugly head.

The success of my talks was a reality, though, and for the following year it was decided that I would come over to the UK every three months for two weeks at a time.

I was appointed a director of Pegasus. In South Africa, Crusader Life continued to use me extensively to run seminars all over the country, business grew and I was asked by other groups involved in insurance to address them. At this stage, Crusader needed more money to finance the rapid increase in the volume of new business and, I believed, our excessive expenditure.

* * *

A year after my first involvement with Pegasus, Geoff Brown and I discussed the need to include a new definition: *child cover.*

This meant that all children born, or to be born, would be covered under this policy from the age of six months to eighteen years at no increase to the premium. As usual, the now well-known critics were out in full force, damning it as a gimmick that would seldom result in a claim. Again, such criticism proved to be unfounded.

Six of our first twenty claims were for child cover and, soon, more and more companies followed our example. In the UK today, it is reported that one in five claims are for child cover and one company has reported an incidence as high as one in four. This comes as no surprise, as diagnosis of leukaemia in young children is ever increasing, with brain tumours coming a tragic second.

Child cover proved to be a great sales tool. Those initially hesitant to buy critical illness insurance were quickly convinced when agents told them that child cover was an added benefit to the policy with no increase in premium.

This is easy to understand considering the economic reality of young couples with children today. Their financial needs generally require a combined income of both parents to pay the bills, the mortgage and all the other monthly expenses. When little Johnny gets ill and is admitted to hospital, we all know who he asks for first – 'Mummy'. His mother has to be with him, she has to take leave and, in the event of more serious conditions, she has to give up work. This results in the loss of half of the couple's income and, all too often, leaves their financial future in jeopardy. If they have a critical illness insurance policy, the immediate cash injection can help them to hold on to their house and eases many other financial and emotional strains.

Today, I am pleased to say that most insurance companies all over the world include child cover in their critical illness insurance policies.

* * *

The year 1991 proved to be the birth of my international acceptance, not only as a presenter of critical illness insurance, but also in the ongoing development of critical illness insurance policies, marketing material and management advice internationally.

This all came to fruition when I was asked to be a main-platform speaker at the Barbican, London, at the annual meeting of the Life Insurance Association (LIA) of the United Kingdom.

Pegasus sponsored me, and it was my first appearance before representatives of other insurance companies, brokerages and even overseas delegates.

When the day for the presentation arrived, I was overawed by the numbers in the audience – a few thousand. The other presenters were highly professional and well known, and had superb audio-visual support equipment.

I, with my sixty or so thirty-five-millimetre slides in my carousel, felt completely outclassed and inferior. When I started my talk, however, I found that I held my audience's attention and that, although I was talking about a policy they had never heard about, they warmed to me. I always include a lot of humour in my talks and they roared with laughter.

At the end of the presentation, I experienced, for the first time in my involvement with the insurance sector, a standing ovation that lasted a few minutes. I felt very embarrassed but was warmly congratulated afterwards. A video recording was made of my talk and I later heard that this video had the highest sales figures of all the talks recorded at that meeting, and that major insurance groups subsequently used it when training their agents.

I was now no longer sought after only in South Africa, but also in the United Kingdom and internationally. Flushed with success, I went out with a few friends from Pegasus to have dinner and missed an Irish Republican Army bomb explosion at the nearby London Stock Exchange by a few minutes.

I believe – and this view is shared by many others – that my talk at the LIA meeting in London was the trigger that resulted in the rapid increase in sales and the acceptance of the product in the UK and Ireland. Looking at the increase in related sales prior to 1991, it certainly suggests this to be the case.

Later that year, I was invited by Irish Life to go on a week-long tour through Ireland, where I addressed their LIA annual meeting. Critical illness insurance was quickly becoming a firmly established product.

There was another significant development that helped tremendously in increasing the agents' acceptance of and confidence in critical illness insurance. Owing to the ever-growing competition, agents became confused about what the best policy to sell was. Each company had different definitions for the same conditions, thus adding to the problem. At a meeting consisting of key role players from companies, re-insurers and agents, it was decided to appoint a committee to revisit the core conditions – cancer, heart attack, stroke and coronary artery bypass graft – in order to standardise their definitions across the policies. This was duly done and approved by all the major companies. The brokers now had greater confidence in the definitions and sales increased correspondingly.[3]

Pegasus continued to lead the field and, due to Geoff Brown's brilliance, we were regularly recognised by our peers as the leading critical illness insurance provider in the United Kingdom. Owing, however, to problems with Crusader Life, Don returned home and appointed a South African lawyer to be CEO of Pegasus.

The new CEO had limited knowledge of insurance and was never accepted by the majority of the senior management at our head office in Bristol. He soon asserted his authority and dismissed Andre Fouche, with whom I had, up till then, enjoyed a very good working relationship. Andre's replacement was a broker consultant who was certainly not of his standard.

Not only was the new CEO an unpopular choice, but he and Geoff Brown, our best asset, were soon at loggerheads. This was hardly the ideal recipe for success. I was not directly involved in the tension and continued, with varying degrees of success, my three-monthly tours through England, Wales and Scotland.

During my first experience on a roadshow with Pegasus in 1991, I was accompanied by their regional broker managers. The manager of the London region was a gentleman named Peter Dodd. I have to admit that at first I did not take to him, as he was flippant and seemed to consider everything a joke. Punctuality, which is so sacred to me, was certainly not his strong point, and we clashed regularly – so much so, that I suggested to Don Rowand that we move him.

But as our time together became more frequent, my opinion of Peter changed completely. He didn't change, but I became aware of his considerable value to me. He was always in a good mood, joked a lot and helped me not to take myself too seriously. He was tall and had a voracious appetite, equalled only by his thirst for pint after pint of dark ale. A few years later I invited him to visit us at our retirement home in Hermanus, where he immediately fell in love with our five-litre boxes of red wine. It was a pleasure for Inez and me to see a man so happy and enjoying every moment of his life.

With the subsequent demise of Pegasus, Peter found other work, but our friendship has lasted. Now, when I am feeling down and he comes on Skype, I am laughing within a few seconds and in a happy mood again. He is my anti-depressant. Thanks, Peter, for tolerating this difficult old man!

* * *

New doors started opening and I was invited to conduct seminars in Australia. This suited me well as my son, his wife and my two grandchildren lived in Sydney. In Australia I met Howard Davy, a former South African, and we teamed up to tour the major centres, which included Sydney, Parramatta, Adelaide, Melbourne, Brisbane and Perth.

During our tour, I again sensed reluctance from their agents and managerial staff to accept trauma insurance, the name given to critical illness insurance in Australia. Until today, the term *trauma* is used in Australia and South Africa. I think that this is a misnomer, as most people relate the term to major injuries and the casualty unit.

The questions were negative and the agents made it very clear to me that they preferred to stick with disability insurance. I did meet a few agents, however, who were excited about critical illness insurance and, as a result, awareness of the policy started to grow in Australia.

For the first few years, I found the talks hard going, but slowly things improved. Trauma insurance was eventually accepted and so was I. Subsequently I visited Australia on many occasions and gave presentations at the Australian LIA and the Asian-Pacific LIA. I also visited New Zealand to address their equivalent organisation.

In Australia, this insurance scheme is very much constrained by 'rating houses'. All products are rated according to their definitions, the number of conditions covered and other criteria. The policy is then rated and agents are, of course, influenced to sell the highest-rated policies.

I had a problem with this and visited these companies to discuss their method of rating and the parameters used. I was astounded by their lack of insight into definitions and other medical terms. I was left with the question, *Who rates the raters?* I believe that this rating system was one of the major reasons why trauma insurance was so slow in being accepted in Australia.

Many other invitations followed to assist with product development, definitions, marketing material, and educating and inspiring agents. I visited Singapore, Malaysia, Thailand, Hong Kong and Taiwan. These were great experiences; I met wonderful people and learnt a lot about all aspects of critical illness insurance in these countries.

After four years, my association with Pegasus ended and I was asked to join Bupa, a very large health insurer in the UK and other parts of the world, for eighteen months. When they talk about health insurance in England, in fact, they don't ask whether you have health insurance, but rather whether you have a Bupa.

I have to admit that, although it was a very large organisation with private hospitals, insurance for medical and dental costs and even travel agencies, it impressed me the least.

My tours around the UK and Ireland were supported by many of Bupa's managers and agents. There was audio-visual support at each venue, with a platform from which to speak. They provided music, multicoloured lights and other equipment that was more appropriate to a rock concert than to my style of presentation. Bupa, however, had the best logo and slogan – clearly visible on large billboards exhibited all over the UK. In my opinion, it was the best motivation for critical illness insurance. It read: 'You are amazing and we want you to stay that way.'

During a one-month period with Bupa, I had the luxury of staying in a spacious flat opposite the company's head office in London. Situated near Charing Cross Road and Trafalgar Court, it was a short walk from there to Temple tube station. Inez, of course, revelled in this opportunity – the shopping wonders of Oxford, Regent and Bond streets were just a short walk away. I have to admit, it was never 'all work and no play'.

One of my requests to Bupa and all other companies and conference organisers was that, for me to present my talks, Inez had to accompany me and that they would pay her airfare and accommodation.

The companies gladly accepted, and Inez and I had wonderful times, visiting many beautiful and exotic places in the process, mostly in luxury, which we otherwise would never have been able to afford. This I consider to be one of the greatest benefits of my presentations all over the world.

During the week, I travelled a lot, but our weekends were free and we were therefore able to explore to the full every place that we visited. My daughter Naudéne and her son lived in London and we enjoyed many happy family weekends together.

In Australia, we discovered the Great Barrier Reef and its surrounding islands, Port Douglas and especially the La Mirage Resort. We visited Queens-town in New Zealand and witnessed all of its surrounding beauty and the spectacular geysers at Rotorua. In Singapore, I fulfilled a lifelong ambition of visiting Raffles, having a gin sling in the Long Bar, eating the peanuts provided and, as is the custom, dropping the empty shells onto the floor. I visualised all the famous people – Ernest Hemingway and others – who had been there over the past decades.

While in Thailand, we discovered Phuket and enjoyed a marvellous meal on the beach, cooked on a Primus stove by its toothless, but very friendly, Thai proprietor – if you could call the owner of a Primus stove and a few plates, glasses, knives and forks a proprietor. Malaysia hardly impressed us and Hong Kong was too crowded for my liking, although Inez was delighted with the vast number of shops.

Taiwan was a blur. We arrived one evening at 10 p.m. I gave my talk at 9 a.m. the next morning and we left at 1 p.m. on the same day. We stayed in a magnificent hotel, however. My meeting was held at the hotel's conference centre and, when I arrived at the venue, there must have been at least ten meetings starting, with thousands of people milling around. I was the only European in attendance and, when I eventually found the hall where I had to speak, my host greeted me and we arranged the preparation of my equipment. We had an audience of about a hundred – of which 90 per cent were young Chinese females.

My host started the proceedings and gave an hour-long speech in what I presumed was Cantonese before introducing me to a hushed and expectant Oriental audience. Again, I did not understand what he said, but proceeded to give my talk, in English, to about a hundred expressionless faces.

When it was over, there was a splutter of applause and that was that – I had to leave immediately for Singapore. I still do not know how many people – if any – in that audience understood a single word I said.

35

My American Dream

I N EARLY 1993, THINGS WERE NOT GOING WELL FOR ME. AT
Crusader Life, strange things that I didn't fully understand were happening. Firstly, Don Rowand resigned and a Mr De Beer, an Anglovaal man, was appointed as our new CEO. Then Bob Rowand resigned. As a consequence of the reshuffling of staff, I began to make use of an unoccupied office at Crusader House to perform my claims assessments.

One morning when I arrived to assess claims, someone else was installed in my office. I had to find another small one in which to work, but it was obvious that my services were no longer needed, and I felt very uncomfortable at having been placed in this situation.

I still, however, presented my seminars and went to Bloemfontein to persuade agents and clients to sell and buy our policies. Our new CEO accompanied sales manager Brian Peters and me to Bloemfontein to introduce himself to our independent financial advisors. He gave his talk in Afrikaans and I remember him saying, '*Ons is klein, maar getrain*' – 'We are small, but organised.' I remember well how he praised Crusader Life and said that the audience could have confidence in us, even though the Rowand brothers had left the company.

I was therefore utterly surprised by a statement he made at a board meeting a few weeks later, in July 1993. Given our financial situation, he said, we would be announcing the following day that we were going to suspend trading. I was astounded, because this would result in financial loss to shareholders. Many policy holders had put their trust in me personally. I felt completely used and abused. I strongly objected to the decision and pleaded that some way could be found to continue trading. But the Anglovaal representatives sitting on the board declined, saying that they were no longer interested in life insurance, or critical illness insurance, for that matter.

A month later, Crusader Life was placed under provisional curatorship. I felt very strongly about this and sent the curators a signed affidavit explaining to them what my perceptions of the situation were. Around this time, I was asked to resign, and I gladly did so.

Many reasons have been provided for Crusader Life's financial collapse. I have my own views. Granted, Crusader was suffering from new-business strain, but Anglovaal, with certainty, had sufficient funds to inject into the company had they wanted to.

Rumours about various forms of impropriety started to spread. Curiously, only the Rowand brothers were held responsible, and the government tasked the National Prosecuting Authority (NPA) to investigate. That body, in turn, appointed a company, Goboda, to conduct a forensic audit of Crusader Life's books. I stood by Don and Bob because I could not believe that they would have resorted to improper business practices. After a protracted investigation, the case was finally thrown out of court and the Rowands' name was cleared. I never doubted that that would be the outcome.[1]

* * *

My next opportunity to spread the word about critical illness insurance fulfilled a dream that I had long cherished – to play a part in the introduction and development of critical illness insurance in the United States of America. During my stay in Houston, Texas, in the 1960s, I came not only to know America but to love the country and its people.

It was difficult to believe that, by 1993, ten years after the introduction of critical illness insurance and its acceptance in many other countries in the world, not a single similar policy had been developed in the United States – or Canada, for that matter. They did have a policy called *cancer insurance*, but this was, as the name indicates, for cancer only. Pioneered by the American Family Life Assurance Company of Columbus, it reached its pinnacle in the 1980s.[2] Fraud and non-payment of benefits by unscrupulous companies and so-called agents gave cancer insurance a bad reputation. Compared to critical illness insurance, it was an inferior product.

When I was approached in mid-1993 by a United Kingdom independent financial advisor and an American multi-agent, who wanted to help me give seminars and develop the first proper critical illness insurance policy in the USA, I was naturally very excited and saw this as a great opportunity.

The American agent was based in Ohio and his office was located in its capital, Columbus. I readily accepted, even more enthusiastically when they promised me equity in a company that would be owned by the three of us. Wow – a company in the USA, a one-third share and a market of nearly 300 000 000 people – and not one with a critical illness insurance policy. I just saw dollar signs, even when they told me that I had to pay my own airfares and accommodation expenses while I was in America. They found an interested re-insurer and we had an initial meeting with them at the Sherlock Holmes Hotel, where I was staying in London.

Having by this stage attained vast experience with critical illness insurance policies all over the world, I had a good idea of what I considered to be the best policy for the United States market. In my arrogance, I forgot that I had no knowledge of this market or the insurance company we were going to use to market it for us in the United States.

The re-insurers, NRG Victory, were very resistant to my demands, but, with a bit of give and take, we agreed on a proposed policy, the number of conditions that would be covered and other details, all of which they promised to take back to their principals.

The next step for me was to go over to Columbus, Ohio, to meet the president and marketing team of American Physicians Life (APL), with whom we were going into business. They would be marketing, distributing and managing the product. APL, whose head office was in Columbus, was owned by the Ohio Medical Association and concentrated predominantly on selling litigation insurance to its members, who were medical doctors and dentists.[3] This should have set the alarm bells ringing but, in my ignorance, it didn't. I was, after all, in the United States and had long dreamt of living, on and off, in this great country, with a large dollar income and a holiday home in Florida, not to mention a private yacht!

Our initial meetings were very enthusiastic and everyone could not wait for the finalisation of the policy and the initial launch. With the re-insurer, we subsequently held a final meeting in London. The policy they were prepared to underwrite was not exactly what I wanted, but I won most of the major points. I was keen for not only the core conditions to be covered, but also life, terminal illness and disability as well. To this, they reluctantly agreed.

They weren't too happy with the inclusion of heart-valve surgery and coronary artery bypass surgery either. But after several arguments, they eventually conceded. I finally won the day when they agreed to allow 25 per cent of the insurable sum to be paid out on the diagnosis of the latter conditions – a win, albeit small. To my utter surprise, they even allowed angioplasty, but with only a 10 per cent payout. Although the inclusion of this condition in the policy was not of extreme importance, it was a good marketing tool.

We now had a good, sellable policy and one that would be difficult to equal in the United States market. We had an insurance company to market it and our own company would supply the necessary support. My task would be to address brokers and agents, to give press, radio and television interviews, and to work on the acceptance of the concept in Ohio, and then all over the United States and Canada. What my two partners would do – aside from enjoying excellent lunches and dinners and spending money freely – I never understood.

I soon discovered a major problem: to get a licence approved to market an insurance policy in the United States, one had to obtain a separate licence in each state. We decided that, because we were small, we would initially launch the policy in Ohio and Kentucky only. To obtain this licence, much documentation and details were needed, which could take a long time and easily be refused. Our application was, however, successful and it was decided that we would carry out the launch in Columbus, Ohio, in the first week of November 1993. I could not believe my luck.

The first launch took place in a hotel in Columbus. I arrived with my two partners and was disappointed to find an audience of less than fifty – and this comprised for the most part of staff from APL. My talk was preceded by an uninspiring introduction by one of my partners about the critical illness insurance experience in the UK. Although the content might have been good, he was a very boring presenter.

I delivered my presentation but could not sense any excitement from the audience. A presenter from APL then delved into the details of commission – a very important point with agents – and their marketing material, as well as mentioning a toll-free telephone number that could be contacted to answer any questions concerning our product.

Question time was a nightmare. 'Who is APL?' was the first question. I was dumbfounded. The location of the presentation was a few miles from the headquarters of APL. The agents had been invited by APL and I had presumed that they supported the company – yet they didn't know who the company was and what they marketed.

Other questions addressed the difference between critical illness insurance and disability insurance, the latter being very popular with agents and clients in the United States. I tried my best to explain, and took the unfortunate step of relating to them how we sold critical illness insurance in England. I was rudely interrupted by an agent who, in no uncertain terms, told me, 'This is not England.' It was the last question, however, that really rocked me: an agent asked us for money to pay his parking fee. I left deflated and saw the red lights begin to flash.

Despite this rocky start, I embarked on a month-long roadshow, visiting Cleveland, Akron, Toledo, Cincinnati and smaller centres in Ohio, and Louisville as well as Lexington in the state of Kentucky. Included in my daily programme were newspaper, radio and television interviews, but the audiences at the talks I gave remained small and most of the questions were negative. The roadshow involved many miles of travelling by car. My two partners often stayed at home to perform some or other 'vital duties' and my disenchantment with them and with APL grew.

I soon discovered that APL not only had very little experience in how to service agents, but it had insufficient personnel to do this adequately. I organised meetings to address the matter with the company's president, shortly after which they appointed broker consultants in the major regions. The majority of these consultants, however, had no knowledge of critical illness insurance and their contribution was, in fact, counterproductive.

During my follow-up visits to the major centres, I received many complaints concerning the poor support that its head office was giving to agents, especially those who posed questions about the policy. One problem was that, when interested parties phoned the helpline, the person who dealt with their queries admitted that she had never heard of critical illness insurance or, as APL called our product, *Survivor Key*.

One thing I had learnt very early on in my insurance career was that you could have the best product and pay the highest commission, but if the head-office management team was unreliable, unfriendly and inefficient, you would lose not only the client but also the agent. If the sales were to increase, as we hoped they would, APL simply wouldn't have the resources or the ability to deal with it.

I became increasingly disillusioned with my two partners – or three, rather. I discovered that we had another UK partner when he pitched up in Columbus to assist us. I couldn't understand where and how he fitted into our company, but was told he was a 'brilliant organiser' who would 'play a major role' in the future of our company.

A clash was bound to happen, and it did, during my fourth week in Ohio. I confronted my partners and explained my frustration with their lack of support, APL's inefficiency and all the other signs of disaster I could see looming. They became very aggressive, especially the UK broker, and I refused to continue my association with them. Of course, they immediately referred me to the agreement I had signed.

I had signed the contract after a twenty-six-hour journey from Cape

Town – via London and Chicago – to Columbus. My partners had collected me from Columbus Airport and hauled me straight to a lawyer's office, where they had asked me to sign the agreement. Not only was I exhausted, but I was very worried, as my luggage had gone missing. So, without reading the contract, I duly signed, in good faith. I trusted them. I therefore had no excuse when they presented me with the agreement.

APL had invested a large amount of money in our joint venture and asked me to return to Columbus early the following year for two weeks. I did so, but on my own this time. I discussed my future association with the president of APL, but we could not find agreement on my terms. To my relief, I left Columbus in late 1993. Sadly, I had not realised my American Dream, but I was glad to escape without losing too much money.

Shortly after my return to South Africa I received an aggressive letter from my partners demanding money and threatening that, if I didn't comply with the terms of our initial agreement, I would no longer be a partner, nor would I continue to be associated with them in any way.

This is what I had already decided to do, but they played their last trump card: they referred me again to our agreement, which barred me from working in critical illness insurance in the United States or Canada for two years should I refuse to comply with the contract. How pitiful it was that they perceived me as a threat: I was a one-man show from South Africa, with only a carousel full of slides used to educate agents and companies about a policy with the potential to mean so much to their clients.

I never saw or heard from my partners again and I do not know what happened to them – or to APL, for that matter. It was a tragedy, though, because we had developed a very good critical illness insurance policy. Their pleasure in barring me from working in North America came to nought because, for the next two years, I was not asked to be involved with critical illness insurance in the United States or Canada.

It was a strange coincidence, and somewhat ironic, that I was invited to become involved with Canada Life in Canada exactly two years later.

* * *

Given the collapse of Crusader Life, I no longer had a job when I returned from the United States at the end of 1993. My involvement in private practice had dwindled: owing to my frequent overseas visits, I was seldom there and cardiologists had started to refer their cases to other surgeons who were more available. In addition, my associate and good friend Rob Girdwood had taken on a partner a few years earlier and, as a result, he required me to assist with surgery less frequently. I could find no fault with that.

Both of my daughters, who were living in Johannesburg at the time, were in the process of leaving to go overseas. My youngest, Marie, her cardiologist husband Darryl and their four children were packing up to leave for the United States, and my eldest, Naudéne, and her family were arranging to go to the UK.

With no work and no family – aside from Inez, as always – I had no reason to remain in Johannesburg. We had already decided to put our house on the market, and it had been sold during my last visit to the United States. I had been in Cleveland, engaged in APL activities, when Inez had phoned to inform me that she had just received an offer. So, from a hotel bedroom in Cleveland, Ohio, USA, I had agreed that she should sign the sale of our house – which we loved – in Auckland Park, Johannesburg, South Africa.

As soon as I had arrived home, the two of us had packed up our belongings and, thirteen years after having left Clifton for Johannesburg and parliament, we arrived back in the Cape to fulfil Inez's dream of living permanently in her holiday home. Although I preferred Knysna, which was written in my DNA, I succumbed to Inez's desire to settle in Hermanus. I am now very glad that we took that decision.

I was now 'retired'. Fortunately, insurance associations and companies did not forget me and I was asked to visit Australia and the Far East on a regular basis. It was during this period that I visited for the last time my dear friends Tom and Doris Sumners, who had taken me in when I'd arrived in Houston in 1966 to work under Michael DeBakey and Denton Cooley. During 1993, we had heard that Doris was not well: she had cancer with liver secondaries, so, when I was asked to speak at a convention in Orlando, Florida, in April 1995, we used this opportunity to visit the couple in Houston. I felt the need to thank them and to say goodbye.

We had kept up our friendship with the Sumners over the years by way of letters. They had visited us, and our two daughters had once stayed with them in America for a few days. So, on the Thursday before Easter, Inez and I walked into the house where I had been welcomed many years previously, and slept in the same room and bed where I had slept during my first night in Houston. But we witnessed many changes.

Tom was in his eighties and had advanced Alzheimer's disease. Tragically, he did not recognise us. Doris was very frail and terminally ill with cancer, but she still remembered my favourite pralines and pecan pie. I was no longer the young, insecure surgeon with no lodgings and very little money.

On Easter Friday, we went to the church I had attended with them in the 1960s. There was a new priest, but some old friends were still there. Tom and Doris slept through most of the service. The next day, we said farewell to these wonderful people, to whom I owed such a large debt, and I knew it would be the last time I would see them.

One month later, I received the message that Doris had died. Tom lived for a few more years. To this day, I remain grateful that we took the opportunity to visit them. Owing to them and all my good friends, I consider myself a Texan in part and I will not tolerate anyone who criticises Texans or Americans. To me, they were always generous and kind and my fervent prayer is that God *will* bless America.

36

Canada

S TRANGELY ENOUGH, IN SOUTH AFRICA, WHERE WE HAD FIRST developed critical illness insurance, I became a forgotten man in the insurance world. Perhaps it was as a result of my previous association with Crusader Life, but for several years not once was I asked to work with any local company or address any local insurance meeting or group.

I had previously given a seminar for Canada Life in Ireland, and it had been very well received. The Irish company was headed by one of the best managers in the industry at that time, a hands-on manager who was very popular with his staff. I am sure that it was he who informed the parent company in Canada about me.

My long-standing ambition to become a part of the North American insurance market became a reality when, in October 1996, Canada Life Insurance's head office in Toronto asked me to deliver a talk at its annual sales conference in Torremolinos, Spain. The presentation was received with great enthusiasm and the management of Canada Life saw this as an opportunity to use me in the expansion of their critical illness insurance market. Critical illness insurance had only recently been introduced in Canada, and Canada Life was determined to become a leading provider of the policy. They asked me if I would consider doing a roadshow for them in Canada.

On my return to South Africa, I had to await further details of my involvement with the company and my pending itinerary. While I was doing a medical locum in Alexander Bay in December 1996, Inez informed me that Canada Life had tried to phone me from Toronto and that she had given them my mobile phone number.

We established contact while I was standing outside my lodgings in the Northern Cape town, facing the desolate and windswept desert. We verbally signed a contract for me to present talks in Canada. The contrast of the dry, arid heat of my surroundings did not deter me from the prospect of ice-cold, snowy Canada.

As always, I insisted that Inez accompany me. Final arrangements were made and, in April the following year, we departed on our two-month tour of Canada, criss-crossing the country and travelling vast distances.

A couple of weeks before we left on the trip, I discovered that I had a raised prostate-specific antigen (PSA) level, which suggested that I had prostatic cancer. I had been to see a doctor for another condition and a routine blood test had been required. While they were performing this test, I asked them to do a PSA test at the same time. The next day, I received the results and was surprised that my PSA levels were raised. Up until then, I'd suffered absolutely no symptoms suggestive of prostatic cancer. As a doctor, I should have known better.

I immediately went to see a urologist for his opinion because I was leaving for Canada in two weeks' time. He was more interested in going out for lunch than in my condition and, after performing a rectal examination on me, he told me that everything was satisfactory and that I could go to Canada – for which I considered suing him a few months later.

In this state of mind, I embarked on my Canadian tour during May 1997. We started in Toronto and proceeded to Ottawa, Vancouver, Victoria, Red Deer, Saskatoon, Calgary, Winnipeg, Quebec, St John's and Halifax, before returning to Toronto. Our return coincided with the celebration of Canada Life's 150th anniversary. It was an exhausting tour, compounded by the fact that I was not at all well. What an opportunity, though, to see the beauty of Canada and in a style that I would never, in my wildest dreams, have been able to afford myself.

During the trip and discussions with Canada Life personnel, I again experienced the perpetual insurance problem: the people in management and those in the marketing team lived in different worlds. It was the usual case of 'us and them'. If things went wrong, it was never 'our' fault, but 'theirs'.

At one point I addressed a group of brokers and, at the end of the meeting, several of the members told me in no uncertain terms that they would now sell critical illness insurance, but not the policy provided by Canada Life. This was not because of the product itself, but as a result of the company's poor management.

I was so frustrated that at the end of my two months I told their president that Canada Life might be 150 years old, but it showed. I even had the audacity to tell him that, if I were in his shoes, I would sack most of the managers. I was informed afterwards that, in a few cases, he actually followed my suggestions.

My visit was otherwise very pleasant and Inez came with me to most places. We always had one Canada Life staff member accompanying and assisting us. This took the delightful form of a very vivacious and bouncy woman named Joanne Regan, who alternated with a serious but equally pleasant and efficient Pierre Andre.

We enjoyed Joanne's company immensely, and we remain very good friends today. She, along with her husband, subsequently visited us twice in Hermanus and they both fell in love with our magnificent Garden Route and South Africa in general.

The highlight of our visit to Canada was witnessing the beauty and spectacular scenery of the vast country. We started our tour through the Canadian Rockies from Edmonton, where I gave a presentation. What is remarkable about Edmonton is that it seemed that people spent most of their lives underground due to the extremely cold weather. I was very impressed with their massive underground shopping centres.

From Edmonton, we travelled to Jasper. The scenery through the Rockies was unbelievably beautiful, with snow-capped mountains and lush vegetation. I had my first sightings of mountain sheep, elks that roamed through the streets of Jasper and even a grizzly bear – and all of this on my first visit.

On leaving Jasper, we witnessed the chocolate-box beauty of Lake Louise on our way to Calgary. The lake's splendour was spoilt for me by a large, ugly hotel built on its shores and I was disappointed that its natural surroundings were so commercialised.

Although I think that Cape Town is the most beautiful city in the world, Vancouver comes a good second place. Here, I gave a few radio interviews and, during one of them, was contacted by a listener, Ronnie Josephs, who was an old friend of mine from the days of student demonstrations in the 1970s. We spent a lovely evening together over a very good meal and a few glasses of wine, and the next day he took us for a wonderful lunch at a restaurant on the nearby ski slopes of the renowned Whistler Blackcomb.

My next talk was in Victoria, on Vancouver Island. Its venue and our accommodation was the Empress Hotel, a fantastic hotel that reminded me a lot of our famed Mount Nelson Hotel in Cape Town. The Empress is renowned for its English afternoon tea, which is presented daily and at which there is always a queue of people waiting to be seated, such is its popularity.

Victoria is a beautiful little city and, if I ever had to leave South Africa, I would live there. Another highlight was visiting the beautiful Butchart Gardens.[1] Originally a quarry that had scarred the landscape with a massive, unsightly hole, the area had been restored into a botanical garden. Today, it is internationally famous for its spectacular botanical wonders. Visited daily by thousands, it is one of the most successful reclaimed projects and we could not imagine that it had ever been a quarry in the first place. Inez and I then flew back to Vancouver from Victoria in a seaplane, a wonderful experience in itself.

After returning to Toronto, we visited St John's, Newfoundland, for a few days, where I saw my first iceberg, which was floating just outside the harbour. This was followed by a visit to Halifax, Nova Scotia. The role played by this community in its support of the rescue of the *Titanic*'s survivors is well documented, and many of the bodies recovered after this tragic maritime disaster now rest in the cemeteries of Halifax. What an opportunity to relive events that I had read about during my youth in faraway Beaufort West.

Part of my duties during this visit – and indeed for many others, as mentioned earlier – was to give newspaper, radio and television interviews to spread the news of critical illness insurance, as it was new and unknown to many people, who found these media interviews very interesting.

Back in Toronto, I was contacted one Friday by an old South African friend of mine now living in the city. He had actually rented my house in Clifton during one summer holiday many years previously. He must have succeeded in re-establishing contact with me after hearing one of my radio interviews.

My Toronto friend invited me to attend his synagogue and, when I arrived there, I felt like I was back at Sea Point, Camps Bay and Clifton. Other than the rabbi and the cantor, the congregation consisted of old Jewish friends of mine from these Cape Town Atlantic Seaboard suburbs. It was a wonderful and emotional reunion.

I reconnected with many old South African friends during my critical illness insurance travels, and the re-establishment of contact often gave rise to the forging of new contacts. This greatly supported the ongoing evolution of this industry and the subsequent development of new concepts. Many of the very big insurance companies in the UK, the US, Canada, Australia and elsewhere are now headed by former South Africans.

One of my disappointments was our visit to the Niagara Falls, which to me comes a pale second to the Victoria Falls. My disenchantment was not with its spectacular beauty, but with the unbelievable commercialisation surrounding it. Can you imagine a Frankenstein castle being built next to the spectacular Victoria Falls? On our way back from the falls, however, we visited Niagara-on-the-Lake, a beautiful, natural area and one free of cheap, commercialised exploitation.

Although not aware of it during our successful mid-1997 trip, I would be fortunate enough to visit a few of these wonderful places in Canada again, during a two-week visit in 2001.

37

Surprise, Surprise

H OW MY LIFE CHANGED ON ARRIVING BACK IN SOUTH AFRICA in 1997. A positive biopsy for cancer of the prostate, a radical pros-tatectomy, a severe post-operative haemorrhage and a near-fatal pulmonary embolus during the first six weeks after my return left me weak, depressed and uncertain about my future. This was not helped when one of my doctors advised me that I could be dead within two years.

When the diagnosis of a malignant prostatic cancer was confirmed, the oncologist gave me a very bad prognosis and suggested X-ray radiation treatment. I agreed, but was not convinced that this was best for me. I discussed the matter with a urologist friend of mine in Johannesburg, on whom Rob Girdwood and myself had once performed a very successful coronary artery bypass graft. He suggested a radical prostatectomy, which involves the removal of the prostate gland and some of the tissue surround-ing it, to which I readily agreed.

As a surgeon, I believed in our old, time-proven saying, 'If in doubt, cut it out.' On 20 August 1997, three months before my seventieth birthday, Dr Gus Gecelter performed the operation.

I was, as always, a dreadful patient, and from day one wanted to be discharged. On the third post-operative day, I went to stay with our good friends the Van Zyls, in Pretoria, only to be back in hospital two days later with a severe secondary haemorrhage.

My mood changed for the worse. I was even more impossible than before and refused any help. On the tenth day I was discharged. Every doctor and nurse, and anyone else who had anything to do with me, must have been only too happy to see the back of me. As I was walking to the car parked at the hospital entrance, I felt a slight pain high up on the right side of my chest. As I sat down on the front seat of the car, it hit me – severe pain all over my chest, shortness of breath and a sensation of impending death.

I didn't say anything to Inez or to my son-in-law's sister, Marcelle Khoury, who had come to fetch me, as I was determined not to be readmit-ted to hospital. As we drove to Marcelle's house, the pain became sharper and, as I struggled from the car to the bedroom, there were more acutely painful areas. I could hardly breathe.

My worst fears were confirmed: I had just experienced a massive pulmonary embolus, known as *drop-dead disease* and acknowledged to occur on the tenth post-operative day. I was a textbook case. I had to tell Inez. My words to her were, 'Inez, I think I'm dying.' My poor wife is not at her best when it comes to illness, but fortunately Marcelle's husband, Alex, was a GP. He was at work that Saturday morning, but when Inez told him that she had a dying husband on her hands, he rushed home.

It didn't take him long to confirm what I had already self-diagnosed, and quickly I was back in the car, heading towards Milpark Hospital, where, ironically, I had worked as a cardiac surgeon for thirteen years.

A lung scan revealed numerous emboli in both lungs and I was rushed to high care. I will never forget the feeling when the hospital staff placed the oxygen mask over my face. After two breaths I felt like a drowning man surfacing.

The management that I had so often administered to my patients started, but this time it was being performed on me: monitoring blood pressure and pulse rate, oxygen saturation and intravenous drips with heparin to thin my blood and providing tubes of blood for other tests. My blood pressure was monitored every thirty minutes by way of a cuff placed around my upper arm. The cuff would tighten and then deflate again. This often woke me, but I did not mind because it meant that I was still alive.

The day I was admitted was Saturday 30 August. That night, while I, an old man, was fighting for my life, a happy, radiant young woman went out with her boyfriend. The next morning I was still alive and my condition was improving. She was dead, killed in a high-speed car accident. By the next Saturday, I was well on the road to recovery and, while I was still in hospital, Inez and I watched Princess Diana's funeral in London on television.

* * *

I spent five days in high care. In the evenings, they wanted to give me sleeping tablets, but I refused, telling them I would keep them and take them later. But I never did as I was too frightened, so I lay awake for most of the night.

With our children all being overseas, Inez was on her own, and she had to tell them about my serious complication. My youngest daughter, Marie, was in the process of moving and had just arrived in North Carolina. When she heard of my setback, she dropped everything and that Sunday was on a plane back to South Africa. I knew she was coming and for hours I lay watching the entrance of the unit. When she finally walked in at 2 p.m. that Monday, my gratitude was so immense that I burst into tears and could not stop sobbing. She will never realise what her love and support meant to us during that anxious period.

I had another problem: while lying in my hospital bed, I monitored all the other patients around me. I could see that some of them were getting into trouble and had potential complications, and my training instructed me to treat them. I observed that one particular patient was restless and kept trying to get out of bed. This was a sure sign that he was anoxic – suffering from a lack of oxygen to his brain. The response of the nursing staff was pathetic. I couldn't stop myself from telling the staff what to do. They eventually responded and, on doing so, the patient immediately showed signs of improving. Whereas I might have been accused of acting unprofessionally, even in my state I remained bound by the Hippocratic oath and was therefore obliged to take proper action.

After five days, I was transferred to a ward that was hidden in the bowels of the hospital. From my own experience, I knew that at night there was a dangerous lack of proper nursing down in the basement and that there would be a much-delayed response if one rang the bell. If one had a cardiac arrest, the chances were very good that one would be discovered cold and stiff the next morning. My solution was to demand a bed for Inez in the ward, where she slept at night. She is a very deep sleeper and I wonder if the outcome, should I indeed have suffered a cardiac arrest, would have been any different!

At last, on the nineteenth post-operative day, I was permitted to leave. While walking to the car, I prayed I would not feel a pain in my chest again. Fortunately, no such thing happened, and on arriving safely at Marcelle's house I went to lie down on the same bed where, nine days previously, I had been so close to death.

But I wanted to get home to Hermanus, to my own bed and the smell of the clean, oxygenated air that comes off the Indian Ocean and blows straight into our house. So I asked Inez to book the earliest flight back to Cape Town. Against resistance from every corner, the flight was booked and, early the next morning, I walked from the car, carrying my own suitcase, into the airport building.

Two hours later we landed, and after another two hours of driving I was home. All the dreams that I had had over the last three weeks of being able to return home had come true. It was a truly wonderful feeling.

* * *

Back home, my strength returned very slowly, but I had nothing to do and I didn't want to do anything. I was in a deep, dark hole, and the only thing I did well was feel sorry for myself.

In early November, one month after being discharged from hospital, I received a phone call out of the blue from a television station in Munich, Germany. The producers asked me to appear on a show, which would be recorded in early December.

This was certainly not one of my priorities, but when it was explained to me what the show was about, I became increasingly interested. I soon realised that it was an opportunity for me to return to reality and to stop feeling sorry for myself. I recognised then that I had two options: either I could sit around feeling sorry for myself and wait for the cancer to spread, or I could start living as if every day were precious. I made my decision and today, thirteen years later, I have never regretted it.

Although in Germany the television programme had a different name, it was similar to a show I had enjoyed watching during my numerous visits to the UK during 1991 and 1992. Hosted by well-known singer Cilla Black, it was called *Surprise, Surprise*. An immediate relative or friend of an aspiring participant would contact the producer of the show after the potential participant had expressed a great desire to make contact with a long-lost friend or relative whom he or she hadn't seen for years. Alternatively, the prospective participant wanted to be introduced to someone famous, or someone he or she greatly admired, but would otherwise have no opportunity of meeting. The participant would then be lured to watch the show live with friends or relatives and told that one of the people accompanying him or her would be appearing on the show. The other 'surprise' party – in this case, me – would duly be invited.

I was told that my part of the programme was to meet the mother of a child on whom I had performed heart surgery in Romania twenty years earlier. The child was now a grown man and his mother expressed a daily desire to thank me personally for the gift of a healthy son.

I arrived in Munich after an all-night flight and a long stopover at Frankfurt earlier in the afternoon. I have to admit that, although they flew me first class, I was exhausted. I was met at the airport and taken to the hotel, which certainly wasn't first class. After a shower and change of clothing, I was fetched from the hotel at 6 p.m. and transported to the studio, where I was more or less dumped.

I was taken to a small room and told to wait – I was not to be seen by anyone as it would ruin the 'surprise'. The room was bare except for a small television and a coffee machine and, after sitting there for about an hour, a woman appeared. In very poor English, she explained to me what to expect.

The programme was a Christmas special that would last about three hours. The good news, she told me, was that I was the highlight and that my appearance would take place last. In the meantime, I could watch the programme and 'enjoy' the coffee from the dispenser. There were no biscuits, sandwiches or any other food. So I sat and waited, watching German television and, of course, not understanding a word.

At last, the *Surprise, Surprise* show started. It was recorded in a large hall packed with people. It was obviously a very popular programme. The host was good, but naturally spoke only German. After a long preamble, he introduced the first 'surprise'.

Although it was in German, I picked up the word *Jackson*. When the participant appeared, I too had the 'surprise, surprise' of my life: it was none other than Janet Jackson, who had her own band and eight bodyguards. She sang songs I'd never heard before to a rapturous audience. I wasn't impressed. After the young man whose lifetime ambition had been to meet Ms Jackson was introduced to her and a few words had been exchanged, Jackson, her band and her bodyguards disappeared.

I couldn't help thinking about how much she must have been paid. I received nothing. But I now jokingly tell my friends that when I appeared on a television programme in Munich, Janet Jackson was a supporting act.

For the next two hours, I sat in isolation, watching a string of surprises that I didn't understand. Eventually, the woman who had spoken to me earlier appeared and told me that I was next. She now joined me to interpret so that I had some idea of what was going on.

The host proceeded to climb down from the platform to a family of four sitting in the second row: a husband and wife and two grown-up sons. The host started to ask the wife questions. She had been told that her younger son would meet Michael Schumacher, the Formula 1 ace, who was his idol. But, instead, she found herself in the hot seat. She was very nervous, surprised and emotional.

The interview went something like this: She was a Romanian girl who had married a German. Her elder son had been born healthy, but when her younger son was born it had soon became obvious that he was a 'blue baby'. As he had grown older, his condition had deteriorated.

She had tried everything in Romania to help her son, but was told that nowhere in the country could he be operated on. As they had no money to have the operation performed in Europe, she had become resigned to the fact that he would soon die. One day, in the village where they lived, she had seen a small group of people clustered around a car, talking to one man in particular.

At this point in the interview, the woman became more emotional and started to cry. When she was asked to continue, she said that when she had enquired who it was, she had been informed that it was a cardiac surgeon who was visiting Romania to perform surgery on children and, more specifically, those who could not be operated on in their own country.

The interviewer at this juncture led her onto the stage, where he seated her on a couch and she continued her story. She related how she had heard about the South African cardiac surgeon and viewed the opportunity to speak to him as an act of God – and a chance for her son to be saved. When she had attempted to talk to him, she had not been allowed to and had been rudely led away. But she had been determined. After a while, she had seen the surgeon getting into the car, but before it could drive away she had run towards the vehicle and sat right in front of it, blocking its path.

She had been grabbed by someone, but before she could be taken away, the South African surgeon had climbed out of the car and asked her handlers to allow her to approach him so that he could hear why she had acted so strangely. In tears, she had explained to him her son's condition and said that there was no hope for him. She had asked him if he could see her son and help him. His response had been that he would gladly see the boy in Bucharest, but she explained that they had no means of getting there.

Now sobbing continuously on stage, she told the audience in a whisper that the surgeon had taken his own air ticket from his pocket and given it to her, saying that he could see her son the following day. He had then left and had duly seen the child the next morning, at the Fundeni clinic. The operation had been performed two days later, and it was a great success. Shortly afterwards, the surgeon had returned to South Africa.

As I sat listening, I thought back twenty years and could vaguely recall the case. I remembered a very desperate woman fighting for her child's life. I recollected that the boy had a congenital heart lesion – a tetralogy of Fallot.

Of her sitting in front of the car and my offering her an air ticket I had no recollection, but the rest of her story was certainly true.

The interviewer asked the woman if she would like to see the surgeon again. Her face lit up immediately and she said yes. When asked why, she responded that, when the operation had been completed and the child was in ICU, they had not been allowed to see me because the unit was strictly out of bounds for family and relatives. Because of this constraint, she explained, she had never seen me again to say thank you, and this had been her greatest wish ever since.

At that moment, I walked onto the stage. She went ballistic. She jumped up and, with tears streaming down her face, proceeded to hug and kiss me. Her husband and two sons did the same – I was kissed by three men more than I cared for. The audience then rose to its feet as one, cheering, with many people in tears. And so ended my 'Surprise, Surprise'.

There was a short reception after the show for participants and television crew. The family of four did not stop hugging me, and it was a memorable and emotional reunion. I was later driven back to the hotel and informed of the time that the car would take me to the airport the next day.

In less than forty-eight hours, I was back in Hermanus, exhausted but confident that I could resume a normal life again in spite of my cancer.

38

Breakthrough in America

D URING MY VISIT TO CANADA IN 1997, THE CEO OF CANADA LIFE
had invited me to his office, saying that he'd arranged a teleconference
with their sister company in Atlanta, Georgia. I had literally run to his office
– this was the opportunity that I had long been waiting for. I was overjoyed.

During the teleconference, I'd discussed a visit to Canada Life USA with
their marketing manager and it had been decided that I would go on a three-
month trip to the United States the following year. The tour would include
visits to thirty-one cities throughout the nation and would be divided into
two six-week sessions with a month's break in between, during which time
I would return to South Africa.

I made it a condition – a demand, in fact – that Inez would accompany
me on the tour. She could travel to whichever centre she desired and could
choose to spend weekends visiting any scenic area of her choice. I felt that
Inez deserved this break after so many years of loyal support and after
having taken care of me during my cancer treatment.

In addition, I was extremely worried about my health and, to be honest,
I felt insecure without her. One of the things that haunted me while I was
away, most often when in a hotel room all on my own, was what would
happen if I should die there.

An added incentive was that Marie and her family were now living in
North Carolina, an important consideration that we factored into our planning. During the week, Inez could either stay with our daughter while I
was on tour, or choose to accompany me. Over weekends, I would have the
choice of staying with my daughter and her family.

In April 1998, we embarked on the tour. My dream of being involved
in the introduction of critical illness insurance to the United States was
finally coming true. The National Conference of Canada Life in Nashville,
Tennessee, was where I gave my first talk, and it was well received. Nashville
is the mecca of country music, and the Grand Ole Opry House, a weekly
country music stage that has seen performances from some of the biggest
artists of the genre, is a major attraction. As a great lover of country music,
I attended a concert at the famous venue and was not disappointed.

The next day we were off to Denver, Colorado. I was accompanied by Marcia Johnson, the marketing manager of Canada Life USA, and Robyn James, her organising assistant. The three of us were seated right at the back of the United Airlines plane, Marcia sitting next to the window and Robyn on the aisle. Just after take-off, when Robyn had got up to go to the restroom, I heard a very loud '*What?*' from her. When she took her seat next to me a short while later, she explained that, on her way to the restroom, a flight attendant had asked her if we were a singing group. Coming from Nashville, she must have thought that this strange-looking threesome could only be singers. There was Marcia, a white woman; me, a grey-haired, elderly gentleman; and Robyn, a pretty black woman in her late twenties. We accepted the notion that we were a singing group and, as our seminars concerned critical illness insurance, we called ourselves 'The Criticals'. Unfortunately, nobody ever asked us to sing.

* * *

Since my previous disappointment in Ohio, where there had been very little progress in the acceptance of critical illness insurance, things were changing: a few companies had critical illness insurance policies and were marketing them to their clients.

Unfortunately, I quickly realised that these policies were very limited with regard to the conditions covered, the maximum insurable amounts, the accessibility of the definitions and the underwriting. If they tried to market their policies in the United Kingdom, for example, they would not sell one.

As I had experienced so often, the management and sales teams were worlds apart and always at loggerheads with one another. Success, of course, was based on sales: when sales were down, management would blame the sales team for not selling enough products and sales would blame management for developing a poor product, or for bad management. Far too often, the latter was, in fact, true.

An important part of a successful sale was the time it would take for the application to be underwritten and brought on the books and, most significantly, how soon the commission could be paid to the agent.

As a rule, the sales team thought that every policy application should be accepted. If declined, they fought this decision and there was always great unhappiness. The salesman felt that he had been done down if the claim was declared invalid, and the prospective client would obviously express dissatisfaction.

During the tour of America, however, the sales team and I were closely associated. Ninety per cent of the agents were a delight to work with and I presented to them my ideas on how we should sell critical illness insurance.

Our thirty-one-stop tour included most of the USA's biggest cities. We visited almost every state where critical illness insurance was licensed. In nine states, the state authorities refused to allow the policy to be marketed, including in Georgia – the state in which Canada Life's head office was located!

The trip required daily commuting between cities, with early-morning breakfast meetings, lunches with major supporters, and radio and television interviews. Then we would head off to the next city, have dinner with local staff and brokers and finally collapse into bed. The same routine was re-peated the next day and every other working day. It was exhausting but I loved it. Whenever I thought the going was tough, I would simply think of my nineteen days in hospital a year prior to the visit.

Over weekends, I would often commute back to High Point, North Carolina, to stay with my daughter Marie, her husband Darryl, and their three beautiful daughters and son. At night, we would enjoy a typical South African *braaivleis* or a meal that my daughter had prepared for us. Marie's husband is a South African–born Lebanese, and her mother-in-law taught her the secrets of Lebanese cuisine. It was excellent, and I almost became addicted to that style of food.

Then it would be back to the airport on the Sunday evening in prepar-ation for our meeting the next morning. Inez joined me in New York, San Francisco and a few other cities, and we could not believe our good fortune. We saw beautiful places, made wonderful lifelong friends, and received kind-ness and warm hospitality – more than from any other country that I had toured promoting critical illness insurance.

Inez and I had long promised each other that we would one day visit the Hawaiian Islands, and the opportunity to do so arose on completion of my last talk, which I gave in Los Angeles. It was too good a chance to miss, and it would give us the additional opportunity to visit our son, Adam, and his family in Australia. So we decided to go to the spectacular and enchanting set of islands in the Pacific Ocean that I had read about and whose beautiful music I had listened to with wonder during my youth.

The afternoon following my talk, we departed Los Angeles and, as soon as the plane descended, the dreams that had been ignited in the dry, dusty Karoo during the 1930s became a reality. The islands were magnificent and far exceeded my childhood expectations. The impressions of lilting Hawaiian music took me back to Mortimer and Hill next door to our home in Beaufort West, where the store's gramophone would often play this music. The exotic scenes from childhood movies on these islands never left me.

Our hotel room overlooked the beautiful beach and tropical blue sea. We visited as many places as possible, where Hawaiian music played and grass-skirted girls danced. The music was exactly as I had imagined, but the dancers were a great disappointment. Instead of the beautiful, hip-swaying girls depicted in the movies, we had to watch tired, middle-aged ladies with plump hips that struggled to sway. The grass skirts hardly moved.

An enthralling highlight, however, was our visit to Pearl Harbour. As a young boy, I had, one hot Beaufort West morning in early December 1941, heard the news of the Japanese's despicable bombing raid. Over the years, we learnt of all the battleships that had sunk, including the USS *Arizona*. Now we stood on its sunken hulk, reading the names of the brave sailors and others who had so tragically lost their lives.

But of greater significance to me was the proud USS *Missouri*, which was now lying gently at anchor. On board this ship on 2 September 1945, the Japanese minister of foreign affairs, Mamoru Shigemitsu, had surrendered on behalf of the Emperor of Japan and the Japanese government to the United States' General Douglas MacArthur, commander in the Southwest Pacific and supreme commander for the Allied powers. Defeat and victory lying side by side – but at what cost?

After Pearl Harbour, which made such a great and everlasting impression on me, the rest of our visit was rather an anticlimax. But what I *can* say is that Inez and I had eventually fulfilled our dreams of visiting this wondrous paradise.

* * *

Our tour of the United States was a great success, largely because of Marcia Johnson. Born and bred in Alabama, and having lived there for most of her youth, she was a down-to-earth, friendly and warm person. She could drink with the men, tell jokes and was excellent at her work. The agents adored her and we immediately developed a strong bond.

We have kept up contact, and today Inez and I converse with her at least once a week using Skype. She has visited us in Hermanus, and we consider Marcia, her husband and their daughter as family. When Marcia stayed with us, I took her along my favourite part of South Africa – the Garden

Route – to Victoria Bay and Plettenberg Bay. She was so impressed with the Beacon Isle Hotel that she wanted to buy a timeshare there. Of course, being a Southern lass, she left our shores with numerous bottles of our best wines.

Marcia became passionate about critical illness insurance from the outset, but was frustrated by the poor management and, in particular, the CEO of the company. This was to prove her downfall: her criticism of her seniors and her increasing clashes with them, in addition to her great popularity with the agents, unfortunately made her unpopular in high places. When I accompanied Canada Life representatives in 2000 on a two-week tour that she had initiated, she was no longer with the company. It was not the same without her.

It seemed to us that our first tour really put this company on the map as a major player in the development of critical illness insurance in the USA. After Marcia's dismissal, however, her successors did not have the same passion and enthusiasm that she had had. I believe that Canada Life USA subsequently missed a great opportunity – due to internal politics and an inability to grasp the impact we had on hundreds of agents – to become involved with critical illness insurance.

Fortunately, many of these agents are still friends of both Marcia and me. To this day, I frequently receive letters from them, thanking me for introducing critical illness insurance to them and saying how impressed they were with the policy. Many are now authorities on critical illness insurance who present seminars and give talks on the subject. They are carrying on the crusade Marcia and I started in 1998.

* * *

Since my early days in the United Kingdom, I had heard about the Million Dollar Round Table (MDRT).[1] Agents could qualify to become a member only by reaching a certain annual commission. If you belonged to the MDRT, you were considered to be among the top agents in the world. Being invited to speak at their annual meeting, which was attended by several thousand agents from all over the globe, placed you in the elite of public speakers, especially if you were a main-platform speaker.

After my initial big meetings in London in 1991, specifically at Life Insurance Association venues, brokers approached me and said they would like to see me speak at the MDRT. Not knowing much about the organisation at the time, I responded with a smile and said that I would appreciate such an opportunity.

Nothing happened until 1999, when I was invited to be a main-platform speaker in New Orleans. Having been back from my trip to the USA for several months, I was very excited by the invitation, as it indicated that critical illness insurance was having an impact in the country. Naturally I accepted, but I was soon informed that my talk was not suitable for the main platform. I was, however, ensured that it was still a great honour to be a speaker at what they termed *break-out sessions*. I was very disappointed and wanted to refuse, but was eventually persuaded to go.

At the meeting, I was amazed at the number of international delegates that attended. But I soon became very disillusioned by everyone telling me what a wonderful honour it was to be a speaker and how fantastic the MDRT and its members were. I had met quite a few of their members around the world and had not been impressed by many of them. To me it was a kind of self-hero-worship meeting with the emphasis on how wonderful they all were because they made a lot of money. For me, unlike for many of them, insurance was an opportunity to provide policy holders with policies that suited their needs and enabled them to receive financial support when they needed it most.

At such meetings, there are the main-platform speakers, whose presentations are delivered in the morning and attended by all delegates. In the afternoons, the meetings are broken up into numerous break-out sessions, where many different presentations are given simultaneously in different halls, the topics relating predominantly to various aspects of insurance. Motivational speeches are also given.

I gave my talk on critical illness insurance at one such afternoon session. It was attended by about 400 agents. My disillusionment at not being a main-platform speaker was tempered by my knowledge that critical illness insurance was not considered a major role player in the United States at the time.

I believe that it was one of the first talks on critical illness insurance to be given at the MDRT. A kind applause followed my presentation, and very few questions were asked. I didn't feel that the response had been positive or enthusiastic, and I left rather deflated. It had become obvious to me that, in the United States, critical illness insurance was, in fact, in trouble.

Although more companies were providing policies, not one of them included the conditions that I believed my future patients deserved. Furthermore, many of their policies were still far inferior to those we had initially developed during 1990 in Ohio with American Physicians Life. The management of most companies was more of a hindrance than a help: their fear of the over-servicing of patients by their doctors – resulting in an increasing number of claims and the threat of litigation against them – was one of their major objections. This resulted in strict underwriting, restrictive definitions that only a medical specialist could understand, and a reluctance to pay claims.

Even under these trying circumstances, however, many agents remained positive and sold policies, and I frequently heard of how patients who claimed were saved financially.

39

Fruits of My Labour

B Y 2002, I BELIEVED THAT MY INSURANCE DAYS IN SOUTH AFRICA were over. This was until I was 'rediscovered' by Old Mutual Insurance, one of the biggest insurance groups in the country, to assist in further promoting critical illness insurance in South Africa. Naturally, I was overjoyed.

Two of my talks in Johannesburg did not go well, however. Attendances were small and it emerged in the feedback that not only did the brokers think they knew more than me about critical illness insurance (which, to my disgust, they still called *'dread disease' insurance*), but they didn't think it held an important place in their presentations. They were more interested in investment insurance and insuring for major medical expenses.

Fortunately, my critical illness insurance seminars must have helped their sales somewhat, and I became increasingly involved with Old Mutual during 2003 and 2004, presenting in cities and towns across South Africa to agents, clients and influential financial advisors. Old Mutual's critical illness insurance product was – and indeed remains – excellent. Their definitions are equal to, if not better than, those anywhere else in the world. During this period they introduced stand-alone critical illness insurance policies and, soon afterwards, child cover.

It is very unfortunate that South Africa, where the first critical illness insurance policy was developed in 1983, still seems to be so far behind places like the United Kingdom, Australia and the Far East with regard to the acceptance and success of the product. Despite the attempts of insurance companies like Old Mutual to promote the policy, there seems to be a lack of understanding among our financial advisors about the necessity for critical illness cover. I hope that this is not because they believe that other policies are easier to sell or that more commission can be made on a policy that is renewable on an annual basis. Insurance is selling a need, and critical illness insurance provides for that need.

* * *

After twenty years of promoting critical illness insurance, I still had two ambitions. Firstly, I wanted to see the product successfully established in the United States. Owing to the lack of significant sales there, I felt that we were failing. I believed that, to achieve this dream, it was necessary for one of the major insurance companies in the USA to develop and market its own critical illness insurance product.

Secondly, it was my ambition to receive an invitation to speak on the main platform at the annual Million Dollar Round Table meeting.

During my visits to Canada, I had had two meetings in the small city of Victoria, in British Columbia. One of them involved addressing a charity gathering organised by Canadian financial advisor Alphonso Franco. The event had been facilitated to collect funds to finance a lung-transplant patient and, although we raised the money, unfortunately the patient died.

Not only was Alphonso enthusiastic about critical illness insurance, but he could talk, think and live it. He was the leading seller of the product in Canada – the whole of North America, even – and was eager to increase awareness of it worldwide. I was, therefore, not surprised when he invited me to be the keynote speaker for the first international critical illness insurance meeting, which he was organising and which was to be held in Vancouver in January 2003.

I gladly accepted the invitation, but had to endure the endless hassles involved in obtaining a visa from the Canadian Consulate in South Africa. Visa problems – which were certainly not peculiar to Canada – aside, my talk in Vancouver was well received, and requests to speak began to flow in. Some of these were from the Association of Insurance and Financial Advisors in New Orleans, the National Association for Critical Illness Insurance in Atlanta, the Protective Life Insurance Company in Birmingham, Alabama, Bradford & Bingley in the UK and ... the cherry on the top, the Million Dollar Round Table's Top of the Table Convention in Palm Springs, California.

The Top of the Table, or TOT, is an association of MDRT members and is exclusive to those who achieve the highest premium income. It includes some of the most elite insurance and financial services professionals in the world.

I had now reached the pinnacle: I was a well-known and respected international speaker.

As always, Inez accompanied me and we revisited some of the places we had so enjoyed seeing while I was working in Houston in the sixties. The difference, however, was that in 1967 we had travelled on Greyhound buses, stayed in the cheapest hotels and had just enough money for basic food. Now we were met at airports by chauffeur-driven cars – we experienced five-star treatment, paid for by the insurance companies and associations that had invited me to speak.

Inez and I revisited New Orleans and saw the magnificent Grand Canyon again, and we fulfilled a lifelong dream of seeing the autumn – or *fall*, as the Americans call it – colours in New Hampshire, commonly known as *leaf-peeping*.

During the change of season from summer to fall, especially in the northern states of America and in Canada, the leaves of many of the trees alter their hues – some stay green, some become yellow, others bright red – collectively producing a tinted kaleidoscope of rich and earthy colours. This spectacular scenery remains for Inez and me one of the major sights in the world, and it made an enormous impression on me. Its beauty made me realise again the wonder of God's creation and how lucky I have been.

Our visit was made even more memorable by the fact that we went by car accompanied by our dearest friend, Marcia Johnson, and Marie, our 'American' daughter. It was the most enjoyable trip we could have wished for, and I pray that I can visit those places again.

I will never forget that, on the first sighting of the spectacular colours everywhere, Marcia played a CD version of the hymn 'How Great Thou Art':[1]

> O Lord my God! When I in awesome wonder
> Consider all the worlds Thy hands have made,
> I see the stars, I hear the rolling thunder,
> Thy power throughout the universe displayed:
>
> Then sings my soul, my Saviour God to Thee
> How great Thou art! How great Thou art!
> Then sings my soul, my Saviour God to Thee
> How great Thou art! How great Thou art!
>
> When through the woods and forest glades I wander
> And hear the birds sing sweetly in the trees;
> When I look down from lofty mountain grandeur
> And hear the brook and feel the gentle breeze …

All of my talks were received positively and we finally arrived at Palm Springs, California, for the TOT meeting. Situated in the desert, Palm Springs is a man-made oasis most famous for its golf courses.

Our hotel formed part of a golf resort and had a large swimming pool warmed by the desert sun. I spent more time at the pool than I should have, but I love swimming and renewed friendships at the poolside with many agents from all over the world whom I had previously met and who had listened to me. Most of them praised my talks and were critical illness insurance converts. Who could not have had a wonderful time!

My speech at the TOT meeting was rewarded with a standing ovation, and I was elated that, although I had not been a main-platform speaker at a Million Dollar Round Table meeting as was my original ambition, I had been a main speaker at their exclusive Top of the Table convention. The best part, however, was still to come.

That night, at a cocktail party, I was approached by one of the organisers of the next MDRT meeting. He asked me if I would consider being a main-platform speaker at their 2004 venue at Anaheim, California.

With cancer, it is difficult to plan a year ahead, and I still felt hurt about the way I had been treated by the MDRT when invited to speak in New Orleans. They had known about me for ten years, and only now was I good enough. I didn't commit myself, but during the evening I thought to myself, *This was always your dream, so swallow your pride, go to Anaheim and give them one of the best talks they have ever heard.* So, that evening, I accepted.

We arrived back home in a glow of happiness and were pleased to be settled for a few months. Our happiness was even greater when my prostate-specific antigen levels were tested. Although higher than normal, they were rising only very gradually. This was far better than we could have expected, and I used the test results as a guide to plan the year ahead.

* * *

If 2003 was a great year, 2004 was even better. My dream of becoming a main-platform speaker at the MDRT was not only fulfilled, but Metropolitan Life (MetLife), one of the biggest insurance groups not only in the United States but in the world, asked me to visit New York to assist them in developing their critical illness insurance product.

We had found New York exciting during a previous visit, but this time it exceeded all of our expectations. We were fetched from the airport and driven to the Waldorf Astoria in a limousine. The driver told us that he and the limousine were at our disposal for the duration of our stay in this great city.

I had read about and seen on television and in the movies the splendour of the Waldorf Astoria. I had heard about all the movie stars and other important people who had stayed there, including former President George W. Bush, who always made the hotel his base during regular visits to the 'Big Apple'. Apparently he would occupy two floors and the roads around the hotel would be closed for the duration of his visit. I was given a bedroom and a large sitting-room-cum-dining-room with computers, a television and all the equipment necessary to run a business. I have to admit that no roads in the vicinity of the hotel were closed during our stay.

Not in our wildest imaginations could we have conceived of the luxury of this famous hotel. We were wined and dined and had frequent meetings with MetLife's product development and marketing teams. I studied their proposed contract and had a frank discussion with them about it. Compared to critical illness insurance policies in South Africa, the UK, Australia and several other countries, their policy was a great disappointment. It covered only six conditions and the maximum insurable amount was $50 000. This did not compare with policies in the UK, for example, which covered twenty or more conditions with maximum insurable amounts of up to – and even exceeding – £1 000 000.

Having promoted critical illness insurance in the USA for several years, I discovered for the first time that there was a big difference between their target market and ours. We in South Africa concentrated on individual insurance policies, whereas the Americans concentrated on worksite insurance and group insurance policies, which involve a group of people contributing funds into a pool from which they all claim. Individual insurance had a very small market penetration in the US. We had tried to promote group insurance policies in South Africa and elsewhere, but had been unsuccessful, as they were considered too expensive by the companies involved.

The six conditions covered by MetLife, with its relatively small maximum insurable amount, however, made this product much more affordable, and one that required a minimum of medical underwriting.

I left with the conviction that MetLife, with its large contingent of agents and financial support, and its prolific name, had the best chance of establishing critical illness insurance in the USA. If they failed, I believed, there was very little future for the product there.

Unfortunately, owing to reasons unknown to me, the company didn't achieve the success that I believe they could have. They failed to make a major impact on critical illness insurance acceptance in the USA and their influence on the future of insurance in their country was not significant. I have to confess that, in addition, I was very concerned about the team they had appointed to manage the critical illness insurance campaign and I wondered whether their failure was due rather to the assigned team's lack of commitment and enthusiasm.

I realise only now that, in very large companies like MetLife, critical illness insurance is hardly 0.5 per cent of their overall business, whereas in smaller companies critical illness insurance *is* a major part, and therefore they put much more effort into promoting it.

* * *

After our time in New York, we visited Marie and her family in North Carolina. I could stay for just a day and a half, but during the first day there I started feeling ill with severe tiredness, a high temperature and coughing. As a result, my son-in-law, also a cardiologist, put me on a course of antibiotics.

When I arrived in Anaheim for the MDRT meeting, I was very ill. I developed a high temperature, was sweating at night and had a cough that kept me awake. In addition, I had severe pain in my right hip, which made it almost impossible to walk.

Inez had not accompanied me to California and I was very much on my own. Fortunately, I had started taking antibiotics and my Canadian friend Alphonso Franco helped me a lot. His attention and concern is typical of the man.

The next day, I felt even worse but attended the opening ceremony. The list of speakers and their CVs made me feel very insecure – it even included the former queen of Jordan.

The auditorium was something I had never experienced before. I attended the morning main-platform meeting for a short time, sitting at the back of the auditorium – one of just over 6 000 attendees. You could hardly see the speakers on the platform; they were too far away. Very large screens, however, were situated at intervals around the hall so that all the audience members could see the speaker.

I sat though the morning session and limped back to the hotel. At 3 p.m., I attended a rehearsal in the main auditorium. I was second on the programme the next morning, immediately before the tea break. I would be preceded by a young autistic boy of fourteen years of age who was considered to be a genius. He had his own jazz band – he played the piano – which performed all over the USA. I soon discovered that he was indeed a genius.

I was told that he was an expert in geography, so I tested him by asking him if he knew what the capital city of South Africa was. Without thinking, he came out with the correct answer. 'There are three,' he said. 'Cape Town is the legislative capital, Pretoria is the executive capital and Bloemfontein is the judicial capital.' I couldn't believe it. I wonder how many South Africans know the correct answer.

That night I was desperately ill. My fever worsened, my coughing became incessant and I was reasonably sure I had pneumonia. I prayed that the antibiotics would work. I was tempted to try to get on a flight back to South Africa as soon as possible despite the fact that, after my talk, Inez and I were due to join Marcia and her husband on a trip to Maui in the Hawaiian Islands. Having come this far and having waited for so long, however, I dragged myself to the Speakers of the Day breakfast and waited for my turn to present.

At last, the master of ceremonies read out my CV and I limped onto a large stage to a designated spot. In front of me, I could see the faces of the first few rows of the audience, but there was darkness in the distance due to the blinding spotlights. I knew, though, that there were in excess of 6 000 people listening to me.

The title of my talk was 'Three Firsts and a Fourth'. Prior to the event, the organisers had insisted that I send them a written speech, as thirty-seven countries were represented and my speech had to be translated into fourteen languages. They offered me a prompter, but I refused. I have experienced that when I read my speech, the passion and emotions disappear.

As a main-platform speaker, one is given twenty-five minutes at most. The organisers are very strict about this so, when practising, I had asked that my speech be timed from the instant it started – five, ten, fifteen and twenty minutes, and then every minute thereafter.

I started my talk with a short summary of who I was and where I came from. I then related my first 'First' – thirty-five years as a cardiac surgeon and a member of the team, led by my brother Chris, that had performed the world's first heart transplant. I then related my second 'First' – nine years as an anti-apartheid politician – before speaking about my third 'First' – how I had developed the world's first critical illness insurance policy and been involved in its success all over the world.

Up till this point, my talk had been going well. The audience had laughed at my jokes and applauded some of my successes. But when I started my 'Fourth', there seemed to be something shifting in the audience, something indescribable.

I told them about my seven-year fight with prostatic cancer. The applause increased in duration and intensity when I related my spiritual renewal, saying that cancer had led me to God and eternal life. I appreciated the audience's applause and it lifted me, but I prayed that they would stop, as it was taking up some of my remaining minutes. Their ovation, however, continued to rise when I said, strange as it might sound, that I thanked God for my cancer because it might reduce my earthly life but would grant me eternal life. That, I considered to be a bargain.

I thanked the insurance world for the privilege and honour it was, after more than twenty-one years, to have been associated with them and conveyed how grateful I was for the financial help they gave to our patients when we, as doctors, had to tell them the worst thing they would hear in their lives: 'You have had a heart attack,' 'Your husband has had a stroke,' or 'Your wife has cancer.'

By this stage, I was feeling terribly sick: I had a high fever and was sweating from the stark lights shining down on me. I was very emotional and started crying. In tears, I ended my speech with the last four lines of the poem 'The Blind Boy' by Colley Cibber:

> Then let not what I cannot have
> My cheer of mind destroy:
> Whilst thus I sing, I am a king,
> Although a poor blind boy.

Totally drained, I had to be helped off the stage. The standing ovation was prolonged and I was mobbed by attendees. Most wanted to shake my hand, while others asked for my signature or for me to pose with them for pictures. When the tea break was over some thirty minutes later, there was still a throng of people surrounding me. After about an hour, Alphonso came to my rescue. It was a truly indescribable and memorable experience.

Mission accomplished. My ambitions had been fulfilled and, to my mind, very successfully. I had achieved in the critical illness insurance world everything and more than I could ever have dreamt of. If I was never invited to speak again, I wouldn't be disappointed. But the invitations did not stop – with the MDRT exposure they actually increased – and at the age of eighty-three years, I am still determined to spread knowledge and understanding to all who want to hear about this wonderful product – critical illness insurance.

40

My Final UK Visit

MY EARLIER HECTIC INVOLVEMENT WITH CRITICAL ILLNESS insurance in the United Kingdom had come to an end in 1996. I had not been surprised, because I had realised that I had nothing new to offer and that most agents in the protection insurance field had already heard my presentations at some time or another. After one of my talks on an earlier occasion, this was cemented for me when an agent came up to me and said, 'Marius, this is the seventh time I have listened to you. You have taught me nothing new, but I am enthusiastic again.' I considered his comment a real compliment.

I had to admit, however, that deep down I wished I could travel around the UK one more time, to meet up with agents I had encountered in the past and to see the beautiful countryside. I missed visiting the English country pubs and enjoying a pint or two of ale and a greasy meal of fish and chips.

Out of the blue, in the summer of 2004, an invitation arrived. It was from Scottish Widows, one of the largest insurance groups in the UK. Scottish Widows is owned by Lloyds Banking Group, which also owns, among other institutions, Cheltenham & Gloucester, a building society. At my talk, agents from Scottish Widows were present in addition to those from Lloyds. It was a dream audience. Many were mortgage agents and thus ideally positioned to sell critical illness insurance policies to their clients who had mortgages.

Fourteen years since having arrived in the UK for the first time, not knowing what to expect with my carousel full of slides, I was once again back on the road. This time, I was a well-known critical illness insurance motivator and equipped with an up-to-date PowerPoint presentation.

I was supported by a most professional and helpful team. Nick Kirwan, who today is with the Association of British Insurers (ABI), was the senior member, but I was accompanied for the most part by Johnny Timpson, Scottish Widows' head of protection insurance marketing. Not only was he extremely competent, but he was the nicest person with whom one could wish to work and he had great relationships with his agents. Two of his team members were bonny Scottish lasses, Jane Flett and Catriona Jeffries.

We travelled through England, Wales, Scotland and Northern Ireland, visiting many of the cities and venues I remembered from ten years earlier. It was the most pleasant of all my visits to the UK.

On a journey north from Edinburgh to Aberdeen, our train stopped at an abandoned, windswept station – Leuchars, in Fife. Over the intercom came a message asking whether there was a doctor on board and, if so, could he or she attend to a passenger who had collapsed in the last coach. I had to disembark quickly and hurry along the platform to the end of the train, where I found a very old gentleman lying on the floor. He was pale and sweating but still conscious.

There was already a nurse in attendance, who diagnosed all sorts of life-threatening conditions. She was reluctant to hand over her patient to me, but my being a doctor established a superior ranking order.

After a few questions and once I'd felt his pulse and made a few other observations, it became obvious to me that the gentleman was most likely hypotensive or hypoglycaemic. This was probably as a result of having spent a long day in Edinburgh. It was a lengthy return trip and he had probably had very little to eat or drink. But for a cup of tea with lots of sugar added, there was nothing else to give him.

I asked him whether I could arrange an ambulance when we arrived in Aberdeen. With a trembling voice, he answered, 'Just send me home.' This is exactly what I had demanded when my doctors wanted to treat me for depression after my cancer surgery.

This episode further strengthened my crusade to let every home-owner know about critical illness insurance, a policy that secures one's house in the event that one is diagnosed with a critical illness that may jeopardise one's financial situation. A home is a person's biggest investment in life. It is where one finds love and affection and where one's children are raised. For me, the comfort of my home is what I want and, now that I am old and sick, it is where I want to die. If one has a critical illness insurance policy to cover one's mortgage, it is guaranteed that one's house will not be repossessed by the banks and others.

The last I saw of my patient was at Aberdeen train station, where he was sitting in a wheelchair surrounded by his loved ones and on his way home. But the story doesn't end there: a day or two later, I was amazed to see that this episode had been covered in the print media.

The Scottish daily newspaper, the *Herald*, reported the story under the emblazoned headline, 'If you have a heart scare on a train, who better to help than Christiaan Barnard's brother?' and *Money Marketing* magazine

announced, 'Barnard in critical rescue on a train'.[1] In addition, the spokesman for First ScotRail was quoted as saying: 'Our staff are trained to deal
with emergencies on board. It was a bonus that a world-renowned heart
surgeon was on board. We are delighted to have been of assistance and
thank all who were involved in the successful recovery of a customer.'[2] The
event was sensationalised, but I do not object to having been made a hero,
even if the stories – in places – lack certain elements of the truth!

So ended my last trip to the United Kingdom, although I subsequently
made two final visits in 2007, where I was honoured for the contribution I
had made to the protection insurance industry with two Lifetime Achievement Awards, from the UK's *Protection Review* and *Cover Magazine*.

41

Travels to China

W HEN IN 1997 I HAD TO EXCHANGE A SCHEDULED VISIT TO
China for an operating theatre and a hospital ward, I was greatly
disappointed. Two months before we had been due to leave for China, my
cancer had decided to reassert itself. The visit to hospital and operation that
followed never dampened my desire to visit this great country, however.

I still cannot believe how I kept going after all my health setbacks. I had
cancelled only one overseas trip during more than twenty years of being 'on
the road', so to speak. Perhaps it was due to the examples set by the farmers,
animals and plants of the Karoo in which I grew up, and their ability to
survive the severe heat, dust and drought.

As the years passed, I realised that my hope to tour China and Japan was
fast fading. My success at the Million Dollar Round Table meeting in Anaheim
in 2004, where thousands of Asian delegates attended, rekindled this fading
dream, and in 2006 my hopes of visiting China were once again raised.

A few years earlier, I had done a tour with General Re Corporation to
Hong Kong, Taiwan, Singapore and Malaysia. My host had been Wolfgang
Dröste and the trip had been very pleasant. He had threatened me with
an invitation to China for years after that visit and, just as I was about to
abandon all hope, his invitation arrived.

I would visit Hong Kong again, China, Japan and, as a bonus, South
Korea. In China, I would give talks for a well-known and respected international insurance group. Foreign insurance companies had been given
licences only a few years earlier. Better still, Inez was invited too.

As was Wolfgang's style, we flew to Hong Kong in business class and
were met at the airport by a limousine, which deposited us at the Grand
Hyatt Hotel. And I can assure you, it *is* grand – very grand.

As our limousine drew up at the hotel, we were met by hordes of people
to carry our luggage. It is the only hotel, in my experience, where, as a guest,
you are guided with a wave to a particular toilet in the bathroom. When
you wash your hands, the water is running from the tap at just the right
temperature and a towel is placed in your hands afterwards. Fortunately,
they allow you to unzip your fly yourself.

The next morning, I delivered my presentation and immediately afterwards we left for the train station. There we were met by a smart, uniformed lady who escorted us to the first-class section of the train and soon we were on our way to China. At last!

A short while later we arrived at the border and, after our escort had navigated customs on our behalf, we made our way into China. It was dark by this stage and we couldn't make out the landscape, but it appeared from the mass of lights that we were in a continuous built-up area. We were offered drinks and snacks and soon arrived at our first destination – the capital city of Guangdong province, Guangzhou, which is also known as Canton. A port on the Pearl River, it is navigable to the South China Sea and is located about sixty miles north-west of Hong Kong.

Our escort accompanied us to the hotel, where there was a big reception party waiting for us. The splendour of the entrance hall left us breathless: a magnificent sculpture of a sailing ship in jade dominated the scene, and there was a waterfall amid flowers, which surrounded us. If the Grand Hyatt was impressive, the White Swan was even more so. It certainly lived up to its reputation as one of the top hotels in the world.

We noticed a dainty young Chinese girl sitting in the passage opposite the lift. Being South Africans, we thought she must be part of the hotel's security. We discovered her actual function soon after our arrival, when we went out for dinner. As we left our room, the girl jumped up and disappeared. When we arrived at the lift, she was standing there keeping the door open for us. I had never experienced this service before then, nor have I since.

We had great difficulty getting Inez out of the reception area of the hotel, as there were so many things to admire and gape at. Once outside, however, it was only a short walk before we arrived at a riverside restaurant.

Again, more magic. There were boats everywhere with beautiful coloured lights, cruising up and down the river. Soft Oriental music floated across the water and sporadic fireworks lit up the sky around us. Inez and I were enthralled and could have stayed there forever. It was so totally different from what we were used to. Wolfgang ordered us very tasty Chinese food and, all too soon, we had to leave – a full programme was planned for the next day.

And so ended our first day in China. We could not have been happier, and spent more than an hour in bed discussing our experiences. In situations like this, I am reminded of my bed in the mission house at Beaufort West, and thank my parents and my God for the wonderful life I have been given.

* * *

The next morning, I was up early. I had a busy day ahead with two talks planned, followed by a flight to Shanghai, so I was sorry that I would not have time to stay and enjoy the luxurious suite. But I was determined to experience a breakfast at the White Swan. The keeper of the lift had it ready for me when I arrived, and a short flight of steps down to the vast reception hall led me to the breakfast area. It was more opulent than anything I had ever seen: large trays filled to the brim, groaning under fruit, smoked salmon, cooked meals, bread rolls and much more. I love smoked salmon with capers and, after two helpings, fruit and several cups of coffee, I reluctantly had to leave – it was 8 a.m. and the two managers from General Re, whom I had briefly met the previous evening, had come to fetch me.

One of the managers, Jenny, was a qualified doctor who had entered into the insurance world. Her medical knowledge, of course, was a great advantage in the context of critical illness insurance. She acted as my interpreter and her English was excellent. As most of my audiences in China were not conversant in English, all of my talks had to be translated. The advantage of this was that it gave me more time to think in between sentences, but the disadvantage was that an hour-long talk now became two hours.

Jenny's male colleague, Tuan, was an actuary. Again, I found a bright and dedicated person and, by the end of my ten days in China, we had become great friends. Jenny and Tuan travelled with us most of the time and the attention they paid to Inez was most admirable.

Both presentations that day were well attended and received favourably. The audience in Asia is different from the West: whereas in the West insurance is male-dominated, my meetings always attended by 80 per cent or more males, in Asia it is exactly the opposite. The females are young and a few are doctors, and many of them find selling insurance a more lucrative livelihood.

My experience in Asia is that the insurance representatives are far more appreciative and eager to learn. You really feel that you are achieving your goals with them. Of course, the meetings ended, as is always the case, with photos and signatures.

I went back to the hotel after the second presentation to collect my belongings and had just enough time to slip in a quick lunch. This was an even greater experience: the tables were now loaded with all the things I love to eat: fruit in abundance, all kind of prawns, oysters, mussels, crabs and more.

As I only had ten minutes, I grabbed as much seafood as possible, but before I could finish I had to leave and was whisked away to the airport. One of the few places I would like to visit again is the White Swan Hotel.

Inez was already at the airport when I arrived, having been taken sight-seeing in the morning. Soon we were in the air, en route to Shanghai.

I knew China well from school history lessons – its profound and re-markable ancient dynasties, the Boxer Rebellion, its war with Japan and the communist takeover. Inez and I had been reminded of the country's vast population by a story that a Canadian patient of mine had shared with me while I was practising in Southern Rhodesia. He told me that in his town in Canada there was a Chinese laundryman. One day, while dropping off his laundry, he told the laundryman a story he knew about a great battle that had been fought between the Chinese and Japanese armies. What was startling to my patient was that, in this battle, fewer than a thousand Japanese soldiers were killed, while the Chinese lost 60 000 of their men. On hearing this, the response of the Chinaman was, 'Pretty soon no Japanese left.'

Our flight to Shanghai was very special. The plane appeared to have come off the assembly line the previous day and the flight attendants couldn't do enough for us. It appeared that the hostesses had been recruited from model agencies.

I had asked Wolfgang to book us into some kind of accommodation where we could live among the average Chinese citizen and not with tourists in their upmarket hotels. This he duly did, and we found ourselves in a business apartment surrounded by shanties. We seemed to be the only Europeans around. The streets had washing lines hanging across them, a man was fixing his BMW on the next corner, and people were selling food, groceries, cooked meals and anything else one could possibly need.

This is exactly what I wanted to experience. Five minutes after we arrived, Inez was out, only to reappear – and receive a good scolding from me, I might add – more than an hour later. Wherever we go, Inez disappears into the area and, when she arrives back, she knows everything about the neighbourhood: where you can buy fruit and groceries, where you can find a dressmaker and, very importantly, where you can find a bargain. I have never found out how she does it. This visit was no exception, and Inez was so excited and happy that my anger at her reckless behaviour subsided. I enjoyed the fruit and the Chinese meal she had bought.

The next day, I was due to give a talk in the afternoon. After that, how-ever, Wolfgang had given me two days off and provided us with a car, driver and guide.

* * *

With the morning free, I rested, but Inez was fetched and shown the shopping delights. In the afternoon, I gave the scheduled presentation to the insurance group's agents. A large and enthusiastic audience greeted me, and the photograph and signature session lasted a lot longer than usual.

While driving to the venue, I was amazed by the thousands of people walking, riding on bicycles and in cars – mostly Volkswagens – through the streets of Shanghai. Everywhere there were people and more people, joined by bicycles and cars. But they were all well dressed and obeying the city's rules, and the streets were clean and litter free. How different from South Africa. Shanghai, with its vast population of 19 million people, was cleaner than Hermanus and its 30 000 residents. We gained the impression that, although few were wealthy, they were not starving either. Unlike in South Africa, these millions of people were well housed and not desperately poor.

That evening, Wolfgang took us out to dinner at an authentic Chinese restaurant popular with the locals. I am sure the restaurant could have seated 2 000 people – it was certainly approaching this number when we were shown to our table. With the usual courtesy and efficiency, a waiter brought us our drinks and menus. I asked for one in English and received a twenty-page description of all their delicacies.

Reading through it, I was startled that I could order pigeon tongues. The next dish that drew my attention was dog paws. If that was not a perfect appetite depressor, the next one was sure to be – bull's penis. I refused to read further and, from then on, I stuck to seafood and vegetables. I did not touch any of the meat dishes – certainly not beef!

I have to admit that I am not a good tourist. I do enjoy seeing the countryside, however, where one can experience the lives of rural people. A trip to the countryside was duly arranged, and on our last day in Shanghai we visited a river village. We walked up and down the canal, took a boat ride with someone's toothless great-grandmother, who paddled the boat both down- and upstream, and saw the dozens of houses and riverside restaurants.

What was a bit disconcerting was that the river was heavily polluted, and we saw a few restaurateurs washing their vegetables and meat in this sewerage-infested water. We had lunch at just such an eatery but the food was delicious. Although I waited for the first rumble in my stomach, both Inez and I escaped any side effects.

All too soon, we were on our way to Beijing, where we found that the Afro-Asian Congress was convening and that thirty-eight African presidents were enthroned in the presidential suites of thirty-eight hotels. The streets were lined with red flags, and red carpets were rolled out in front of every hotel – we even walked the red carpet at our hotel.

Of course, each president was accompanied by dozens of officials, relatives and who knows who else. The CEO of the South African Broadcasting Corporation (SABC) was staying in our hotel, and I met him a few times in the special facility reserved for residents staying in luxury suites. There, light breakfasts, snacks and drinks were available at all times, and there were a dozen or so very attractive, hand-picked Chinese ladies serving guests continually. It was worth going to have a drink just to look at them.

I have to be honest that, during my five days there, I frequented this facility often. This was not because I was hungry or thirsty, but because the locals spoke English as only the Chinese do, and I was very eager to talk with each person, as they took every opportunity to improve their English.

* * *

The visit to Beijing was a repeat of Shanghai. I gave presentations at two meetings, one with General Re and the other with insurance agents. Both were well attended, with more than 700 people at each venue.

Again, we were afforded a two-day sightseeing opportunity, so Inez and I visited museums containing all the wonders of the histories of previous dynasties, silk factories and jade shops, as well as the Forbidden City, the Summer Palace and Tiananmen Square. Unfortunately, the square was closed as a result of preparations for the Olympic Games, which were due to take place the following year.

We saw the magnificent Olympic stadium, which was reaching completion, and visited the Great Wall of China. It was a cold, windy day and climbing up and down steps was not easy for me. The wall was impressive, but my condition wasn't, unfortunately. Inez carried on while I went back to sit in a restaurant until she came back and told me all that she had seen. I enjoy listening to her speak of her experiences and observing her full enjoyment of every moment.

My last talk was at the General Re headquarters, after which I had to rush back to meet people at the hospitality room, who, I was told, wanted to see me. I was enjoying the snacks and coffee with other senior people of General Re when in marched the hostesses, singing 'Happy Birthday'. They presented me with a birthday cake and a large bouquet of flowers. Photos and kisses followed and that is where, and how, I celebrated my seventy-ninth birthday.

The CEO of the SABC was there with a few friends, and as the ladies surrounded me I turned to him and quipped, 'Not too bad for a *boytjie* from Beaufort West!' They enjoyed this aside and I shared my birthday cake with some of them.

My impressions of Beijing will always be dominated by the thick clouds of pollution that hung over the city, day in and day out. How people can live in such pollution will always be a mystery to me. Our visit to China, however, left me in wonder at the progress there and the wonderful people with whom I had worked, and their ancient culture and history. Waiting all those years for the visit had certainly been worthwhile.

My trips to Japan and South Korea were spent predominantly at airports, in planes, at hotels and in lecture halls. I therefore didn't have the opportunity to experience anything of its people, nor was I able to visit historical sites. Japan was effectively a one-day, two-night visit, which I spent in Tokyo, while Seoul was half of that time.

We experienced the same friendly, courteous people with efficient service. My lectures were followed by receptions and, in both cities, the food – especially the prawns, crab meat and other dishes – was excellent. This was far removed from the biscuits and weak tea offered after such talks in other countries.

There was, however, one other highlight for Inez and me. A company for which our eldest daughter, Naudéne, often worked in Holland had asked her to travel to Tokyo to assist in editing a documentary. This just so happened to coincide with our visit, so by some twist of fate we were in Japan at the same time. It was wonderful to spend our two evenings together. We realised that it would be most unlikely that we would ever be in Japan again – and certainly not together. Of my many highlights during this long-awaited tour, this one was probably the best.

Critical Illness Insurance:
The Way Forward

Although my involvement with protection insurance has now virtually come to an end, critical illness insurance policies are still thriving, and many of the changes I wanted to introduce are now being made.

Living in a town to which many people retire and having lived in a retirement village for ten years, I am daily alerted to the deteriorating effects of ageing and the increasing costs of caring for the aged. The developed world is facing an 'ageing tsunami' and most governments seem to be blind to or do not care about the gigantic financial storms that are already facing us. In most countries of the western world, human life expectancy is well into the eighties. I read a newspaper report recently which stated that 50 per cent of children born today can expect to live until the age of 100.

More than twenty-five years ago, I had a dream to provide money for those patients who had been diagnosed with a critical illness. Critical illness insurance was the result. After a slow start, it is today recognised as the protection policy of the new millennium and millions of policies are sold throughout the world. Daily, thousands of claims are paid out, bringing the financial security that is so needed. Mortgages are paid, bankruptcy is avoided and numerous financial futures have been saved.

As can be expected, more than 80 per cent of claims are for cancer, heart attack, stroke and coronary artery bypass graft. What is alarming is that the average age of the claimant is fifty. This is just the age at which one's financial needs are the greatest: payments on a large mortgage, children's school and university fees, and savings for one's retirement. A critical illness, its treatment, and the drastic and often traumatic lifestyle changes that follow can shatter all of one's dreams.

I am still restless, however, as I see the need for an insurance product that will provide financial aid when age and illness makes it impossible for people to care for themselves. I helped to develop such a product years ago but, with the exception of the USA and perhaps Canada, it has not been the complete success we had hoped for. It is called *long-term care insurance*, although I would prefer it to be termed *frail-care insurance*.

Long-term care comprises a variety of services, including medical and non-medical care for people who have a chronic illness or disability. It dramatically helps to meet health or personal needs and is a form of medical insurance where the purchaser pays premiums in exchange for benefits related to long-term care.

Once the policy holder meets the definitions, the sum insured becomes available and the money can either be used to provide home care, or the patient can be cared for in a retirement home with staff and facilities to make his or her twilight years happy and comfortable. The benefits vary from policy to policy and can include a daily amount for nursing-home or assisted-living care, home care, or day programmes for the elderly.

Long-term care (or frail care) is not easy to define and the boundaries among primary, acute and long-term care have, until fairly recently, been blurred. As a result, individual countries have established their own interpretations, including those for the concept of 'frailty'.

In Germany, for example, the Social Security Code defines a frail person as 'a person who requires for a minimum period of approximately six months, permanent, frequent or extensive help in performing a special number of "Activities of Daily Life" … and "Instrumental Activities of Daily Life" … due to physical, mental or psychological illness or disability'.[1] Such a person is dependent on assistance with personal care, nutrition, mobility and housekeeping.

It is critical that we care more for the frail and aged, and that frail-care insurance be fully incorporated in the spectrum of protection insurance policy options. Slowly, the problems associated with ageing are being recognised by governments today. Some of them are considering, or have established, obligatory national contributions to fund such facilities.

I so much wanted to remain involved in spreading the word about long-term care, as I am convinced that it should be made compulsory. It is of great sadness to me, however, that the insurance providers are dragging their feet in developing these policies. They are more than willing to provide large sponsorships for sport, for instance, but when it comes to society's most vulnerable people they do not seem to give a damn. In many western countries, only one or two companies provide such policies and, even then, the financial advisors seem reluctant to offer it to their clients.

Despite its necessity, long-term care insurance has, regrettably, come too late for me, as I am fast reaching the stage where I might need such care.

PART V

Matters
of the Heart

Living and Dealing with Cancer

I T WAS AS A SECOND-YEAR ANATOMY STUDENT THAT I FIRST LEARNT
about the prostate gland. I was taught that it is situated just below the
bladder and in front of the rectum, partially surrounding the urethra, which
carries urine from the bladder out of the body via the penis. At birth it is the
size of a pea and in adulthood that of a walnut. I also discovered that the
prostate plays a role in the male reproductive system: it is responsible for
producing a clear liquid that makes up about a third of the seminal fluid
used to carry and protect the male sperm during intercourse.

During my third year at medical school, I learnt that this gland is
prone to infection and enlargement and, in my fifth year, I was introduced
to urology and the basic diagnosis and treatment, such as it was then, of
prostatic cancer.

All of this made little impression on me, as there were far more important
organs and diseases to study and treat. Never did I think that from the age
of sixty-nine until now – more than thirteen years – this little organ would
form such a significant part of my daily life.

I am one of the millions of men who are diagnosed with prostatic cancer
every year. Unfortunately, I am not one of the 80 per cent that, according to
United States statistics, will be cured. In South Africa, 4 000 cases of prostatic
cancer are diagnosed annually and, because our early-diagnosis campaign
is not as advanced as those in North America and Europe, 2 500 men lose
their lives from this form of cancer every year.

Fortunately, prostatic cancer is slow-growing. In its early stages, however,
it is symptomless. It is estimated that 50 per cent of men with prostate cancer
do not know that they have it. To achieve the United States' high cure rate
of 80 per cent, it is therefore imperative to educate men about the disease
and to urge them to have regular screening tests.

As with most cancers, the cause of prostatic cancer is unknown. There
are, however, some factors recognised to increase the risk, namely age – the
incidence increases rapidly in men who are over fifty – a lack of exercise and
a family history of prostatic cancer. Although often symptomless, there are
warning signs, such as frequent urination, especially at night; blood in the

urine and semen; lower backache; and pain in the pelvis or upper thighs, among others. These signs are not diagnostic, however; they can also signal non-cancerous infection and enlargement of the prostate.

Screening tests are vital. For those over the age of fifty, testing should be an annual event, although I actually recommend that tests be performed from forty years of age and onwards. I know a few men of this age whose cancer is incurable because of late diagnosis.

Included in the screening tests is a rectal examination of the prostate by a doctor. This is not diagnostic, though, and in my case was totally unreliable. My prostate, on rectal examination, was normal – even after my advanced prostatic cancer had been confirmed.

My experience is that the measurement of prostate-specific antigen is the most important screening test. If I had my way, it would be a requirement for all males of fifty or over to be tested, and even younger men if risk factors apply. Although there is much speculation about the value of the test, without it I would not be alive today.

The prostate gland secretes a small amount of PSA in the blood. The accepted value of PSA is between 0 and 4 nanograms. I believe that test results indicating a value exceeding 4 should be taken seriously, as this level can signal cancer or enlargement of the prostate. Recent information suggests that, for people under fifty, a value in excess of 4.8 is a warning sign. Prior to my trip to Canada in 1997, when I had a routine PSA test, my results revealed a PSA level of 8.9. After a brief rectal examination, however, my urologist declared my condition satisfactory and said that I could proceed with my trip to Canada. As mentioned briefly in Chapter 37, I found his opinion strange and very unsettling, as the warning signs were self-evident – I probably had prostate cancer. While the preparations for Canada kept me busy, a feeling of dread lurked in the back of my mind for the trip's entire duration.

My belief is that there are two ways to follow up a test result showing a raised PSA level: either wait for a few months if it is between 6 and 8 and then do another PSA test to establish whether it is still rising, or have an immediate rectal prostatic biopsy, a painless procedure whereby a biopsy needle is inserted into the prostate via the rectum and four to six samples are removed from both lobes of the gland. I recommend the latter option.

The microscopic examination of specimens procured during the biopsy can be positive or negative for cancer, but a negative result does not necessarily exclude cancer. If after three months the PSA is measured and there is a further increase, another biopsy must be performed. In my case, three out of the four biopsies I had on my return from Canada were positive. This, combined with the raised PSA, was sufficient evidence to confirm the diagnosis of prostate cancer. I was devastated.

An important recent advancement is the grading of the disease according to the Gleason classification, which evaluates the prognosis of men with prostate cancer.[1] A Gleason score is given to the cancer on the basis of microscopic appearance. The higher the Gleason score, the more aggressive the cancer – and, of course, the worse the prognosis. Further scanning of the prostate may reveal whether the cancer has spread outside the capsule – the membrane surrounding the prostate gland – which is a bad prognosis sign, and a bone scan will indicate whether it has spread to the bones. After I'd received news of a worryingly high Gleason score of 8, my doctors immediately scanned the prostate and discovered that the cancer had spread outside the capsule. The bone scan, much to my relief, was negative.

Once the diagnosis of cancer is confirmed and the grade and stage of malignancy evaluated, the treatment is not always clear. In my experience, urologists will advise surgery whereas oncologists will recommend radiation therapy. In older men with a Gleason score of 5 or less, a 'wait-and-see' approach or hormone therapy is recommended.

My initial consultation with an oncologist in mid-1997, after I had received my test results, was very depressing. He talked of a prognosis of no better than two years, and suggested a six-week course of daily radiation therapy. He did not recommend surgery as a result of my advanced age of seventy at the time and the possible complications of incontinence and loss of erectile functions. During surgery, both the muscular sphincter, which contracts after urinating, and the nerves that stimulate the rush of blood to the penis to bring on an erection can be damaged.

* * *

In August 1997, some six weeks after returning from Canada, I opted to have surgery – a radical prostatectomy – despite the oncologist's discouragement. As described earlier, a severe post-operative haemorrhage and a near-fatal pulmonary embolus followed.

When the prostate was examined microscopically after its removal, the doctors were not very hopeful of a cure. The Gleason 8 score was confirmed, but the cancer was found to be in both lobes of my prostate and had spread outside the capsule and into the adjacent tissue – my formal diagnosis was thus 'metastatic carcinoma of the prostate with localised spread'. A plus, however, was that the adjacent lymph glands and surrounding organs were clear of cancerous cells.

Of the immediate complications, I was spared incontinence, but there was a price to pay: soon afterwards, I became impotent. This condition has not changed.

Inez and I have never found this a great burden. We compensated by becoming much closer and our love intensified. Touching each other more often when together and enjoying each other's company became a replacement for the sexual act.

I dreaded the result of the first PSA test after my operation. If all the cancer cells had been removed, the PSA should have been 0. Unfortunately, my PSA levels were a 0.6. After three months, they had further reduced to 0.1. I knew then that I had to live with cancer and, if I lived long enough, that it would eventually kill me.

Once you have incurable cancer you live with it every day. You wake up with it and you go to bed with it. For the first few years, it dominated my life, and the PSA test every three months was a dreaded experience. I felt like a convicted murderer who, having already been found guilty, now awaited his sentence: execution or life imprisonment.

For the first year after my operation, things went well. My PSA levels stayed down, but the dream that things would be fine was shattered when they soon started to rise again. The truth was now confirmed: my radical prostatectomy had not been as radical as we had prayed for – some cancer cells had been left behind and were increasing. As they multiplied over the next nine months, all of the doctors that I consulted said that I was to wait before further treatment. My answer was, 'Wait until when – till I die?'

I was determined to receive radiation to the area where the prostate had been removed. My medical advisors recommended that I first have a bone scan. With my PSA being well below 20, however, I considered it most unlikely that I had bone secondaries. I didn't even want to know if this was the case. Instead, I relied on the hope that the radiation treatment would be successful – it was a chance I was prepared to take.

After much soul-searching, I found a very sympathetic and understanding oncologist, Dr Visser, at Karl Bremer Hospital in Bellville, near Cape Town. She was prepared to put me through a six-week course of radiation. This would occur daily, except on Saturdays and Sundays. I have never understood why these two days are excluded. My experience is that cancer never takes a weekend off.

As I live in Hermanus, the radiation treatment in Bellville would mean commuting five days a week to the hospital. Our great friends Jack and Tessa Marks came to my rescue when Tessa offered us the use of her brother's flat in Camps Bay.

My radiation, which started on 1 September 1999 and ended on 15 October, was painless and lasted only a few minutes at a time. I didn't even need to undress. The staff who attended to me were wonderful and made the experience a friendly and non-traumatic event but, as with everything in medicine, nothing is for free – there is a price to pay.

The radiation attacks not only the cancer cells but the adjacent, normal cells as well. In my case, this applied not so much to the bladder as to the rectum and anus, and I developed extremely painful diarrhoea. It was like passing a packet of razor blades every few hours. Except for blood in the urine, thankfully urinating was not too painful.

On my way back from Karl Bremer Hospital to Hermanus, however, I had an excruciating problem. Before each treatment, one has to drink a few glasses of water so that the bladder becomes fully extended. This is necessary to minimise the risk of radiation to adjacent structures, such as the rectum.

With all the water I'd had to drink, however, a pit-stop en route to Hermanus became a desperate necessity. The nearest facility was ten miles away at a roadside service station on the N2 highway. This was my salvation, but the nearer we drew to this point of relief, the worse my need became. Fortunately I just made it, but I still wonder what people thought of this elderly, grey-haired man screeching to a stop and racing to the toilet as fast as he could run. I didn't care, though – the need was greater than my dignity.

I then had to wait for three months until my next PSA test. I must admit that I just couldn't wait, so I went for the test two weeks early. My blood had to be sent from Hermanus to Cape Town and the result would be ready the following morning. The twenty-four-hour wait was agonising. I phoned the lab at the earliest opportunity and then had to endure a further unbearable thirty-second wait for them to find the results on their computer.

I burst into tears when the results showed that the treatment had been a great success: my PSA had dropped from 6.9 to 1.3. Over the next six months, it dropped further to 0.1. My cancer and I were now at peace with each other, and I resumed travelling the world and giving my talks on critical illness insurance. But this truce didn't last forever.

* * *

After about two years, I noticed that I was experiencing difficulty in passing urine. I again visited Dr Gecelter, who had performed my radical prostatectomy, and he confirmed what I already knew – that I had a bladder-neck obstruction, where the neck of the bladder does not open properly, blocking the flow of urine. A minor operation improved this problem for a short time.

In 2003, during a trip to the USA, Inez and I went to Chattanooga, Tennessee, to celebrate with Daniel and Anca Constantinescu their twenty-fifth anniversary of residency in the United States. And what a great occasion that was! Afterwards, Daniel took us by car to the Atlanta airport. While walking to our departure gate, I became aware of a few drops of urine dripping out of me, causing a small wet spot in my underpants. It soon stopped, however, and we boarded the aeroplane for our short flight to Greensboro, North Carolina, to spend a few days with Marie and her family. This visit was foremost in my mind and I soon forgot about the episode.

After our arrival in Greensboro that afternoon, Inez and I went for a short walk. It was then that my bladder emptied itself uncontrollably. Immediately I knew that I was incontinent. I crept back to my daughter's house. Not even pieces of toilet paper or pads could stem the flow or remove the very obvious, and very visible, embarrassment.

For a man – and perhaps even more so for a woman – incontinence is a dreadful complication: it is humiliating, demoralising and depressing. Fortunately, I was later able to control it by frequent visits to the toilet. I hated it then, as I do now.

Once back home, I visited a urologist, who suggested a penile clamp to give me control in passing urine. I found it to be of great help and could travel, walk, swim and live a normal life with it. Fortunately, at night, when lying on my bed, I was completely continent.

My PSA stayed down and my bladder function was under control, but, with cancer, the moments of calm are only a lull before the next storm. It turned out not to be a flood, however, but a drought.

Slowly but surely, I noticed my urinary stream becoming weaker. Ultrasound scans confirmed another obstruction in the bladder neck, caused by fibrous tissue developing and narrowing the lumen of the urethra. The oncologists blamed the surgery, the surgeons the radiation. But I was left with the problem.

My condition worsened, and one morning there was complete obstruction. My bladder did not take kindly to this and contracted violently and frequently to empty itself, causing agonisingly painful cramps. I tried every trick known to me to relieve this painful condition, including turning on a tap to hear the sound of running water, and sitting in a hot bath. But to no avail.

So it was back to hospital. To my utter relief, a doctor was able to insert a urethral catheter to relieve the urine retention.[2] The relief was immediate and the contractions disappeared. I could not believe it. The catheter was removed after three days, and things went back to incontinence and the penile clamp. But I now had to have the obstruction periodically dilated to ease the blockage. At first, I did this myself at monthly intervals, but it became so uncomfortable that I needed the urologist to help me.

After returning from a two-week stint in the UK with the insurance company Scottish Widows, the urologist had great difficulty passing the dilator through the obstruction. He used increasing force and, although I asked him to stop, he continued. I recall it was a Friday and, for a few hours afterwards, I passed bloody urine without too much difficulty. But then, most likely due to increased swelling resulting from damage done by the extreme force, I entered two days of absolute agony. With unbearable cramps, I was able to pass only a few drops of urine. To my relief, it was better by the Sunday, but come Monday evening I could no longer take the pain, and again it was back to hospital.

With me under anaesthetic, the urologist tried to pass a trans-urethral catheter to allow urine to drain freely from the bladder, but my urethra was so damaged by the previous urologist's excessive force that he had to use a supra-pubic catheter, which was inserted via an incision in my abdomen directly into my bladder. When I woke up, my worst fears had become a reality: I had a catheter protruding from my abdomen. Somehow this was unacceptable to me, but I was told that a 'supra-pubic' was far easier to manage and that patients preferred it, in fact.

In my days as a general surgeon, I had inserted many abdominal drains; I had even performed a few permanent colostomies on patients. I therefore insisted that another attempt be made to replace the troublesome catheter. It was becoming urgent, as I was due to leave for my eagerly anticipated seminar tour to Hong Kong, China, Japan and Korea in three weeks' time.

This catheter was successfully inserted while I was under anaesthetic, and I had to come to terms with the fact that I would have to live with it. Not the greatest prospect. Instead of my bladder being in my pelvis, it was now a plastic bag strapped to my leg.

But a complication arose, which further delayed my departure to the Far

East: my PSA levels started to increase again, and I had to face the prospect of hormonal therapy. With a PSA of 6, and against the urologist's advice to wait, I started the therapy, which consists of an injection of anti-androgen every three months to block the testosterone that causes the prostate to grow. I had to pray hard that it would work. With the exception of chemotherapy, there is no further treatment possible, and I will not consider chemotherapy as I believe that the results do not justify the side effects. This is my personal view, and may not be shared by other patients.

After three months, my PSA was back down to 0.6 and, three months later, to less than 0.1. My present regime is to use the anti-androgen intermittently when the PSA is well down, then to stop treatment and to start again when it is raised. The PSA level at which I resume treatment, however, is not fixed. Most doctors tell me to wait until it is 10, but I prefer to start the treatment when it is between 4 and 6. Although I have to admit that I do not have clinical evidence to support this method, it works for me. I then have the treatment at intervals of three months until the PSA is down again, preferably less than 1.0. Unfortunately, the treatment loses its efficacy after a while, but I will cross that bridge when I have to.

My response has been better than I could have expected but, again, a price has to be paid. Since the anti-androgen is a female hormone, there is a complication of hot flushes – the same at those experienced by menopausal females. Not pleasant, but one can live with it.

Now, five years later, and having had no injection for eleven months, my PSA levels are rising again. Things have worsened over the past year, as I have developed recurring bladder infections. The catheter in my bladder is a foreign body and, while it is there, it is virtually impossible to get rid of the infection.

Several months after my initial bladder infection, I developed severe bladder-neck contractions due to the infection, which resulted in excruciating pain lasting about fifteen seconds at a time, with diminishing intervals between contractions. The pain was unbearable, and I had to do something about it.

In hospital, the catheter was removed and, with the help of antibiotics, the infection cleared up. But I was left completely incontinent. This, for me, was a terrible complication: there is a constant dribble of urine and, in spite of a pad and nappies (yes, eighty years plus and having to wear a nappy), it is virtually impossible to stay dry. To make sure that the infection cleared, I tolerated the depressing experience. But after four weeks I could no longer take it, and the catheter was reinserted. It is unbelievable to imagine that I actually couldn't wait for it to be reinstated.

Thirteen years after my initial diagnosis, I am as well as a man of my advanced years can expect to be. What my cancer has in store for me in the future I do not know, but I will not give in. And, as in the past, I will counter every move it makes with determination and all my remaining strength. My great dream is, of course, to kill my mortal enemy – my cancer. Succumbing to a heart attack or any other fatal disease to achieve this dream I would consider a great victory.

* * *

When I started treatment for prostatic cancer in 1997, I decided to keep the bad news to myself and told only three people of my diagnosis. The diagnosis of cancer is not limited to the affected area only; the brain is also affected. I was shattered. I could not sleep and became very emotional. Cancer never leaves you and, as a doctor – knowing what to expect – this only served to disturb my already fragile peace of mind. I needed emotional help, but from where?

I remembered what I was told on my mother's knee about how finding God brings inner peace. So the next Sunday, Inez and I attended the United Church in Hermanus, even though we lived close to the Dutch Reformed Church. I hadn't been to church for years – I had left the Dutch Reformed Church decades earlier, not only because of their endorsement of apartheid, but following a rather acrimonious meeting with my *dominee*.

In 1972, I asked the *dominee*, who had come by on *huis besoek*, not to raise issues that I was against. But he couldn't resist the opportunity. The more I asked him to stop, the more he continued to do so, which served only to anger me further. When the situation risked becoming very unpleasant, he played his trump card. 'Doctor,' he said, 'you must be placed under church censure.'

'*Dominee*,' I replied, 'this is the first time that I have to agree with you.'

It was the last time I ever saw him, and I didn't return to his church either.

While listening to the United Church's pastor that Sunday morning, full of fear and doubt, and screaming inside for help, it was as if his sermon had been written especially for me. My fears and doubts disappeared and hope replaced despair. I immediately became convinced that this was the only crutch I needed. My physical life was in danger and my earthly life could be cut short at any time, but I now had the promise of eternal life.

Since then, I have attended church every Sunday, when and where possible, to have my spiritual battery recharged. I have found tremendous peace in being able to pray. I am convinced that there is a God, that he loves me and that he rules my life. If I should die, it is only the beginning and not the end of my existence.

Another reason for my desire to go to heaven is to see my parents again, to thank them for all they did for me and to live with them, Inez and my family forever. Many non-believers will say that this is gobbledygook and that there is no life after death. They ask us what we are going to do should we find out after death that there is no such thing as heaven or hell. My response has always been that this would be a great disappointment. But what would they do, I ask, should they find out that I was correct?

Because of my belief in eternal life, I do not fear death. How can I? After thirteen years of cancer – with all its pain, complications and humiliation – I can say with conviction that I thank God for my cancer because it reunited me with Him and the promise of eternal life. What a bargain!

In Memory of Chris

I LOVE NATURE AND WILDLIFE. I LIKE TO GO INTO THE BUSH, AND the flowers of Namaqualand are a wonder. On Friday 31 August 2001, Inez and I drove up to Kamieskroon in the Northern Cape to see the kaleido-scopic West Coast spring flowers. We stayed at a farm bed and breakfast and went to admire the flowers, which I believe to be one of the wonders of God's creation and a 'must see'. It was an unbelievably beautiful sight.

We returned home late on the Sunday afternoon and, as we approached Cape Town, I switched on my cell phone. There were several messages waiting. The first was from a colleague of mine, Ray Swart, who had been the Progressive Federal Party's MP for Berea when I was in parliament. He remains a good friend. 'Marius,' he said, 'I just want to sympathise with you over the death of your brother.'

The messages that followed were all from the press, who wanted to talk to me. But there were no messages from any of my relatives, so I phoned Louwtjie, Chris's first wife, and got through to their daughter, Deirdre. She confirmed that her father had died that day, Sunday 2 September.

I was shocked. The person who should have died was me – I had had a life-threatening disease for more than a decade. I was incensed that not one member of the family had taken the courtesy to inform me of my brother's death. Why had I heard about it via a recorded message from a friend?

That night Inez and I, both very distraught, stayed over at the home of Ina Vosloo, a friend of ours who lives in Durbanville, a northern suburb of Cape Town. She had known Chris and had been one of the nursing sisters when I was in private practice in Johannesburg's Milpark Hospital. We all felt numb.

The press hounded me when I arrived home in Hermanus. I had been very ill with influenza, which had been with me for weeks, and I had gone straight to bed. I begrudgingly spoke to one of the reporters covering Chris's death. What a mistake! The journalist, a nasty man, asserted that Chris and I hadn't spoken in two years. I retorted that this was a complete lie, as Chris had phoned me the previous week. But he trapped me with his next question: 'Are you going to the funeral?' he asked. I told him that I hadn't decided yet, and started explaining my great annoyance with Beaufort West – the way that my father had been treated during all the time he had lived there and the most unpleasant way in which his schools and church had been removed from the centre of the town. This proved to be another mistake.

The headline in the following week's *Sunday Times* read, 'Barnard to shun brother's funeral' and the article alleged that there was an ongoing fight between Chris and me. I wanted to sue the writer and, in fact, reported him to the newspaper ombudsman, who in the event proved to be worse than the reporter.

Chris had four funerals: one at Groote Schuur Hospital, one in the Dutch Reformed Church's Mother Church at the top of Adderley Street in Cape Town, and two in Beaufort West – one was for the public, and the other was a private ceremony.

Despite being very ill, I went to the funeral at Groote Schuur. I didn't attend the service at the Dutch Reformed Church because I was running a high temperature that day, but Inez and I went to both funerals in Beaufort West, which took place in my father's church. It was strange to be back. I knew this church intimately from my childhood and associated it with my father in the pulpit and my mother at the organ. It had now been converted into a museum. Despite the comfort of having Inez by my side, I still felt very much alone.

Most of the people that attended Chris's public funeral were strangers. Very few of the inhabitants of Beaufort West knew us, as they were born after we left the town or had moved there in more recent times. They knew only the stories of the heart transplant as it had been presented in the press. Many attended purely out of curiosity.

At Chris's private funeral in Beaufort West, most of Chris's family, with whom I had nothing to do either professionally or socially, seemed like strangers to me. With the exception of Louwtjie and her family, Chris's relatives weren't part of the original Barnard family that to me were associated with that little Dutch Reformed missionary church from years ago.

Chris's more recent family had made no contribution to the historic transplant nor the fame and fortune that went with it. But here they were in the front seats, while poor Louwtjie and her family were essentially ignored. Louwtjie, who had made so many sacrifices to support Chris – particularly during the hard times – looked understandably out of place in their midst.

Chris's third wife, Karen, from whom he was divorced, seemed to have taken over Chris's family duties. A late inclusion in the Barnard family, she, in my opinion, knew little if anything about Beaufort West, nor the history of our family. In this respect, I don't think my parents would have felt very comfortable with some of the attendees.

An unwelcome person at all of Chris's funerals was the late television producer Dirk de Villiers and his crew, who recorded the services on video. To my mind his actions, which were probably performed with a view to financial gain rather than historical value, were unsympathetic and completely out of place at an event such as this. But perhaps my judgement was clouded due to my dislike of the man.

A notable exception to my otherwise negative sentiments about my brother's extended families appeared in the form of his eldest son, Frederick, from Chris's marriage to his second wife, Barbara. He spoke well and provided a very balanced perspective of his late father. I thought it was rather cruel of his family, however, to expect Frederick – then twenty-eight – to be the one to bare his soul in public at these occasions, but he acquitted himself with great composure and dignity. His father, I believe, would have been immensely proud of him.

* * *

It is difficult to believe that I am still alive and Chris has been dead for more than ten years. At the time of his passing, and given my cancer, I would have been an odds-on favourite to die before him. But I am still around today and able to provide my final tributes to and criticisms of my famous brother.

Since his death, the media has managed to keep Chris in the news, but the memory of him is fast fading. Over 50 per cent of people today were born after the first heart transplant was performed forty-four years ago. To many, the event has little significance, and the name *Chris Barnard* has even less. Chris did, however, play a major part in the history of cardiac surgery. Whenever the subject of heart transplants arises, he will be remembered as having performed 'the first' and, in this way, his name will live on.

My brother will also be remembered for less laudable activities, however. His personal life was manna to a remorseless press, who first built him up with endless praise and adoration and then gleefully set out to destroy him. Unfortunately, he played to their tune and became aware of the dangers of man-made fame only during the last few years of his life.

My brother then became very lonely and felt rejected. He was of the opinion that his great contribution to medicine was no longer appreciated. I believe that at that moment, after years of estrangement, he made a sincere attempt to repair our poor relationship. He started to phone me regularly to complain bitterly about his personal problems and the way the media and others were treating him. He started to open his heart to me and I listened but gave nothing in return. My attitude was dismissive: *When you were in the limelight, you turned your back on me,* I thought. *I have now had my own life without you for twenty years and I am content.*

Today, one of my greatest regrets is that I did not respond to his endeavour to restore our relationship. I kept him at a distance. Since the heart transplants, he had disappointed me so often that I could not forgive him. But I am now convinced that he was crying out for help, and I failed him.

Chris had discovered that rejecting his roots and relishing in fame could not preserve his good looks – his handsome, boyish features, which he tried so hard to maintain, became disfigured from cancer and surgery – nor provide him with the affection and compassion of a loving family. The people he considered loyal turned on him, but he found love and care with Louwtjie and Deirdre. The wheel had come full circle.

These days I think of Chris often – mostly about what could have been. I wish that I could relive the last few years of his life. I would certainly welcome him back into the real Barnard family with open arms.

But it is too late now. Chris was my brother, but we were always strangers to each other. He was a great doctor and a brilliant scientist, but he had feet of clay. Fortunately, I am now at peace with him and have forgotten the bad times. Today I only remember, with love, being his young *boytjie*. Sorry, Chris.

The man who at one time didn't want to set foot in Beaufort West again ended up leaving his ashes, interred in a cask, in the town. They are buried in the garden of the old parsonage in Beaufort West next to a little monument, on which is inscribed: 'I came back home.'

Friends of the
Red Cross Children's Hospital

'But if anyone causes one of these little ones who believe in me to sin, it would be better for him to have a large millstone hung around his neck and to be drowned in the depths of the sea.' — MATTHEW 18:6

ONE OF THE BETTER INSTINCTS OF HUMAN BEINGS IS THEIR LOVE for children. To love a child is not difficult: children are so helpless, and they give their love in return so freely and abundantly. During my thirteen years as a cardiac surgeon at the Red Cross War Memorial Children's Hospital in Rondebosch, I experienced the human love, devotion and sacrifice for children on a daily basis. For me, the best part was to see the children's response to my twice-daily visits to them during their recovery period. Smiles of recognition, outstretched arms to welcome me and a few seconds with them in my arms must be some of the most joyous experiences of my fifty years as a doctor.

When I returned to Cape Town in 1967 after my year's specialist study in cardio-vascular surgery in Houston, my work each day started at the Red Cross. What saddened me at the time was that so many of these children spent aimless hours in their cots, with no visitors, toys, music or audio-visual stimulation. Only the nursing staff, overworked as they were, willingly undertook to spend a few minutes with them every day to make them feel loved.

It was while writing a weekly column for the *Cape Times* ten years later that I was approached to support the founding of a group that would give time, money, toys and other forms of support to the children of the Red Cross. I gladly responded and, as described briefly in Chapter 14, my article – titled, 'If you love children, do "adopt" the Red Cross' – received a warm and instantaneous response.[1] The organisation that we formed was called *Friends of the Children's Hospital Association* (FOCHA).

On arrival at the hospital, one is immediately confronted by the plaque in the foyer, on which is inscribed, 'This hospital has been established by the Cape Region of the South African Red Cross Society as an enduring memorial to the sacrifice, suffering and service of our people in World War II,

1939–1945'. One hopes that future generations, in their gratitude for the great work done in this hospital, will be mindful of those in whose memory it was erected.

The Red Cross is built in the shape of a cross. While the children's wards were part of the outstretched arms of the cross, our cardiac ICU and operating theatres were right in the heart of its centre. Although overshadowed by its more famous mother hospital on the slopes of Devil's Peak, the Red Cross has grown to maturity since its inception in 1956. The hospital admits children up to twelve years of age from all over South Africa and from many other parts of the world. Dedicated doctors and nurses travel from across the country and from abroad to be trained there to care for sick children. They are assisted by ancillary staff, including laboratory assistants, radiographers, social workers, occupational therapists, physiotherapists and many others.

There, in the arms of that great symbolic cross, it has been shown that a hospital built specifically for children and staffed by people who love to work with children is the best place in which to care for a sick child.

I am delighted to report that, in 2011, the Friends of the Children's Hospital Association remains not only very much alive, but a thriving movement led by its able director, Mrs Fundiswa Phillips, with a core team of extremely dedicated and compassionate personnel, most of whom are volunteers.

The FOCHA, or the *Friends* as we like to refer to it, is probably one of the most active volunteer organisations in South Africa and has grown significantly over the past thirty-three years. Needs are now, however, far greater, as the hospital sees a total of approximately a quarter of a million inpatients and outpatients annually – a vast majority of these requiring assistance from the Friends. The number of registered volunteers totals sixty and these numbers are growing steadily. Clearly the Friends is in excellent hands and it is my hope that this organisation continues to prosper in taking care of our young patients at the Red Cross Children's Hospital.

* * *

I am pleased to say that in my hometown, Hermanus, there is a Friends of the Hermanus Hospital Association where, with the help of dedicated volunteers, the same devoted service is provided to patients.

When we see the good work done by this and other organisations, it is difficult to understand that we live in a country where child abuse and rape is so rife, and committed in the most inhumane forms. Almost daily there appear newspaper headlines such as: 'One Child Is Raped in South Africa every 3 Minutes' and '530 Child Rapes Occur Every Day'. According to Childline South Africa, there has been a 400 per cent increase in child abuse in South Africa over the past ten years.

Individual cases of child abuse, rape and murder are regularly reported, revealing shocking brutality. One such case is that of an infant who was raped and left in the bush to die. When discovered, the baby was taken to hospital and lovingly restored, where possible, to some form of health. Other victims are not so fortunate. What will stay with me forever, though, is the photograph of this baby on admission, her tiny legs apart and one or two loops of her small bowel protruding from between them as a result of her torn vagina. Such senseless cruelty and murder: in a recent episode a young girl who was the victim of a robbery was so badly beaten up that she almost died and will probably be blind for the rest of her life. I can find no words to describe the monsters who commit such crimes. Nothing can justify their despicable deeds.

The work performed by the volunteers at the Friends and other similar groups restores one's faith in humanity. I feel proud to have been a founding member and patron of that organisation, and I laud the Friends for their outstanding work in nurturing and restoring the shattered lives of these unfortunate victims – our precious children, our future.

* * *

Since the late 1960s, therefore, when I began working as a paediatric cardiac surgeon at the Red Cross Children's Hospital, it has held a special allure for me. Throughout my life I have striven to embody the ideals embraced by my father, whose passionate belief in God, compassion and the resilience of the human spirit was matched only by his boundless love for children. From his early years in the Salvation Army, he was well recognised for his devotion to them, and his love for his own children was infinite. I have endeavoured to convey this love to my children, and I hope that this, the most precious of God's gifts, will be passed on to our future generations for eternity.

Unlike Frank Sinatra, who sings that he did it his way, I can, now that my end is near, say with total conviction that I did it God's way. I could never have had the life I've had without His help and guidance.

Notes

CHAPTER 1

1. Although there were other harbour pilots in the intervening years, John Benn and his descendants – John II, Conning and Reuben – ruled the Knysna mouth until the harbour was finally closed in 1954. Not one person lost his or her life in the Heads under their watch.
2. The *sitee*, the *vastrap* and the *Hotnot's riel* were popular traditional dances at the time. *Vastrap* music unites Afrikaner folk music with Khoisan trance dance.
3. Mafeking has since been renamed *Mafikeng*.
4. *Furlough* refers to the leave of absence granted for a soldier to return home.
5. The valedictory speech was submitted by A.T. Cooper, for the Commanding Officer.

CHAPTER 2

1. Termed the *NG Sendingkerk* in Afrikaans, the church was built in 1871.

CHAPTER 3

1. The *Groote Kerk* (literally the 'Large Church' or 'Great Church') in Cape Town's Adderley Street was the first Christian place of worship to be erected in the Cape, following the arrival of Jan van Riebeeck in 1652. The building's cornerstone was laid in 1700.

CHAPTER 4

1. A *tetralogy of Fallot* is a congenital heart defect that involves four anatomical abnormalities (although only three of them are always present). It is the most common cyanotic heart defect, representing 55–70 per cent, and the most common cause of 'blue baby' syndrome.

CHAPTER 8

1. The Helpmekaar movement was founded in 1916 to pay for the legal costs of those Afrikaners who were arrested and tried by the Botha–Smuts government. They had rebelled against the government's decision to join the British to fight in the First World War in German South West Africa and Europe. When the court case concluded, there was money remaining, so the trustees decided to set up a fund for poor Afrikaans boys who needed financial help with their studies. Many of South Africa's key economic institutions emerged from the Helpmekaar movement. The organisation remains in existence today.

2. Groote Schuur Hospital (also known as *GSH* or, colloquially, *Grotties*) is a large, government-funded teaching hospital situated on the slopes of Devil's Peak in Cape Town, South Africa. Founded in 1938, it is the chief academic hospital of the University of Cape Town's medical school. The boarding-house premises in Clee Road, where I shared a room with Chris for two years, now form part of today's new, enlarged Groote Schuur Hospital.

3. By the 1960s, District Six had become like a boil on the nose of the architects of apartheid: it didn't coincide with the government's warped definition of 'separate development'. In 1966 it was proclaimed a 'White Group Area'. Over 60 000 inhabitants were wrenched from their homes, livelihoods, community centres and societal networks when their houses were bulldozed. They were relocated to the bleak plains of the 'Cape Flats', several miles away. In 1970, the remains of District Six were razed to the ground and the area was renamed *Zonnebloem* in an effort to attract developers. Would-be developers were successfully dissuaded, however, and the site remains barren as a stark reminder of a brutal, unworkable policy.

4. My wife, Inez, is not directly related to Beyers Naudé, even though they share the same family name.

5. That this highway was recently renamed *Beyers Naudé Drive* is a delicious irony, in that it was previously known as *D.F. Malan Drive*.

6. *Riem* in Afrikaans literally refers to a strip of skin such as leather, as in *riempie* chairs, for example. From here on, I will simply call him *Riem*.

CHAPTER 11

1. In medical terms, clots are called *thrombi*, while smaller clots are referred to as *emboli*. *Ischaemia* denotes a restriction in blood supply to an organ, i.e. a restriction in oxygen, glucose and other blood-borne fuels. The lack of oxygen and nutrients results in tissue damage.

2. Since the 1950s, more than eighty models of prosthetic heart valves have been developed. These valves are either devised from biological tissue or they are mechanical.

3. In 1994, Jan Smuts Airport was renamed *Johannesburg International Airport*. Its name changed again in 2006, when it became *O.R. Tambo International Airport*.

CHAPTER 12

1. A retractor opens the field of operation by retracting surrounding tissue so that the operating area can be better seen. In the case of an aneurysm, for example, it is used to retract the small bowel to expose the aneurysm at the back of the abdomen.

2. The term *paracorporeal*, which denotes the external pump's positioning at the side of the patient, is applicable to artificial hearts and specifically an LVAD. In October 1966, DeBakey and Liotta implanted the paracorporeal

Liotta–DeBakey LVAD in a new patient who recovered well and was discharged from the hospital after ten days of mechanical support.

CHAPTER 13

1. Today this cricket ground is officially named *Sahara Park Newlands*, although South Africans, and Capetonians in particular, still tend to refer to it simply as *Newlands*.
2. This Act was officially named *The Reservation of Separate Amenities Act.*

CHAPTER 14

1. These fatty deposits are called *plaques of atheroma. Atherosclerosis* is the condition involving the build-up of these deposits on the innermost layer of the arterial walls. See also Chapter 32.
2. The Vineberg procedure was named after eminent Canadian cardiac surgeon Arthur Vineberg.
3. Also termed *lidocaine*, lignocaine is a common local anaesthetic and anti-arrhythmic drug.
4. Marius Barnard, 'If you love children, do "adopt" the Red Cross', *Cape Times*, 30 October 1978.
5. Palliative surgery is any form of surgery that concentrates on reducing the severity of disease symptoms rather than striving to halt, delay or reverse progression of the disease itself or provide a cure. Coronary bypass, for example, would be palliative, as atherosclerosis can still recur, while a heart transplant is not palliative as it provides a complete cure.
6. Total anomalous pulmonary venous drainage (TAPVD) is one such rare congenital heart defect. All four pulmonary veins are irregularly positioned and make anomalous connections to the body's venous circulation.
7. See also Chapter 4, note 1.

CHAPTER 15

1. The remaining 10 per cent consisted of non-ethnic blacks, i.e. coloureds and Asians. The 80 per cent referred to is the percentage of black Africans.
2. In the United States in 1980, the National Conference of Commissioners on Uniform State Laws formulated the Uniform Determination of Death Act. It states: 'An individual who has sustained either (1) irreversible cessation of circulatory and respiratory functions, or (2) irreversible cessation of all functions of the entire brain, including the brain stem, is dead. A determination of death must be made in accordance with accepted medical standards.' This definition was approved by the American Medical Association in 1980 and by the American Bar Association in 1981.
3. Many years later, when I was in parliament, the law was amended. We debated these issues and the Human Tissue Act was passed. An inclusive statute, it legalised the transplant of all tissues, including blood transfusions

and artificial insemination. I believe it is one of the very best South African Acts. Importantly, it serves to control and prevent the abuse of transplantation.

4. Medically, *perfusion* refers to the passage of fluid through the vessels of an organ. In this case, the recipient's blood diffused through the donor heart.

5. The greater the evolutionary gap, the more vigorous the cellular-rejection response.

CHAPTER 16

1. Hamilton Naki died on 29 May 2005, aged seventy-eight.

2. The article, which is titled 'Africa's uncelebrated hero' and dated 4 July 2005, is available at http://www.atdforum.org/spip.php?article147.

3. Titled 'South Africa: Hamilton Naki, the unsung hero' and dated 13 December 2009, the article is available at http://newafricanperspective.blogspot. com/2009/12/black-shero-south-africa-hamilton-naki.html.

4. 'Hamilton Naki, 78, self-taught surgeon, dies', www.nytimes.com, 11 June 2005.

5. Johann Abrahams (producer), 'The Hamilton Naki Story', *Special Assignment*, 2 June 2009.

6. David Smith, 'Film on black surgeon in first heart transplant team rekindles controversy', *Guardian*, 1 June 2009. Available at http://www.guardian.co.uk/ world/2009/may/31/black-surgeon-first-heart-transplant.

7. Don McRae, *Every Second Counts* (London: Simon & Schuster, 2006).

CHAPTER 17

1. Peter Hawthorne, *The Transplanted Heart* (Johannesburg: Hugh Keartland Publishers, 1968).

2. The stately home Groote Schuur was bequeathed by Cecil John Rhodes and has been used as the official residence of the leaders of South Africa since 1911.

3. The tahr is a deer that, until recently, roamed the slopes of Table Mountain.

CHAPTER 18

1. Peter Hawthorne, 'Another Dr. Barnard transplants a human heart', *Life*, 25 February 1972, p. 81.

2. Johan Brink, 'Don't Ever Give Up', *Journal of Heart and Lung Transplantation*, April 1996, pp. 430–431. *Idiopathic cardiomyopathy* is a disease of the heart muscle with no known cause, leading to a weakened and often enlarged heart. It is one of the principal reasons for heart transplantation.

3. At the time of his death on 10 August 2009, Tony Huesman was the world's longest-living heart transplant recipient, having survived for thirty-one years with a transplanted heart. Huesman received a heart in 1978 at the age of twenty after viral pneumonia severely weakened his heart. The operation was performed at Stanford University under American cardiac surgeon Dr Norman Shumway.

4. Dr Blaiberg died on 17 August 1969, having survived for nineteen months.

5. A xenograft involves a donor and a recipient of different species. In this case, a

chimpanzee heart was transplanted into a human, resulting in hyperacute rejection. See also Chapter 15, note 6.

CHAPTER 19

1. William J. Cromie, 'Heart transplants: A dim record', *Chicago News*, 12 June 1970.
2. *Ibid.*
3. See also Chapter 15, note 3.

CHAPTER 20

1. The test that Rodney Hewitson performed on Robert Sobukwe was a diagnostic bronchoscopy, a procedure during which an examiner uses a viewing tube to evaluate a patient's lung and airways, including the voice box and vocal cords, trachea and many branches of bronchi.

CHAPTER 21

1. 'International discussion between heart surgeons in Hague hotel', *Het Vaderland*, 25 March 1968.

CHAPTER 22

1. Marius Barnard, 'Marius: The other Professor Barnard', *Cape Times*, 18 March 1980.
2. A Blalock–Taussig shunt (also referred to as a Blalock–Thomas–Taussig shunt) is a surgical procedure to alleviate the symptoms of cyanotic heart defects, which are common causes of 'blue baby' syndrome.
3. An atrial septal defect (ASD) is a form of congenital heart defect that enables blood to flow between the left and right atria via the interatrial septum, resulting in the mixing of arterial and venous blood. This prevalent condition is commonly known as *hole in the heart*.
4. An angiogram is performed by injecting dye via a catheter into the various chambers of the heart. This enables one to observe the functioning of the heart, its valves, the arteries and the other structures, and to measure intra-cardiac pressures, all of which are necessary for a correct diagnosis.
5. Septicaemia is a potentially life-threatening infection involving large amounts of bacteria being present in the blood. It is commonly referred to as *blood poisoning*. Fulminating septicaemia cases can often die of complications including septic shock and intravascular problems within hours of being apparently well.
6. The 'sins' to which I was alerted by the superintendent of Groote Schuur Hospital related largely to my political involvement while working at the hospital, which brought me to loggerheads with the hospital authorities. This is discussed further in Part III.
7. An intravenous pyelogram (IVP) is a test that uses dye injected into the veins

to determine, by way of X-rays, the anatomy of the urinary system. It is also used to locate kidney stones.

8. The Popular Movement for the Liberation of Angola (*Movimento Popular de Libertação de Angola*) is an Angolan political party that has ruled the country since independence of the then Portuguese Angola in 1975.

CHAPTER 23

1. Sieg Hannig, 'Poles highlight working trip by Marius Barnard', *Star*, 6 June 1980.
2. The oxygenator, as described elsewhere in this book, was a key component of the heart–lung machine.
3. Also known as the *Cathedral Basilica of Saints Stanisław and Vaclav*, Wawel Cathedral is located on Wawel Hill in Kraków.
4. The Hussites, a Christian movement, followed the teachings of Czech reformer Jan Hus (*c.* 1369–1415), who became a forerunner of the Protestant Reformation. The group bolstered Czech national awareness.
5. The Mustard procedure was developed in 1963 by Dr William Mustard at the Hospital for Sick Children in Toronto, Canada. It was the first procedure to show that congenital heart defects could be fully repaired.
6. Viv Prince, 'Alive – the boy Marius wept over', *Sunday Tribune*, 8 June 1980.
7. 'Surgeon recalls wartime friendship', *Cape Times*, 11 June 1980.

CHAPTER 24

1. Marius Barnard, 'A piece of bread', *Reader's Digest*, February 1975.
2. Not his real name.
3. Marius Barnard, 'Soul of his feet', *Reader's Digest*, December 1976.

CHAPTER 25

1. In those days, fervent supporters of the SAP (and, later on, the UP) were given the name *bloedsappe*. *Bloed* literally means *blood*, which indicates that we were 'true-blue' supporters of these parties.
2. UCT Administration Archives, Medical Faculty Board minutes, 12 May 1927, from L. London *et al.*, 'Truth and Reconciliation: A Process of Transformation at the UCT Health Sciences Faculty' (Cape Town: University of Cape Town, 2003), p. 35.
3. The original Groote Schuur Hospital building was constructed with the aid of public subscription and government funds. Construction began in 1932 and the hospital was opened in 1938, replacing the New Somerset Hospital in Green Point as the teaching hospital for UCT. Building of the existing hospital commenced in 1983 and was finally completed in 1989.
4. UCT Administration Archives, Medical Faculty Board minutes, 8 October 1942 and 9 March 1943, from 'Truth and Reconciliation: A Process of Transformation at the UCT Health Sciences Faculty', p. 37.

5. 'Truth and Reconciliation: A Process of Transformation at the UCT Health
   Sciences Faculty', p. 37. There were ninety-four black students registered
   at UCT by 1944. Twenty-four of these were in the Faculty of Medicine.
   Segregated teaching continued until the 1960s, despite the medical school's
   belief in 1947 that the racial admission policy would be temporary.

CHAPTER 26

1. The National Union of South African Students (NUSAS) was founded in 1924.
   Aimed at representing and promoting the interests of university and college
   students, it was open to students of all races and was particularly active at UCT
   and other 'liberal' universities during this period.
2. Bob Toms, 'TEACH: A year of generosity and challenge', *Argus*, 4 June 1973.

CHAPTER 27

1. Neil Lurssen, 'Dr Marius Barnard: Why I withdrew as U.P. candidate', *Weekend
   Argus*, 16 February 1974.
2. Lucille Bell, 'Barnard resigns', *Argus*, 15 March 1980.
3. Chief reporter, 'Barnard not happy at work', *Cape Times*, 17 March 1980.
4. Staff reporter, 'Marius Barnard to quit hospital', *Cape Times*, 17 March 1980.
5. Medical reporter, 'Barnard loss sad, says UCT', *Argus*, 17 March 1980.
6. Translated from '*Marius Barnard bedank; noem g'n redes*' ('Marius Barnard
   resigns; gives no reasons'), *Die Burger*, 17 March 1980.
7. 'Parktown rejects Cape transplant', *Zoo Lake Advertiser* and *Hillbrow News*,
   April 1980.

CHAPTER 28

1. Eschel Rhoodie served as the secretary of the Department of Information
   between 1972 and 1977, while Dr Connie Mulder was minister of this
   department.
2. The name *Muldergate* was coined by the local newspapers in reference to then
   US President Richard Nixon's Watergate scandal.
3. Those belonging to the Reformed Church were referred to as *doppers* and were
   known for their conservative views. They advocated, for example, that dancing
   was a sin.

CHAPTER 29

1. Quoted in Viv Prince, 'Barnard and the pain of apartheid', *Sunday Tribune*,
   4 May 1980.
2. The South African Medical Council was a statutory body consisting of elected
   medical doctors and administrators. It functioned under the jurisdiction of the
   minister of health.
3. Eugene Hugo, 'Barnard says apartheid is worst sickness', *Sunday Times*,
   4 May 1980.
4. *Ibid.*

CHAPTER 30

1. Becoming a nominated member was a means of occupying a seat in parliament without being elected as an MP. This was essentially a reward for services rendered to the party and a position proportionally awarded by each party.

CHAPTER 31

1. The South West African People's Organisation (SWAPO) was a black liberation movement that fought against the South African armed forces in Namibia in the 1980s and supported the MPLA in the Angolan conflict during the same period.
2. The 1989 election was to be the last 'whites-only' general election.

CHAPTER 32

1. Preamble to the Constitution of the World Health Organization as adopted by the International Health Conference, New York, 19–22 June 1946; signed on 22 July 1947 by the representatives of sixty-one states (Official Records of the World Health Organization, No. 2, p. 100) and entered into force on 7 April 1948.
2. On 11 January 1964, the landmark report of the Advisory Committee to the Surgeon General of the United States, 'Smoking and Health', was released. The report concluded that cigarette smoking was a cause of lung cancer and laryngeal cancer in men, a probable cause of lung cancer in women and the most important cause of chronic bronchitis. The Canadian Veterans Study was one of seven studies cited in the report.

CHAPTER 33

1. The same Zach de Beer is referred to in previous chapters, in relation to his role in South African politics.

CHAPTER 34

1. *Underwriting* in this context refers to the use of medical- or health-status information to evaluate a claimant for insurance coverage.
2. Barings Bank, founded in 1762, was brought down in 1995 due to unauthorised trading by its head derivatives trader in Singapore, Nick Leeson.
3. Acceptance of critical illness cover by independent financial advisors was further enhanced by the work carried out by the major IFA trade body NFIFA – the National Federation of Independent Financial Advisers – when in 1994 it achieved standardised definitions for the six 'core' illnesses that followed the initial four. This work was furthered in April 1999 by the Association of British Insurers (ABI), which developed its Statement of Best Practice for Critical Illness Cover.

CHAPTER 35

1. Robert W. Vivian writes in 'Short-Term Insurance Market 1990–2000', *South African Journal of Economic History* 18 (1&2), September 2003: 'Crusader Life Assurance Corporation Ltd was placed under provisional curatorship on the 25th August 1993 and under judicial management on the 29th March 1994. On the 6th May 1997 a scheme of arrangement was approved by the High Court in terms of which its business was transferred to Hollard Life Assurance Company Ltd and The Southern Life Association Ltd. It was subsequently acquired and renamed Clientèle Life Assurance Company Ltd.'

2. This company was founded in 1955 by three brothers, John Amos, Paul Amos and Bill Amos, in Columbus, Georgia. In 1964, the company name was changed to American Family Life Assurance Company of Columbus.

3. Litigation insurance is essential in the United States due to the high rate of claims that are brought against doctors for malpractice.

CHAPTER 36

1. The Butchart Gardens is a group of floral display gardens in Brentwood Bay, Canada, near Victoria on Vancouver Island. The gardens receive more than a million visitors each year.

CHAPTER 38

1. The Million Dollar Round Table (MDRT) is a professional trade association that was formed in 1927 to help insurance salespeople and financial advisors establish best business practices and develop ethical and effective ways to increase client interest in financial products, specifically risk-based products such as life insurance, disability and long-term care.

CHAPTER 39

1. A Christian hymn based on a Swedish poem written by Carl Gustav Boberg (1859–1940) in 1885.

CHAPTER 40

1. Helen Puttick, 'If you have a heart scare on a train, who better to help than Christiaan Barnard's brother?', *Daily Herald*, 17 June 2006; and Sam Shaw, 'Barnard in critical rescue on a train', *Money Marketing*, 15 June 2006.

2. *Ibid.*

CHAPTER 42

1. As quoted in M. Arntz, R. Sacchetto, A. Spermann, S. Steffes and S. Widmaier, 'The German Social Long-Term Care Insurance: Structure and Reform Options', *Discussion Paper Series*, IZA DP No. 2625, February 2007, Forschungsinstitut zur Zukunft der Arbeit (Institute for the Study of Labour), pp. 1–25.

CHAPTER 43

1. The Gleason score is based on the degree of loss of the normal glandular tissue shape, size and differentiation of the glands as originally described and developed by Dr Donald Gleason in 1974.

2. Catheterisation involves the insertion of a plastic tube known as a urinary catheter into a patient's bladder via his or her urethra to allow the patient's urine to drain freely from the bladder out of the body. In males, the catheter-tube insertion into the urinary tract is through the penis. Supra-pubic catheters can also be used to drain urine. They are inserted directly into the bladder via an insertion in the abdomen.

CHAPTER 45

1. 'If you love children, do "adopt" the Red Cross', *Cape Times*, 30 October 1978.

Abbreviations

ABI: Association of British Insurers
ANC: African National Congress
APL: American Physicians Life
ASD: atrial septal defect
BOSS: Bureau of State Security
CABG: coronary artery bypass graft
CCF: congestive cardiac failure
CCU: coronary care unit
CP: Conservative Party
CPA: Cape Provincial Administration
CPR: Canadian Pacific Railways
DP: Democratic Party
ECG: electrocardiograph
EEG: electroencephalograph
FOCHA: Friends of the Children's Hospital Association
FRCS: Fellow of the Royal College of Surgeons
GP: general practitioner
ICU: intensive care unit
IFA: independent financial advisor
IVP: intravenous pyelogram
LIA: Life Insurance Association
LVAD: Left Ventricular Assist Device
MBChB: Bachelor of Medicine, Bachelor of Surgery
MCh: Master of Surgery
MDRT: Million Dollar Round Table
MEC: member of the executive council
MP: member of parliament
MPLA: Popular Movement for the Liberation of Angola
NBC: National Broadcasting Corporation
NFIFA: National Federation of Independent Financial Advisers
NPA: National Prosecuting Authority
NUSAS: National Union of South African Students

NUSED: National Union of South African Students' Education Secretariat
PAC: Pan Africanist Congress
PFP: Progressive Federal Party
PMH: Peninsula Maternity Home
PRP: Progressive Reform Party
PSA: prostate-specific antigen
SAA: South African Airways
SABC: South African Broadcasting Corporation
SAP: South African Party
TB: tuberculosis
TEACH: Teach Each African Child programme
TOT: Top of the Table
UCT: University of Cape Town
UP: United Party
WHO: World Health Organization

Glossary

arrhythmia: a disturbance of the normal electrical rhythm of the heart

atrial septal defect (ASD): congenital heart defect that enables blood to flow between the left and right atria via the interatrial septum, resulting in the mixing of arterial and venous blood; also known as 'hole in the heart'

Bantu: derogatory term applied by the Nationalist government to black South Africans during the apartheid era; used outside South Africa to describe group of Niger–Congo languages and their speakers

biopsy: removal and examination of a tissue sample from a living body for diagnostic purposes

Blitzkrieg: tactic used by Nazi Germany during World War Two that included 'lighting-fast' surprise attacks to strike the enemy as if by lightning; literally 'lightning war' in German

Bo-Dorp: Upper Town

boer(e): literally 'farmer(s)'; also used as a term for an Afrikaner

boeremusiek: literally 'farmer's music', very popular among Afrikaners

bossies: bushes

boytjie: young lad; slang for jock-like person, equivalent of 'buddy'; literally 'little boy'

braaivleis: barbecue

cannula: flexible tube inserted into a body cavity, used to drain fluid or introduce medication

carcinoma: invasive malignant tumour consisting of transformed epithelial cells

cardio-thoracic surgery: field of medicine involved in surgical treatment of diseases affecting organs inside the chest, or thorax, generally the heart and lungs

cardio-vascular surgery: field of medicine involved in surgery on the heart and blood vessels to treat valvular heart disease and complications of ischaemic heart disease, and to correct congenital heart disease; includes heart transplantation

coloured: term for grouping of South Africans of mixed racial descent

confinement: final phase of a woman's pregnancy, including delivery and birth

congenital: a condition that is present at birth as a result of heredity or environmental influences

coniglio: Italian for 'rabbit' or 'hare'

cyanosis: bluish discolouration of the skin and mucous membranes due to lack of oxygen in the blood

dagga: marijuana

dominee(s): minister(s) of the Afrikaans Dutch Reformed Church or similar denomination

dondering: hammering, giving one a hiding

dop: drink, tot

doringbome: thorn trees

dorp(e): village(s), town(s)

eerwaarde: reverend

Eisbein: pickled ham hock; literally 'ice leg/bone' in German

electrocardiograph (ECG): instrument used to detect and diagnose cardiac abnormalities by measuring electrical potentials on the body's surface

electroencephalograph (EEG): instrument that measures and records the electrical activity of the brain

embolus (pl. emboli): small blood clots; piece of a thrombus that has broken free and is carried towards the brain by the bloodstream

gannabos: lye bush

gooingsak: jute bag

harders: southern mullet; small edible fish found in South African coastal areas and salt-water lagoons

Helpmekaar movement: literally 'Helping One Another' movement; South African organisation established to provide financial support to Afrikaners to further their education

Hotnot: shortened form of 'Hottentot'; derogatory term historically denoting the Khoikhoi people; also used to refer to coloured people

Hotnot's riel: traditional South African dance

Hotnotsvye: sourfig; widespread in the south-western and Eastern Cape areas of South Africa

houseman: medical intern; graduate of medicine undertaking supervised practical experience

huis besoek: literally 'house visit'; Dutch Reformed Church ministers' traditional routine of visiting members of their congregation at their homes

ischaemia: restriction in blood supply to an organ resulting in tissue damage

japies: Afrikaans slang implying 'rough-and-ready' sort of person with few social graces

jingo: derogatory name historically given by Afrikaners to a pro-English Afrikaner

kaalgat: naked

Khoi: Khoikhoi; 'Hottentot'

kindermeid: childminder

Klippies and Coke: mixed drink of brandy and Coke; 'Klippies' is colloquial slang for the popular South African–produced brandy Klipdrift; also locally coined 'spook and diesel'

koppie(s): hillock(s)

laaitie: child, young person

ligature: cord, wire or bandage used in surgery to close or tie off blood vessels

locum: short for *locum tenens*; temporary substitution, typically for absent doctor, cleric or teacher

maagskoon maak: stomach cleansing

mal: mad

melkbos tree: small, graceful tree with drooping branches; also known as a wild rubber or horn pod tree

meneer: mister; also a polite form of address in Afrikaans to a man

metastatic carcinoma: carcinoma in a region remote from its site of origin

mielie meal: maize flour

mieliepap: maize porridge

mielies: maize (cobs)

mobilise: medical term denoting the release of a body part through separation from its surrounding tissues

motor neuron disease (MND): group of neurological disorders that selectively affect motor neuron cells, which control voluntary muscle activity including speaking, walking, breathing, swallowing and general movement

myocardial infarction: death of, or damage to, the heart muscle due to a reduced blood supply to the heart; a heart attack

neonate: baby between nought and four weeks old

occlusion: obstruction or closure of passageway or vessel; degree of opening and closing of tubes through which blood flows

oom(s): uncle(s); also popularly used by Afrikaners to address respectfully an elder male

Oros: popular South African orange-flavoured juice concentrate

osse: oxen

Ossewabrandwag: literally 'Ox-Wagon Sentinel'; Afrikaans paramilitary organisation

ossewa-trek: ox-wagon trek

ouderling: elder of the Dutch Reformed Church

Ou Plaas: Old Farm

palliative surgery: surgery reducing severity of disease symptoms rather than halting, delaying or reversing progression of disease or providing a cure

paracorporeal: positioning of external pump at side of patient; also applicable to artificial hearts, specifically a Left Ventricular Assist Device (LVAD)

pathogenesis: mechanism by which a disease is caused; also used to describe development of disease, such as 'acute', 'chronic' or 'recurrent'

perfusion: act of pouring over or through; especially passage of fluid through vessels of an organ

pericardium: fluid-filled sac surrounding the heart

platteland: country districts or rural areas; literally 'flat country'

primêre skool: Afrikaans for primary school

radical prostatectomy: operation to remove the prostate gland and some of the tissue surrounding it

ringkommissies: executive district commissions of the Dutch Reformed Church

rooibos: type of South African tea; literally 'red bush'

rooinekke: derogatory name given historically by Afrikaners to English people because of their sunburnt necks; literally 'rednecks'

ryperde: saddle horses

sadsa: maize-based dish, staple Zimbabwean food

Sauerkraut: traditional German dish of fermented cabbage

sitee: traditional South African dance

sjambok: leather whip, traditionally made from hippopotamus or rhinoceros hide

springers: type of fish, also known as 'ladyfish' or 'ten-pounder'

Standard 6: level of schooling according to old South African system; equivalent of today's Grade 8

supra-pubic catheter: tube inserted through a small incision in the abdomen into the bladder to release urine

suurklontjies: sour drops; a sweet

syphilitic kind: syphilis-infected child

tannie(s): aunt(s); also popularly used by Afrikaners to address respectfully an elder female

tetralogy of Fallot: congenital heart defect involving a lack of oxygen in the blood; most common cause of 'blue baby' syndrome

thrombus (pl. thrombi): blood clot formed in a blood vessel or the heart; does not move to another area of body

trans-urethral catheter: tube inserted into the bladder via the urethra allowing urine to drain freely from the bladder; in males, catheter insertion into the urinary tract is through the penis

Tsitsikamma: Khoisan word meaning 'place of much water'

underwriting: in medical insurance context denotes use of medical- or health-status information in evaluation of an applicant for insurance coverage

urethra: tube connecting the urinary bladder to the genitals for removal of fluids out of the body; in males, the urethra travels through the penis, carrying semen as well as urine

vascular surgery: specialty of surgery in which diseases of the vascular
   system – arteries and veins – are managed by medical therapy, minimally
   invasive catheter procedures and surgical reconstruction
vastrap: traditional dance drawing on Afrikaner and Khoisan influences;
   literally 'trample'
veld: bush
volksspeletjies: folk dancing
Voortrekkers: Boers who trekked from the Cape Colony to the north from
   1835 onwards
vrektes: death of animals

xenograft: surgical graft of tissue between donor and recipient of different
   species, resulting in hyperacute rejection. The greater the evolutionary
   gap between the species, the more vigorous the cellular-rejection
   response

Index

short-term insurance 313
  see also critical illness insurance
Shumway, Dr Norman 119, 134, 144, 156, 175, 176, 412
Singapore, MB's visit to 340
Slingsby, Dick 322
smallpox 312
Smith, Dr Dolf 106
smoking and health 295–296, 315–316
Smuts, Jan 37, 53, 263, 301
Sobukwe, Robert Mangaliso 179–181
Sobukwe, Veronica 180
soccer, MB's love for 48–49
'Soul of his Feet' 254–258
South African Airways (SAA) 295–296
South African Broadcasting Corporation (SABC) 112, 385–386
South African Institute of Race Relations 273
South African Medical Council 288
South African Medical Journal 143–144
South African Party (SAP) 78, 261
South African Railways 15, 25, 27
South America, heart transplants in 175
Southern Life 310, 319, 326
Southern Rhodesia *see* Salisbury, Rhodesia
South West African People's Organisation (SWAPO) 300
Spain
  heart transplants in 175
  MB's visit to 185–188
Spanish flu epidemic 312
Special Assignment 154
Springbok rugby team 48
Standard Bank Insurance Brokers 323
Standard (Stander) family 63
Stanford University 175, 412
Stanton, Lacon 276, 294
Star newspaper 267
Steytler, Dr Jan 271
St Joseph's Home 300–301
St Luke's Episcopal Hospital 175
St Martin's Hospital 92, 332
Stopforth from Scotland 7
Streek, Barry 266, 271

Streicher, Myburgh 271, 273, 274
Sumners, Doris 116, 118, 124, 348–349
Sumners, Reverend Tom 116, 118, 124, 348–349
sunday services, in Beaufort West 59–66
Sunday Times 289, 402
Suppression of Communism Act 193
Surprise, Surprise 358–361
Suzman, Helen 181, 266, 272, 283–284, 287, 295, 297, 298, 302
SWAPO *see* South West African People's Organisation
Swart, Dr Chris 129, 241, 242, 245, 247–248, 280
Swart, Ray 283–284, 298, 302, 401
  introduction by 259–260
Szczecin, Poland, MB's visit to 239–240

tahrs 164
Taiwan, MB's visit to 341
TAPVD *see* total anomalous pulmonary venous drainage
Teach Each African Child (TEACH) programme 267
Temperance Sunday 62–66
Terblanche, Prof. John 172
tetralogy of Fallot 25, 140–141, 194–195, 204, 246–248, 310–311
Teubes, June 98
Texas Children's Hospital 121–123
Thailand, MB's visit to 340–341
theatrical companies, touring 35
The Economist see Economist, The
Thesen, Paul 169–170
Thesen wood factory 7, 170
Thomas from Wales 7
Thompson, Prof. J.G. 142
'Three Firsts and a Fourth' 375–376
thrombi 410
tied agents 323
TIME magazine 164
Timpson, Johnny 377
Tirgu Mureş, Transylvania 193, 216–217, 222, 232, 235–236
tissue rejection *see* immunosuppression